Canadian Liberalism and the Politics of Border Control, 1867-1967

Christopher G. Anderson

Canadian Liberalism and the Politics of Border Control, 1867-1967

UBCPress · Vancouver · Toronto

21 20 19 18 17 16 15 14 13 12   5 4 3 2 1

Printed in Canada on FSC-certified ancient-forest-free paper
(100% post-consumer recycled) that is processed chlorine- and acid-free.

Library and Archives Canada Cataloguing in Publication

Anderson, Christopher G. (Christopher Gordon)
    Canadian liberalism and the politics of border control, 1867-1967 /
Christopher Anderson.

Includes bibliographical references and index.
Also issued in electronic format.
ISBN 978-0-7748-2392-0 (bound); ISBN 978-0-7748-2393-7 (pbk.)

    1. Canada – Emigration and immigration – Government policy. 2. Aliens – Civil rights – Canada. 3. Immigrants – Civil rights – Canada. 4. Refugees – Civil rights – Canada. 5. Citizenship – Canada. 6. National security – Canada – History. I. Title.

JV7233.A53 2013   325.71   C2012-904137-8

Canadä

UBC Press gratefully acknowledges the financial support for our publishing program of the Government of Canada (through the Canada Book Fund), the Canada Council for the Arts, and the British Columbia Arts Council.

This book has been published with the help of a grant from the Canadian Federation for the Humanities and Social Sciences, through the Awards to Scholarly Publications Program, using funds provided by the Social Sciences and Humanities Research Council of Canada.

UBC Press
The University of British Columbia
2029 West Mall
Vancouver, BC V6T 1Z2
www.ubcpress.ca

Contents

Acknowledgments / vii

Four Notes on the Text / ix

Introduction: Reconsidering the Control/Rights Nexus / 1

1 The Study of Liberal-Democratic Control over International Migration / 12

2 The Liberal Internationalist Foundations of Canadian Control (1867-87) / 31

3 The Expansion of Liberal Nationalism in Canada (1887-1914) / 58

4 The Domination of Liberal Nationalism in Canada (1914-45) / 93

5 A New Era of Human Rights (1945-52) / 129

6 The Return of Liberal Internationalism in Canada (1952-67) / 158

7 Contemporary Canadian and Comparative Concerns / 190

Notes / 205

Works Cited / 234

Index / 253

Acknowledgments

I first became interested in this area of study in the mid-1990s, when I took a course on Canadian (with an added dash of comparative) citizenship, immigration, refugee, and multiculturalism policy. The course was taught by Jerome H. Black at McGill University, and the interest that he sparked in me then has carried forward to the present, as those themes and the numerous issues that they generate have come to define my work as an academic. My first expression of gratitude therefore goes to Jerome. Without his encouragement and enthusiastic support, I might never have embarked upon this path. Apart from his scholarship and mentorship over the years, he has also offered his friendship, which has been especially rewarding.

The attention with which Elisabeth Gidengil read and responded to earlier drafts of what has become this book only deepened my respect for her sharpness of mind and commitment to helping students sharpen their own; her example has taught me much about how to pursue a more meaningful scholarly life. Yasmeen Abu-Laban offered comments that were as supportive as they were critical, which enabled me to approach my work with a much wider perspective. For their parts, Sandy Irvine, Kim Rygiel, Dagmar Soennecken, and Phil Triadafilopoulos have provided – in ways direct and indirect – valuable and valued input along the way. I also want to acknowledge the role played by Brian Tanguay, who – as Chair of the Department of Political Science at Wilfrid Laurier University – helped to find me a place to complete this book and contemplate the next ones.

I have learned a lot about how to write a better book from everyone that I have come into contact with at UBC Press. From the original proposal onward, Emily Andrew has shepherded me through the various stages with great kindness and skill – I have often heard her praises sung and now add my voice to that chorus. As the manuscript moved into production, Holly Keller, Anna Friedlander, and Lesley Erickson guided me very well, and I thank them for their many contributions. As for the two anonymous readers, they raised thoughtful questions and sought important clarifications from two different perspectives, which encouraged me to pursue lines of argumentation that I might not otherwise have followed. This book also received support in the form of a Book Preparation Grant from the Office of Research Services at Wilfrid Laurier University, for which I am grateful.

An undertaking such as this is hard to sustain without the assistance, forbearance, and companionship of family and friends. Eugenia, Alexander, and Matthew have borne the uncertainties and vagaries of the past few years well and have given me renewed purpose in countless ways. My heartfelt thanks also goes to my parents, Kenning and Marion Anderson: with children of my own now, I am beginning to understand all that they have done and continue to do on my behalf. Finally, I want to raise a glass or three to the H69 brethren, who have offered a most humorous (if frequently shocking) commentary since 1987 – *sans aucun doute!*

This book is dedicated to the memory of W.M.M. and A.E.H.

Four Notes on the Text

1 Parts of the Introduction and Chapter 1 are reproduced from "Restricting Rights, Losing Control: The Politics of Control over Asylum Seekers in Liberal-Democratic States – Lessons from the Canadian Case, 1950-1989," *Canadian Journal of Political Science* 43, 4 (2010): 937-59. Material in Chapter 2 was previously published in "The Senate and the Fight against the 1885 Chinese Immigration Act," *Canadian Parliamentary Review* 30, 2 (2008): 21-26.

2 For House of Commons and Senate of Canada debates, I have used in-text citations with the date and page or column number as reported in the official printed version (it varies over time). The text itself makes plain where the debate in question took place.

3 The following abbreviated forms are used to identify the party affiliation of parliamentarians referred to or quoted in the text:

C	Conservative Party of Canada
CCF	Co-operative Commonwealth Federation
I	Independent
L	Liberal Party of Canada
LCP	Liberal-Conservative Party
NDP	New Democratic Party
P	Progressive Party of Canada
PC	Progressive Conservative Party of Canada
SC	Social Credit Party of Canada
UP	Unionist Party

4 Immigration was, in turn, the responsibility of six different government departments during the core period covered in this book. While changes

are noted at appropriate points in the text, a list is provided here for easy reference:

1868-92	Department of Agriculture
1892-1918	Department of the Interior
1918-36	Department of Immigration and Colonization
1936-50	Department of Mines and Resources
1950-66	Department of Citizenship and Immigration
1966-67	Department of Manpower and Immigration

Canadian Liberalism and the Politics of Border Control, 1867-1967

Introduction: Reconsidering the Control/Rights Nexus

On 17 October 2009, seventy-six Tamil asylum seekers arrived in British Columbia aboard the *MV Ocean Lady* and were promptly detained by Canadian officials. On 30 March 2010, the Canadian government introduced its *Balanced Refugee Reform Act,* which, according to Amnesty International (2010, 1), would "sacrifice a fair process for all [refugee] claimants in the name of speed and efficiency." On 13 August 2010, the *MV Sun Sea* docked in British Columbia carrying 492 Tamil men, women, and children, who also claimed asylum and were immediately detained. On 21 October 2010, the Canadian government presented its *Preventing Human Smugglers from Abusing Canada's Immigration System Act,*[1] which the Canadian Civil Liberties Association (2011) concluded contained measures that would "violate both international and Canadian constitutional standards by denying ... individuals their right to liberty, to be free from arbitrary detention, and their due process rights." In each case, official and public discourse emphasized themes of threats to, and abuse of, Canada and Canadians, and the government sought to increase restrictions on the rights of non-citizens at and within Canada's borders. In the process, officials argued that such tools were needed to confront new challenges in *controlling borders* – in determining the conditions under which international migrants can enter into and remain within the territory under a state's authority – and that without them the government would, as Citizenship and Immigration Minister Jason Kenney told the House of Commons, "put at risk the broad public consensus, which has historically existed in Canada in favour of immigration and refugee protection" (27 October 2010, 5417).

These responses form part of a consistent pattern in Canada's contemporary approach to border control, in which rights-restrictive policies have been used to limit the ability of individuals, interest groups, and the courts to engage in *rights-based politics* – to challenge state control measures through the promotion of the rights of non-citizens (and, in some cases, citizens as well). Thus, when 599 Chinese migrants arrived in British Columbia by boat in 1999, the government initiated "an enforcement response to human smuggling with a strategy that entailed detention, the control of flows of information, and deportation" (Mountz 2004, 334). In 2000, it unveiled its *Immigration and Refugee Protection Act,* which contained features that in the opinion of the United Nations High Commissioner for Refugees (UNHCR 2001, 13-14) would broadly interfere with a person's "right to seek and enjoy asylum from persecution" under Article 14 of the 1948 Universal Declaration of Human Rights. In 1986 and 1987, two separate sets of arrivals by boat and the government's reaction to them helped to produce a "popular image of an assault on Canada's borders by dishonest and bogus refugees (and ... perhaps even criminals)" (Creese 1992, 130). The government undertook a virtually unprecedented emergency recall of Parliament to speed through restrictive legislation aimed at limiting access to the inland refugee status determination system (even as it increased the system's fairness by institutionalizing an oral hearing for claimants within the process; see Dirks 1995, Chapter 7).

Although asylum seekers have been a central target of rights-restrictive control policies in recent years, this approach has been employed against other international migrants as well. Since the mid-1990s, Canada has, for example, increased its powers of detention and deportation over non-citizens (Pratt 2005), especially with respect to criminals (Chan 2006) and presumed security cases (Aiken 2007). A rights-restrictive approach can also be seen in efforts to make Canadian citizenship harder to obtain (Galloway 2000) and, for naturalized Canadians, easier to revoke (Anderson 2008). These policies, moreover, have had gendered and racialized discriminatory features (Abu-Laban 1998a; Pratt and Thompson 2008; Razack 2010). Thus, although many significant rights are recognized for non-citizens under Canadian immigration and refugee law (see Galloway 1997; Goslett and Caruso 2010), the government has sought to increase its control over the country's borders by decreasing both the rights that non-citizens can claim against the state and the efficacy of rights-based politics.

To be sure, Canada is not the only country to adopt such an approach. As border control has become an increasingly controversial and political issue in and among liberal democracies, many states have sought to "simultaneously appease public anxieties over migration, short-circuit judicial constraints on migration control, and still keep open wanted trade, labour, and tourist flows" (Guiraudon and Joppke 2001, 12). Since at least the 1970s, and certainly with the end of the Cold War, a "global migration crisis" is said to have arisen, in which traditional control measures at the border have become less effective, prompting states "to take more rigorous steps to control entry" (Weiner 1995, 207). While privileging the migration of "desirable" (often economic) migration, liberal democracies have erected rights-restrictive barriers to migration within, at, and beyond their territorial borders (Andreas and Snyder 2000; Brochmann and Hammar 1999; Cornelius et al. 2004; Spencer 2003). With respect to refugees and asylum seekers, the UNHCR (2006, 2) has observed that state responses have seen "a gradual movement away from a rights-based approach towards more discretionary forms of refugee protection" during the past few decades. Furthermore, restrictive policies have been pursued to make it more difficult for the foreign-born to acquire national citizenship and the rights protections that it affords, thus serving as additional instruments of control (Joppke 2010). As in Canada, these trends have intensified since 11 September 2001 (Guild 2009). Such a rights-restrictive approach is often justified on the grounds that domestic politics – including the recent rise of rights-based politics – has been "a cause of weak sovereignty and ineffective immigration policy" (Freeman 1998, 103).

What if, however, this interpretation of how control and rights intersect – the *control/rights nexus* – is inadequate? What if control difficulties stem not simply from rights-based politics but from the rights-restrictive policies pursued by states as well? What if the rights-based claims of non-citizens are not just a distinctive and recent phenomenon but reflect deeply embedded ideas and traditions within liberal-democratic states? These are important questions from any number of perspectives.[2] In the case of international migrants, for example, a rights-restrictive approach could limit their ability to fulfill their human potential and could even have life-or-death consequences, especially for asylum seekers and refugees. For citizens in liberal democracies, their commitment to uphold principles such as equality and liberty could be seriously compromised. As for decision makers, repeated control policy failures might erode the trust and security of citizens. Finally, policy analysts are unlikely to develop sustainable control policies within liberal-democratic political systems if they do not adequately appreciate how control and rights intersect.

That rights-restrictive control policies in recent years have been only a qualified success in preventing the arrival of "unwanted immigration" (Joppke 1998b) lends initial support to such concerns. For example, as states have made it more difficult for people to enter legally from the 1980s onward, the number of illegal or irregular migrants is understood to have grown (Castles et al. 2003). Of course, the growth in such migration has been produced through a range of interrelated factors, including increasing economic disparity between countries, ineffective systems of sanctions on employers who hire illegal migrants, the development and extension of transnational social networks, technological advances in communications and transportation, and the activities of people smugglers and human traffickers (Ghosh 1998). It can also be connected, however, to the rights-restrictive policies pursued by liberal-democratic states. In this sense, states may have been less successful in preventing non-citizens from entering and remaining within their borders than in altering the conditions and status under which this can be done, thereby contributing to the production of the illegal and irregular movements that states ostensibly seek to prevent, and fostering "a self-fulfilling cycle of restriction and control" (Squire 2009, 4; see also De Genova 2002).

The idea that limiting rights can contribute to a decrease in control refines one of the central conclusions drawn in the comparative literature on liberal-democratic control policy. The notion that there is an essential link between border control and the rights of non-citizens – that "rights must be considered in any theory of international migration" (Hollifield 2000, 148) – occupies a prominent place in this field of study. In practice, however, an unduly narrow reading of the range of dynamics that can exist – and have existed – between control and rights has prevailed: namely, that the recent rise of rights-based politics has undermined liberal-democratic state control and produced serious control policy failures. This formulation rests on a particular modelling of the relationship between control and rights that emphasizes the relatively novel role that the latter play in constraining the former, mostly through the efforts of special (migration-supporting) interest groups and the courts. It also can lend justification to a rights-restrictive approach by privileging state control over the rights of non-citizens. Such a rendering of the control/rights nexus is insufficient, however, insofar as it masks more than it reveals in its representation of this crucial aspect of the politics of control. In particular, it downplays or limits its conceptualization of how the rights-based choices made by states can affect policy outcomes. As well, it tends to stress the contemporary rather than historical foundations of the relationship between control and rights.

An alternative case can be made that the restriction of non-citizen rights within a liberal democracy can contribute to a decrease in control by creating opportunities for rights-based politics, encouraging circumvention of restrictive measures, and prompting additional decision-making stages that generate administrative inefficiencies. In other words, rights-restrictive policies can increase the risk of control failure when they open up avenues along which state authority and capacity can be challenged effectively. Furthermore, a loss of control may lead to additional restrictive measures, creating a negative feedback loop within the control/rights nexus. Thus, while rights-restrictive policies alone cannot explain problems of control, they merit much more attention than they have received to date. Rights-based politics can also produce an *increase* in control when rights-restrictive policies are sustained, for example, by the courts or by a sufficiently broad coalition of political actors, a common enough occurrence that receives little attention in the literature. Finally, rights-based politics is not simply a recent phenomenon but has deep roots in liberal-democratic institutions and traditions.

This formulation reflects a more comprehensive understanding of the control/rights nexus and offers the possibility of greater conceptual and empirical clarity in the description and explanation of liberal-democratic control. It situates the relationship between control and rights-based politics within a more complex political environment, which provides for the possibility of an improved understanding of control policy outcomes. In the process, it ensures more explicit and substantial recognition of the role of the state in the emergence and perpetuation of perceived failures of control. It suggests that a more extensive and historical analysis of control politics is needed in order to grasp the evolution, and thus the nature, of liberal-democratic control. To explore further these and other dimensions of the control/rights nexus, this book presents a detailed examination of the first century of Canadian border control, from 1867 to 1967.

This choice can be justified on several counts. First, Canada has generally remained on the sidelines of the comparative control literature, which is odd. After all, it is one of the few traditional countries of immigration, and its policies with respect to the admission and integration of immigrants and refugees as well as their exclusion have been studied and adapted in other migrant-receiving countries (Kymlicka 2004; Mountz 2010). Although its marginal position in the literature reflects a general tendency in the field of comparative politics, where "Canada remains somewhat off the beaten track" (Vipond 2008, 14), the possible dividends from increasing its presence are not insignificant. It would add breadth to the attempt to determine what is distinctive about liberal-democratic control, and could add depth by uncovering previously overlooked and testing currently identified dynamics and patterns.

Second, the Canadian literature lacks explorations of the liberal-democratic foundations of the country's control policies, especially their rights-based aspects. A great strength of the study of immigrants and refugees in Canada lies in its detailed examinations of the migration experiences of a diverse range of groups over time across numerous dimensions (see Magocsi 1999). A significant weakness stems from the limited number of analyses that focus on the politics surrounding the policies that affect such migration. This is reflected in the fact that Canadian political scientists have rarely published in this area over the years. As will be suggested in Chapter 1, it is also seen in the more descriptive than analytical tendencies of much recent writing on Canadian control policy, which often focuses on the abuses and dysfunctions of the system to the virtual exclusion of other policy-oriented considerations. As a result, Canadian and comparative scholars are left with little insight into the evolution of control politics and policies in Canada. For its part, the Canadian literature has all but ignored comparative studies of control.

Third, most comparative and Canadian analyses provide inadequate historical context for their findings, which results in a more limited understanding of how liberalism itself structures the control/rights nexus. At times, this leads to the granting of almost normative status to restrictive approaches in the analysis of recent policy developments (Bonjour 2011). While it is certainly true that "the expansion of immigrant rights marks a significant change in post-war liberal states" (Joppke 2001, 339), this process has noteworthy prewar origins. Indeed, it will be seen in the Canadian case that this postwar shift extended from ideas and traditions that had shaped expansionist approaches to control since the time of Confederation, if not earlier. In certain important respects, then, the rights of non-citizens re-emerged more than emerged during the second half of the twentieth century, although within significantly different policy and political settings. The relationship between control and rights during the contemporary period is thus part of a larger historical narrative that needs to be established.

Finally, as for the choice of Canada's first centenary, it marked an important turning point not only in the country's national development (Berton 1997) but also with respect to border control, as the government instituted an official policy of non-discrimination in immigrant selection and reintroduced effective judicial oversight over this policy area. Although the liberal nature of subsequent control policy developments is often highlighted in the literature, their pre-1967 liberal foundations have received very little attention.[3] If an examination of the past can be shown to have potential for shedding light on the interpretation of the present in the Canadian case, then the possibility of its doing so for other liberal-democratic states needs to be taken more seriously.

Although the research presented here incorporates much from the substantial secondary Canadian literature, its primary source material is drawn from an extensive investigation of parliamentary debates and published state documents relating to control during Canada's first century. By exploring how the relationship between control and rights has been discussed and practised over time, considerable insight into the ways in which the *liberalness* of a liberal-democratic state affects control can be gained. Indeed, it offers an essential but underutilized window onto how control policies have long been entwined with debates over the meaning of liberalism (and, indeed, of "being Canadian"). It is not a perfect window, of course, as control politics has often marginalized certain actors and interests – frequently the migrants themselves – and treated them as objects of control rather than as political subjects in their own right (Iacovetta 1998; Sharma 2006b). At one level, then, this was a largely male and elite-dominated political undertaking by those of British and, to a lesser extent, French colonial descent. Some compensation for this bias can be realized, however, through the secondary literature, which enables marginalized political subjects to be heard and their roles in control politics to be explored, as does a more careful reading of the primary literature. More specifically, a focus on the rights-restrictive policies of states helps to ensure that the responses of Canadian citizens and non-citizens alike remain more constantly and fully in view. This in no way diminishes, however, the continuing need for studies of immigrant communities that overcome the conceptual and empirical limitations of the "white settler society" framework by treating their members as political actors engaged with one another, Canadian citizens, and the state (Stasiulis and Jhappan 1995), and that undertake the requisite empirical research (see, for example, Mar 2010).

To structure the analysis presented in this book, the concept of the universe of political discourse (Jenson 1989) is employed to trace the evolution and interaction of two competing perspectives on liberal-democratic state control that have long defined policy debates and developments. *Liberal Internationalism* posits a strong positive link between the state and the rights of non-citizens, forged by liberal ideas of equality and freedom alongside cognate international norms, whereas *Liberal Nationalism* is rooted in a more insular interpretation of state sovereignty that supports a narrower range of rights that non-citizens can claim against the receiving state. Within this framework, the evolution of the control/rights nexus is traced through the arguments of participants in their efforts to shape policy decisions, the actions of decision makers in their attempts to regulate the conditions under which international migrants can enter and remain within Canada's borders, and the reactions of international migrants and others with interests in this policy area.

This research reveals that control at Confederation was generally understood in terms of a Liberal Internationalist perspective that challenged restrictions on the rights of non-citizens. Although Liberal Nationalism came to dominate Canadian control debates and policies from the beginning of the twentieth century until well after the Second World War, Liberal Internationalism never disappeared from the universe of political discourse and by 1967 had returned to a prominent position. Although interest groups were an important part of this political shift, the courts were virtually excluded from this policy area for much of the period covered and it was primarily within the parliamentary domain that this contest unfolded. In tracing the evolution of the control/rights nexus, this study details a long-standing discussion over the rights of non-citizens and reveals that rights-restrictive policies have often generated a rights-based politics that has challenged state control. It demonstrates, moreover, how such policies have produced control failure by encouraging both circumvention and administrative inefficiencies. In doing so, it uncovers previously unexplored dimensions of Canadian immigration and refugee history and sheds new light on some familiar aspects. It shows how the success of rights-restrictive policies has often depended on their extreme nature, which has rendered them subject to more effective contestation over time. It concludes, therefore, that rights-based politics is neither new nor an adequate focal point for attempting to understand the control/rights nexus in Canada. Rather, the rights-based nature of state control policies can provide a better analytical point of departure for examining control outcomes. Although this is not a comparative study, the Canadian case is explored in the context of liberal-democratic control, which renders its findings relevant when considering the experiences of other liberal democracies in the past and present. Indeed, this research demonstrates that when situated within more adequate historical and political contexts, tensions within liberal–democratic states between control and rights – often recognized in the literature – can be better understood.

The empirical and conceptual justifications for this approach are presented in Chapter 1. First, the basic dimensions of liberal-democratic control politics are established through a brief survey of recent liberal-democratic control experiences, which highlights a general turn towards a more rights-restrictive approach. Second, the tendency in the comparative literature to focus on rights-based politics to explain control failure is reviewed critically against this backdrop, and an alternative emphasis on rights-restrictive policies is advanced. In the process, the limited extent to which the Canadian literature has addressed the control/rights nexus is noted. Third, the conceptual and methodological considerations that underpin the analysis in the chapters that follow are presented. Most importantly, the notion of the universe of political discourse is introduced, alongside the Liberal Internationalism/ Liberal Nationalism distinction, which provides an analytical framework for tracing how the control/rights nexus has been defined and debated over time and offers possibilities for viewing the Canadian experience through a comparative liberal-democratic lens.

Chapter 2 explores the foundations of Canadian control and identifies commonly overlooked factors that gave shape to a predominantly Liberal Internationalist approach during the first two decades after Confederation (1867-87). While objectives such as populating the land and ensuring access to cheap labour are emphasized in the literature, they neither tell the whole story nor provide an adequate baseline against which to assess subsequent developments. Decision makers did not view border control as a major policy problem at the time, and in any event were not sure that much could be done to increase it. As a reflection of this, the country's first immigration law, the 1869 *Immigration Act,* spoke more of protecting than restricting immigrants to Canada. Such an expansionist approach fit comfortably with a Liberal Internationalist outlook that stemmed from the country's British liberal traditions, which posited a positive link between the state and the rights of non-citizens. This is most clearly seen with the passage and amendment of the 1885 *Chinese Immigration Act,* the first explicit rights-restrictive feature in Canadian immigration law. Although the law's inherent racism is often highlighted, the Senate's attempt to first defeat and then repeal it on Liberal Internationalist grounds has been inexplicably ignored. This case not only constitutes an important addition to the history of race and racism in Canada but also underscores the idea that the liberal roots of control are more complicated and much deeper than is generally recognized.

Chapter 3 traces the expansion and consolidation of a rights-restrictive approach to Asian and European immigration (1887-1914). Following the 1885 *Chinese Immigration Act,* the government steadily expanded the scope of its race-based approach by creating increasingly extensive regulatory frameworks for Chinese, Japanese, and East Indian arrivals up to the First World War. It did so on the grounds that the equality and due process rights of non-citizens were secondary to the sovereign right of states to control their borders. While struggling to curtail such migration, the state employed an elastic definition of "Asian" that encompassed Jews, Syrians, Armenians, and others, many of whom were refugees seeking an escape from persecution. In the meantime, as European (especially eastern and southern European) immigration grew substantially, the government constructed an approach to control that was rooted in expanded executive discretionary power shielded from effective judicial and parliamentary oversight. These efforts were eventually codified in the 1910 *Immigration Act* and seriously constrained the avenues along which state control policies could be challenged effectively. Such Liberal Nationalism supplanted but never wholly displaced Liberal Internationalism. Even at this early stage in Canadian history, rights-restrictive policies generated rights-based politics, most prominently in the case of the East Indian community. Aside from serving as a reminder that immigrants have long reacted against restrictionist policies, this material shows that they often did so in Liberal Internationalist terms stemming from British liberal traditions. It also reveals why the courts played such a marginal role in control politics until the late 1960s, when the severe limits on judicial oversight instituted in 1910 were removed.

Chapter 4 reviews how a small legislative amendment in response to the 1919 Winnipeg General Strike expanded the scope of Canada's restrictive control policies to British-born immigrants and produced a new wave of rights-based politics (1914-45). During the interwar period, the government consolidated a highly effective system for rejecting and removing immigrants (both European and non-European) from the country. Its success was underwritten by the extreme nature of its rights-restrictive character, with both the due process and equality rights of non-citizens being tightly circumscribed. This led to an expansion of Liberal Internationalist critiques and rights-based politics, which anticipated more effective challenges to the legitimacy of Liberal Nationalism in the post–Second World War period. Control was also undermined by increasing circumvention on the part of

"Asian" migrants. When the government refused admission to Jewish refugees from Europe and instituted a policy of internment and then removals of Japanese Canadians (many of whom were Canadian-born), Liberal Internationalism underwent further renewal. The material presented in this chapter thus shows how the specific rights-based concerns of due process and equality protections that came to prominence after the war – with respect to both non-citizens and increasing calls for a written bill of rights – were firmly embedded in Canadian politics well before that time.

Chapter 5 traces the onset of the slow decline and transformation of Liberal Nationalism soon after the Second World War, alongside the rise of Liberal Internationalism in the debate over Canadian control policies (1945-52). It begins by identifying the emergence of an expanded human rights discourse in Canada, one that drew on the experiences of the recent war and merged with an ongoing debate over the meaning of British liberalism. It would take some time, however, for Liberal Internationalism to have much more than a discursive effect. Indeed, Canada maintained a Liberal Nationalist approach during this period even as it eventually opened its doors to thousands of Europeans displaced by the war. This is exemplified by both the decision not to sign the 1951 United Nations Convention Relating to the Status of Refugees (which codified the rights of asylum seekers vis-à-vis the receiving state) and the passage of the 1952 *Immigration Act* (which maintained the restrictive focus of its 1910 predecessor). Nonetheless, this approach became increasingly difficult to sustain in the face of continued rights-based politics and circumvention, along with administrative inefficiencies stemming from the discretionary nature of control decision making. It is important to trace these developments as their existence and significance are often overlooked in the literature – especially the fact that such rights-based politics occurred largely through non-judicial means anchored in Canada's parliamentary system. This underlines the need to situate the role of interest groups and the courts within a broader analytical framework than is commonly employed in the comparative control literature.

Chapter 6 traces the further marginalization of Liberal Nationalism and increased institutionalization of Liberal Internationalism in the period leading up to Canada's centenary year (1952-67). New due process and equality provisions for non-citizens that hearkened back to claims that had been made on behalf of non-citizens since the late nineteenth century provided the foundations for a new era in Canadian control and, as a result, Canadian national development. In particular, the government instituted an official policy of non-discrimination in immigrant selection and vastly expanded judicial oversight within this policy area. This generated a Liberal Internationalist context for the development of subsequent control policies and prompted shifts in the discourse and demands of Liberal Nationalism. These important developments did not simply unfold through interest group politics or the courts but were more the product of robust parliamentary debate over what it meant to be a liberal democracy. In completing this analysis of the first century of Canadian control politics, Chapter 6 offers a better foundation for exploring the continued tension between control and rights – between Liberal Internationalist and Liberal Nationalist approaches – during Canada's second century.

Chapter 7 considers the lessons drawn from the preceding analysis in the light of more contemporary developments. The need to undertake a more detailed and contextual approach to the study of liberal-democratic control is underlined through a brief survey of various ways in which due process and equality issues still define Canadian control politics. The continued evolution and resurgence of Liberal Nationalism – especially with respect to asylum seekers – is highlighted through a brief assessment of the control politics surrounding recent Canadian legislation – the 2010 *Balanced Refugee Reform Act* and the 2012 *Protecting Canada's Immigration System Act*. This is followed by the identification of important future research directions, both in the Canadian and comparative liberal-democratic contexts.

In sum, the research presented in this book shows that rights-based politics has existed ever since Canada first instituted rights-restrictive control policies and highlights the need to pay more attention to the rights-based character of a country's policies when trying to understand liberal-democratic state control outcomes. Moreover, it reveals the dangers of focusing too exclusively on rights-based politics and perceived control failures, as other important dynamics (such as circumvention and administrative inefficiencies) and outcomes are thereby unjustifiably downplayed or ignored. In the process, it demonstrates how rights-restrictive policies can increase the risks of control failure when they open up avenues along which state authority and capacity can be challenged effectively. As a result, this study not only contributes to how Canadian immigration and refugee history is understood but speaks more generally to research on liberal-democratic control policies and politics. In doing so, it implicates the choices made by states in the production of the control problems that restrictive control policies are supposed to rectify. This, in turn, expands the political parameters within which control debates might unfold by de-centring state rights in the face of the rights of non-citizens, which calls attention to a broader range of policy options in the politics of control.

1
The Study of Liberal-Democratic Control over International Migration

International migration constitutes an issue of high politics between states and a highly political one within them. A core contemporary concern among states is that of regulating population movements across national boundaries, while the presence of foreigners is often the subject of strenuous and sustained public debate within states. Although the term "control" has long been employed in the study of how states respond to international migration, its use as a conceptual or theoretical tool to assist in describing, evaluating, and explaining the behaviour of states is not so old. One prominent argument holds that the recent rise of rights-based politics has made it more difficult for liberal democracies to control their borders and that such states have, as a result, pursued an increasing range of rights-restrictive policies. As observed in the Introduction, however, such a conceptualization does not adequately capture the diverse ways in which control and rights intersect. This chapter provides a critical examination of the comparative control literature and suggests how it might better guide empirical and theoretical work on the politics of control. In doing so, it draws attention to the need to situate contemporary developments more securely within a deeper and broader history of liberal-democratic control.

The chapter opens with a brief summary of recent trends in international migration, focusing on the growth in the number and diversity of international migrants in liberal-democratic states and the tendency to pursue rights-restrictive policies in response. This is particularly apparent with the increased securitization of international migration as a policy area, especially after 11 September 2001. The analysis then turns to examine how the control/rights nexus has been conceptualized in the comparative and Canadian literatures. The former generally employs too narrow an understanding of the relationship between control and rights, whereas the latter rarely addresses the subject directly. In response, an alternative formulation of the control/rights nexus is presented that begins with the rights-restrictive policies pursued by states. It is suggested that this allows for a greater appreciation of how the particular rights-based choices made by states can influence control policy outcomes. Finally, the chapter establishes an analytical framework rooted in the notion of the universe of political discourse, describes the Liberal Internationalist and Liberal Nationalist perspectives that can be seen to structure control debates and policies, and outlines how these conceptual tools are applied to the Canadian case in this book.

Trends in International Migration and Liberal-Democratic State Responses

The end of the twentieth century was marked by the consolidation of an "age of migration" (Castles and Miller 2003) in which international population movements – immigrant and refugee, temporary and permanent, regular and irregular – continued to grow and diversify. The effects on receiving countries in the developed world have been many and varied, and subject to numerous and often divergent interpretations. This has been an important feature of the politics of control as controversy over the possible ethno-racial, economic, and security effects – among others – of international migration on receiving countries has shaped public discourse and policy decisions. In seeking to control their borders by attracting certain types of migrants and excluding others, liberal-democratic states have often adopted a rights-restrictive approach that limits the claims that non-citizens can make against the state.

In 2010, there were an estimated 214 million international migrants globally, representing roughly 3.1 percent of the world's population, up from 2.3 percent some two decades earlier (UN DESA 2009, 1). Since the 1980s, developed countries have received a growing proportion of working-age international migrants, reaching a figure of 62 percent in 2010 (UN DESA 2010, 1). This has fundamentally altered the demographic characteristics of receiving countries. For example, in 2008 the foreign-born constituted 25.4, 20.2, and 13.7 percent of the national populations of Australia, Canada, and the United States, respectively (OECD 2010, 299, Table A.1.4). In 2010, there were around 72.6 million migrants living in Europe and Central Asia (a 5.1 million increase over 2005), and about one-third of all international migrants are found in Europe, constituting some 8.7 percent of the regional population (IOM 2010, 183). The country origins of migrants to the developed world have also diversified, with a general shift in the post–Second World War period from Europe to Africa, Asia, and Latin America and the Caribbean (Castles and Miller 2003, 77). While an estimated 10-15 percent of international migrants in developed states are deemed irregular (IOM 2010, 120), 80 percent of refugees – who constitute about 7.6 percent of international migrants – remain in developing countries (ibid., 119). The meaning and significance of the presence of the foreign-born and their descendants in liberal democracies are often the subject of heated debate, especially within the context of their increased ethnoracial diversity, and this has "compelled these countries to reinterpret their traditions, to reshape their institutions, to rethink the meaning of citizenship – to reinvent themselves, in short, as nation-states" (Brubaker 1989, 1). In doing so, liberal-democratic states have often taken a rights-restrictive approach.

This can be seen, for example, in a general shift away from family immigration and towards selective skilled and unskilled economic migration in response to perceived labour market needs and the anticipation that such migrants will draw less on welfare benefits, among other factors. Whereas Australia and Canada rapidly undertook such a reorientation in the 1990s (Abu-Laban 1998b; Birrell 2001), the process has been slower in the United States, where family immigration has accounted for about two-thirds of annual intake fairly consistently since the 1980s (Reinemeyer and Batalova 2007). Although family immigration remains relatively high in some European Union member states, many have shifted towards attracting more economic migrants (IOM 2008, Chapter 8). Thus, the Organisation for Economic Co-operation and Development (OECD) reports that "changes in family reunification policies have tended to impose restrictive criteria, such as residency and income requirements. The use of language or civics tests as a precondition for family reunification and for naturalisation continues to expand" (OECD 2010, 22). In contrast, the mobility rights of high-skilled economic migrants have increased in many developed countries, especially within "global cities" (Sassen 1996).

Liberal-democratic states have also put considerable effort into responding to irregular or "unwanted immigration" (Joppke 1998b). Their ability to do so has been limited by factors such as budgetary constraints, which set political and practical boundaries around viable policy options (Castles 2004). Moreover, many national economies benefit from, may even depend on, irregular migrants to meet labour market needs (Düvell 2006; Hanson 2007). Nonetheless, irregular migration calls attention to a state's inability to control its borders, which can lead to public and political pressure to act. One response has been to undertake "symbolic" actions directed more towards appearances of control in response to immediate border control issues than, for example, addressing perceived root causes of such movements (Andreas 2001). Nonetheless, states have increased border control resource commitments, especially after 2001, and much greater effort is now put into identifying and removing those not selected by the state to enter and remain (Broeders and Engbersen 2007). This has been pursued in part by removing state action from judicial oversight through interdiction techniques and by defining the rights of non-citizens more narrowly in law. These and other policies have reduced the range of rights accessible to irregular and regular migrants seeking to move between countries (Bogusz et al. 2004).

Such practices have been especially prominent with respect to refugees and asylum seekers, who often use irregular channels to seek protection from persecution. Since the 1980s, liberal-democratic states have worked to decrease the number of asylum seekers in their inland refugee status determination systems on the grounds that too many claimants are at best "asylum shoppers" and at worst "false claimants." By the late 1990s, the United Nations High Commissioner for Refugees (UNHCR 1997, 155) had observed a significant decrease in opportunities for protection:

> Anxious to protect their borders from unwanted immigration, and suspicious of the motivations of many of those seeking asylum, governments of industrialized countries have adopted a range of new measures to control and restrict access to their territory. For refugees fleeing persecution, these measures have in many cases severely affected their ability to gain access to asylum procedures and safety.

This became all the more apparent after 2001. UNHCR statistics show a drop in asylum applications in industrialized countries from some 620,000 in 2001 to around 358,800 in 2010, a decline of about 42 percent (UNHCR 2011, 5). Among other factors, the wide range of restrictive policies that have been enacted since the 1980s have collectively served to circumscribe the right of individuals to seek protection from persecution by limiting their access to inland determination systems and their legal rights within them (Bohmer and Shuman 2008; Squire 2009). As a result, rights at the heart of the international refugee protection regime have been challenged, if not diminished (Kelley 2007).

Alongside restrictive actions at the national level, there has been increased policy coordination and cooperation across borders. This can be seen most clearly in the EU, where free movement between member states has been achieved through the development of common rules to govern both the entry of temporary migrants and external border control (Geddes 2003). This has included the negotiation of agreements to coordinate asylum policies around a shared set of principles (Guild 2006). In North America, joint border management has occurred primarily on a bilateral basis centred on the United States (Andreas 2005); recently this has involved efforts to construct a common security perimeter around Canada and the United States, with extensions to be developed to Mexico (Gilbert 2007). With regard to asylum seekers, Canada and the United States have implemented a Safe Third Country Agreement since 2004 to coordinate the processing of asylum applications (Macklin 2005). For its part, Australia has pursued its "Pacific

Strategy," working with other regional states to prevent the arrival of asylum seekers (Kneebone and Pickering 2007). There is also evidence of greater policy coordination and cooperation among states more generally with respect to international migration, although the literature remains slight (see IOM 2011). In the process, liberal-democratic states have established a range of practices to "buffer" themselves from unwanted international migration, which has had a restrictive effect on the mobility of non-citizens and their ability to enter into rights-based relationships with receiving states (Guiraudon 2001).

Already apparent in many liberal democracies in the 1980s and 1990s (e.g., Huysmans 2000; on the Canadian case, see Irvine 2011), these trends within and between countries and across international migration categories intensified following 11 September 2001. Although international migration had become a securitized policy domain before then, the subsequent inten-sification of this process has shielded or removed administrative and execu-tive action from judicial, political, and public scrutiny to an even greater degree, as control policies have been crafted with "an emphasis on security and a narrower reading of the rights and interests of non-citizens" (Crépeau et al. 2007, 315). Although this is recognized in the comparative control literature, a narrow interpretation of the relationship between control and rights, focusing on rights-based politics and control failure, has unnecessarily limited the study of the politics of control at this crucial juncture.

The Literature on Liberal-Democratic Control

It was not until the early 1990s that a dedicated effort was made to pursue "a systematic theoretical analysis of both the external pressures impinging on the state and the internal dynamics of the legislative and administrative bodies dealing with immigration" (Portes 1997, 817). Previously, politics and the state had been marginal considerations in the literature on inter-national migration, largely due to lack of attention from political scientists (Freeman 2005; Massey 1999; however, see Zolberg 1981). Instead, explana-tory efforts more often sought to elucidate economic and sociological dimen-sions without touching on "the fact that the streams were flowing through gates, and that these openings were surrounded by high walls" that rested on a foundation of state sovereignty (Zolberg 1999, 73). Since the early 1990s, in contrast, much work has been published that speaks to the political dimensions of control, especially perceived control policy failures, and a prominent explanatory claim has focused on the constraining effects of rights-based politics. Although this literature has shed considerable light on the politics of control in liberal-democratic states, albeit rarely with regard to the Canadian case, it possesses conceptual and empirical limitations that need to be addressed.

Conceptualizing Control: The Comparative Literature

The control/rights nexus was first explored in detail by Hollifield in his comparative investigation of the political economy of control, *Immigrants, Markets, and States.* "Rights-based politics and more expansive citizenship policies," he wrote, "have worked to stimulate immigration and weaken the capacity of democratic states to control their borders" (1992, 222). Although not the only factor involved (markets also feature prominently in his analysis), rights-based politics was seen as constituting an unprecedented and central challenge to the justifications that had long underpinned state control policies: "Liberal states have tried to regulate migration according to the realist principles of sovereignty and the national interest, yet liberalism in its rights aspect forces these states to recognize migrants as individuals. Their own cultures and institutions have compelled the liberal states to modify or abandon statist policies" (ibid., 228). This "new brand of liberal politics" could be seen "at every level of democratic polities" but Hollifield underlined an important "shift in the arena of political conflict – from parties and legislatures to courts and administrative agencies" (ibid., 170). He argued that liberal democracies like the United States had become subject to a "judicial assault on the sovereignty and autonomy of the state," which undermined their control capacity (ibid., 186). By focusing on rights expansion and control failure, Hollifield established an interpretation of the control/rights nexus (see Figure 1) that has since figured largely in the literature.

Figure 1

The Control/Rights Nexus: The Traditional Formulation

rights-based politics → control failure

For example, in an important comparative edited volume, *Controlling Immigration,* Cornelius, Martin, and Hollifield proposed that various push/pull dynamics in the international system of states (including the end of the Cold War and growing economic inequalities), transnational social networks, and the demand for cheap labour were "necessary but not sufficient" explanatory factors of the "crisis of immigration control" (1994b, 8). A fundamental shift had occurred since the Second World War, making human rights criteria an intrinsic part of the standards of political behaviour used to judge actions between and within liberal-democratic states. At the international level, there had developed a "postwar order [that] has, embedded within it, certain liberal notions of rights, norms, and principles, which have been partially institutionalized" (ibid., 31). At the national level, a human rights discourse had been advanced through both judicial and legislative means, resulting in an expansion of the range of recognized rights possessed by resident non-citizens. Cornelius and colleagues concluded that this domestic process – especially in the form of judicial activism – had served "to constrain the executive authorities of democratic states in their attempts to achieve territorial closure and to exclude certain individuals and groups from membership in society" (ibid., 10). Thus, the recent ascendancy of a rights-based politics inclusive of non-citizens was held to be a crucial component in explaining the finding that liberal democracies were losing control.

Subsequently, Joppke argued that control policies were "self-limited by interest-group pluralism, autonomous legal systems, and moral obligations toward particular immigrant groups" (1999, vii). He explored how the judiciary created situations of "self-limited sovereignty" where, "once admitted, an alien enjoys the equal protection of the law, and the state has 'self-limited' its capacity to dispose of her at will" (1998a, 19). He concluded that "independent courts have clashed with restriction-minded state executives, and rights expansion for immigrants [has been] achieved against rather than with the latter" (2001, 340).[1] Once again, the rights of non-citizens were seen to limit the extent to which liberal-democratic states could control their borders. For example, "instead of being subject to contestation," Joppke suggested, "the norm of non-discrimination functions as a fundamental, taken-for-granted assumption, even by those who are opposed to its effects" (2005a, 7). Any retreat from this norm "would immediately be branded as a violation of fundamental liberal-democratic norms and be tantamount to a civilization break" (ibid., 19). The prominence of rights, he reflected, now constituted "the mark of the liberal state" (2005b, 48). In its conceptualization of the relationship between control and rights, Joppke's work has therefore been consistent with the idea captured in Figure 1: as an embodiment of rights expansion, rights-based politics has undermined state control.

Although this idea constitutes a core contribution to the study of liberal-democratic control, it has certain limitations. For example, with its focus on rights expansion and rights-based politics, little if any differentiation is made between kinds of rights or degrees of expansion. As a result, the possibility that some forms of expansion could be more problematic than others from a control perspective is largely left unexamined. Moreover, with its emphasis on control failure, the literature does not adequately explore the extent to which rights-restrictive policies result in control success. As well, it is increasingly recognized that states have developed ways to shield their actions from the effects of rights-based politics by shifting the authority and practice of control "to venues more favourable to restrictive control policies" (Guiraudon 2001, 33). This has included "a shift of decision making in monitoring and execution powers upward to intergovernmental fora ... downward to local authorities ... and outward to nonstate actors" (Guiraudon and Lahav 2000, 176). Of particular importance has been the practice of "deter[ring] immigration by regulating embarkation at or near the point of origin," or "remote control" (Zolberg 1999, 73).

In addition, much less attention has been paid to instances in which rights-based politics has not been sufficient to counter rights-restrictive policies. For example, such policies might succeed when opposing groups fail to mobilize sufficient political support or when restrictive measures receive consensus-like backing from politicians or are sustained by the courts. This again suggests the need to expand the analysis to account for different ways in which control and rights intersect. Finally, with its focus on rights-based politics, the literature has done too little with respect to "bringing states directly into the analysis as independent entities" (Freeman 2005, 122). In particular, it is important to examine more keenly the executive and legislative contexts within which rights-based politics arises and unfolds (Boswell 2007). Moreover, the literature infrequently reflects critically on the meaning of control failure itself, often assuming that it occurs when states do not meet expressed control objectives or particular popular demands for restriction. This sidesteps the possibility, for example, that a supposed control failure might be consistent with other important economic and political objectives (De Genova 2002). The concerns raised here are offered not to challenge the centrality of the connection between control and rights in liberal-democratic states but rather to suggest that the study and understanding of this relationship needs to be refined and expanded.

Thus, an important research path has been developed for the study of liberal-democratic control, one of probing "how far ... liberal democracies [can] go in limiting rights of foreigners as a strategy for immigration control" (Hollifield 1999, 57). Although it is clear that "regulating international migration requires liberal states to be attentive to the (human and civil) rights of the individual" (Hollifield 2004a, 901), it is necessary to move past a simpler problematization of rights expansion. While control is said to be bounded by "ideas, institutions, and culture, as well as certain segments of civil society" (Hollifield 1999, 58), the task of providing firmer conceptual and empirical (especially historical) foundations remains. Some important leads have nonetheless been established. For example, Hansen (2002, 270) advocates a path dependence approach to the study of control in accordance with the idea that "the range of options available at any point in time is constrained by extant institutional capabilities, and these capabilities are themselves a product of choices made during some earlier period." This is reinforced by Zolberg (1997) and Fahrmeir and colleagues (2003), who stress that too little is known about earlier periods of control and their effects on the present and how it is understood. Moreover, such a historical approach needs to recognize that "ideas, ideology and ethical considerations play a much more significant role in the making of migration policies than has hitherto been accounted for" (Bonjour 2011, 111).

Unfortunately, after a productive burst of scholarship, there has been too little development on the operation of the control/rights nexus in liberal-democratic states. This is partly because much attention was initially paid instead to whether rights-based politics has primarily national (Freeman 1998; Guiraudon and Lahav 2000; Hollifield 2000; Joppke 1998a) or international (Jacobson 1996; Jacobson and Ruffer 2003; Sassen 1996, 1998; Soysal 1994) foundations. The lack of advancement can be seen in a number of recent "state-of-the-art" surveys, in which the role of rights in shaping control policies is acknowledged but barely discussed as the impressive expansion of the literature on the politics of international migration is canvassed (e.g., Castles 2004; Cornelius and Tsuda 2004; Cornelius and Rosenblum 2005; Lahav and Guiraudon 2006). Thus, while rights-based politics occupies a central place within the comparative literature, the relationship between control and rights in liberal-democratic states – in both the past and present – requires greater clarification. This is just as true in the case of Canada as elsewhere.

Conceptualizing Control: The Canadian Literature

As observed in the Introduction, Canada scarcely figures in the comparative control canon. For example, although both editions of *Controlling Immigration* (Cornelius et al. 1994a; 2004) include a chapter on Canada, neither fully addresses the issue of control. The first essentially provides a selective description of contemporary policy trends (García y Griego 1994), while the second focuses more on explaining the distinctiveness of Canadian immigrant selection policies (Reitz 2004).[2] Each suggests that Canada has seen less of a gap between its control objectives and outcomes or between control outcomes and public opinion than other receiving states. Moreover, control problems that have arisen, such as those involving asylum seekers, are traced to rights expansion rather than restriction. The Canadian case merits being explored more systematically, however, and its marginal place in the control literature has not facilitated this process.

This poor record is matched – perhaps even exceeded – in the Canadian immigration and refugee literature, which rarely engages comparative work on control. In general, the Canadian literature is more descriptive than theoretical on questions of control, and pays little heed to how the country's liberal-democratic foundations have influenced policy. Although a rich body of work on the history of international migration to and settlement in Canada exists, it tends to concentrate on specific migration groups, periods, and/or themes, and is infrequently marked by contributions from political scientists. Furthermore, it rarely explores the specific intersection of rights and control. For example, although classic works by Hawkins (1972) and Dirks (1995) provide detailed and insightful analyses of the administration of immigration and refugee policy, these are done more from a political-bureaucratic than a liberal-democratic perspective, and important texts by Whitaker (1987) and Avery (1995) take a similar approach to security and immigrant labour. Although rights issues are increasingly explored for some migrant groups, such as asylum seekers, detainees, and migrant workers (e.g., Aiken 2007; Basok 2003; Dauvergne 2005; Mountz 2010; Pratt 2005; Stasiulis and Bakan 2005), such studies generally do not engage broader questions of, or the comparative literature on, control or Canada's liberal-democratic foundations.

As an exception, one recent and prominent strain in the Canadian literature addresses the relationship between control and rights in the context of asylum seekers but exhibits many of the limitations found in the comparative canon. During the past decade, numerous authors have promoted the idea that Canada is unable to control its borders adequately because its policies towards asylum seekers provide too many rights protections. Politicians are said to be unwilling to take a more restrictive approach due to the influence of the courts and interest groups, which are said to promote the rights of non-citizens over the national interest (e.g., Bauer 1997; Bell 2005; Bissett 2010a; Francis 2002; Gallagher 2003; Moens and Collacott 2008; Stoffman 2002). It is maintained that this has constrained public discourse so that those promoting a more restrictive approach have been sidelined from the policy debates. Like the comparative literature, then, this body of work concludes that rights-based politics inhibits or even undermines state control. It similarly employs an unduly narrow interpretation of the control/rights nexus, both conceptually and empirically, and therefore provides at best a very partial explanation.

There are, however, two dimensions of the Canadian literature that are particularly useful in understanding the evolution of the control/rights nexus, each reflected within the chapters that follow, where they are woven into a more comprehensive narrative that focuses on how Canada's liberal-democratic political system has structured its authority and capacity to control. The first consists of work that assesses the effects of rights-restrictive policies on particular immigrant groups. Generally written by historians, these analyses provide important insights into how migrants themselves have often responded by opposing or even circumventing restrictive measures. The second, which intersects with the first, traces the emergence and consolidation of human rights discourse and instruments in Canada from the interwar period to the early 1960s. This literature calls attention to the relationship between debates concerning the rights of non-citizens and the evolution of liberalism in Canada. In exploring the relationship between control and the rights of non-citizens since Confederation, this book both reinforces and expands on these themes (see also Anderson 2011). It draws direct lines between the wealth of information available on the Canadian case and the conceptual and empirical perspectives presented in the comparative control literature. In doing so, it seeks to help clarify the concept of liberal-democratic control.

Clarifying the Concept of Control

The idea that the rights-restrictive policies of liberal-democratic states contribute to the generation of rights-based politics, and thus influence control policy outcomes, has not gone unnoted in the comparative literature. For example, Joppke and Marzal (2004, 839) observe that "the constitutionalization of immigrant rights has to be put into the dynamic context of states' discriminatory practices triggering court intervention." The implications of this insight have not been pursued very far, however. As a result, a particular feature of the control/rights nexus – the relationship between rights expansion and control failure – has garnered the lion's share of attention while others have been all but ignored. If the relationship between control and rights is extended to include rights-restrictive policies, however, at least four distinct analytical advantages emerge, as captured in Figure 2.

Figure 2

The Control/Rights Nexus: An Alternative Formulation

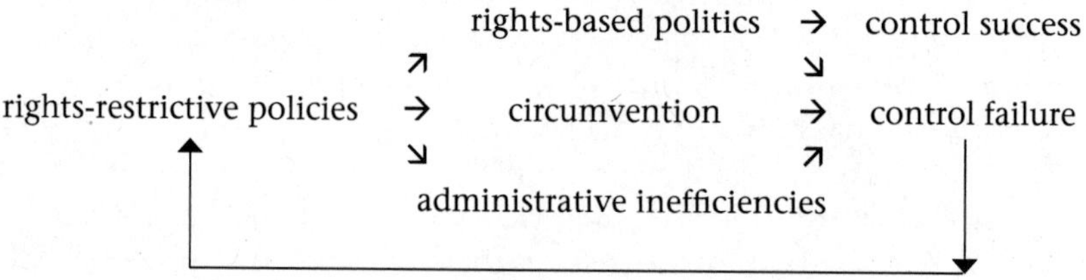

First, a more adequate context for rights-based politics can be provided by enabling the comparison of policies in terms of the extent to which they restrict different types of rights, foster rights-based politics, and produce a loss of control. In doing so, the focus is expanded from individuals, interest groups, and the courts to include the roles played by the executive and legislative arms of the state.

Second, it becomes possible to assess the extent to which rights-restrictive policies contribute to control failure along other avenues, such as encouraging circumvention of the law or creating administrative inefficiencies within the state itself as it seeks to reconcile rights restriction with important liberal values such as due process and equality. After all, as Castles (2004, 860) has noted, international migrants have agency in that they are "social beings who seek to achieve better outcomes for themselves, their families and their communities by actively shaping the migratory process." Moreover, as Lahav and Guiraudon (2006, 208) have suggested, "administrative decisions, policy implementation, and the network of actors involved in these processes may provide us with a more accurate picture of the character of immigration control." This underscores the need for a much broader and deeper consideration of the processes involved.

Third, it anticipates that a government could find itself within a negative feedback loop, wherein control failure prompts further rights-restrictive measures, which in turn result in failure, and so on, until a more serious or systematic loss of control occurs. Of particular note here is the possibility of restriction thresholds that can be sustained within a liberal democracy until the conditions that support them, such as the formation of a political consensus around the particular rights involved, change or falter. Alternatively, the initial success of restrictive practices could generate new forms of circumvention or administrative inefficiency, leading to further calls for restriction. Thus, control policies may contribute to the creation of the very problems that they are said to be designed to resolve. This highlights the need to trace such dynamics over time, especially in the context of identifying possible control/rights patterns.

Finally, the focus in the literature is overwhelmingly on control failure due to rights-based politics. Much less consideration is given to instances in which such politics produce control success as executive and legislative measures are sustained – for example, through judicial approval or broad political consensus regarding their legitimacy. Moreover, the very meaning of failure and success in a control policy context needs to be problematized, rather than read directly off expressed state objectives and presumed public preferences (De Genova 2002).

For these various reasons, then, it is necessary to move beyond the constraining effects of rights-based politics to understand the broader policy and political contexts within which control and rights intersect in liberal-democratic states. By establishing rights-restrictive policies as the analytical point of departure, a much richer understanding of control politics is made possible.[3] In the process, a historical approach to the politics of control needs to be taken so that factors involved in shaping patterns of continuity and change into the contemporary period can be more accurately identified and assessed. This requires a framework that can capture how control policy has been debated, practised, and challenged over time in the context of the liberalness of liberal-democratic states.

Reframing the Study: Liberal-Democratic Control

In a review of the Canadian public policy analysis literature over thirty-five years ago, Simeon stressed the importance of studying the prevailing ideas in a given policy area in order to understand state decision making: "Policy is a function of the dominant ideas, values, theories, and beliefs in the society... [and] these factors may be seen as providing the basic assumptions and framework within which policy is considered" (1976, 570). Although their role has largely remained on the margins of the policy analysis literature (Berman 2001), more attention is now being paid to how ideas, "as articulated in policy discourses, can serve as contributing factors to policy change, even in the absence of changes in institutions and interests" (Bhatia and Coleman 2003, 715-16). This has been an understood, if underdeveloped, feature of the comparative control literature (e.g., Bonjour 2011; Hollifield 1999). Although ideas alone are unlikely to account for policy decisions, they nonetheless structure debates and choices throughout the policy process, from problem definition to policy evaluation (Pal 2006). To appreciate their influence, however, it is necessary to specify their content, identify their operation through policy debates and decisions, and, ultimately, explore their expression in policy outcomes. In this book, ideas are used as a lens through which to view the evolution of Canadian control policy, and to appreciate both why some forms of control have been pursued over others and the implications of such choices for how control can be understood. In the process, light is shed on how the liberal-democratic character of the political system shapes control policy actions and outcomes – how it has defined and continues to define the evolution of the control/rights nexus.

According to Jenson (1989, 238), state and non-state actors operate within a *universe of political discourse*, "a space in which socially-constructed identities emerge in discursive struggle." In this context, she suggests, debates take place over the meaning of difference and its political significance, and power relations that define relationships between collective identities in society are shaped. One way to approach such power relations is to study what she calls the societal paradigms that operate within the universe of political discourse, those "shared set[s] of interconnected premises which make sense of many social relations" and their related practices (ibid., 239).[4] Politics can be examined, then, through the efforts of state and non-state actors to define which societal paradigm will become hegemonic, will operate as the basic template off which policy decisions are made. As Phillips (1996, 257) puts it: "The political struggle that occurs within the universe of political discourse sets the boundaries of what are considered to be legitimate claims and relevant actors, determines the possibilities for alliances and advocacy strategies, and limits what are deemed by policy makers to be feasible policy options." Such a discursive approach to policy analysis is in keeping with a broader contemporary commitment in the field of policy studies to "moving beyond objectivist conceptions of reality" (Orsini and Smith 2007, 3).

Examining the nature of the universe of political discourse that defines the relationship between the state and non-citizens can assist in understanding how control has been and is pursued in liberal-democratic states; it can help delineate the control/rights nexus. First, however, the dominant perspectives (or, in Jenson's terms, societal paradigms) that define control discourse need to be identified.

In the Canadian case, two main perspectives have dominated the politics of control since Confederation. Each stems from a particular set of assumptions about the ties that bind non-citizens and the state (and thus its citizens), and each has been and continues to be – albeit in evolving formulations – prominent in justifying divergent policy choices. Despite the danger that can arise in viewing policy debates as unfolding in such a binary fashion, in that a diversity of interests and opinions can become artificially reduced, thereby introducing distortion into the analysis, it can nonetheless capture an underlying structure in political discourse. This can be seen with respect to Canadian control policies since Confederation, where the central debates have revolved around whether Canada should be more or less receptive to the claims of non-citizens who wish to enter into and/or remain within the country.[5] The terms "Liberal Internationalism" and "Liberal Nationalism" are assigned in this book to these relatively expansionist and restrictionist camps, respectively. These basic outlooks, like the concept of control itself, do not exist in a political vacuum but reflect evolving yet bounded assumptions about how the relationship between non-citizens and the state ought to be realized. In addition, they are not mutually exclusive, as Liberal Internationalists will advocate certain restrictive measures, while Liberal Nationalists will support certain expansive options.

Liberal Internationalism, which extends from the notion of "humane internationalism" that Pratt (1989, 13) employed in his work on comparative overseas development assistance, is premised on "an acceptance by the citizens of the industrialized states that they have ethical obligations towards those beyond their borders and that these in turn impose obligations upon their governments."[6] It is rooted in an assumption that only in meeting such commitments can liberal democracies act in a manner consistent with the basic principles upon which their political systems are founded. With respect to international migration, Liberal Internationalism exhibits certain central concerns. First, it holds that control policies ought to reflect a recognition of the common humanity of citizens and non-citizens. This could stem, for example, from a universalist approach to liberal values or specific human rights instruments, such as the 1948 Universal Declaration of Human Rights and the 1951 United Nations Convention Relating to the Status of Refugees.

Second, it insists that citizens and non-citizens generally be treated alike under domestic law. For example, due process and equality protections should not be denied to non-citizens on the basis of citizenship status but extended to them as fellow human beings. Third, it sees the settlement of immigrants and protection of refugees as being in the long-term interests of the receiving state and society. This is thought to assist in the creation and extension of peaceful relations between peoples of the world. Emphasis is also placed on the positive contributions that the foreign-born can make to the economic, political, and social well-being of the receiving country.

Liberal Nationalism, in contrast, holds that domestic interests take priority over commitments to the global community, and that liberal-democratic governments generally ought to attend to these before addressing the needs of strangers.[7] It is rooted in an assumption that only by meeting such commitments can liberal democracies ensure long-term support for the basic principles upon which their political systems are founded. From such a starting point, the three principal features of this perspective with respect to international migration stand largely in opposition to those at the core of Liberal Internationalism. First, Liberal Nationalism holds that border control ought to privilege the perceived national interests of citizens over the interests of non-citizens. This could, for example, extend from a close association between citizens and the responsibilities of the state, or an assertion of state sovereignty that renders international human rights instruments more advisory than obligatory. Second, it insists that citizens and non-citizens need not be treated alike under domestic law. The full protection of the law, then, is held to extend only to citizens as members of the national political community, while the position of non-citizens might vary from much less to minimal protection. Third, Liberal Nationalism considers it to be in the country's self-interest to see to the needs of its own citizens before extending assistance to foreigners at or within its borders. This is rarely understood to imply that no help should be offered, but rather that it should be on a limited scale and more focused (through, for example, foreign aid or trade agreements) on those who remain abroad. In addition, emphasis is placed on the potential threat that the foreign-born might represent to the economic, political, and social well-being of the receiving country.

This contrast between Liberal Internationalism and Liberal Nationalism fits comfortably within recent debates concerning the "illiberal liberalism" practised by liberal-democratic states. Although inconsistencies and tensions have long existed within liberal political systems, including with respect to control (as explored by Hollifield and Joppke, for example), the notion of illiberal liberalism has begun to be used in examining state responses to international migration. For example, it has been employed to explore immigrant integration policies (Bauböck and Joppke 2010) and migration-related security policies (Bigo and Tsoukala 2008), among others. It has perhaps been explored most extensively by King, who starts with the assumption that "a liberal political system provides equality of treatment of individuals and access to the due process of law for the redress of violation of individual rights. It is premised on the impartial treatment of its members and places a high value on individual autonomy" (1999, 8). Liberal-democratic states often pursue "illiberal" control policies that contravene such principles, however, especially but not simply with respect to non-citizens and the foreign-born. For King, this is not an aberration or perversion of liberal-democratic politics; rather, "illiberal policies are intrinsic to liberal democracy itself" (ibid., 26) because such a system is open to (democratic) public contestation and therefore to the pursuit of policies that meet a wide range of political demands. Others trace illiberal liberalism to the imperatives of a capitalist economic system as well (De Genova 2002). In either case, "while liberals have certainly been concerned to promote some kinds of liberty and private property, they have generally located these concerns within the broader task of governing populations," which can involve both liberal and illiberal principles and techniques (Hindess 2004, 33).

The potential for illiberal policies may be even greater when liberal-democratic states address control because non-citizens are not members of the national political community and their access to liberal standards of justice within that community is therefore less complete.[8] Rather, they are governed by migration law, that "bold expression of the sovereign power of the nation, and of its absolute ability to control, to choose, who will be admitted to the community" (Dauvergne 2005, 57). Thus, the rights of non-citizens in liberal-democratic states operate on a complex analytical and political terrain that includes liberal standards of due process and equality protections as well as commitments to a humanitarian response to the claims of non-citizens. Whereas the former extend uncertainly from the obligations associated with justice within the national political community, the latter are rooted more in charity (because non-citizens are not members of the national political community) and thus "can expand and contract easily with the domestic political environment" (ibid., 72). The Liberal Internationalism/Liberal Nationalism framework employed here functions well on this terrain because it is focused on tracking changing patterns in how rights-based relationships between citizens (through the state) and non-citizens are understood and institutionalized over time. As such, it permits insight into how the (il)liberalness of liberal-democratic states shapes – and has long shaped – their control policies and politics.

Indeed, Liberal Internationalist and Liberal Nationalist perspectives can be traced throughout the history of Canadian control policy, from Confederation to the present. Each has changed over time, of course. While Liberal Internationalism originated in British liberalism, it eventually came to incorporate a broader commitment to international human rights, especially as conceptualized after the Second World War. Liberal Nationalism began with concerns over the moral and ethnoracial character of non-citizens and citizens alike, but has come to focus more on a presumed willingness of non-citizens to abuse the generosity of the receiving state, and on the purported negative effects of ethnoracial diversity on social cohesion and even state security. This shift reflects the marginalization of explicitly discriminatory perspectives that emerged during the postwar period. In order to examine and understand the importance of these two perspectives in the evolution of the control/rights nexus in Canada, it is necessary to engage in a fairly detailed study of its control policies over time, as the literature on Canadian immigration and refugee policy is not sufficiently developed along these lines. In doing so, Brubaker's advice (1995, 903) that greater attention be paid to "contextual rather than generalized structural features of liberal democratic politics" is followed. In particular, focused attention is given to how those engaged in the politics of control have justified their actions and arguments, and the extent to which these positions have been reflected in policy choices.

For this analysis of the first century of Canadian control politics, the primary emphasis is on parliamentary debates and public policies. The focus on Parliament can be readily justified. It is the central institution of governance in Canada, and as such it articulates and defines collective interests for the country. Indeed, although it does so in a far from perfect manner (Docherty 2005; Skogstad 2003), Parliament, especially the House of Commons, is "the only [representative body] that can claim to speak on behalf of all Canadians" (D. Smith 2007, 4).[9] This discursive feature of Parliament, conducted through the structure of government and opposition, creates a "complex dialogue [that] teaches and informs both nation and government" (Franks 1987, 15). As a result, policy debates undertaken through Parliament offer an exceedingly rich source of material for an examination of the politics of control. Unfortunately, it has only infrequently been the focus of systematic study, even of such repositories of policy and political information pertaining to the control/rights nexus as parliamentary committees.[10] Although Parliament embodies politics conducted at an elite level, it nonetheless incorporates, directly and indirectly, a diverse range of actors, including ministers, parliamentarians, and senior decision makers from the civil service, as well as critics and supporters in society. Even though certain actors – especially women, non-British immigrants, and non-citizens – were all but excluded from this institutional setting in the past, their presence has grown over time and, as noted in the Introduction, other sources can be used to incorporate them into the analysis to a greater extent.

Thus, the parliamentary record can be used to trace the evolution of the control/rights nexus in Canada through the arguments of participants in their efforts to shape policy outcomes, the actions of decision makers in their attempts to regulate population movements across and within Canada's borders, and the reactions of international migrants and others with interests in this policy area. This is undertaken through an extensive reading of the published primary and secondary record on Canadian immigration and refugee policy during the country's first century. In terms of primary materials produced by the Canadian state, this book concentrates on the debates of the House of Commons and the Senate, the reports of numerous standing and special parliamentary committees, a wide range of documents published by government departments responsible for immigration to Canada, and the various statutes and regulations that have grounded the country's control policies. A selective examination of relevant judicial decisions has also been conducted. In terms of the secondary literature, published works on Canadian immigration and refugee policy have been supplemented with surveys of the histories of specific immigrant and refugee groups in Canada. The result is a reading of Canadian immigration and refugee history that provides a more solid foundation for the study of, and additional insights into, contemporary control politics in Canada and other liberal-democratic states.

Conclusion

The role of the receiving state in structuring the complex world of international migration and shaping its effects for citizens and non-citizens alike probably cannot be overestimated: "Policy and institutional environments are as important a determinant of the success of migration as, for example, the socio-economic performance of migrants. Making the right policy choices is ultimately the best way for governments to steer migration in the direction of benefits over costs" (IOM 2005, 21). Although liberal-democratic states have pursued an array of rights-restrictive policies in recent years to exert greater control over their borders, it is not yet clear how successful these policies have been, or will be. While such states have often been able to alter the numbers, types, and conditions under which migrants can legally enter and remain, the goals of control in *liberal* democracies necessarily include broader commitments to freedom and equality – to human rights. The determination of policy failure and success, therefore, needs to consider such aspects, which are, however, often overlooked or downplayed in the analysis.

Thus, although considerable attention has been paid to the relationship between control and rights in recent years, there are still considerable gaps in how it is studied and understood. By providing a more extensive conceptualization of the control/rights nexus, the ideas presented in this chapter offer a framework to assist in the development of mid-range immigration theories "that can help explain specific empirical findings by linking them to appropriate bodies of historical and contemporary research" (Castles 2004, 872, in reference to Portes 1997). Although the ways in which the institutions, practices, and principles of rights are embedded vary across different political settings and traditions (Hollifield 1999), the basic tension between the state and non-citizens – between control and rights – exists within each (Crépeau et al. 2007). With the advent of an increasingly rights-restrictive approach towards international migration since 2001, the study of the control/rights nexus has only gained in significance. If the analysis presented in this book has merit, then it becomes all the more important to recognize that any liberal democracy that seeks to control its borders by implementing rights-restrictive policies risks having its authority and capacity challenged successfully – and not just, as the literature too often suggests, through rights-based politics. This has grave human rights implications for many international migrants, the most vulnerable of whom include refugees and asylum seekers, making this an issue of considerable importance for policy makers and citizens alike in Canada and other migration-receiving states.

2
The Liberal Internationalist Foundations of Canadian Control (1867-87)

The standard tale told concerning the defining features of Canadian immigration and refugee policy prior to the First World War centres on "the willingness of the Dominion government to give businessmen a free hand in the recruitment of the immigrants they needed for national economic development; and the determination of the Immigration Branch to recruit agriculturalists, particularly for the settlement of Western Canada" (Avery 1995, 23). This is usually recounted against the backdrop of a pervasive racism that saw various non-white and non-Christian peoples (especially Asian and Jewish migrants) endure a range of restrictive and discriminatory practices. In this narrative, the liberal context is generally downplayed or omitted. For example, Kelley and Trebilcock (1998, 108) write that "while liberal values may have played a role in determining the direction of American and British immigration policy throughout the nineteenth century, there is little to suggest that it exerted great influence in Canada." "A commitment to liberal values," they continue, "when expressed, was more likely to be used as a rhetorical flourish rather than an accurate reflection of genuinely held principles" (ibid.). Thus dismissed, the subject is scarcely examined as the authors pursue their story into the twentieth century. Such characterizations are too casual, however, and have limited how the origins and subsequent evolution of control in Canada have been understood.

This chapter begins to rectify this situation by identifying the general features of international migration to, and the place of British liberalism in, Canada at the time of Confederation. This provides a benchmark against which the history of Canadian control policy can be assessed. Following this, the statutory foundations and limitations of immigration control during this early period are reviewed, and the specific case of Jewish refugees is raised. It was only after the government instituted an explicitly rights-restrictive approach towards Chinese migrants during the 1880s, however, that the influence of Liberal Internationalism on Canadian policy became a more evident feature of control politics. Thus, the chapter concludes with an examination of the struggle that took place in the Senate to prevent the passage of, and then to repeal, the 1885 *Chinese Immigration Act*. Although these interventions were ultimately unsuccessful, they reveal the nature of Liberal Internationalism at that time, knowledge of which is crucial to understanding the advance, dominance, and eventual retreat of Liberal Nationalism during the remainder of Canada's first century.

The General Context of Control at Confederation

The creation of the Dominion of Canada in 1867 is obviously an important historical and political marker. It constituted, however, more an evolution than a radical break with the past (Lipset 1968). It maintained political continuity with Britain as the British Crown remained the highest authority in the Canadian political system, which itself was defined by an act of the British Parliament – the 1867 *British North America Act* (*BNA Act*). Moreover, despite the presence of a large francophone population, Canada was largely understood to be a *British* country, and Canadians would remain British subjects into the post–Second World War period. Despite some debate at Confederation over the country's national identity, few rejected the political identity that it should assume, that, as the *BNA Act* declared, it should have "a Constitution similar in Principle to that of the United Kingdom." Furthermore, a sense of being British was reinforced through Canadian immigration policy. Prior to Confederation, the settlement of British immigrants was a strategic colonial response to secure the territory from French and, after the American Revolution, American territorial ambitions. Such immigration helped foster a national political community primarily rooted in British interests and traditions (Berger 1970), which would have important implications for how the rights of non-citizens were understood.

International Migration Trends

The eighteenth and nineteenth centuries were periods of great European mobility, temporary and permanent (Moch 1992). Although much of this migration took place within Europe, massive population movements extended throughout the world. During the hundred years prior to the First World War, some 50 million people boarded ships and left for the Americas, Australia, New Zealand, and other parts of the world colonized by Europeans, the majority going to the United States (Sassen 1999, 42-43). Around 5.5 million were destined for Canada, although many journeyed onward to the United States, either immediately or not long after their arrival (Widdis 1998). While British and German immigrants dominated migration to North America early in the nineteenth century, increasing numbers soon arrived from eastern and southern Europe (Cohen 1995, Parts 2 and 4).[1] Many of these were refugees, including those persecuted for their religious or political beliefs as well as those targeted on the grounds of their status as national minorities (Marrus 1985; Zolberg et al. 1989). In addition, there was increased migration from colonized to imperial countries (Dowty 1987, 52). The arrival of growing numbers of migrants from outside northern Europe fostered a more entrenched ethnoracial dimension to the politics of control in receiving states at the end of the nineteenth century, one that directly influenced Liberal Nationalist policy pursuits until well after the Second World War. Canada was no exception to this pattern.

The terms "country of immigration" and "settler society" are often used to describe Canada, since, with the important exception of Aboriginal peoples, everyone in the country is either foreign-born or descended from those who arrived from the fifteenth century onward. Before the late nineteenth century, immigration to Canada was almost wholly European, either directly from Europe or through the United States. Although francophones constituted the majority population in British North America in 1800, British migration soon changed this. Between 1815 and 1867, more than 1.3 million individuals officially emigrated from Britain to the North American colonies (Carrothers 1965, 305-6). This contributed significantly to a growth in population from some 350,000 to around 3.8 million over the same period (Macdonald 1966, 86).[2] Other northern European immigrants – primarily German and Swiss – were present in much smaller numbers, as were perhaps a thousand or so Chinese in British Columbia (Burnet and Palmer 1988, Chapter 2). The predominance of British (and more generally northern European) immigration by 1867 was not simply due to the efforts of the state. Rather, "in spite of spasmodic attempts to the contrary, the policy in force was in substance one of indiscriminate immigration, unorganized and uncontrolled" (Macdonald 1966, 90). This would continue for some time under Confederation.

By 1867, Canada had also developed a tradition of receiving refugees, and this had already had a profound influence on its political development.[3] Most notably, about forty thousand Loyalists resettled in the Canadian colonies at the time of the American Revolution, helping to consolidate the British character of the population vis-à-vis both the United States and the numerically dominant francophone population (Moore 1984). They were accompanied by some three thousand Mennonites, Quakers, and other pacifist religious minorities that had suffered for their refusal to take up arms for American independence, along with Aboriginal peoples who had fought on the side of the British (Dirks 1977, 16-22). Finally, during the eighteenth and nineteenth centuries, thousands of escaped slaves and free blacks came to Canada, where their liberty was more readily protected even if their equal treatment was far from assured (Winks 1997). The reception of such refugees from the United States reinforced a non-American identity and a stronger sense of Canadian identity rooted in British traditions, including a Liberal Internationalist approach to the rights of non-citizens and the duties of the state towards them. In this sense, "to accept the runaway slave was one way to demonstrate the superiority of British liberties and to strike at the Republic, economically as well as morally" (ibid., 149).

The priority of successive Canadian governments during the early years of Confederation was, however, to attract agriculturalists of British or northern European origin.[4] As one of the three major facets of what came to be known as the "National Policy" (the other two being protective tariffs and a nationwide railroad network), immigration was to provide the means of settling lands from Ontario to British Columbia, which would protect against American territorial ambitions and foster domestic economic growth by increasing agricultural output as well as western Canadian demand for eastern industrial products. The majority of annual arrivals during this period – anywhere between 60 and 90 percent, depending on the year – were British; other significant groups consisted of Germans, Scandinavians, and, during the 1870s, Russian Mennonites (see figures reported in Canada 1870, 5; 1878, xx; 1887, xxiii). As a result, British, French, and northern Europeans constituted about 97 percent of a national population of 4.3 million at the time of the 1881 census, down slightly from around 98 percent of 3.5 million in 1871 (Canada 1873, 332-33; 1882a, 300-1). The corresponding figures for those with British ancestry were roughly 59 and 61 percent, respectively (ibid.). These settlers

> made British North America *British*. By the beginning of the 1860s the British emigrants and their descendants were not only proportionately represented in the colonial élites; they were disproportionately well represented, particularly in all commercial activities and in the professions. (Buckner 1997, 22; emphasis in original)

Although the presence of a sizeable francophone population and political traditions derived from French colonial heritage are undeniable, when control debates occurred after Confederation, it was British political ideas and traditions that defined their basic discursive parameters. In the decades both preceding and following Confederation, then, immigration helped reinforce the idea that Canada was, culturally and politically, a British country.

British Liberalism in Canada at Confederation

It has been argued that the traditional attempt to understand Canadian political thought at Confederation as being the product of an interplay between liberal and conservative (Tory) ideas has diverted attention from more fruitful avenues of research (Ajzenstat and Smith 1995). Moreover, the common view that Canada was founded more on a pragmatic than on a philosophical basis – that it lacked defining political ideas – is said to be a severe misrepresentation (P. Smith 1987, 3). Indeed, it appears that core features of Canadian political thought from Confederation to the late nineteenth century remain to be delineated (see McKay 2000; Moore 1997; Romney 1999). This book contributes to this process by exploring the intersection of British liberalism and Canadian control policies with respect to non-citizens during Canada's first century.

At its core, liberalism "implies not only the feeling of liberty but the idea of equality. This feeling and this idea develop together" (Ruggiero 1981, 51). Thus, liberalism proposes that individuals equally possess inherent rights to pursue their interests (generally within certain, contested limits) in an effort to achieve their human potential. Such an outlook dominated political debate, if not political practice, in Britain during the Victorian era, wherein a commitment to liberty and equality was to be secured through parliamentary government, the history of which is itself difficult to disentangle from that of liberalism. Moreover, the principles of British liberalism were generally held by its advocates to be profoundly human and therefore not tied to any one nation, fostering an impetus to extend them in the world, "spreading progressive commercial and constitutional values internationally, and entrenching those values particularly firmly in the empire" (Parry 1993, 3). While free trade gave definition to its commercial values, its constitutional values stemmed from parliamentary government rooted in British political traditions and the rule of law: "Good law regulated passion, suppressed barbarism and encouraged the development of human character; it bolstered true liberty" (ibid., 6). Indeed, the British saw themselves as exemplars in organizing relations between and within society and the state.[5] This commitment to liberty and equality did not apply only to British citizens but also extended to non-citizens.

Although Britain had a long history of attempts to control its borders against the "King's enemies," a shift occurred after the Napoleonic Wars that resulted in very little official oversight being exercised by the middle of the nineteenth century (Roche 1969). Although an unmitigated right to remain did not exist, foreigners were understood to possess a right to enter Britain (Dua 1999, 148). In general, the government showed little interest in denying foreigners such rights for much of the nineteenth century.[6] Moreover, as early as the fifteenth century, a British tradition of asylum had taken root, which shaped how the rights of non-citizens were conceptualized under liberalism. By the end of the nineteenth century, "the view of Britain as a refuge and haven for the oppressed and persecuted from other lands ... [had] congealed as a widely-held tradition" (Holmes 1988, 67). Even when Britain came under intense pressure to extradite or expel certain refugees, it maintained the principle, expressed in 1851 by Home Secretary Lord Palmerston, that "the laws of hospitality, the dictates of humanity, the general feelings of mankind, forbid such surrenders; and any independent government, which of its own free will were to make such a surrender, would be universally and deservedly stigmatised as degraded and dishonoured" (quoted in Schuster 2002, 48).

Of course, practice often diverged from principle in the treatment of non-citizens. For example, Holmes (1988, 84) writes that "there was little evidence between 1871 and 1914 of the much-vaunted tradition of toleration in Britain, let alone acceptance. But, at the same time, there was little indication of a blanket, unremitting hostility towards immigrants and refugees."[7] Indeed, British liberalism could at times operate less as a guiding principle and more as a tool employed to serve various political ends, including discrediting political opposition (Garrard 1971). Still, despite sometimes significant pressure from domestic and foreign actors, it remained a central feature of British control policy for most of the nineteenth century.

In contrast to the history of Britain (and of the United States), where liberalism's historical role in framing and shaping politics and political debate has been extensively explored, there have been few such studies of Canada. Nonetheless, there is increasing recognition that liberalism was an important feature of Canada's Confederation debates. There was a general consensus among the architects of Confederation "that the British connection was to be maintained, that British institutions were to be preserved, and that whatever new institutions might be necessary were to be shaped, so far as possible, on British models" (Trotter 1971, 111). In line with contemporary British liberals, "Canada's founders believed that it [was] the primary and overriding purpose of parliamentary government to uphold liberties" and to benefit individuals equally (Ajzenstat 2007, 53). Thus, a language of rights was present during the Confederation debates, with Parliament being tasked with ensuring that rights were secured equally in accordance with unwritten British constitutional conventions and practices.[8]

As for the rights of non-citizens, much would depend on who counted as a member of the national political community. While "being Canadian" remained inexact but certainly British at Confederation, tighter boundaries around the idea of who belonged – and thus who possessed which rights vis-à-vis the state – were soon drawn, as they were in various European countries. In 1905, Britain began to limit the rights of non-citizens to enter and remain, and expanded these during and after the First World War, even for refugees (Garrard 1971; Holmes 1988). In the United States, control politics became exceedingly fractious from the late 1800s to the early 1900s, and policies became increasingly restrictive (Higham 1988). More generally, the late nineteenth century saw a rise in ethnonationalism throughout the West, producing an increase in laws and policies that defined national political communities in more circumscribed fashion (Hobsbawm 1992). This, in turn, affected immigration control policies and even, as noted earlier, gave rise to new refugee movements. Nonetheless, British liberalism continued to anchor a Liberal Internationalist approach to control in Canada, even as its influence waned in the face of an ascendant Liberal Nationalist outlook.

The Regulation of International Migration (1867-87)

After Confederation, Canada did not have a very extensive or structured system of immigration control. This was unexceptional, as such regulation was not consistently pursued in most Western states at the middle of the nineteenth century.[9] The US government did little more to regulate entries between 1819 and 1875 than collect vital statistics.[10] Although commercial and geographic isolation limited passage to the Australian colonies, the flurry of restrictionist measures pursued to curb Chinese migration during the last third of the century suggests that there were few effective barriers to entry (Jupp 1998). As for Britain, for the first fifty years after the end of the Napoleonic Wars, "Britannia needed no bulwarks, no towers along the steep, and she evidently did not need any immigration officers either," as only a handful were employed to check arrivals (Roche 1969, 56). At the same time, however, some governments directly encouraged international migration. For example, Britain promoted the emigration of its own nationals through various private and public schemes, while Australia and Canada sought to benefit from these efforts (Carrothers 1965). Thus, the characterization of this period as one in which "Canada maintained a laissez-faire philosophy towards immigration in allowing market forces of supply and demand to determine migration flows" (Li 2003a, 17) does not quite reflect the complexity of control during this period.

Legal Foundations of Control

The constitutional basis of Canadian control policy lies in Section 95 of the *BNA Act,* which established immigration as one of two areas of concurrent authority (the other being agriculture) between the federal and provincial levels of government, with the laws of the former being paramount in any case of conflict.[11] The connection between agriculture and immigration seemed, at the time, self-evident. In the 1860s, Canada was primarily a rural and agricultural society (Norrie and Owram 1996, 203-5). Moreover, there were large areas of unsettled territory that might be put into production, especially once rights to lands controlled by the Hudson's Bay Company were acquired by Ottawa in 1869. The link was reinforced when responsibility for immigration was placed within a new federal Department of Agriculture in 1868, a practice that dated back to 1853 within the United Canadas (Hodgetts 1955, 250-51). This association was tied to nation-building concerns: "Land was a means of absorbing immigrants, and immigrants were a means of occupying land and developing the country"

(Stevenson 1993, 303). Although jurisdiction was concurrent, it was understood that the federal government would play the primary role. Thus, during the 1865 Confederation debates, Canada East representative J.O. Bureau complained that "the local legislatures will have the powers of making laws on the subjects of Immigration and Agriculture, but the Federal Legislature will have the same power, and it is evident that it will have the upper hand" (quoted in Sampat-Mehta 1972, xxvi-xxvii).

At first, the provinces (except Nova Scotia, which initially sought to withdraw from or renegotiate the terms of Confederation) and the federal government placed a fairly high priority on immigration, creating a Standing Committee on Immigration and Colonization[12] during the first session of Parliament and acting on a Quebec request in early 1868 to discuss the division of powers under Section 95. Although the subsequent conference established an active role for the provinces in overseas recruitment (with Ontario and Quebec appointing immigration agents in London and Paris, respectively), this practice was discontinued in 1874 and the federal government assumed full responsibility for immigration promotion (Canada 1869, 3-5; 1875a, 1-8). The 1868 arrangement was problematic, Agriculture Secretary John Lowe claimed, because "the employment of Provincial and Dominion agents in the same places, not only led to waste of strength, but in some cases to actual conflict of opinion, which was bewildering to intending immigrants" (Canada 1875b, 7). In addition, both levels of government were less interested in funding extensive immigration programs at a time of considerable economic uncertainty (Stevenson 1993, 315-18). Moreover, with the creation of Manitoba in 1870, Ottawa acquired its own public lands to administer. After 1874, then, the federal government's primary role in immigration was firmly established and remained relatively uncontested by the provinces – with a few important exceptions, especially regarding Asian migration to British Columbia – for close to a hundred years.

Canada's first federal immigration law, the 1869 *Immigration Act,* reflected a desire to increase immigration and a generally laissez-faire outlook on control. It also was the product of several practical border control problems. The law focused not on regulating who entered but on ensuring that immigrants arrived in a humane and orderly manner. This stemmed from a tragedy two decades earlier, when thousands of cholera-infected Irish immigrants escaping the Great Famine in 1846-47 had died during the process of resettling in Quebec (Hodgetts 1955; Macdonagh 1961). The 1869 *Immigration Act* dealt at length with the responsibilities of the Masters of Vessels transporting immigrants and the Medical Superintendents at Canadian quarantine stations, detailing financial penalties that might be imposed on the former if their duties were not fulfilled. Much of the rest of the law enumerated protections to be afforded immigrants on board and upon arrival.

The legislation, in short, addressed how people arrived much more than who was arriving.

As for border regulation, only two types of persons were identified who could be denied landing:

> any Lunatic, Idiotic, Deaf and Dumb, Blind or Infirm person, not belonging to any Immigrant family, and ... [who] is, in the opinion of the Medical Superintendent, likely to become permanently a public charge (Section 11.2)

> [any] pauper or destitute Immigrants ... until such sums of money as may be found necessary are provided and paid into the hands of one of the Canadian Immigration Agents ... for their temporary support and transport to their place of destination (Section 16)

Primary responsibility for identifying the former fell on Masters of Vessels (who also assumed any costs associated with such unwanted immigrants) and Medical Superintendents.[13] As for paupers, that section of the law had to be invoked by Cabinet before coming into force, which was first done in late 1879 (Kelley and Trebilcock 1998, 81). This action expired, however, in April 1880, having been created, Agriculture Minister John H. Pope (C) told the House (25 February 1880, 200-3), to stop immigrants from arriving during the winter months, when there was little work available. Finally, the law did not require the removal of members of either prohibited category; it merely raised the possibility in the case of the former under particular circumstances (Section 12).

For their part, Immigration Agents were charged with welcoming more than screening newcomers. As Deputy Agriculture Minister J.C. Taché put it:

> The immigrants ... are met by the Agent whose duties are to see that the laws which protect the immigrant are fully complied with, and that any breach of the obligations contracted towards them by the transport companies, previous to their arrival, are dealt with in accordance with such laws. Our Agents are besides to give to the immigrants all required information to protect them against impositions, direct them in their further steps towards their intended destination, and procure for them any medical or other assistance of which they may be in need. (Canada 1868, 7)[14]

This facilitative role is further underscored in the annual reports submitted by Immigration Agents during the early years of Confederation, which scarcely mention people being refused entry while often noting expenditures to feed, shelter, and transport inland whatever "paupers and destitute Immigrants" had arrived.

Limitations of Control

Even if Canada had wanted to regulate arrivals more closely, its capacity was limited in several respects. First, overseas officials could only discourage unwanted immigration. Future Prime Minister Charles Tupper (C), then Canada's High Commissioner in London, reminded the Agriculture Minister in 1888 that "under the existing arrangements it is possible for any person to go to Canada without coming at all in contact with the Canadian Government agents" (Canada 1888a, 241).[15] All that officials could do was to refuse state-subsidized travel for people considered to be undesirable.[16] It was not until well after the First World War that immigrants travelling through major European ports were screened more systematically before departure. Second, passengers could be let off anywhere along the way as long as their names were entered in the manifest submitted at the ship's final destination.[17] This limited the ability to establish the health and wealth of newcomers.

Third, first-class passengers were not routinely screened and were not even counted as immigrants in official statistics.[18] Although paupers were unlikely to occupy such berths, those with "undesirable" medical conditions or – a concern that emerged in the early 1870s – criminal records might. Fourth, until a 1902 amendment, there was no established procedure to check each immigrant's health upon arrival. After the government passed the 1872 *Quarantine Act,* only those vessels "(except Canadian mail steamers) that had come from an infected port, or that had experienced a death or outbreak of disease on board, [were required] to report for inspection at Grosse Île," the country's main quarantine station (Kelley and Trebilcock 1998, 84). Thus, many ships disembarked without any medical examination by Canadian officials.[19] In 1882, Frederick Montizambert, the Medical Superintendent at Grosse Île, warned of "the undoubted evasions of the quarantine laws during the last few years" and recommended strengthening the law considerably (Canada 1882b, 119). Indeed, annual quarantine reports provide little evidence that people were refused admission during this period for health reasons.

Fifth, Canada struggled to attract immigrants, especially during the mid-1870s. With the proximity of the United States and aggressive advertising campaigns from some South American countries, Canada had difficulty convincing immigrants to come. In 1872, in an effort to increase arrivals from continental Europe, Canada instituted the first of many systems of "bonus payments" that rewarded booking agents and shipping companies for each person brought to Canada.[20] The government also transferred significant tracts of western land to private interests to promote settlement, a policy that was as limited a success as it had been in pre-Confederation Canada (see Macdonald 1966). Immigrant recruitment was undertaken, then, without much government oversight at points of embarkation or disembarkation.

Control over immigrant selection had essentially been delegated to the private sector, which had little incentive to regulate arrivals.[21] Commercial agents were joined by "philanthropists, charitable organizations and other public bodies" that "collected funds, organized local clubs to help deserving families to emigrate, and sought to rouse public opinion to the urgent need of immediate and extensive relief" in Britain through the emigration of the poor (ibid., 93; see also Johnson 1966). It was only in the late 1880s that Canada sought to regulate such migration.

Finally, the law did not apply to land borders with the United States. Although individuals with goods were supposed to check in with customs officials at particular stations, passage could easily be made at other points along the more than six-thousand-kilometre border. Thus, departmental officials admitted that "no means exist of ascertaining and recording arrivals of settlers along our inland frontier" (Canada 1871, 8) except where an Immigration Agent was established, and even then little more than "a count of heads" could be performed (Canada 1874a, vi).[22] In effect, very little control was practised or possible over American entries, and this did not begin to change until a border patrol system was instituted in the early twentieth century.

In several appearances before the Standing Committee, Secretary to the Department of Agriculture John Lowe (later its Deputy Minister) provided further explanations for the limited control exercised during this period. First, impoverished immigrants might nonetheless make good immigrants: "As a general rule, passengers first coming to the country need the greatest care and assistance, and my own opinion is, that it is far better to err on the side of overdoing than in underdoing this duty, wherever else we may save expenditure" (Canada 1879b, 21).[23] For example, Lowe cautioned against rejecting a group of poor Irish arrivals, maintaining that "they may be, nevertheless, very valuable immigrants" (Canada 1883, 24). Second, the positive reports he received from front-line Immigration Agents led him to believe that the domestic labour market could absorb such immigration. Third, the number of undesirable immigrants, he felt, bore "a very small fractional relation to the total immigration" (Canada 1888b, 76). It was not a major problem. Finally, he suggested that it was unrealistic to expect the state to exert great control over the "quality" of arrivals: "In all large immigrations there will be a considerable proportion of the very poor, and perhaps a percentage of immigrants who would not be so desirable as some others. This is absolutely to be expected, or at least it is a concomitant of all immigration" (Canada 1884, 9).

For the first decades after Confederation, then, there were very few restrictions, rights-based or otherwise, on non-citizens in Canada's immigration laws, policies, and practices. Although this extended from a desire to people the land, it was also the product of conceptual limitations concerning the notion of who counted as an immigrant as well as numerous technical difficulties surrounding control itself. In addition, it was consistent with a prevalent sentiment in British liberalism that saw impediments to the free movement of people as antithetical to liberal political values. Because there were no significant rights restrictions controlling movement across the border, however, rights-based politics did not arise.

This is not to suggest that control was of no concern to the public or decision makers. Segments of society could readily turn against immigrants deemed to present economic competition or challenge dominant social norms. Organized labour, especially at the local level, was "constantly on guard against what it term[ed] excessive immigration" (Corbett 1957, 4). Its protests were especially sharp concerning contract immigrant labour and Asian migration but could also arise on a sectoral basis (Goutor 2007). More generally, fears were often voiced over non-British/non-French arrivals (particularly Asian, Black American, and Jewish immigrants), and there continued to be anti-Catholic prejudice in society. In Parliament, the question of pauper immigration (especially from Britain) was raised on occasion,[24] as was that of Chinese migrants in British Columbia (see below). More often, however, the focus was on whether the government could control the country's population loss (of citizens and non-citizens alike) to the United States, and whether it would control its own spending (and alleged cronyism) in this policy area.

Moreover, despite the limitations outlined above, immigration officials were neither inattentive nor powerless against "undesirable" immigrants, and specific actions were taken at times to stop their arrival. In 1880, for example, the Hamilton Immigration Agent reported that a steamship company was transporting pensioned soldiers from Britain to Canada (a type he felt would not make good immigrants) by lowering its fares; a year later, he noted that the department's direct intervention had stopped the practice (Canada 1880, 31; 1881, 29). More generally, Lowe claimed that with respect to steamship companies, "we do not control them, but we have influence with them" (Canada 1886, 13). Officials also occasionally claimed to have deported paupers and those deemed to be insane, although they rarely produced evidence.[25] Indeed, even in a case where the state might have sought to act more restrictively – in response to the movement of Jewish refugees from Europe – it did not do so.

Controlling Jewish Refugees

The 1869 *Immigration Act* contained no specific provisions for refugees, and in this Canada was not unique. The conceptualization of the relationship between refugees and the state was, during the late nineteenth century, at a very basic stage of development (Zolberg et al. 1989). Refugees had historically been understood to include those seeking sanctuary from religious persecution, a general definition that was expanded in the mid-nineteenth century to include political persecution. Soon thereafter the concept was again enlarged to incorporate those persecuted on ethnoracial grounds. Although a few European countries had refugee-related legislation around the time of Canada's Confederation, this was generally geared towards the handling of political exiles, those "well-educated, cultured elites ... who were politically motivated to leave their own countries" during the nationalistic and revolutionary upheavals of the early to middle 1800s (Sassen 1999, 36). Such exiles generally fled to a nearby (liberal) European country, often hoping to return to their countries of origin, and they faced few restrictions on their activities.[26] Those who travelled further generally went to the United States, which "held a worldwide reputation as a haven for the victims of political oppression and religious persecution" (Kraut 1982, 13). Besides Jews fleeing Russia and eastern Europe, many American immigrants were "Germans living in Slavic countries, Greeks residing in Romania, Croats and Serbs in Hungary, Turks in Bulgaria, and the French in Canada, among others, [who] often felt the sting of discrimination and sometimes were the target of official and unofficial acts of repression" (ibid., 19).

While relatively few refugees probably arrived in Canada during the mid-1800s, those who did would have faced few restrictions, since there were – as seen above – few formal barriers to entry. In keeping with the experience in European liberal countries, such exiles were likely to have been welcomed rather than shunned by their fellow elites in Canada. Furthermore, and as will be seen in more detail below, Canadian political culture contained a strain of the same Liberal Internationalism identified earlier in the case of Britain. There was, in short, no prominent political position against the resettlement of refugees in Canada at this time; this would have to be constructed. Indeed, in the past, such groups as the Loyalists, pacifists, and escaped slaves and free Blacks from the United States had been generally accepted, if not enthusiastically welcomed.

Besides the arrival of European refugees on a more or less individual basis, two large movements occurred during this early period. The first consisted of some seven thousand Mennonites from Russia, who arrived between 1873 and 1880 (Epp 1974).[27] These Russian Anabaptists had originally moved from Prussia to Russia during the reign of Catherine the Great, who accorded them certain privileges concerning religious freedom, control over education, local government, and an exemption from military service, but beginning in 1870 these privileges were terminated under the Russification policy of Czar Alexander II. Anxious to secure a large population of Mennonites to settle the west,[28] Canada promised an exemption from military service, land grants in Manitoba, their own religious schools, the right to affirm rather than to swear oaths in court, and travel assistance.[29] Such exceptional conditions underline how much the government wanted these potential settlers.[30]

Much less enthusiasm and support was seen in the Canadian government's response not long after to the plight of Jewish refugees seeking to escape from Russia and eastern Europe. From the onset of the infamous Russian pogroms in 1881, Jewish emigration to the West reached around 2.5 million by the outbreak of the Great War (Marrus 1985, 27). After arriving in western Europe,

> it did not take long before such uninvited guests became unpopular. By the end of the century, European opposition to the Jewish emigrants was widespread, nourished by popular antisemitism, xenophobia, fears about diseases carried by the Jews, and hosts of legends about their supposedly nefarious customs and habits. (Ibid., 35)

The translation of such negative sentiments into political action was limited, however, as many of the refugees continued onward (often encouraged and assisted by governments and private organizations) to North America: "So long as America received virtually everyone who came, Europeans seldom had to define refugees, worry about their responsibilities, and ponder who qualified for aid and who did not" (ibid., 39). This helped increase the size of the Jewish community in Canada from a reported 1,233 in 1871 to 6,501 in 1891 (Klein and Dimant 2001, 263, Table 1).

From the first settlements in New France until Confederation, anti-Semitism was a relatively muted (compared with other parts of the world) yet standard feature of European political culture in the New World (Godfrey and Godfrey 1995). As news of the plight of Russian Jews arrived in the early 1880s, there were probably fewer than 2,500 Jews in Canada (Kage 1962, 18). Canada's first High Commissioner in London, Alexander Galt, strove to convince the Canadian government to allow agricultural and wealthy Jews to resettle in Canada. Although Prime Minister John A. Macdonald (C) opposed any large movement, he hoped that Galt's proactive approach might encourage Jewish financiers to invest in Canada.[31] The beginning of what became a mass movement of thousands at the turn of the century began with the departure of 240 refugees from Liverpool in April 1882, bound for settlement in western Canada (Abella 1990, 79). In contrast to the considerable planning involved in the resettlement of the Mennonites, the government did little if anything to prepare for the Jewish refugees or assist them after arrival. Instead, the refugees had to rely extensively on their co-religionists in Canada and abroad.

Despite the Jewish community's efforts to minimize the potential negative impact that the arrival of so many impoverished refugees would have on perceptions of Jews in Canada, the reaction of the general public to continued and increasing Jewish immigration was largely negative. "As the number of Jews in the country increased," Abella observes (ibid., 103), "so did the opposition to their presence." As the situation grew worse, "officials blamed Jews for their own administrative bungling" in failing to establish the refugees on the land (Tulchinsky 1992, 128). Although the government's initial acceptance of Jewish resettlement soon turned into unease and even opposition, direct restrictions were not placed on this movement until the twentieth century. By 1911, the Jewish population in Canada was reported at 74,760 (Klein and Dimant 2001, 263, Table 1). Meanwhile, the difficulties experienced by Jewish refugees in rural and urban areas alike contributed to an emerging Liberal Nationalist perspective that sought – through a lens of cultural and ethnoracial discrimination – to ensure that only (or primarily) "desirable" immigrants of British and northern European origin were settled in Canada.

During the first two decades after Confederation, then, low-key (albeit persistent) concerns were expressed as to the types of European immigrants being admitted to Canada, but little was done in response. In 1872, *An Act to amend the Immigration Act of 1869* was passed that, even as it added "any criminal, or other vicious class of immigrants to be designated [by Cabinet]" to the list of those who might be denied landing (Section 10), broadened the protections afforded newcomers. In 1887, *An Act to amend "The Immigration Act"* expanded the deportation provisions that could be employed against such immigrants.[32] However, in the absence of evidence that either amendment was put to much use during the period under review in this chapter, neither can be considered to have constituted a serious control initiative. Although the government did take action in response to particular cases on occasion, little effort was made to establish a system of immigration control during these early years.[33] The one exception concerned Chinese immigrants to Canada.

The Liberal Internationalist Defence of Chinese Migrants (1867-87)

The entry into, and continued presence of Chinese migrants in British Columbia in the late nineteenth century placed control firmly on the political agenda in Ottawa, and remained problematic for both Liberal and Conservative governments until well into the twentieth century. The arrival – even the anticipated arrival – of Chinese migrants was often understood to threaten the economic and social well-being of the resident white population, and thus to require the restriction, exclusion, or even expulsion of the Chinese from Canada. Energetic debates about control arose, and entries were eventually severely curtailed. Despite an extensive literature on the various restrictions put in place, a key moment in this history has been overlooked, namely, Senate efforts to first reject and then repeal the 1885 *Chinese Immigration Act*. If only for this reason, the act's passage (and subsequent amendment) merits attention, but there are at least three additional reasons that it should be considered here.

First, the law constitutes an early effort by Canada to assert its sovereignty. Not only was control limited in the various ways noted above, but Canada's authority over its borders remained incomplete. In part, this was because Confederation had left unresolved the country's territorial limits, as several British-controlled lands in North America were not included within the scope of the *BNA Act* and disagreements with the United States concerning the precise demarcation at certain points remained. Moreover, Canadian independence from Britain in the area of foreign relations had not yet been established.[34] Under such circumstances, control over Chinese (and, more broadly, Asian) immigration represented a small but important step in asserting Canada's sovereign authority over its borders.[35]

Second, the legislation introduced a new racial dimension to Canadian immigration law. Although ethnoracial discrimination had existed in this policy area prior to 1885 – for example, "the manner in which promotional activities and incentives were distributed exhibited strong racial preferences" towards northern Europe and the United States (Kelley and Trebilcock 1998, 107) – the 1885 *Chinese Immigration Act* was explicit. Once the principle of discrimination on the basis of race was established for one group, it became relatively easy to extend it to others. Thus, the assertion of state sovereignty and the expression of racism were tightly intertwined, even mutually reinforcing: because Canada was a sovereign state, it could discriminate against other races in the name of the national community; because the national community saw Asian migration as a threat, Canada had to uphold its sovereignty by controlling its borders. This close connection between sovereignty and explicit racial discrimination would be a central tenet of Liberal Nationalism until well after the Second World War.

Third, the rise of a Liberal Nationalist argument for restriction on the basis of race was opposed by a Liberal Internationalist perspective that has almost been completely overlooked in the literature. Although Liberal Nationalism existed at Confederation, primarily in terms of religious discrimination, it was not initially reflected much in Canadian debates or policies. Indeed, it first had to overcome the prevailing political norm of Liberal Internationalism rooted in British liberalism, which was found in all white settler countries at the time.[36]

Thus, the politics surrounding the 1885 *Chinese Immigration Act* reveal that control has long raised questions of the rights of non-citizens in Canada. Moreover, even in this early period, rights-restrictive policies produced rights-based politics pursued through judicial, legislative, and other means, as well as efforts to circumvent state control. This, in turn, would lead the state to take an increasingly restrictive approach. To appreciate these developments, this section traces the emergence of the issue of control over Chinese migration in the House of Commons both before and after the passage of the 1885 *Chinese Immigration Act*, before turning to the Liberal Internationalist grounds on which it was challenged in the Senate.

Chinese Migrants and British Liberalism (1867-84)

Chinese migrants began settling in British North America, especially British Columbia, as early as the 1850s, but their numbers began growing appreciably only with the gold rush of the 1860s and construction of the western section of the Canadian Pacific Railway during the 1880s. Precise numbers do not exist but contemporary reports suggest a Chinese population of between 1,700 and 4,000 in the 1860s, and between 3,000 and 6,000 during the late 1870s, with 4,383 being counted in the 1881 Canadian census (Roy 1989, 5, 269, Table 1B; Canada 1879a, 1-2). As railroad construction picked up steam in the early 1880s, the number grew to around 10,550 by September 1884 (Canada 1885a, viii). Overall, some 16,000 to 17,000 Chinese migrants arrived during the early 1880s to work on this construction project (Roy 1989, x-xi).[37]

For geographic and economic reasons, Chinese migrants generally arrived and lived in British Columbia. At first, their reception was relatively cordial: "Colonial British Columbians were initially remarkably tolerant of the thousands of Chinese who came. British officials refused to countenance any discrimination, and whites, rather than pressing for hostile action, boasted of the British justice enjoyed by the Chinese" (ibid., 4).[38] Although there was racism, including violence against the migrants, Liberal Internationalism formed the basis of the government's response. Thus, when Governor Anthony Musgrave met in 1869 with Chinese residents in Barkerville, where the largest number then resided, he informed them "that the denizens of whatever nationality residing under our flag should possess ... equality and protection" (quoted in ibid., 5). While Britain itself had very limited experience with receiving Chinese migrants (Holmes 1988, 81), official acceptance of the rights of foreigners to enter and remain within its borders mitigated against any wholesale restriction in Canada. With growing numbers of American and Chinese migrants arriving, greater competition in the gold fields, and the establishment in 1871 of a provincial government that felt less bound by British traditions, this began to change. Not long after British Columbia joined Confederation, local politicians (at the provincial and then federal level) began pressuring Ottawa for legislation to restrict the ability of the Chinese to immigrate to or work legally in Canada.[39]

The first major effort, by British Columbia Member of Parliament Arthur Bunster (L), sought and failed to convince the House to make it illegal to hire people to work on CPR construction if their hair was longer than 5.5 inches – an obvious attack on the Chinese, whose hair was often worn in long queues (18 March 1878, 1207).[40] Prime Minister Alexander Mackenzie (L) replied categorically that the motion "was one unprecedented in its character and altogether unprecedented in its spirit, and at variance with those tolerant laws which afforded employment and an asylum to all who came into our country, irrespective of colour, hair, or anything else" (ibid., 1209). Mackenzie "did not think it would become us, as a British community, to legislate against any class of people who might be imported into, or might emigrate to, this country" (ibid.).[41] His statement stands as perhaps the earliest clear expression in Parliament of Liberal Internationalism on the subject of border control. Although such arguments would become more sophisticated over time, two core features were already present: that all individuals should be treated equally before the law, and that a country should not pursue policies that contradicted its founding principles. These ideas have influenced the politics of control ever since.

The following year, Amor de Cosmos (L) called upon the government to enact such "repressive measures" as curtailing Chinese arrivals, preventing their becoming naturalized, and disenfranchising those who had already acquired citizenship (16 April 1879, 1259). Joshua S. Thompson (LCP) went further in maintaining that the "Chinese were a nuisance and a curse, and that getting rid of them, by any means, was an end that must be accomplished" (ibid., 1261).[42] Again, Mackenzie, now leader of the Opposition, responded, stating that "he did not see how it was possible to accede to the proposition to expel [the Chinese] without at once giving up all [that Parliament] held sacred as to the rights of man in their own as in other countries" (ibid., 1262). He was joined by Samuel MacDonnell (L), who argued that this would be

> a very unprecedented act on the part of the Dominion, and at variance with the policy of other nations, to pass a law to prevent the immigration of people from any portion of the world. If some people came into this country, bringing with them practices or habits of immorality, or any other peculiarities which we could not tolerate, we should rather suppress such peculiarities by legislation than legislate for the exclusion of such people. (Ibid., 1264)

Thus, if Canada wanted to restrict certain types of behaviour, then it should do so under the rule of law in conformity with its own founding norms rather than by denying entry to a particular group.[43] For Mackenzie and MacDonnell, the Chinese ought to be judged by their merits as individuals (indeed, a language of rights was employed by Mackenzie), and not according to their ethnoracial background. As with any other people, Mackenzie said, "while the Chinese had bad, they had, no doubt, also good qualities" (ibid., 1262).

De Cosmos was not convinced, asserting that old principles did not suit modern problems. Mackenzie, he said, "was the personification of the old-fashioned notion that the moment a slave touched British soil he was free; that Britain, to-day, was an asylum where everyone could at once gain a foothold, and be recognised as living under the protection of the British flag" (ibid., 1264). This was a misguided response, he insisted, when Canada needed "that due protection we all ought to give, irrespective of politics, to our race in our own country against an Asiatic and pagan horde that would overrun and crush us whenever opportunity was afforded" (ibid.). This exemplifies the close connection in Liberal Nationalism between state sovereignty and racial discrimination: excluding foreigners on the basis of race was legitimate in the presumed interests of the (white) national community. David Mills (L) expressed disquiet over the dehumanizing language employed by de Cosmos and others, stating that it brought no credit to the House to "give the Chinese a bad name, and then hunt them down like rabid dogs" (ibid., 1263). This was, he protested, "to deal with these people as [our] Christian ancestors [sic], to their dishonour, did with the Jews" (ibid.).[44]

Prime Minister John A. Macdonald openly sympathized with de Cosmos and his supporters. Indeed, Macdonald's expressed opinions show no trace of the Liberal Internationalism voiced by Mackenzie, and yet his racism (later quite evident) was constrained by practical considerations. Initially, he simply agreed to establish a special committee, one that de Cosmos himself would chair, to investigate the question.[45] Although the committee recommended against the encouragement of Chinese immigration and the use of Chinese labour to construct the Canadian Pacific Railway, some of the reported testimony was more ambivalent (see Canada 1879a). In response, the government took no action, and as Chinese arrivals decreased in 1880 and 1881, just as the economy in British Columbia experienced modest growth, the question all but disappeared from parliamentary debate until 1882, when de Cosmos again appealed for restrictive legislation. Prime Minister Macdonald then replied that Chinese labour was necessary if the railway was to be finished, but that measures might be taken upon its completion.[46]

The House of Commons and the 1885 Chinese Immigration Act (1884-87)

With work on the Canadian Pacific Railway nearing completion in 1884, Macdonald agreed to an Opposition motion that it was "expedient to enact a law to restrict or regulate the incoming of Chinese to Canada" (12 April 1884, 974, 1289).[47] As a first step, another investigative committee was appointed. The Chapleau Commission, named after co-chair Secretary of State Joseph A. Chapleau (C), submitted two separate reports, differing in some details but not in their essential conclusions. Although the commissioners questioned and ultimately sought to refute suggestions of the alleged negative effects of Chinese immigration, they concluded that public sentiment was so wholly against such arrivals that the government should regulate it. This could be accomplished "by imposing a head tax of $10 on all Chinese immigrants, preventing the objectionable – the diseased, deformed, and impoverished – from landing, and creating a special tribunal to register the Chinese and then enforce laws, administer justice, and collect taxes among them" (Ward 1990, 40).

In response, the government first altered legislation to create an *Electoral Franchise Act,* already before the House, so as to deny any person of Chinese origin the right to vote in federal elections. Macdonald justified this on the grounds that the Chinese migrant "is a stranger, a sojourner in a strange land ... he has no common interest with us ... he has no British instincts or British feelings or aspirations, and therefore ought not to have a vote" (4 May 1885, 1582). If given the vote, he warned, the Chinese would likely elect a sufficient number of Chinese MPs in British Columbia to force "eccentricities" and "immorality" that were "abhorrent to the Aryan race and Aryan principles, upon this House" (ibid., 1588). He received support from many MPs (especially from British Columbia) but also faced vocal opposition. Louis H. Davies (L) argued that "if a Chinaman becomes a British subject it is not right that a brand should be placed on his forehead, so that other men may avoid him" (ibid., 1583). Peter Mitchell (I) declared that "we should make our laws comprehensive enough to include all classes of foreigners. So long as they comply with the naturalisation laws, they can become British subjects, and I would give them the vote" (ibid., 1582). While he did not find them "the most desirable class of citizens," Arthur H. Gillmor (L) maintained that "as British subjects in British colonies, we ought to show them fair play" (ibid., 1585).[48] Despite such protests the motion was carried. For reasons that are not clear, the voice of Liberal Internationalism then became all but mute as the House turned to consider the government's legislation to restrict Chinese immigration.

Chapleau discussed the need for *An Act to restrict and regulate Chinese Immigration into Canada* with such an open expression of regret that Edgar C. Baker (C) commented that "one would almost imagine [that he] were in opposition to the Bill rather than in favour of it" (2 July 1885, 3013).[49] Chapleau began from a Liberal Internationalist position, expressing his surprise when

a demand was made for legislation to provide that one of the first principles which have always guided the English people in the enactment of their laws and regulations for the maintenance of the peace and prosperity of the country, should be violated in excluding from the shores of this great country, which is a part of the British Empire, members of the human family. (Ibid., 3003)

Although he agreed that it was a good thing to ensure the continuance of a "white" British Columbia, he took issue with how the Chinese had been demonized.[50] The Chapleau Commission, he said, had found little evidence to support the uniformly negative image put forward by those in favour of restriction, and had concluded that Chinese migration had had a generally positive impact on the regional economy. He had come to see, however, that when it came to the Chinese, Canadians were "naturally disposed, through inconscient prejudices, to turn into defects even their virtues" (ibid., 3006). Such prejudice was hardly a noble sentiment but had to be acknowledged – the government could not ignore the antagonism felt by the white population in British Columbia and must therefore act.

The government proposed to make all Chinese migrants – with a few exceptions – pay a $50 "Head Tax" (or "Capitation Tax") before being landed,[51] while no more than one Chinese passenger was to be allowed per fifty tons weight of an arriving vessel (Section 5).[52] Responsibility for identifying Chinese passengers on board was delegated to Masters of Vessels (under threat of stiff penalties), and no Chinese immigrant could be landed before having been medically examined (Sections 6 to 9). The law would also establish a certificate system to control those leaving from and returning to Canada without paying the Head Tax again (Section 14). Restrictionists were not wholly satisfied but recognized in the legislation, as Noah Shakespeare (C) noted, "the thin end of the edge" of a more extensive system of control (2 July 1885, 3011). Indeed, amid various concerns over the administration of the proposed law, the only opposition (aside from that expressed by Chapleau) came from those who wanted to make it even more restrictive, and it was passed in the House easily.

Amendments were soon introduced to the 1885 *Chinese Immigration Act* in 1886 and 1887. At first, the government sought to enforce compulsory registration of those already in Canada (with penalties for non-compliance), to expand the scope of the law to cover trains as well as ships, and to remove merchants from the exemption list (see 12 May 1886, 1229). These suggestions were supported by restrictionists but sparked some opposition from MPs who had earlier opposed the disenfranchisement of the Chinese, such as Louis Davies and Peter Mitchell. Although the House passed the bill, it was (as will be explored further below) held up in the Senate by opponents of restriction. The government's next effort lacked almost any suggestion of additional restriction, except for a change to allow Chinese immigrants only three months' leave from Canada before they had to pay the Head Tax again (see 4 May 1887, 277).[53] Even these proposals barely made it through the Senate, however, and the lone restrictive feature – the three-month limitation – was removed from the bill. In the House, the only opposition took the form of a protest that the wife of a Chinese migrant would not be allowed to enter without paying the Head Tax, a restriction that would, it was felt, result in a lowering of moral standards within the Chinese community if male Chinese migrants did not, as a result, bring their wives with them (see David Mills in 31 May 1887, 642-43).

The absence of much debate on this issue in the House can be seen in part as a reflection of the ambivalence of Canadians outside British Columbia, with the notable exception, at times, of calls for greater restriction made by segments of organized labour (Goutor 2007). According to the 1881 census, only thirty-three Chinese individuals lived in Canada outside British Columbia; ten years later, this figure was 219 (Roy 1989, 62). It is therefore not surprising that most Canadians did not spend much time considering the issue,[54] and when they did, people were likely to have relied on stereotypes of "John Chinaman" that were part of the European and North American cultural norm (Ward 1990). Certainly, there is little indication in the literature that many were willing to defend the Chinese in Canada, aside from some church and business leaders. This portrayal, however, does not adequately take into account one source of considerable political support at the end of the nineteenth century – the Senate. The opinions expressed in that chamber are interesting in their own right as they provide greater depth to the historical record of race relations in Canada, but they are also important in an examination of control for what they reveal about Liberal Internationalism.

The Senate and the 1885 Chinese Immigration Act (1885-87)

Support for the Chinese was apparent when the Senate debated the 1885 *Electoral Franchise Act*. "I cannot myself see the propriety," Alexander Vidal (C) commented, "of excluding the Mongolians, who have shown themselves to be patient, industrious and law-abiding, from privileges which are given to every other member of the human family in this country" (13 July 1885, 1276). Lawrence G. Power (L) did not think that "the Parliament of Canada should make any distinction of race at all; that the Chinese, Negroes, Indians and Whites should be on the same footing; that no exceptions should be made in favor of one or against another race" (ibid., 1280). Having opened up China to trade, Richard W. Scott (L) observed, Canada should not "set up a Chinese wall on our side," which would be "entirely contrary to the principles of the Empire" (ibid.). Despite such protests, however, the franchise legislation passed.

These objections paled, however, compared with the palpable sense of outrage expressed by many Senators over the proposed Chinese immigration legislation. Often, their comments reflected the same brand of Liberal Internationalism heard earlier from Mackenzie. "I think it is entirely inconsistent with the very fundamental principle of the British constitution," declared Alexander Vidal, "that legislation of this kind should find a place on the statute book" (ibid., 1297). William J. Macdonald (C) of British Columbia argued that "in a free country, Chinamen as well as persons of other nationalities, have their rights and privileges, so long as they conform to the laws of the country" (30 January 1885, 6). The law, claimed James Dever (L), would tarnish Canada's reputation:

> We, who pride ourselves on the freedom of our institutions, and the abolition of slavery in the United States, and who fancy we are going over the world with our lamp in our hand shedding light and lustre wherever we go – that we should become slave-drivers, and prohibit strangers from coming to our hospitable shore because they are of a different colour and have a different language and habits from ourselves, in deference to the feelings of a few people from British Columbia, is a thing I cannot understand. (13 July 1885, 1298)

There would, some Senators maintained, no doubt be some "undesirables" among the Chinese, but as with any immigrant group many would make positive contributions to Canada. Such discrimination, concluded William Almon (LCP), remained "contrary to the genius of the nineteenth century" (ibid., 1295) – British liberalism.

Although Liberal Internationalists in the Senate could not prevent the bill's passage, it returned to the House only because of some clever procedural moves on the government side. William Almon had "given notice that [he] would oppose it at the third reading, and that [he] would move that it be read the third time three months hence" (18 July 1885, 1411), meaning that it would not pass that session. Almon, however, was told that he had committed procedural errors, which allowed the legislation to emerge from the committee stage unscathed and pass Third Reading without discussion: he did not give notice in writing of his intentions and had assumed that debate could not pass through two stages on the same day.[55] Thus, his efforts to scuttle the bill were sidestepped and it passed without a word altered, despite considerable opposition to the very principles on which it was based.[56]

Almon's chances of success might seem to have been slim, for government bills rarely failed to pass in the Senate, especially when the same party controlled both chambers;[57] however, the fate of the government's attempt to amend the law the following year suggests otherwise. As noted, the 1886 amendments were mostly restrictionist in nature, involving mandatory registration of those Chinese already in Canada, removal of merchants from the exemption list, and expansion of the scope of the act to include railway passage. Rather than simply debate these measures, opponents attacked the very need for any such legislation. While much of the criticism was familiar – "It is so repugnant to all that is English, and honourable or right that one can hardly discuss it in a proper frame of mind" (Richard Scott, 21 May 1886, 692) – there were important developments as well.

Vidal challenged Canada's right to restrict entry, suggesting that this was not absolute but must conform to the principles on which the country had been settled:

> By what royal right have we and our fathers crossed the ocean and taken possession of this western continent? What right had we to come here and dispossess the Indians, native proprietors of this country, and take possession of their lands? ... [Do we] consider that we have a better right to it than they have, but to consider it so exclusively our own as to shut out from sharing in the advantages of this country others of God's people who have as much right to it as we have? (Ibid., 687)

The land was taken "because we believed that where our civilization and enlightenment have been introduced we have carried with us the blessings of Christianity to the people amongst whom we have settled" (ibid.). To exclude others on the basis of race, he concluded, was so "utterly inconsistent with our professions as Christians and with the vaunted freedom we profess to cherish as a British people" that it undermined the basis on which the land had been occupied (ibid.). For Scott, the 1885 law was "such a gross violation of the law of nations, of the comity of nations, a law which we ourselves have been endeavoring to hold forth as being the true principle on which the nations of the world should trade" (26 May 1886, 746).

Finally, many Senators saw restrictionism as a form of "special interest" politics, as a protectionist appeal by British Columbia workers, and protested that they should not dictate the terms of policy to the rest of the country.[58] It would not be long, however, before the tables would be turned and opponents of restriction were deemed "special interests," a moniker they have been unable to escape to the present. Indeed, one of the great successes of Liberal Nationalism has been its ability to project its approach as embodying the "national interest," which initially grew out of its keen association between state sovereignty and racial discrimination.

Opposition to the 1886 bill was therefore rooted in a rejection not only of the specific amendments but also of the 1885 legislation itself. Even George W. Allan (C), who introduced the bill on behalf of the government, said that he had "no special leaning towards this Chinese legislation" (ibid., 747).[59] Scott suggested that it would be "a service to the empire if we allow this question to stand over for another year" (ibid.), when passions in British Columbia might have calmed and a more reasonable examination of the question might be essayed. The Senate let the debate stand for six months, which effectively killed the bill.

When the government introduced its 1887 amendments, opposition to the 1885 *Chinese Immigration Act* – which had "not a shadow of justice or right on its side" (William Macdonald, 10 June 1887, 311-12) – appeared to have increased. Future Prime Minister John J.C. Abbott (C), who sponsored the bill for the government, agreed that the principle behind the law was offensive to the chamber but suggested that amendments might help temper its severity. If too many changes were demanded, he cautioned, the House would reject them and thus the modest positive changes contained in the bill would be lost (13 June 1887, 347). Such reasoning found sympathy but little support as "the sentiment of the Senate seemed to be that the Act should be wiped off the Statute Book," Scott claimed (ibid., 349). Indeed, Vidal introduced legislation to do just that, and Abbott admitted that it would likely pass on a vote. The justification for repeal was succinctly expressed by Robert P. Haythorne (L): "It is a difficult thing to amend a Bill based upon a wrong principle, and the principle upon which [the 1885 law is] based is a bad and cruel one" (10 June 1887, 312). Even if rejected by the House, Vidal argued, his bill would "show that we have proper views of British freedom and the responsibilities that are attached to our professions as Christians" (ibid., 307).

The government side was again able to steer its legislation through the chamber, however. It argued successfully before the Speaker that since the law involved the collection of revenue – the Head Tax – the Senate could not repeal it.[60] Although the rationale for the Head Tax was clearly one of policy (to restrict the entry of Chinese migrants) rather than revenue generation,[61] the Speaker supported this line of reasoning. Thus, Vidal's initiative was ruled out of order, the possibility of meaningful change to the law was thwarted, and Third Reading was speedily accomplished.

The Senate's response to the government's attempts to restrict Chinese immigration is instructive in at least two major respects. First, it reveals an important feature of the history of Canadian state relations with Chinese migrants that has been overlooked for too long. Although it is true that the Chinese had few supporters in Canada, they could count on a large number of Senators. Thus, William Macdonald took note of the role played by many of his Senate colleagues: "I wish to express my satisfaction at the fact that a people who have been treated so rigorously and ungenerously, who are unrepresented, and who have been hunted to the death, should have found representatives to stand up on the floor of this House and speak on their behalf" (ibid., 311). Of course, Liberal Internationalism was not the sole motivation for opposition to the 1885 *Chinese Immigration Act* and its amendments (as noted above, there was also a distrust of organized labour as well as a desire on the part of business for cheap labour). Moreover, a commitment not to discriminate against the Chinese did not necessarily imply admiration for them either as individuals or a group, although it was sometimes joined to such sentiments (Ward 1990). It was often connected to an opinion that "whites" were superior to the Chinese,[62] and for some Senators their arrival provided a means of converting them to Christianity. Nonetheless, basic tenets of Liberal Internationalism – a commitment to individual rights and a responsibility towards the international community – found widespread support and underpinned expansionist alternatives concerning Chinese migration.

Second, it demonstrates that Liberal Internationalism has deep roots in Canada. Because there is a tendency to concentrate on the restrictionist features of the history of Canadian immigration policy, some of its more expansionist – especially rights-based – dimensions have come to be viewed as almost uniquely modern political phenomena. As the history of the parliamentary debates surrounding the country's first efforts to control Chinese immigration shows, and as will be seen in what follows, Liberal Internationalism has been an important part of the universe of political discourse ever since border control was first seriously discussed in Canada. In short, the rights of non-citizens have long been a central feature in the politics of control.

Conclusion

Two decades after Confederation, the Canadian state exerted only a limited degree of control over its borders. For the most part, it had neither the infrastructure in place nor the requisite determination to do so. Aside from financial and technical difficulties, it was not yet clear who exactly ought to be controlled. Even when certain non-citizens were deemed to be undesirable, such as Jewish refugees, they faced few barriers to entry. Border regulation was also limited by a desire to attract immigrants to populate the land. Furthermore, it took time for control problems to be identified, policy objectives to be determined, and responses to be crafted and implemented. As Deputy Interior Minister James A. Smart remarked in 1898, "all immigration work is largely experimental" (Canada 1898, 238). Moreover, an alternative to the prevailing norm of Liberal Internationalism inherited from Britain had yet to gain political traction. For most of this early period, then, the statement of Gavin Fleming (L) in the House that "since Confederation, it has always been the policy, or at least the professed policy of those at the head of the Emigration Department, to aid and assist the poor emigrant when he came to our shores" (25 February 1880, 199) remained generally true. The first steps in the construction of a Liberal Nationalist approach were taken with the 1885 *Chinese Immigration Act,* but a concerted effort was required to overcome the dominant Liberal Internationalism in the Senate. This challenges suggestions that there is a primary connection between liberal democracies and restrictive control policies, and underlines the importance of a historical approach to understanding contemporary control.

3
The Expansion of Liberal Nationalism in Canada (1887-1914)

The common view that "Canadian immigration policy served, above all else, the dictates of the capitalist labour market" (Avery 1979, 37) during the period covered in this chapter reveals only so much about the politics of control. A focus on the record numbers of arrivals between the 1890s and the First World War has meant that important changes in Canada's approach to control have remained underappreciated. Without doubt, there was an incredible expansion of the numbers and diversity of immigrants to Canada, with significant population movements from central, eastern, and southern Europe, as well as non-European immigration from China, India, and Japan, among other countries. Concurrently, however, the conceptual and legislative foundations of a rights-restrictive approach that would remain in place until the 1960s – and that continues to shape the politics of control – were established. This was a reflection of the growing prominence of Liberal Nationalism within the universe of political discourse that defined the control/rights nexus.

This new system of control was based on an assumption of the state's unfettered right to regulate its borders, even at the expense of the due process and equality rights of non-citizens. This chapter begins by exploring Canada's approach to controlling European immigration between 1887 and 1914, as discretionary powers were increasingly centralized within Cabinet and the immigration bureaucracy (which shifted from the Department of Agriculture to the Department of the Interior in 1892), and new restrictive legislation was passed that insulated executive actions from judicial and parliamentary oversight. Control policies directed towards Asian immigration between 1887 and 1908, as the government struggled to limit Chinese and then Japanese and East Indian arrivals, are reviewed next. Although each group presented particular control challenges, Canada consistently responded with rights-restrictive policies that were reinforced when they failed. The analysis then focuses on how East Indian immigrants in particular responded through various tactics of rights-based politics before the government succeeded in undermining their effectiveness. This material provides further substantiation for the idea that a Liberal Nationalist approach had to be constructed in Canada against a Liberal Internationalist norm.

Restricting European Immigration (1887-1914)

The most significant control-related event between 1887 and 1896 was probably the shift in ministerial responsibility to the Department of the Interior in 1892, aimed at fostering a closer connection between immigrants and land settlement. Otherwise, immigration continued to be "left largely to chance or caprice" (Macdonald 1966, 6) as entries remained minimally regulated and relatively few immigrants seemed to want to come to Canada. This began to change with the appointment of Clifford Sifton (L) as Minister of the Interior in the newly elected Liberal government in 1896, after which the numbers and diversity of immigrants increased significantly. Annual intake levels had dropped from around 84,500 to less than 17,000 between 1887 and 1896, but rose to almost 141,500 in 1905 and more than 272,000 in 1907 (see Citizenship and Immigration Canada 2003, 3). After the Conservatives gained power in 1911, intake reached a record high of over 400,000 in 1913, twenty-four times the number in 1896 (ibid.). There was also significantly greater intake diversity, especially with respect to non-northern European groups such as Italians, Poles, and Russians. As it opened the country's doors wider, however, the government began to build its walls higher from 1902 onward, especially under the watch of Minister Sifton's successor, Frank Oliver (L).

The Sifton Years (1896-1905)

Clifford Sifton saw a large and productive agricultural community as the backbone of a robust economy and thus of a strong country: "It was, he believed, in the pioneer's struggle and determination to survive, in the farmer's ceaseless toil and devotion to his faith, that the character of the nation was both determined and regenerated" (Hall 1981, 3). Indeed, Sifton was a lifelong advocate of a more expansive immigration policy, at least with respect to Europeans, and even as he laid the foundations for a more restrictive approach, he promoted the large-scale immigration of farmers to take up land in the Prairies. First, however, he had to address two problems that had long challenged his predecessors. In doing so, he initiated two approaches that would shape control for years to come: a centralization of discretionary power within the immigration bureaucracy and the delegation of immigrant selection to the private sector.

The first problem was administrative. As Minister of the Interior, Sifton later recalled in the House, he found "a department of delay, a department of circumlocution, a department in which people could not get business done, a department which tired men to death who undertook to get any business transacted with it" (31 May 1906, 4270). He immediately initiated a massive shakeup of the department, replacing top civil servants with individuals with whom he had worked before and who shared his expansionist outlook (Avery 1979, 18). In the process, he centralized power within the department, seeking to fulfill his electoral promise that "instead of the department running the minister, the minister would run the department" (quoted in Hall 1981, 124). He also expanded his capacity for action by augmenting the department's discretionary power.

The second problem was one of scope. If the government wanted to settle western Canada but could not attract British or northern European farmers, then it had to look elsewhere. Sifton undertook an extensive promotional campaign in the United States to tap into a demand for land that increased as settlement opportunities in the American West diminished. Recruitment was delegated to Immigration Agents and, in turn, to sub-Agents, and Sifton took a results-based approach by tying salaries to the number of immigrants resettled in Canada. This paid significant dividends as close to 1 million people relocated from the United States between 1901 and 1914, including many recent immigrants from Europe (Knowles 1997, 66). The delegation of immigrant selection, however, limited how much control the government would have over arrivals, as "immigration personnel were often very individualistic in their response to immigrants and interpretation of policy" (Troper 1972, 15). Elsewhere, Sifton looked to central and eastern Europe to attract the "stalwart peasant in a sheepskin coat, born on the soil, whose forefathers have been farmers for ten generations, with a stout wife and a half-dozen children" (Sifton 1922, 16). This epitomized his "businesslike assessment of ethnic differences" (Hall 1977, 77): he was not "disposed to exclude foreigners of any nationality who seemed likely to become successful agriculturalists" (quoted in Hall 1985, 68).

His opposition to non-European and non-white immigration shows, however, that settling farmers was but one of the principles that defined his outlook. Sifton's attitude towards the Chinese will be seen in his support for restrictive measures such as a $500 Head Tax in 1903. His more general rejection of "Asiatics" stemmed from a belief that "they are not adapted to our country, and they will create difficulty and wholly unnecessary economic and social problems" (quoted in ibid., 302). His objection to non-white immigration even extended to potential agriculturalists, such as Black American farmers, who faced an unofficial policy of discouragement and exclusion from the late 1890s onward. Although no laws prevented their admission, provided that they fulfilled the basic requirements established under the 1869 *Immigration Act* and its regulations, "there were no Negro agents or sub-agents nor was there any white agent authorized to work among members of the black community. Indeed, agents were instructed to use their influence to prevent Negro settlement" (Troper 1972, 128).[1]

Encouraging European immigration was difficult, however, as many countries made it illegal for foreign governments or individuals to promote emigration.[2] In 1899, therefore, Sifton engaged the North Atlantic Trading Company (NATC), a secret consortium of European steamship and booking agents (whose identities could not be revealed, it was claimed, lest they be prosecuted for encouraging emigration), to arrange passage for people wanting to move to Canada. The NATC played a significant role in European immigrant selection and, according to Sifton (1922, 16), "winnowed out this flood of people, picked out the agriculturalists and peasants and sent them to Canada, sending nobody else." In return, the consortium received a bonus per agriculturalist that arrived in Canada, whether or not it had brought them over.[3] Sifton long considered the work of the NATC to have been a singular success (Hall 1985, 65).[4]

Few parliamentarians shared this view, however. Indeed, the NATC agreement was the focus of criticism from the time it first was made public in 1905 to its termination in 1906.[5] Among many complaints, opponents questioned how the government could justify paying people to break the law in other countries, and how Parliament could be sure that no corruption or fraud was practised when insufficient information, such as the identities of those involved, was furnished.[6] The lack of control over immigrant selection was repeatedly raised: "How does your [Immigration Agent] at the seaport know that a certain man and his wife and family belong to the agricultural class?" George Foster (C) asked. "What evidence has he? None, absolutely none" (20 April 1906, 1807). By delegating immigrant selection to private interests with a financial stake in resettling as many people as possible, and by not establishing any independent means of screening arrivals, the government had further diminished its control.[7]

Criticisms also arose concerning immigrant diversification, beginning with the arrival of Galicians. As early as 1897, Frank Oliver had complained of their poverty. Besides claiming that the Galicians took jobs from young British men in Canada, he ascribed characteristics to them as a Slavic race that made them less desirable than British or German immigrants.[8] He made a clear distinction between "our people" and the immigrants, stating "that our own people are the best, that the best the country has is not too good for them, and that if there is any preference, they are the parties who should have it" (2 June 1898, 6842). For Oliver, "the primary object of inducing immigration is not simply to produce railroad traffic, but for the purpose of building up a kindred, and as far as possible, a higher, and a better civilization" (26 July 1899, 8521). To resettle people "who are not progressive, whose ambition is not civilization," he proclaimed, was to put "a collar around the neck of your civilized and your progressive settlers" (ibid., 8522). Such an immigrant was "inferior to ourselves in his knowledge of government, in his ideas of liberty" (29 April 1902, 3740), and might eventually become so numerous as to "control us instead of our controlling them" (26 July 1899, 8524).[9] To those who argued that Galicians would "assimilate," Oliver warned against "the intermarriage of your sons or daughters with those who are of an alien race and of alien ideas" (12 April 1901, 2934).

Oliver was not alone in his fears of Galician immigration. Alexander McNeill (LCP) claimed to have had it on sound authority that "a good many of these people have been criminals in their own country," but was unwilling to reveal his source to Sifton, even in private (26 July 1899, 8505).[10] Thomas S. Sproule (C) suggested that Galicians were of a "poorer and more helpless class, who are unable to do anything for themselves" (2 June 1898, 6824). Edward G. Prior (C) went further in suggesting that the Galicians' manners were "very little removed from the habits of animals" (7 July 1899, 6841). The idea of a racial hierarchy was becoming more encompassing and entrenched within Liberal Nationalism as it expanded from its consideration of Chinese migrants to include Europeans. What distinguished it from the racism of Liberal Internationalists was the assertion that it was in the national interest to exclude such "inferior" peoples.

Although he privately tried to decrease such immigration (Petryshyn 1991, 21), Sifton publicly supported the Galicians, arguing that they would, with their skills and the opportunities that lay before them, soon "develop into a thoroughly prosperous agricultural community" (2 June 1898, 6829). Moreover, he charged his critics with fostering public prejudice.[11] Although Sifton did not openly oppose Oliver, a fellow Liberal,[12] others did. Oliver and his supporters were routinely admonished for promoting unrealistic expectations of immigrants. For example, Duncan C. Fraser (L) objected that Oliver "spoke about settlers as if he wanted them to be perfect angels when they came to this country ... if we insist that every man who comes in must be as good a citizen as the people who are here, I think it says very little for the manhood of our people and for our idea of true citizenship" (26 July 1899, 8546). "If we bring only in to this country those who enjoy all the advancement in civilization and religious training and everything that makes a gentleman and a scholar," he argued, "we will never settle this country" (12 April 1901, 2941). Others, like John V. Ellis (L), suggested that Canadians could do more to help newcomers adjust (7 July 1899, 6900). In Sifton's "businesslike assessment of ethnic differences," then, and in the arguments of those who supported his immigration policies, the Liberal Internationalist belief that ethnoracial differences (at least among Europeans) were neither inherently dangerous nor set in stone was expressed, albeit within a framework of Anglo-Saxon superiority.[13]

Sifton's group resettlement policy for Doukhobor refugees also drew significant criticism. Like the Mennonites, the Doukhobors are a pacifist Christian religious sect that endured persecution during the late nineteenth century at the hands of the Russian government for refusing to place the authority of the state above that of God. In 1899, Sifton agreed to resettle more than 7,500 Doukhobors in western Canada. "The Canadian government was anxious to attract immigrants," recalled British Quaker Aylmer Maude, who took part in the negotiations, "and the officials that we met took much trouble to meet the unusual circumstances and give every possible assistance" (quoted in Dirks 1977, 33). The refugees were allowed to take up block settlements and were exempted from military service, among other exceptional measures.

Sifton's decision soon came under attack in Parliament along two Liberal Nationalist fronts. First, he was criticized for having granted the refugees special concessions. "I do not see why any persons settling in our country should be allowed privileges which are not granted to our own people," Uriah Wilson (C) protested: "If there are any privileges to be given to anybody, our own people should be preferred" (12 April 1901, 2886). Others claimed that group settlement would inhibit integration into mainstream Canadian life: "If they are a desirable class of settlers," Nathaniel C. Wallace (C) said, "they should be sent to mingle with the other people, so as to be taught Canadian instincts; the value of the liberty we enjoy, and the kind of institutions we live under" (ibid., 2964). Second, the Doukhobors were labelled undesirable, not only for some of their social practices but also because they were said to have no respect for the law. "Any people who are too good to conform to the laws of this country," Oliver argued, "are too good to live in this country, and we do not want them at any price" (ibid., 2937). In this vein, Wallace approvingly quoted a *Halifax Chronicle* editorial:

> It is revolting in the extreme to think of blood such as this being destined to mix with our good, clean British and French Canadian blood to its certain corruption ... Better let the prairies lie fallow as they have lain since the waters receded from their face than plant them with residents who will be in but not of Canada; and whom shall we be ashamed to acknowledge as bearers of the Canadian name. (Ibid., 2966)

For such Liberal Nationalists, the Doukhobors' refugee status was irrelevant to the question of resettlement. The presumed interests of the national community were to take precedence over the needs of the persecuted, and these national interests were interpreted along predominantly ethnoracial lines.

Sifton took Wallace to task for inflaming public sentiments against immigrants for political gain; indeed, the intense focus on the Doukhobors, as well as on Galicians, was, he felt, aimed at undermining the government by appealing to public prejudice. He was joined by Arthur W. Puttee (Independent Labour), who maintained that "you cannot draw up an indictment against a whole people ... Certainly, they do not speak our language or wear our dress, but that is not a crime" (ibid., 2946). The onus was on Canada, he suggested, to show its superiority by making them feel welcome. Indeed, Senator David Mills (L) proposed that

> if they grow up where freedom has full play, where there is no attempt to persecute or impose disabilities upon them, on account of any peculiar view which they may hold, they are very likely to adjust themselves to the views and feelings and sentiments of the rest of the population, and those peculiarities, if they do not entirely disappear, become proportionately weak and unimportant. (29 March 1901, 178)

"There is no better way to make good citizens," Duncan Fraser suggested to the House, "than to remove people from despotism and give them liberty to expand their energies" (12 April 1901, 2943). Thus, two Liberal Internationalist arguments still resonated in Canadian control debates: that the receiving population had a responsibility to ensure successful integration, and that in their search for freedom, refugees could make ideal citizens.[14]

Sifton was also criticized when, against his express wishes,[15] Italian (especially southern Italian) immigration increased.[16] Although only 2,795 Italians were recorded in the 1891 census, the total rose to 10,834 in 1901 and 45,411 in 1911 (Ramirez 1989, 8, Table 2). Italian immigration was generally organized through a *padrone* system, whereby private Italian labour agents recruited workers for particular contracts with companies in Canada, especially in construction and natural resource extraction. The government frequently made exceptions to its agriculturalists-only rule in response to requests from such businesses, many of which were actively engaged in immigration promotion, a situation that further diminished control.[17] As a result, "the long-standing goal of bringing into the country only the settler-labourer type of immigrant was displaced by a policy of importing an industrial proletariat" (Avery 1979, 37). When hundreds of Italians were left stranded in Montreal in early 1904, however, a Royal Commission was struck to investigate Italian labour in Canada (see Harney 1994). Sifton claimed to be powerless to turn back Italian immigration and denied that the government had encouraged it. In response, critics such as Thomas Sproule increasingly expressed frustration with Sifton's refusal to admit that there was a problem, let alone act upon it: "It is the minister and his supporters, not the opposition, who have the power to change the law to make it effective, and why do they not do so?" (21 July 1904, 7297).

These concerns extended to the Canada-US border, which could still be crossed with minimal oversight.[18] This was partly due to the delegation of power to Immigration Agents and sub-Agents, as mentioned above. For example, it was discovered in 1903 that many of them "did little actually to promote immigration, simply issuing certificates to intending immigrants to collect the commission – and there was evidently considerable falsification and abuse of the system" (Hall 1985, 64). Similar problems existed in Europe, as no serious effort at inland or overseas screening was made; indeed, Sifton declared to the House that such screening would be impractical.[19] Nonetheless, as criticisms of the government's policies grew, he acknowledged that

> it is extremely desirable that some method should be devised that will enable us to exercise a little more authority than we have in regard to foreign immigrants. At the present time[, however,] there is nothing in the law that authorizes me to stop them at all; the law would have to be amended in order to confer authority upon me to do so. (26 July 1899, 8515)[20]

While officials sought to exclude criminals and paupers, Superintendent of Immigration Frank Pedley maintained that "so long as a man is healthy and is not likely to become a public charge, then there is no reason why he should not be admitted" (Canada 1902, 314).

Deputy Minister James A. Smart stated before the Standing Committee that the government could not take too hard a line if the land was to be settled. "We undertook to prevent persons who were not possessed of sufficient capital from coming in [last year]," he recounted, "but we found that the restriction was going to have a bad effect upon all immigration" (Canada 1898, 226). A few years later, he noted that rumours of new medical provisions were having a deterrent effect on potential settlers (Canada 1903, 12). Even with greater scrutiny, he revealed, "it is pretty hard to say who are undesirable ... Of course, it is always desirable to have people come to the country with means, but past experience has shown that the people who have gone to the west with means have not made the same success as those who have gone in with no means at all" (Canada 1899, 277). Although monetary requirements were imposed on eastern European and Jewish immigrants at the beginning of the new century, Smart said that they were difficult to enforce because immigrants were often wary of showing officials their money (Canada 1900, 320). It was also hard to distinguish poor from pauper: "Because a man has not much money in his pocket it does not make him a pauper" (Canada 1903, 106).

Sifton's most significant restrictive legislative change was a 1902 amendment to the 1869 *Immigration Act* "to enable the government to deport immigrants from foreign countries, who may be suffering from any dangerous or infectious disease" (16 April 1902, 2850). Since Confederation, Canadian policy had generally looked to secure the welfare of new arrivals, with quarantine stations established so that diseased foreigners could be cured before being landed.[21] With the exception of the Chinese (who had long been blamed for carrying diseases), it was immigrants with mental health problems who first became a concern. Indeed, prominent Canadian psychiatrist Charles K. Clarke spent much of his professional life promoting stiffer medical inspections and the deportation of "mental defectives" and the "feeble-minded" so that they did not weaken Canadian society (Dowbiggin 1995).[22] Outside the medical profession, immigration restriction was promoted by an influential eugenics movement that "provided apparently new, objective scientific justification for old, deep-seated racial and class assumptions" (McLaren 1990, 49). Thus, those promoting increased control over arrivals could draw on a powerful discriminatory discourse and rationale expressed in medical terms.

An Act to amend the Immigration Act was introduced in 1902 after reports surfaced that immigrants rejected by the United States on health grounds were being admitted. "Why," demanded Uriah Wilson in the House, "should we consent to admit the off-scourings of creation into this country?" (16 April 1902, 2962).[23] Sifton replied that the reports had little substance: "It will easily be understood that men stationed as officers along the Canadian frontier line are desirous to show their government that they have a great deal to do, as otherwise their offices would be abolished, and we may therefore look constantly for indications in the press that these gentlemen are extremely busy" (ibid., 2975). Nonetheless, the government soon introduced legislation, initiating an eight-year process that gave the government an unprecedented array of powers over non-citizens wishing to come to or remain in Canada.

The legislation empowered Cabinet to "prohibit the landing in Canada of any immigrant or other passenger who is suffering from any loathsome, dangerous or infectious disease or malady, whether such immigrant intends to settle in Canada, or only intends to pass though Canada to settle in some other country" (Section 1). Anyone admitted despite being a member of this excludable category could "be apprehended, without a warrant, by any immigration agent or other government officer, and ... compelled to return or be taken on board the vessel, and by force, if necessary" (Section 2). Subsequent regulations empowered front-line officials to determine whether immigrants were inadmissible on medical grounds. Although Deputy Minister Smart claimed that upon arrival "our doctor takes charge and examines every one" (Canada 1903, 6), only three paid medical officers worked at the country's eastern seaports, and no inspection occurred on the west coast, except through quarantine operations conducted by the Department of Agriculture.[24]

For Liberal Nationalists, these changes did not go far enough. Edward F. Clarke (C) maintained that Canada should screen immigrants overseas and "not continue to be, as has been asserted again and again, a dumping ground, or a place from which immigrants who could not go from European points direct into the United States may scheme to obtain entrance into that country" (1 May 1902, 3928).[25] The laxity of the Canadian system was revealed, some suggested, by the fact that the United States turned back immigrants coming through Canada and had recently increased the number of inspectors screening Canadian admissions from 66 to 116 (21 July 1904, 7311).

Sifton maintained that the problem was "of a most trifling character, such as is bound to occur under any administration" (29 April 1902, 3748). Moreover, to check those rejected for admission to the United States would be expensive and require new legislation (21 July 1904, 7333). Although inland medical inspections were also supported by Liberal Internationalists, they often argued that foreign diseases did not present a great threat. Thus, Arthur S. Kendall (L) found concerns over unhealthy immigrants to be "ridiculous" when Parliament refused to deal with the more serious question of public health – in comparison, problems stemming from immigration were "mere bagatelles," the physician said (ibid., 7290).[26] Deputy Minister Smart observed that "we have never heard in Canada of any epidemic of any kind resulting from the introduction of persons inflicted with" diseases (Canada 1903, 13). Such opinions, however, flowed against the rising tide of support for a more restrictionist approach.

This was evident in the Senate, where the Liberal Internationalism that had dominated debates over the 1885 *Chinese Immigration Act* had all but disappeared. Senator James A. Lougheed (LCP) began by declaring that "the liberality which is practiced by our government on this particular subject leads to Canada receiving the refuse of European immigration" (6 May 1902, 400). During its deliberations, Senators sought to make it easier to compel transportation companies to return rejected migrants. While arguing that the government should "take power to pass the most stringent regulations" (9 May 1902, 441), Lougheed successfully amended the bill to allow people to be turned back at the border "for any cause whatsoever," as long as the grounds were proclaimed by Order-in-Council (10 May 1902, 447). During the subsequent debate in the House, however, Sifton maintained that "the government does not consider that the executive authority should have such unlimited powers for the exclusion of people coming into Canada" (13 May 1902, 4802), and was supported by the Opposition. Within four years, however, both sides in the House had changed their positions.

Although non-citizens were increasingly likely to be deported for medical reasons after 1902, critics failed to convince Sifton to take a more restrictive approach. Moreover, by the early 1900s his attention had shifted from immigration to other issue areas relevant to his ministerial portfolio, such as transportation and natural resource exploitation.[27] Meanwhile, the numbers and diversity of immigrants continued to grow, reflecting Sifton's belief that immigration "was a business, and the immigrant a long-term investment for Canada" (Hall 1977, 81). His influence should not be reduced simply to numbers, however. Although his support for greater diversity in European immigration provided continued space for Liberal Internationalism in the universe of political discourse, he also increased the centralization of discretionary power within the immigration bureaucracy and took steps towards a more restrictive approach to control. It is on this foundation that institutions of control were constructed that would shape Canada's response to immigrants and refugees up to the 1960s.

The Oliver Years (1905-11)

Liberal Nationalists could be forgiven for thinking that immigration policy would change when Oliver became Interior Minister, as he had long been one of the most consistent and vocal opponents of Sifton's policies. Oliver, however, oversaw large if somewhat erratic increases in annual intake levels and continued diversification. Moreover, his description of the Sifton period bore little resemblance to his earlier backbench comments. Although still advocating the selection of only "desirable" immigrants, Oliver now declared that expansion under Sifton had produced "the most happy results" (19 June 1905, 7687). Soon, however, he embarked upon the most substantial reworking of Canadian immigration policy in the country's history.

Oliver had long agreed with Sifton that the 1869 *Immigration Act* did not authorize the type of control so often demanded in Parliament, and he found support for change from officials. Superintendent of Immigration William D. Scott, who would largely be responsible for designing the rights-restrictive approach to come, had clearly expressed views on the inferiority of all but British and northern European immigrants and on Canada's need to exert more control over entries (see Scott 1914), while Chief Medical Officer Peter H. Bryce took a eugenics-based approach that accorded well with Oliver's outlook (McLaren 1990; Roberts 1986). In 1906, Oliver introduced *An Act respecting Immigration and Immigrants* to replace the 1869 *Immigration Act*.

"This is not an Act to promote immigration," he declared, "it is an Act to regulate immigration, and has nothing to do, except in a secondary way, with efforts that are put forward to promote immigration. This is, as it were, a brake upon the wheel" (13 June 1906, 5205). It would provide the "means for controlling immigration generally and respecting undesirable immigrants, which did not exist in the old Bill" (ibid., 5196). It gave the department increased discretion in regulating the border and, by extension, the Canadian population.

Although protections for immigrants in transit and upon arrival were retained, greater attention was now devoted to establishing the conditions under which people could be refused admission. Under "Immigrants Prohibited from Landing," the law stated (with limited exceptions) that "no immigrant shall be permitted to land in Canada" who is feeble-minded, an idiot, or an epileptic, or who is insane, or has had an attack of insanity within five years; ... who is deaf and dumb, or dumb, blind or infirm ...

who is afflicted with a loathsome disease or with a disease which is contagious or infectious and which may become dangerous to the public health or widely disseminated, whether such immigrant intends to settle in Canada or only to pass through Canada to settle in some other country ...

who is a pauper, or destitute, a professional beggar, or vagrant, or who is likely to become a public charge ...

who has been convicted of a crime involving moral turpitude, or who is a prostitute, or who procures, or brings or attempts to bring into Canada prostitutes or women for purposes of prostitution ... (Sections 26-29)

As a consolidation of recent legislative changes and parliamentary debate, these provisions provoked little controversy (especially after those who were simply deaf were removed from the list). For Liberal Internationalists, such prohibitions were of less concern than the types of restrictions proposed and their relation to notions of due process and equality.

The new law would grant the government the power to expand the definition of who was undesirable without seeking the approval of Parliament, as had been proposed by the Senate in 1902. Specifically, the Governor-in-Council would be able to, "by proclamation or order, whenever he considers it necessary or expedient, prohibit the landing in Canada of any specified class of immigrants" (Section 30).[28] Cabinet could also establish minimum monetary qualifications for immigrants, "which may vary according to the class and destination of such immigrant, and otherwise according to the circumstances" (Section 20). Those found to fall within a prohibited category could be removed up to two years after their arrival (Section 71). Anyone who within the same period had "become a charge upon the public funds, whether municipal, provincial, or federal, or an inmate of or a charge upon any charitable institution" (Section 28), or who had "committed a crime involving moral turpitude, or become an inmate of a jail or hospital or other charitable institution" (Section 33), could similarly be deported. Furthermore, those deemed to be in contravention of the law could be apprehended without a warrant (Section 70), while an entire family might be deported should "the father or head of a family" be removed (Section 72). The concept of the border, then, was being pushed inland in terms of both space and time, providing much greater scope for the state's authority to regulate the future of the Canadian population.

Many parliamentarians expressed concerns over the removal of these and other areas of government action from parliamentary oversight. Criticisms emerged over the minister's being granted the authority (in Sections 3 and 6) to appoint various departmental officials: "Here again you give the minister a personal power which is as wide as the world," George Foster complained (13 June 1906, 5204).[29] David Henderson (C) worried that the authority – subsequently removed – to charge a duty on immigrants was "placing power in the hands of the Governor in Council that we should not place in his hands" (ibid., 5219). Considerable disquiet was evoked by the new deportation provisions. Haughton Lennox (C) opposed the removal of people who had, within two years of their arrival, become a public charge, arguing that it was "contrary to all natural justice that we should deport him because forsooth he had the misfortune in the meantime, or even through improvidence, to become a charge upon the public funds" (ibid., 5250). "Canada should not try to establish a reputation for being perfectly inhuman," Senator Lawrence G. Power (L) observed (29 June 1906, 1005), but should take responsibility for those admitted. "When does a man," he inquired, "become our own criminal?" (ibid., 1008).

Oliver maintained in the House that the government could be trusted to use these new powers with "due discretion" (13 June 1906, 5251).[30] Unless provided such authority, he warned, it could not be held responsible for evasions of the law.[31] In the Senate, Richard Scott (L) argued for the government that "very full and arbitrary powers must be given to officials to prevent such persons [with diseases] landing, or, if having landed, to send them back" (29 June 1906, 993). "You must," he said, "have some sort of confidence in the government administering the law in a humane and proper manner" (ibid., 1013). Despite the range of misgivings expressed, however, few suggestions were advanced to alter the bill's restrictive features.[32]

Soon thereafter, Oliver introduced amendments to the 1906 *Immigration Act* to facilitate the removal of immigrants who had become a public charge or had been incarcerated. This provided Liberal Internationalists with another opportunity to voice their views. The 1907 *Act to amend the Immigration Act* was, Foster protested, "altogether too drastic" (3 April 1907, 5718). Punishing people with removal for events that occurred in Canada, he argued, was nonsensical: "In order to make this logical, you have to connect the disability with his previous domicile, it must be something he has brought over with him" (ibid.). Senator William Macdonald (C) declared it "monstrous" to deport people who had arrived with good intentions: "They were honest people when they left, and they became dishonest or immoral in this country, and it is improper for us to deport them" (9 April 1907, 657).[33] In response to such concerns, Oliver once again asked for trust: "My hon. friend has stated a case which is quite possible under the wording of the law, but of course he understands as every one will understand, that such a case does not come within the spirit of that enactment and it is to be assumed that the administration of the law would be according to the spirit" (3 April 1907, 5719).

This failed to satisfy Thomas Sproule: "If you are going to carry out only the spirit why make the letter of the law more drastic than the spirit?" (ibid.). John Ellis (now a Senator) observed that deportation "involves so many serious consequences to the family that we do not like to look upon it" (15 April 1907, 729).[34] Oliver told the House, however, that the power had "to be in a drastic form in order that it may be acted upon effectively and satis- factorily" (3 April 1907, 5719).[35] The 1906 law and 1907 amendments cer- tainly affected deportations, which rose from 137 in 1906 to 1,748 in 1909 (Roberts 1988, 44, Table 3). Although annual figures varied to the end of the Great Depression, they never dipped below 500 and peaked at around 6,500 in 1933. The most prominent reason for deportation was medical initially, but soon "public charge" and "criminality" cases came to the fore.

Although the new legislation succeeded in reducing parliamentary influ- ence over the state's control efforts, it did not isolate them from the judiciary, and non-citizens could still – as will be seen below – use the courts to chal- lenge the state's actions effectively. This led to a jaded view of the judiciary within the department, and the government responded aggressively. Oliver went so far as to argue that "if you so frame the law that the right or power of deportation becomes a subject of legal dispute, you might nearly as well not have the power" (3 April 1907, 5719). Rather than give non-citizens recourse to the courts, he suggested, everyone should "trust to the judgment and fairness of the authorities in administering the law" (ibid.).

In an effort to court-proof its actions, the government introduced legisla- tion in 1910 to replace the 1906 *Immigration Act*. Although the new *Immi- gration Act* contained several new control measures, Oliver stressed the need to restrict judicial oversight: "The law requires amending in order to make it more satisfactory in enforcement when tested by opposition which brings it under review of the courts" (4 March 1909, 2009).[36] The new law would ensure that "until a man has actually and legally entered Canada, he is not entitled to claim the protection of the courts" (19 January 1910, 2135). This "somewhat radical provision," one that Oliver worried "may not meet the approval of the House" (14 March 1910, 5504), would effectively bar the courts from reviewing departmental decisions relating to non-citizens:

> No court, and no judge or officer thereof, shall have jurisdiction to review, quash, reverse, restrain or otherwise interfere with any proceeding, decision or order of the Minister or of any Board of Inquiry, or officer in charge, had, made, or given under the authority and in accordance with the provisions of this Act relating to the detention or deportation of any rejected immigrant, passenger or other person, upon any ground whatsoever. (Section 23)

This roadblock to rights-based politics through the courts would stand for almost sixty years, until immigration matters were again made more fully subject to judicial review in 1967.

The government also proposed to establish administrative boards of inquiry to oversee cases of detention and deportation: "Our object is to give the person ... an opportunity to present his case, to give him, so to speak, a fair trial, rather than, as at present, the department takes the responsibility of an arbitrary action without a form of trial" (21 March 1910, 5817).[37] It was, Oliver explained, a trade-off for taking away access to the courts. The boards would consist of three or more officers at a port of entry and were to be held in camera with, where practicable, the non-citizen in question present. When evidence or testimony was introduced, the immigrant would have the right to counsel, and in non-medical cases an appeal to the minister could be lodged following a decision (see Sections 13-24).

The government also wanted to "clearly and definitely provide for the exclusion of undesirables who arrive in Canada by rail or by road" (19 January 1910, 2134) so as to regulate cross-border movements from the United States. Henceforth, an individual crossing the border where there was no Canadian official would be required to "forthwith report such entry to the nearest immigration officer and present himself for examination" (Section 33.6). In 1907-08, there were 175 immigration officials working at 107 points along the border, and 4,580 people were found to be inadmissible to Canada (Canada 1909, 198). By 1910-11, this number had risen to 15,004 (more than 12 percent of all applications for admission from the United States), while staff had increased to over 200 officers at 134 points (Canada 1912, 128-29). The department also began to prosecute more aggressively those suspected of having entered along the border in contravention of Canadian immigration law (ibid., 132).

Finally, the 1910 *Immigration Act* expanded the grounds for keeping non-citizens out of Canada, and this elicited scarcely any opposition.[38] Cabinet was given authority to "prohibit for a stated period, or permanently, the landing in Canada, or the landing at any specified port of entry in Canada, of immigrants belonging to any race deemed unsuited to the climate or requirements of Canada, or of any specified class, occupation or character" (Section 38.c). This was done, Oliver explained, "to give the government arbitrary power to prohibit the landing of any class of people. Suppose there was a sudden influx of people from some undesirable Asiatic or African country, we could, without ceremony, simply say: You cannot land" (22 March 1910, 5853).[39] He acknowledged that "it is impossible to enforce a harsh statute in a soft way" and that the "drastic exclusion provisions" would result in "terrible hardships" (ibid., 5860-61).

The problems that could arise with the expanded discretionary powers of the department and its officials were soon seen in Oliver's efforts to bar Black

Americans from resettling despite being qualified to do so under the law. In 1911, Alfred H. Clarke (L) inquired about reports that immigration officials had been sent to prevent the arrival of a group of such immigrants from Oklahoma. "If it is correct that the officers of this government have taken the steps to prevent the entrance into this country of these people on account of their colour," he warned, "then I think it will require a very great deal of explanation from the department to justify it" (22 March 1911, 5911). In Liberal Internationalist tradition, he reminded the minister that "it has always been the boast of British institutions that unfortunate men will find a haven within our borders" (ibid.). Oliver justified his actions with an ambiguous description of Canadian policy:

> There are many cases where the admission or exclusion of an immigrant depends on a strict or a lax interpretation of the law, so that if the immigrant is of what we would call the desirable class it may be that [the law is] administered laxly, and if he is of the presumably less desirable class then [it is] administered more restrictedly. (Ibid., 5912)

"The only idea I have from the statement of the minister," George Foster replied, "is, that he is above the law" (ibid., 5913).[40] Oliver's difficulty stemmed from the fact that the department did discriminate on the basis of race, but behind the scenes, through tactics of administrative stalling and by making it known that health inspections at the border would be strictly enforced against Black Americans and then doing just that (see Troper 1972, 121-45). Thus, despite formal denials, little effort was made to hide the fact that discrimination occurred.[41]

By 1913, Senator Lougheed observed that "our immigration machinery is sufficiently efficient to prevent anyone from coming into Canada against the wishes of the Canadian government" (2 June 1913, 937). Oliver agreed, declaring upon his return to the House after his government's 1911 defeat at the polls "that although our immigration has doubled in the past six years, that increase has taken place under a policy of restricted and selective immigration, probably more drastic than that imposed by any other country in the world" (30 November 1911, 607-8). The department "had now evolved from a recruitment agency to a security service" (Avery 1979, 88). Nonetheless, as the legal foundations for a more rights-restrictive approach were established and its implementation was extended and refined, and despite the dominance of a Liberal Nationalist discourse, the proportion of British immigrants continued to decrease while the government's control capacity was still limited by minimal screening in Canada and overseas. This trend continued under the Conservative government of Robert Borden in the few remaining years before the outbreak of the First World War.

The Conservative Years (1911-14)

The Conservatives initially did little to change the orientation of the previous Liberal government with respect to immigration. The major control issue that arose prior to the First World War was East Indian immigration, and this was ultimately resolved in the government's favour, as will be seen below. As for European immigration, after years of criticizing Liberal expansionist policies, the Conservatives now highlighted in the 1912 Speech from the Throne the "copious and welcome stream of immigration [that] has poured into our country during the past summer" and boasted that its size "during the present year is greater than during any corresponding period of our history" (21 November 1912, 2). As annual intake levels jumped from 208,500 in 1910-11 to 251,800 in 1912-13 before declining to 225,600 in 1913-14, the percentage of non-British/northern European arrivals rose from around 23 percent to around 37 percent (Department of Mines and Resources 1946, 240, Table 3). An explanation for this growth could lie in the fact that although the Liberals had been subject to continual pressure from the business community to increase immigration, the Conservatives gained office when such demands were particularly strong. Moreover, the party had considerable corporate connections, particularly new Interior Minister Robert Rogers (Avery 1995, 32). This soon provoked criticisms in the House.

In March 1914, Eugène Paquet (C) asked to discuss the question of immigrant selection since "race assimilation, in this immense and young country of ours, is a social problem of the greatest moment" (9 March 1914, 1437). Although he welcomed farmers, Paquet claimed that immigrant workers were "too often indifferent to sanitary requirements and constantly at variance with them," and too often were connected to crime (ibid., 1438). He suggested that all immigrants be required to show a certificate from their homeland to attest to their moral qualities. Herménégilde Boulay (C) called on the government to shut out "that class of immigrants that is swarming into our cities, those Jews who are a curse to the trade; those ruffians and thugs who terrorize our peaceful citizens; those criminals whom we are constrained as a last resort, to confine to our penitentiaries, after costly lawsuits, at the expense of honest people" (12 March 1914, 1620). Interior Minister William J. Roche's response harked back to Sifton: "How are we to exclude them unless we pass a prohibitory Act entirely, if they are able to pass the monetary qualification and the medical examination?" (ibid., 1627).

Prior to the First World War, the Conservatives did nothing to decrease European arrivals. Neither did they alter the rights-restrictive system of control erected under the Liberals. The tendency to focus on the expansionist outcomes of Canadian control policies during these years should not detract, however, from a full appreciation of the rights-restrictive control framework that was institutionalized at the same time. Although it was not fully implemented at first, it would soon be, and it shaped government policy and practice for decades to come. Its creation reflected the continued ascendancy of Liberal Nationalism in Canada, which held the rights of non-citizens to be of secondary importance compared with the sovereignty of the state and its ability to act in accordance with the "national interest." This was very much reflected in policies aimed at restricting Asian immigration during this same period.

Restricting Asian Immigration (1887-1908)

After coming into effect in January 1886, the 1885 *Chinese Immigration Act* probably decreased Chinese migration to Canada for the rest of the decade. It is difficult to assess its direct effect since a reduction was anticipated with the completion of the Canadian Pacific Railway. With work on the railroad winding down, many Chinese were expected to return to China or move on to the United States.[42] By the 1890s, however, the number of arrivals had begun to grow again, and by 1901 the Canadian Census reported the presence of 16,375 Chinese in Canada, up from 4,383 in 1881 (Roy 1989, 269, Table 1B). During this same period, Japanese immigration began to increase, followed by East Indian arrivals. Although different policy tools would be used for each group, collectively they contributed to the continued development of a much more restrictive approach to control. By the outbreak of the First World War, this had been expanded to include such groups as Armenians, Jews, and Syrians.

Consolidating Control (1887-96)

As Chinese immigration grew, numerous proposals were advanced by British Columbia MPs to amend the 1885 *Chinese Immigration Act*. In 1892, David W. Gordon (LCP) introduced a Private Member's Bill to increase the tonnage restriction to one person per one hundred tons and decrease to four months the time provided for return visits to China on a certificate. Secretary of State Joseph Chapleau (C) assumed sponsorship of the proposal for the government, removing the tonnage provision and increasing the number of months' leave to six while replacing the certificate system with detailed registration before departure from Canada. This was a response to concerns that extensive certificate fraud existed (5 July 1892, 4631). Although opposition was not widespread, Liberal Internationalist voices could still be heard in the House. Thus, Thomas Christie (L) decried the Head Tax as being excessively onerous, constituting "a heavy penalty for the crime of being born a Chinaman" (ibid., 4637). "I have no sympathy," he affirmed, "with any legislation which discriminates against any class, creed or nationality, and I hold that all classes and all nationalities should be placed exactly on the same basis" (ibid.). The government carried the day, however.

In 1896, George R. Maxwell (L) called for a $500 Head Tax. He linked the protection of the national community to the exclusion of foreigners, arguing that "it was our self interest to do all the justice to our own people that we possibly could" and that it was "a narrow-minded policy to fill the land with semi-barbarians" (9 September 1896, 895-96). It was only, he said, through the pursuit of "self preservation that any one of us can attempt to feel and act the impulses of what is called altruism or the higher life" (ibid., 896).[43] John Charlton (L) similarly maintained that "it is the instinct of self-preservation that compel[s] the Anglo-Saxon to demand that barriers shall be set up against this flood that would pour in upon them and subvert their institutions" (16 September 1896, 1352).[44] Therefore, he averred, to restrict the entry of the Chinese was not a human rights issue.[45] Indeed, offered William W.B. McInnes (L), "if the question of humanity be considered, I would suggest that the highest and most practical kind of humanity requires that we protect the interests of those who are nearest and dearest to us" (ibid., 1366).

In contrast, Liberal Internationalists viewed the success of the Canadian nation as being directly tied to the welcome offered foreigners. "It would be a retrograde move," Duncan Fraser claimed, "for us to pass laws to keep these people out on the ground that they are Chinamen" (9 September 1896, 904). To be a great nation, Canada had to lead by example in opening its doors to people from all over the world.[46] By the late nineteenth century, however, such ideas were receding in Canadian politics, overtaken by a Western ethnonationalism that promoted ethnic and linguistic conformity as ideal features of the modern nation-state (Hobsbawm 1992). In this context, Liberal Nationalists soon broadened the focus of their concerns to include the rising number of Japanese arrivals in Canada.

Extending Control (1896-1903)
After his 1896 motion, George Maxwell introduced two more bills to restrict Chinese migration. He was joined by William McInnes, who presented legislation in 1898 and 1899 to expand Canada's restrictionist policies to include people of Japanese origin. The possibility that "the case of the Chinese to-day may be quoted as a precedent for excluding some other race in the future" had been anticipated earlier by Senator George Howlan (L) (26 May 1886, 705), but the types of restrictions employed against the Japanese would be very different from those used against the Chinese, even if their objectives and outcomes were virtually the same.

Japanese migrants had lived in Canada since at least the mid-1880s but their presence acquired political significance only in the 1890s. Like the Chinese, the vast majority settled in British Columbia, and by the mid-1890s their numbers had probably never grown beyond 1,100 and were usually around 300 (Ayukawa and Roy 1999, 845). The community grew to some 4,500 by 1901 (representing 97 percent of all Japanese in Canada), while

11,272 arrived by ship during a thirteen-month period between 1900 and 1901 (Roy 1989, 92). Although most were destined for the United States, their presence underscored the question of control for many in the province. Arrivals were quickly curbed, however, by the Japanese government, which played the primary role in controlling Japanese immigration to Canada until well into the twentieth century. Thus, only 6 Japanese were reported to have arrived between 1901 and 1904 (Ayukawa and Roy 1999, 846). Nonetheless, by 1895 Japanese immigrants were provincially disenfranchised in British Columbia and over the next few decades the province passed numerous restrictive laws, many of which were disallowed by the federal government or ruled *ultra vires* by the courts (see Adachi 1976, Chapters 1 and 2).

In contrast with the Chinese, support for the Japanese outside British Columbia was more widespread. Although MPs like Frank Oliver claimed that the Japanese "are not our people, they do not belong to our civilization, they do not strengthen our country, and we are here for ourselves and not for them" (25 June 1900, 8206), others offered both cultural and political reasons for not equating the Japanese and Chinese. Prime Minister Wilfrid Laurier (L) stated that "Japan is one of the rising nations of the present day. It has shown itself to be very progressive, it does not seem to me at all doubtful that within a short period Japan will have placed itself in the fore front among the civilized nations of the earth" (27 March 1903, 599).[47] When a proposal was made in the Senate to bar the Japanese from taking up mineral claims, Senator David Mills replied that "Japan is recognized as a civilized state lying within the domain of international laws, and subject to the same rights, privileges and duties as every civilized state within that same domain" (16 February 1898, 156).[48] This idea was reinforced by the Japanese consul in Canada, Tatsugoro Nosse, who argued that his co-nationals were more European (Roy 1989, 98). Moreover, the Japanese government sought to shape the course of Canadian immigration policy during this period by ensuring that it was linked to broader imperial questions of defence and trade between Britain and Japan.

Thus, while control over Chinese and Japanese arrivals was prominent on the parliamentary agenda during the early 1900s, only the former were touched by legislative action. In 1900, when Laurier introduced *An Act respecting and restricting Chinese Immigration* to amend the 1885 *Chinese Immigration Act,* he said that he was "not prepared to come in conflict with the Japanese government, when, perhaps, there may be complications in the Orient which may involve England in a war, and when, possibly, the best ally she would have in the Orient might be put in jeopardy" (14 June 1900, 7408-9).[49] In contrast, he planned to double the Chinese Head Tax to $100, overruling Sifton, who wanted it raised to $250 alongside a restrictive language test (Hall 1981, 263). The law would also cover arrivals by land (Section 11) and ensure that all people of Chinese origin came under its aegis "irrespective of allegiance" (Section 6), thereby voiding exemption claims by Chinese British subjects.

The legislation revealed that Liberal Internationalism was a greatly diminished force in Canadian politics. William C. Edwards (L) declared that such "retrograde and inhuman legislation" was "abhorrent to the principles of free trade and the commonest rights of all men who occupy this earth" (25 June 1900, 8166-67). It was based on ideas that were no different, he said, than those motivating the Boers in South Africa, against whom Britain was then at war.[50] Thomas Christie called for the repeal of that "oppressive and ... tyrannical" law, arguing that it was "both unjust and unBritish, and, therefore, cannot fail to be detrimental and injurious to the best interests of Canada and be a reproach to the good name of our country" (ibid., 8190-91). It was not, he said, "in accordance with our free, liberal institutions in Canada" (ibid.). These were familiar Liberal Internationalist ideas, however; whereas Liberal Nationalists brought new dimensions to the debate.

John Charlton claimed that those supporting the Chinese were too idealistic. He admitted, for example, that Christie's views did "at least credit to his heart and aspirations in favour of humanity and his love for freedom; and speaking in the abstract, his arguments may perhaps be considered unanswerable" (ibid.). But non-citizens were not the only ones with a stake in this matter, he continued, as there were also those

> who have a preemptive right as residents, as citizens of the country, and as having built up its institutions with the desire of founding a free country and free institutions, to hand down to posterity. They too have rights and are warranted, when determining what their action may be with reference to permitting others to share with them the blessings they have created and the country they have opened up, in taking into consideration what the influences are likely to be of those who propose to seek an asylum and a home with them. (Ibid.)

Charlton thus recognized few (if any) limitations on the actions that could be taken to control a nation's borders in the interests of its citizens.[51]

A more explicit link between racial discrimination and state sovereignty was made by Thomas Sproule: "I have always held that every country has a perfect right to exclude from its borders any undesirable element of humanity whether it be a criminal class, a pauper class, or a class that will be found to be to the disadvantage of the people of that country. Every civilized country does that to-day" (ibid., 8194-95). Similarly, George Casey (L) argued that "we have a right, as every other people inhabiting a country have, to object to the introduction among our population of any race whom we may consider hopelessly barbarian, or not capable of assimilating with our population" (ibid., 8203). For Liberal Nationalists, then, the country's sovereign right to control its border became conflated with the manner in which it exercised this right. These two issues would not begin to be separated again until after the Second World War, and they often continue to be merged in the politics of control today.

In 1903, Laurier introduced *An Act respecting and restricting Chinese immigration* to increase the Head Tax to $500, claiming that it was impossible to secure an agreement with China to control migration because of civil strife in that country. By now, no opposition to such measures was expressed in the House.[52] The same was not true in the Senate,[53] but opinion had clearly undergone a significant shift since 1887. According to some, partisan politics had made the Senate less willing to oppose the government.[54] In 1900, the Head Tax increase was discussed but no substantial amendments were offered. In 1903, the debate was longer and more heated but the only amendment passed sought to allow Chinese servants accompanying British subjects not to be taxed (Section 6.d). The dominant Liberal Nationalist view in the Senate was expressed in the conclusion of Pascal Poirier that "this Bill is nothing but a polite way of inviting the Chinamen to stay at home" (11 June 1903, 318). Even as the government worked to limit Chinese and Japanese immigration, however, a new control problem was emerging with the arrival of migrants from another part of the British Empire – India.

Expanding Control (1903-08)
The first East Indians arrived in Canada early in the twentieth century but their numbers remained small until 1906, when, it was reported in the House, 2,193 "Hindoos" had come to British Columbia (28 November 1906, 234).[55] Although often referred to as "Hindoos," the migrants were primarily of the Sikh faith, and also included some Muslims.[56] By 1906, East Indian immigration had provoked considerable agitation in British Columbia. Even more than the Japanese, however, East Indians received support from a number of quarters in Canada.

Some within the military promoted the admission of those who had fought with the British army in India, and there was more support from the churches than in the case of the Chinese or Japanese (Ward 1990, 84-85). Moreover, some in the East Indian community had gained access to elite Canadian society, such as Sunder Singh, an Oxford University graduate who helped establish a Canada-India Committee in Toronto.[57] As well, like other immigrant groups, East Indians established voluntary associations in Canada to protect their interests. Foremost among such "strong, defensive community institutions" (Buchignani et al. 1985, 20) was the Vancouver Khalsa Diwan

Society, created in 1907 to serve the community's economic, religious, and social needs and to provide a vehicle for political action concerning matters of "self-defence in Canada and Indian nationalism" (Ward 1990, 81). Despite growing agitation in British Columbia, little action was taken by federal or provincial governments during the early 1900s, as British Undersecretary of State for the Colonies Winston Churchill promised tighter regulation of emigration from British-controlled India (J. Morton 1974, 201).

Although people of Asian ancestry declined as a percentage of the total population of British Columbia during the early twentieth century, their absolute numbers grew, as did the fears of the majority population.[58] This was especially apparent when sudden and visible increases in Asian immigration occurred, as in 1907, which saw the Vancouver anti-Asian riots in September.[59] British Columbia had disenfranchised East Indians in April 1907 and included them in measures to limit Asian participation in various professions, on juries, in receiving government contracts, and in buying property (N. Singh 1994, 33). Tensions erupted when, just before a planned anti-Asian immigration protest in September, it was rumoured that a few hundred East Indians had entered from the United States after being driven out of Bellingham, Washington. After the riots, to maintain good diplomatic relations with Japan, Laurier instructed immigration officials to ensure that all Japanese with legal documents were admitted in accordance with the 1894 Anglo-Japanese Treaty of Commerce and Navigation, which recognized that citizens of each country had "full liberty to enter, travel or reside in any part of the dominions and possessions of the other contracting party" (quoted in Adachi 1976, 41). He also expressed his government's regrets to Japan, appointed William Lyon Mackenzie King (then Deputy Minister of Labour) to investigate reparations for the Japanese in Vancouver,[60] and sent Minister of Labour Rodolphe Lemieux to Tokyo to negotiate future limitations on Japanese arrivals.[61]

The result appeared to be a fairly comprehensive system of control. Although negotiations were anything but easy (Sugimoto 1978), Lemieux arranged that no more than four hundred labour migrants could come to Canada annually.[62] Besides determining appropriate reparations, Mackenzie King recommended and was appointed to an investigation into the causes of Asian labour migration to Canada, which subsequently highlighted the problems experienced by Japan in regulating its citizens who were living and working abroad in places such as Hawaii. This contributed to the Canadian government's decision to issue a 1908 Order-in-Council (PC 27), declaring that "immigrants may be prohibited from landing or coming to Canada unless they come from the country of their birth, or citizenship, by continuous journey and on [a] through ticket, purchased before leaving the country of their birth or citizenship" (quoted in Sampat-Mehta 1972, 133-34). Although the regulation could be enforced against Europeans (for example, when labour conditions were unstable), the Deputy Interior Minister let it be known that it was always to be applied against Asians (ibid., 134-35).

The measure affected primarily the East Indian community, as it was nearly impossible to arrange for direct passage from India to Canada. This "shattered any illusions that South Asians' status as British subjects meant anything. Even Chinese and Japanese aliens could immigrate" under certain conditions (Buchignani et al. 1985, 24). Since the East Indian population in Canada was overwhelmingly male, its very survival was threatened. East Indian arrivals had increased considerably since the beginning of the twentieth century, from a few dozen in 1904-05 to 2,124 in 1906-07 and 2,623 in 1907-08 (Department of Mines and Resources 1946, 239, Table 2), including two ships carrying some 900 and 500 migrants, respectively, that arrived just before the 1907 riots. This led to renewed discussions between the Canadian and British governments over imperial relations and state sovereignty, and Mackenzie King was duly sent to London in March 1908.

Mackenzie King was instructed to request assurances that the British would ensure a virtual exclusion of migration to Canada from India. The Laurier government wanted permission to state that

> the Government of India and the British authorities at Hong Kong, Shanghai and other ports had resolved: (1) to prohibit Indians proceeding to Canada without passports; (2) to limit the number of passports issued to a number to be agreed upon by the Government of Canada and India, and (3) to request the Government of Canada to deport all Indians arriving in Canada without passports. (Quoted in Sampat-Mehta 1972, 132)

The justifications for such restrictions were twofold. First, they were said to be humanitarian, since "experience has shown that immigrants of this class, having been accustomed to the conditions of a tropical climate, are wholly unsuited to this country, and that their inability to readily adapt themselves to surroundings so entirely different inevitably brings upon them much suffering and privation" (Canada 1908b, 5). Second, such migrants might create economic hardship and, as a result, social unrest for Canadian (i.e., European) families. Thus, a rights-restrictive policy was repackaged as a humanitarian response. For its part, Britain did not want to take (and did not want Canada to take) actions that might foster colonial discontent, and sought to convince Canada that open and aggressive control policies could undermine imperial stability.

Although Mackenzie King's mission produced no new British policies, his report conveyed a clear message: "That Canada should desire to restrict immigration from the Orient is regarded as natural, that Canada should remain a white man's country is believed to be not only desirable for economic and social reasons, but highly necessary on political and national grounds" (ibid., 7). It also secured recognition from British authorities that "in matters which so vitally affect her own welfare, Canada is the best judge of the course to be adopted, and that as a self-governing dominion she cannot be expected to refrain from enacting such measures in the way of restriction as in the discretion of her people are deemed most expedient" (ibid.). Canada was reminded, however, that membership in the Empire came with responsibilities and that "the exercise of her plenary powers in this particular [should] not be without a due regard to the obligations which citizenship within the empire entails" (ibid.). In his report, Mackenzie King suggested increasing the $25 monetary requirement then in place; it was soon raised to $200 by Order-in-Council. Whereas some 4,700 East Indians had arrived in 1906 and 1907, only 125 would be admitted during the following seven years (Ward 1990, 79).

Thus, a new Asian migration control regime had been created by mid-1908, consisting of the amended 1885 *Chinese Immigration Act,* arrangements with the British and Japanese governments, and regulations for the continuous journey and monetary requirements. The Liberals did not escape the politics of Asian immigration unscathed, however. Although five Liberal MPs from British Columbia tried to protect their political futures by introducing a motion in Parliament that "steps should be taken to restrict the influx of oriental immigrants into Canada" (16 December 1907, 701), voters returned only two of seven Liberals in the province in the 1908 general election.[63]

Sovereignty, Rights-Based Politics, and East Indian Immigrants (1908-14)

In response to increasing restrictions, Asian communities in Canada engaged in rights-based politics through judicial and legislative means as well as circumvention. This was most evident in, but not confined to, the case of East Indians. The government responded in 1910 by effectively removing judicial oversight of immigration control. Such extreme rights restriction proved effective for some time but was difficult to sustain in the long run as its contrast with core liberal principles became more apparent. It was only in 1967, however, that this restriction was removed; before then, it seriously hampered the pursuit of rights-based politics through the courts in Canada for more than half a century. In the context of increasing restrictions against Asian migration up to the First World War, the analysis now turns to examine the tactics employed by the East Indian community, especially its use of the courts, to overcome such barriers, and the responses they provoked from the Canadian government. Following the arrival of the *Komagata Maru* in 1914, the government at last secured a firm statement from the courts regarding the legitimacy of a rights-restrictive (and race-based) approach to control, signifying the clear ascent of Liberal Nationalism in Canada.

Adjusting Control: Chinese and Japanese Immigration (1908-14)
As the government continued to adjust the *Chinese Immigration Act*,[64] Chinese migration began to increase. In response, Mackenzie King – elected as a Liberal MP in 1908 and representing Canada at a 1909 international conference in Shanghai on the opium trade[65] – tried to convince Chinese officials to regulate emigration to Canada. Meanwhile, a scandal erupted in British Columbia over Chinese immigration, resulting in the appointment of a Royal Commission in late 1910. During the commission's hearings, "the evidence made it clear that with the connivance of some officials and the inefficiency of others, many Chinese had entered Canada without paying the head tax" (Roy 1989, 235). Thus, Chinese migrants were already beginning to circumvent Canada's restrictive policies. Revelations concerning the Liberal Party's involvement in appointing some of the customs officials involved, and continued unease over the effectiveness of the 1908 Gentlemen's Agreement with Japan, combined to put the Liberals on the defensive in British Columbia during the 1911 general election, which brought the Conservatives to power under Robert Borden.

In opposition, Borden had been cautious on the subject of Asian immigration, using it to his party's advantage without pushing as hard as some of his western colleagues. For example, although he favoured restriction, he did not exploit opportunities such as the 1907 riots or the 1910 scandal as tools in a campaign against Asian immigration. Borden was critical of the 1908 Gentlemen's Agreement, however, and wary of replacing the 1885 *Chinese Immigration Act* with any such deal. Aside from transferring responsibility for administering that law from the Department of Trade and Commerce to the Department of the Interior (the Royal Commission had called attention to the "divided authority and no definite responsibility" that characterized the old system and undermined its effectiveness; quoted in Sampat-Mehta 1972, 63) and requiring photographs on all documents related to Chinese migration control, the Conservatives appeared willing to let Chinese immigration increase.[66] This provoked protests when the British Columbia economy began to falter in 1913, but the outbreak of the First World War soon interrupted Chinese arrivals.

As for the Japanese, Borden had previously expressed uneasiness with Laurier's decision to pass a 1906 law confirming Canada's commitment to the terms of the 1894 Anglo-Japanese Treaty of Commerce and Navigation without reservation, on the grounds that Article 1 of the agreement ensured that the subjects of each country were secured "full liberty to enter, travel, or reside in any part of the dominions and possessions of the other Contracting Party, and shall enjoy full and perfect protection for their persons and property." Laurier had argued that the Japanese had proven faithful in their adherence to the 1908 Gentlemen's Agreement and that trade with Japan was important to Canada's economic development. Borden worried that "under the treaty subjects of the Empire of Japan have exactly the same right to enter, travel and reside in Canada as citizens of Canada have" (8 April 1908, 6449) – they were empowered to contest the authority of the Canadian government to control its borders.[67] Interior Minister Oliver responded that if Canada felt that it had lost control, then it could repeal the 1906 law confirming Canada's adherence to the treaty. Although the Laurier government did not encounter any great difficulties along the lines outlined by Borden,[68] it chose not to sign the 1911 successor to the treaty when it could not secure written guarantees that the mobility rights included would not result in an increase in Japanese immigration to Canada.

This was subsequently accomplished by the Conservatives, who received explicit confirmation from Japan in 1913 that the provision relating to mobility did not trump Canadian immigration law (Canada 1967, 737-47), and this was clearly stated in the 1913 *Japanese Treaty Act*. The difference from past policy was slight, however: "Control still ultimately rested with Japan, and Borden found himself tied – as was his Liberal predecessor – to the bounds of imperial policy" (Adachi 1976, 94). The number of Japanese arrivals decreased soon thereafter as the 1913 economic recession made Canada a less attractive destination. Furthermore, by 1914 Canada had come to rely on Japan's military assistance, secured through the 1905 Anglo-Japanese Alliance, as Japanese ships patrolled the Pacific for much of the war (Sarty 1984). Thus, neither Chinese nor Japanese immigration troubled the Borden government much in the years before the First World War, but the same could not be said about East Indian arrivals.

The East Indian Challenge (1908-14)
Between 1908 and the First World War, only 125 East Indians were landed in Canada, which suggests that control policies were rigidly enforced; the East Indian population reached around 4,000 before the war and then declined to around 2,000 after it began (Ward 1990, 79). Nonetheless, the level of attention paid to this community by immigration officials remained high, with the department hiring William C. Hopkinson to observe and report on the activities of East Indians in Canada.[69] The government was concerned that Sikh activists might use Canada as a staging ground for fomenting revolt against the British occupation of their homeland. This added a particular political dimension to East Indian control policies. Immigration officials also worried about the frequency with which East Indians were taking the government to court over its discriminatory policies – and winning.

Asian immigrants' use of the courts to assert their rights within Canada went back to pre-Confederation British Columbia and continued after it had become the country's sixth province. For example, in 1878, Tai Sing (one of twelve Chinese applicants then before the court in separate cases) successfully challenged the province's 1878 *Chinese Tax Act,* arguing that it was *ultra vires* of federal jurisdiction (*Tai Sing v. Maguire*). As for the Japanese, one of the most famous cases involved Tomey Homma, a naturalized Japanese Canadian, who challenged provincial legislation that denied the franchise to Chinese and Japanese Canadians. Although twice victorious before Canadian courts, Homma ultimately lost before the Judicial Committee of the Privy Council in London in 1902 (see Adachi 1976, 53-55). Beyond British Columbia, when a Saskatchewan law prevented Chinese restaurant owners from hiring white women, Quong Wing argued (unsuccessfully) before the Supreme Court of Canada that this deprived him "of the rights ordinarily enjoyed by the other inhabitants of the Province of Saskatchewan" and thus was *ultra vires* of the federal government's authority to define the rights of naturalized citizens (*Quong-Wing v. R.,* 443).[70]

East Indians seemed to go the furthest in pursuing rights-based politics through the courts and were "portrayed as the most litigatious of Vancouver's Asian minorities" in the local press (Indra 1979, 170). There are likely several reasons for this. First, with the continuous journey and $200 regulations, East Indians suffered the most restrictive control policies. They had to contest such policies if they were to persist as a community in Canada. Second, the Sikhs may have had a more clearly defined group identity than the Chinese or Japanese, stemming from a long history of protecting their interests as a minority population in South Asia. Third, the British had justified colonial occupation on the basis of British justice with equality and fair play for everyone within the Empire: "For half of a century the British in India had cultivated the fiction that Indians were equal members of the Empire; as the thesis went, Indians were British subjects, with the same rights, privileges, and responsibilities as Canadians and New Zealanders" (Buchignani et al. 1985, 21). The sense of injustice was therefore probably more acute.

For the East Indian community, the central question was the right to enter into and remain within Canada on terms of equality with other (especially white) British subjects. After the 1907 riots, the government sought to organize the community's voluntary departure to British Honduras (rather than India, where they might agitate against the Crown). For its part, the community was in the process of consolidating its presence in British Columbia, building Sikh temples in Vancouver (1908) and Victoria (1912) that "were meeting places and refuges, open, in the Sikh tradition, to anyone, Hindu, Christian, Muslim, or Sikh" (Johnston 1979, 5). This openness was rarely reciprocated, however, and East Indians remained isolated from mainstream society.[71] Community consolidation was further spurred by immigration officials, who threatened that any East Indian found to be a vagrant would be deported, resulting in the creation of mutual aid societies.

More importantly, the community engaged in a six-year battle with the federal government, using tactics that included written petitions, letters to the press, public rallies, meetings with officials and politicians in Britain,

Canada, and India, and recourse to the courts (see Buchignani et al. 1985, Chapter 2). It even used direct action techniques, such as circumventing the continuous journey regulation by arranging for a ship to make a direct journey from India. As well, wives of East Indians in Canada were brought over by indirect means to challenge government policies. In December 1911, a four-person delegation arrived in Ottawa to encourage a less rights-restrictive approach, especially in terms of family reunification, right of entry, and the $200 monetary requirement (Josh 1975, 9).[72] Locally, the community was "spending money and time, sending petitions and deputations, holding meetings and passing resolutions requesting the British Columbia government to allow admission to the new Indian entrants but to no avail" (ibid., 12).

While the Canadian government resisted and contained such rights-based politics, it had more difficulty when challenged before the courts. This became apparent following the arrival of the *Monteagle* in March 1908, carrying some 180 East Indian migrants. Initially, despite knowledge to the contrary, immigration officials barred most of the passengers on the grounds that they had not made a continuous journey from India (Sampat-Mehta 1972, 137). In detention, the migrants applied for release, arguing that the powers delegated to the Interior Minister by the Governor General under the continuous journey regulation contravened the law. The Supreme Court of British Columbia agreed and they were released (see *In Re Behari Lal et al.*). The government responded by reaffirming the disputed regulation[73] and Oliver introduced "a little amendment to the Immigration Act; a trifling little matter of some four or five lines" in the House (13 April 1908, 6708) to give the powers a statutory foundation. According to Robert Macpherson (L), this was done "to exclude Hindus and all kinds of Asiatics, and all kinds of undesirable people ... It is purely and simply a restriction on Asiatics" (8 April 1908, 6435-36).[74] It would also make it easier to force transportation companies to take such migrants back to their point of departure.

Although few MPs voiced support for the rights of East Indians,[75] many questioned whether the government could compel other countries to take back migrants. Oliver had complained that "when immigrants come from a country which is not that of their citizenship and the conditions are such as to require their deportation, the country from which they sail refuses to accept them and it is not possible for us to deport them" (26 March 1908, 5657), and claimed that the changes would solve this problem. But without the agreement of the other state, Borden observed, no law would accomplish this end. Instead, the government was once again creating a situation in which a migrant might be left in legal and physical limbo, caught, in Laurier's phrase, between the restrictive policies of two countries, "left between the two places like Mahomet's coffin hanging between heaven and earth" (8 April 1908, 6441).[76]

These changes were reconfirmed in the 1910 *Immigration Act* and the government immediately instituted regulations to put them into effect. The regulations were also used against European migrants, particularly those coming to work on the railways as well as Jewish refugees (Belkin 1966, 46). Although Canadian control policy continued to exclude East Indians effectively, the case of Hasan Rahim brought the authority of the state before the courts again (see Johnston 1979, 9). Rahim had been apprehended several months after he had been granted entry as a tourist under the 1906 *Immigration Act,* and was ordered deported under the 1910 law without the required formal hearing. When a lower court dismissed the state's case and ordered him released (see *In Re Rahim*), immigration officials apprehended him again on the same charge but with a hearing. This was criticized when the case was brought back to the courts, and Rahim was once again ordered released (see *In Re Rahim [No. 2]*). Among immigration officials, these rulings fostered the idea that border control was undermined when department actions were measured independently against the law and regulations that were supposed to govern them.[77]

In the next significant case, a British Columbia Supreme Court judge overturned a lower court ruling in November 1913, with the result that some three dozen East Indians were released from detention. The migrants had arrived on the *Panama Maru* and had been found not to possess the required $200 or to have travelled by a continuous journey. Although the court rejected other arguments presented by J. Edward Bird on behalf of his clients,[78] key objections were accepted by Chief Justice Gordon Hunter. Hunter ruled that the new regulations were *ultra vires* because the authority they granted to immigration officials exceeded that laid down in the 1910 *Immigration Act.* He also challenged government deportation procedures: "Common justice requires, and I think Parliament intended, that when a person is ordered to be deported out of the country, the reasons for so doing should be clearly stated, in order that he might at least know what was the reason" (*In Re Narain Singh et al.*, 510). As for the jurisdiction of the court, he opined that "it would, indeed, be strange to find that the doors of the Court were shut against any person of any nationality, no matter what the act complained of might be" (ibid., 510-11).

Former Interior Minister Oliver felt that these were "trifling" reasons (2 March 1914, 1223) for overturning departmental decisions and that forceful government action was required lest "some other judge in Vancouver, or Victoria, or Prince Rupert, or Halifax, or Sydney, or some other place" again thwart its will:

If it is a fact that the courts of Canada are above the Parliament of Canada, all we have to do is to sit down and accept the situation, but I believe that the mind of the people of Canada is that the Parliament of Canada shall dictate the law of Canada, and particularly that it shall dictate what shall be done within the boundaries of Canada with regard to this supremely important subject of immigration. (Ibid., 1224)[79]

While admitting that "individual rights must be protected, and must be protected by process of law," Oliver maintained "just as strongly that public and national rights must be protected, and must be protected just as sacredly as the law right of the individual by processes of law" (ibid.). Foreigners could draw on habeas corpus protections only once they had been admitted legally to the country by an immigration official; any other position, he said, was not reasonable.

> To say that any person in all the wide world, let him be of whatever character he pleases, has the right to come into this country of Canada in the face of regulations designed to keep him out, designed for the well-being present and future of the people of Canada, and that he shall have all the protection of all the complicated machinery of law that is found to be necessary in the transactions of citizens of the country, is absurd, is unjust to the country and places a burden upon administration that should not be so placed. (Ibid., 1225)

When non-citizens used the courts to challenge such discrimination, he lamented, Canada was made "a laughing-stock to the world" (ibid., 1224).

Oliver's comments sparked modest but revealing debate on the role of the courts and the nature of the rights of non-citizens in Canada. Henry H. Stevens (C) complained that East Indians were abusing the legal system: "It is not a case of getting a square deal; it is a case of trying to dig a hole or find a flaw in our regulations, and of upsetting them in that way" (ibid., 1239).[80] It was "this Parliament and the Government which should control the right of entry into this country, and that right should not, in any sense, be left to the courts" (ibid.).[81] One of the few to voice concerns was Rodolphe Lemieux, who, while wanting to restrict Asian migration, felt that the right of habeas corpus ("the palladium of British liberty") was inherent to all British subjects, whether Asian or not, "in accordance with British justice and freedom" (ibid., 1230). This was, however, a mild interjection in a debate that generally gave full support to the government.

The *Komagata Maru* (1914)

The Conservative government moved quickly to respond to the *Narain Singh* decision. It altered and re-enacted the two regulations declared null and void in order to meet the court's objections. It had also introduced a regulation in late 1913 to prevent artisans and other labourers from landing at

British Columbia ports. These regulations came under attack following the arrival of the *Komagata Maru* in British Columbia on 23 May 1914, carrying 376 East Indian migrants. The ship had been chartered and accompanied by a wealthy Sikh, Gurdit Singh, to challenge Canada's restrictive immigration policies.[82] Its arrival constituted more than a simple question of border control, as it was feared that Canada's response could stir up Sikh nationalist feelings in India. After tracking its progress to Canada, the boat was, upon arrival in Victoria, brought to lie offshore at Vancouver under quarantine, where it remained for two months.

The trepidation with which immigration officials contemplated an eventual court case was expressed by Vancouver Immigration Agent Malcolm R.J. Reid, who had demonstrated his willingness to push the limits of the law in 1913 by deporting an East Indian migrant despite two writs of habeas corpus ordering his release. With the arrival of the *Komagata Maru*, Reid advised Ottawa that if the "matter goes to court at all, it should only go under compulsion and that immigration authorities ... should use every means to avoid court procedure" (Josh 1975, 37).[83] He suggested delaying proceedings until Singh's creditors could confiscate the ship, saving the government the trouble of administering its own laws and defending them before the courts. J. Edward Bird (who had successfully argued *Narain Singh* in 1913) was hired to assist the passengers in their dealings with immigration officials, but found that he was obstructed at every turn, with access to them denied and his communications with them monitored. Moreover, once the boards of inquiry that were to determine the right of the migrants to enter the country began their work, the government refused to render any decisions lest they be brought before the courts.

> The Act said that any passenger detained by an immigration officer had to be examined "forthwith" and "immediately" landed or rejected. That was not happening, but the public did not care, and Reid felt himself impregnable. When counsel Bird threatened to get a writ to compel him to make a judgment, he said bluntly that he did not consider himself obliged to pay the slightest attention to any court orders, if any were made. (Johnston 1979, 47)[84]

Bird also objected to the evident partiality of the boards of inquiry system, calling it "a travesty of justice. The prosecutors are the judges" (Josh 1975, 33). He felt that the standards of justice that ought to be observed in Canada, with its British traditions, were not being met.

By late June, Superintendent of Immigration William Scott worried that excessive delays might themselves be brought before the courts and ordered Reid to complete some hearings. Eventually, a test case was settled upon in negotiations with Bird, and Munshi Singh was ordered deported under the continuous journey, monetary requirement, and labour regulations passed in 1913.

Meanwhile, Oliver raised the question of state sovereignty and border control in the House, declaring it "a question of racial dominance and national existence" (1 June 1914, 4563). The *Komagata Maru* represented "an organized movement for the purpose of establishing as a principle the right that the people of India, and not the people of Canada, shall have the say as to who shall be accepted as citizens of Canada" (ibid.). Within the Empire, each part was "guaranteed the opportunity to work out the destiny of that particular part according to the ideals of the people and the material possibilities of that particular part" (ibid.). Thus, he called upon the government to ignore any court proceedings and deport the passengers. Prime Minister Borden, however, upheld the principle of judicial oversight: "It will be for the judge of the court to consider the statute in view of the circumstances disclosed and determine whether the court has or has not jurisdiction to proceed" (ibid.).

In contrast to his earlier success in *Narain Singh,* Bird, with lead counsel Robert Cassidy, was less effective this time. They argued before the British Columbia Court of Appeal that Singh had rights in Canada as a British subject, that the law did not authorize the types of racial discrimination being practised against him, and that in the absence of supporting evidence officials could not find him to be a labourer instead of the farmer that he claimed to be. On this last point, Bird raised the idea of "the common law that a man shall not be convicted without proof such as would satisfy natural justice" (*Re Munshi Singh,* 253). His case was not as strong as it had been in *Narain Singh,* however, and Bird was seen to be "openly groping for arguments" (Johnston 1979, 59). The government simply argued that it possessed sovereign authority to control arrivals and that the courts had no jurisdiction over decisions made by a legally constituted board of inquiry. Thus, the government sought to sidestep the larger equality and due process aspects of the case.

The court rejected all the arguments marshalled on Singh's behalf and upheld the government's actions. Although their reasoning was relatively straightforward, the justices spent considerable time defining the state's authority in this policy area. Chief Justice James A. Macdonald declared that "Canada's authority to admit immigrants of any or every race or nationality, on any terms she pleases, is complete" (*Re Munshi Singh,* 255). Moreover, the court agreed that under Section 23 of the 1910 *Immigration Act,* it had no authority to question the board of inquiry's decision. A number of justices stressed that simply being present on Canadian territory did not provide non-citizens with civil rights protections under the *British North America Act.* Indeed, restrictions of this sort were well tempered, some said, by the provision of a direct appeal to the minister. That at least some of the justices held racist views on the subject of Asian immigration was revealed by Justice Albert E. McPhillips, who suggested that the government's restrictive approach "may be well said to be safeguarding the people of Canada from an influx which it is no chimera to conjure up might annihilate the nation and change its whole potential complexity, introduce Oriental ways as against European ways, eastern civilization for western civilization, and all the dire results that would naturally flow therefrom" (ibid., 291).[85]

Thus, the *Komagata Maru* – amid concerns that the passengers might seek to escape rather than be forced to depart, and about violence erupting in the local Sikh and majority populations in Vancouver – was made to leave on 23 July.[86] Although Gurdit Singh later said that the passengers "were adjudged guilty without a trial" (Josh 1975, 21), the government, by means that probably did little to promote the cause of British justice, had achieved a significant victory.[87] Against the fear, expressed by MP Henry Stevens, that "in the Orient – at our doors – there are 800 millions of Asiatics [who at] the very least tremor ... would unquestionably swamp us by weight of numbers" (Ward 1990, 91), Canada had erected a firm barrier.

Gurdit Singh appears not to have sought to undermine imperial authority but rather to provoke a reconfiguration of Canadian immigration practices so that they might conform to long-standing notions of British justice and specific British declarations as to the equality of all subjects within the Empire. His actions were undertaken with neither a deep understanding of Canada's immigration law nor an appreciation of the political situation in British Columbia. Rather, they reflected his own positive experiences of British justice in various civil suits during his business career. Although the *Komagata Maru* would play a role in the independence struggle in India, for the East Indian community in Canada it signalled a defeat that initiated a gradual erosion in community solidarity and size. Nonetheless, although the courts were now effectively closed as an avenue for rights-based politics, between the two world wars the East Indian community would slowly work to rebuild its capacity to contest rights-restrictive policies, and some East Indians would defy these policies and enter the country illegally.

In early 1914, Oliver, from the Opposition benches, initiated a debate in the House of Commons on what he saw as the negative effects of Asian immigration. He declared that "as the civilization of the West differs radically from the civilization of the East, it will be agreed that if western or European civilization is to prevail on this continent, it must be without the influence of Asiatic civilization" (2 March 1914, 1220). Canada must protect itself against Asian immigration, he warned, because "there are conquests other than those achieved by force of arms ... and hundreds of millions of people on the other side of the Pacific ocean are looking for an outlet" (ibid.). In short, he argued in Liberal Nationalist fashion that under the Liberals, "whatever measures were necessary to attain [the protection of European civilization in Canada,] those measures were taken not only of right but of right with due authority" (ibid., 1221). Although not everyone went quite as far, this view set the tone for Canadian policies towards Asian and other immigration during the interwar period.

Conclusion

The end of the nineteenth century and the onset of the twentieth was a period of extraordinary growth in immigration to Canada, especially just before the First World War. At the same time, the government was engaged in a conscious effort to enlarge its authority and improve its capacity to control, beginning with the centralization of power within the Interior Department in the late 1890s and culminating in the *Munshi Singh* case, with a wide range of rights-restrictive measures enacted in between. For European immigrants, the government equipped itself with the tools to curtail arrivals (although it would not use them extensively until after the war) and remove immigrants should they prove to be, or to have been perceived to be, "undesirable" on any number of grounds (as it had done before the requisite statutory foundation had been laid). As for "Asian" immigration, the government used a variety of means to curtail quite severely the arrival of Chinese, Japanese, and East Indian migrants, along with other groups deemed to be "Asian." Indeed, as Hawkins (1972, 94) notes, prior to the late 1940s, "Asia meant almost everything in the Eastern Hemisphere outside Europe," including the African continent. Thus, these restrictions were used to exclude many Jewish migrants as well as Syrian and Armenian refugees prior to the war (Abu-Laban 1980; Kaprielian-Churchill 2005). Although these groups had some supporters in Canadian society and Parliament,[88] with the politics of control now predominantly defined by Liberal Nationalism, their modest efforts to confront the rights-restrictive policies of the state had little effect.

As in the case of Chinese migration in the 1880s, however, the construction of a Liberal Nationalist approach to control elicited a Liberal Internationalist reaction that provided an alternative understanding rooted in core ideas of British liberalism. Moreover, once established in Canada, "undesirable" immigrants challenged simplistic constructions of "the nation" rooted in the country's British (in particular) and white colonial heritage. Thus, from very early on, the issue of control was debated in terms of what it meant to be a liberal country, requiring that important decisions be made on the rights of non-citizens vis-à-vis the state. Although such rights would long be circumscribed quite closely in Canada, this chapter and those that follow demonstrate that the rights-restrictive policies of the state never remained unchallenged.

4
The Domination of Liberal Nationalism in Canada (1914-45)

During the interwar period, Canada's border control capacity increased dramatically with the implementation of new restrictive policies and practices targeting Asian as well as European immigration. While measures directed at the former continued to reflect the belief that ethnoracial discrimination was a sovereign right of states, those aimed at the latter revealed a determination to limit the due process protections of all non-citizens severely. With a growing commitment to screening immigrants overseas, and more developed routines for removing them after arrival, by the 1930s Canada could all but close its borders to foreigners (including Jewish refugees) and, just after the Second World War, could engineer the removal of thousands of Japanese Canadians. The extreme nature of this rights-restrictive approach, however, rendered it susceptible to renewed rights-based politics and circumvention, which eventually helped to undermine its effectiveness and legitimacy. Such rights-based politics was enmeshed in a slow realignment of rights discourse in Canada from British liberal traditions to international human rights, and contributed to the creation of a bill of rights in Canada after the war.

This chapter begins with a review of Canadian policies towards "enemy aliens" during the First World War, which constituted one of the earliest examples of rights-based politics related to European immigrants. At the war's end, there was a shift in focus to controlling political radicals, which further anchored rights-based politics concerning Europeans in questions of due process protections for non-citizens. The significant decade-long parliamentary debate that this produced has been largely overlooked in the literature. In the meantime, the government's continued efforts to regulate Asian immigration saw success, which, however, came only through increasingly drastic rights-restrictive measures. Although these worked to reduce legal arrivals, they also encouraged circumvention and laid the foundations for a more extensive rights-based politics. The rights-restrictive measures pursued with respect to Jewish refugees and Japanese Canadians before, during, and immediately after the war helped to set the stage for a new era of control politics in Canada, in which Liberal Internationalism rose to prominence at the expense of Liberal Nationalism.

Closing the Doors to European Immigration (1914-39)

The First World War was a watershed for border control in most liberal democracies. Many of the restrictions put into place to secure national borders in a time of war were maintained, or only adjusted, once hostilities ceased. In Britain, the *Aliens Restriction Act* was passed in 1914, replacing the narrow control powers authorized under the 1905 *Aliens Act* with "very wide powers to control the movements and activities of aliens during the emergency, embracing in some particulars British subjects as well" (Roche 1969, 79). In 1919, a new *Aliens Restriction Act* was passed, establishing a control system that would be expanded and refined for decades, and increasing the discretionary power of front-line officials and the deportation powers of the Home Office. In the United States, a new immigration law was passed in 1917 that, through a new literacy test, introduced "the first general restriction that applied to all immigrants" (Daniels 2004, 39). This was followed by the country's "greatest triumph of nativism," the restrictive quota system, in 1924 (ibid., 49). In many countries, new entry restrictions (including passport and visa requirements) were bolstered by increased financial and personnel commitments. Canada likewise expanded the scope of its rights-restrictive approach to "enemy aliens," "foreign agitators," and the unemployed, including, for the first time, the British-born. This prompted an extensive parliamentary debate concerning the rights of non-citizens under British liberalism (especially with respect to the notion of due process), one that would inform a broader societal debate over the rights of European and non-European immigrants alike in the years leading up to the Second World War.

Restricting the Rights of "Dangerous Foreigners" (1914-21)

With Europe at war, immigration to Canada dropped significantly (along with parliamentary debate over its effects), as transportation became more difficult to obtain and many countries enacted exit restrictions, especially on those age-eligible for military service. After Britain (and therefore Canada) entered the war on 4 August 1914, Ottawa quickly passed a *War Measures Act* (officially titled *An Act to confer certain powers upon the Governor in Council and to amend the Immigration Act*), through which the Governor-in-Council would "have the power to do and authorize such acts and things, and to make from time to time such orders and regulations, as he may by reason of the existence of real or apprehended war, invasion or insurrection deem necessary or advisable for the security, defence, peace, order and welfare of Canada" (Section 6). The executive was granted authority to censor all sorts of publications and documents, and to effect the "arrest, detention, exclusion and deportation" of non-citizens (Section 6.b) with minimal judicial over-sight.[1] At the same time, the 1910 *Immigration Act* was amended to prohibit residents who left Canada to aid "enemy aliens" from returning without ministerial permission (Section 12). Although these new measures gener-ated little parliamentary debate, William Pugsley (L) questioned the sus-pension of the right of habeas corpus, a move that "strikes at the dearest liberties of a British subject" (20 August 1914, 22).[2] This concern would come to be shared by those critical of the government's rights-restrictive approach to control during the interwar years.

Despite official assurances that German and Austro-Hungarian immigrants would be left alone provided they did not assist their countries of origin in the war, restrictions on the rights of such "enemy aliens" were enacted through a series of orders-in-council under the authority of the *War Measures Act*. While many of the estimated 550,000 people of "enemy alien" origin in Canada experienced various forms of discrimination in their everyday lives during the war (many suddenly found themselves unemployed; those who had been naturalized since 1902 were disenfranchised through the 1917 *War-time Elections Act*), some 8,500 were interned in camps across the country, even though "not more than 3,179 of them could be regarded, even under a generous interpretation, as prisoners of war; the remainder were civilians, taken from their homes and deprived of their property" (D. Morton 1974, 32).[3] The internment policy was not simply encouraged by public prejudice but also used by municipalities seeking to reduce social assistance costs and employers hoping to have labour activists apprehended (Martynowych 1991). Ukrainians were most likely to be interned (Minenko 1991), and few in Parliament or the general population raised objections (Swyripa 1983, 49). In their own defence, Ukrainians used rights-based politics to present their case directly to political leaders (including Prime Minister Robert Borden), challenged the government's actions in the courts, and organized strikes in internment camps (Melnycky 1983). Although these efforts oc-casionally helped to overcome specific grievances, they did little to under-mine political or public support for internment, which was maintained until the end of the war.

In the context of widespread labour unrest, the return of thousands of veterans looking for work, and the 1917 Russian Revolution, the government came under increasing pressure to target foreign workers. In June 1918, Borden initiated a special investigation into the mobilization of the foreign-born by domestic and international socialist organizations, and enacted two orders-in-council to shut down the "enemy alien" foreign language press and outlaw several leftist organizations. This approach won general support from Canadians: "Anglo-Canadians who had learned to despise the Germans and Austro-Hungarians had little difficulty transferring their aroused pas-sions to the Bolsheviks" (Avery 1979, 76). As it sent troops to Siberia in 1918 to undermine the new Russian regime, Canada considered deporting all "enemy aliens," including Russians. The plan was deemed unfeasible, however, for both international political and practical transport reasons. It was against this backdrop that the newly established Department of Immigration and Colonization (created in 1918) sought to define Canada's postwar immigration policy through several amendments to the 1910 *Immigration Act* in April 1919.

Immigration was creating, the department's inaugural minister, James A. Calder, told the House of Commons, many "social, educational and industrial questions" in Canada (29 April 1919, 1866-67). Population growth, he felt, was essential for postwar economic recovery but thought had to be given to

> what class of people we are going to get, where they are to come from, what steps should be taken to see that they are properly absorbed into the life of the community, how we may pick and choose these people who are to become citizens of Canada, and how we can place them in the life of the nation with the greatest advantage to themselves as well as to Canada. (Ibid., 1868-69)

Above all, immigration "of such a nature that our citizenship will be swamped by elements coming in from outside which will destroy or at least tend to destroy it" (ibid., 1869) had to be avoided. The government therefore proposed a return to the policy in force at Confederation: settling farmers (particularly those with capital) from Britain and the United States, and domestic servants. Canada should have, Calder maintained, "the absolute right as a nation to determine for ourselves what our future citizenship shall be" (ibid., 1871).[4]

The 1919 *Act to amend The Immigration Act* considerably broadened the conditions under which a foreigner could be excluded. For example, Prohibited Classes would now cover, among others:

- Persons who in the opinion of the Board of Inquiry or the officer in charge at any port of entry are likely to become a public charge;
- Persons of constitutional psychopathic inferiority;
- Persons with chronic alcoholism;
- Persons over fifteen years of age, physically capable of reading, who cannot read the English or the French language or some other language or dialect. (Section 3)

People could also be excluded for their (presumed) political opinions, and the government would gain, Calder said, "very large powers ... at any time to prohibit the entry of any class or section of people or people of any occupation and coming from any country" (30 April 1919, 1947). It would be authorized to "prohibit or limit in number for a stated period or permanently ... immigrants belonging to any nationality or race of immigrants of any specified class or occupation" if they were

> deemed unsuitable having regard to the climatic, industrial, social, educational, labour or other conditions or requirements of Canada or because such immigrants are deemed undesirable owing to their peculiar customs, habits, modes of life and methods of holding property, and because of their probable inability to become readily assimilated or to assume the duties and responsibilities of Canadian citizenship within a reasonable time after their entry. (Section 13)

Although some opposed exclusion based on religious beliefs (which was eventually removed from the bill), these far-reaching powers appeared to comfort more than trouble parliamentarians.

Calder garnered considerable support for his suggestion that Canada had let in too many undesirable immigrants. "We do not want in this country ... an inferior class who will only increase our difficulties and troubles," John W. Edwards (UP) declared. "There is no necessity for us to cheapen Canada in the eyes of the world" (30 April 1919, 1931-32).[5] Thomas M.M. Tweedie (UP) argued that the Ukrainians "have not become Canadianized or Anglicized to the extent that they can become part and parcel of the social and economic life of this country" (ibid., 1940). Hume Cronyn (UP) proposed an amendment to exclude all eastern and southern Europeans on account of "certain ethnic and sociological characteristics, largely due to racial origin and climatic condition and indelibly fixed during the course of many centuries" (9 May 1919, 2282). In the Senate, James Lougheed (LCP) lamented Canada's previous open-door policy, claiming falsely that

> when the war broke out we found that Canada had become the shelter, so to speak, for an almost innumerable class of aliens who did not hesitate for a moment to express their hostility and antipathy to our institutions, who showed no sympathy whatever with the country, and no desire to assimilate themselves with the population, of which they formed a part. (16 May 1919, 399)

Such beliefs led parliamentarians like Senator Edward L. Girroir (C) to fear that immigrants brought with them "the germ of immorality and the germ of revolution" (19 May 1919, 427).

The most vocal opponent of the proposed restrictions was Samuel W. Jacobs (L), the second Jewish MP elected in Canada: "So long as we can assure ourselves that the people brought into this country are law-abiding citizens, healthy, and able to take part in the work of developing the country, that is all we require" (29 April 1919, 1881).[6] Moreover, it was unrealistic to focus on attracting wealthy immigrants: "Who ever heard of a man of wealth leaving his home in Europe and coming out to Canada either to live in a large city or to go on the land?" (ibid., 1882). The proposed legislation, he suggested, legitimized those who spread fear and hatred of foreigners. William D. Euler (L), a third-generation Mennonite, similarly observed that "the war has brought about a great many prejudices and has bred racial hatred" and "those feelings are not a safe guide for those who are legislating for the best interests of Canada" (30 April 1919, 1927).

Some worried that the state was gaining too much discretion in determining admissions, and this was voiced by both Liberal Internationalists and Liberal Nationalists. As a Liberal Internationalist, Jacobs argued for greater clarity, since

> even ministers of the Crown sometimes change, and a king may arise who knows not Joseph, and who would apply the law more rigorously than at present. Many of these sections are satisfactory if handled intelligently, but I think cases of very grave hardship might arise if they were interpreted by a department not sympathetic to the immigrant. (Ibid., 1944)

Senator Frederic Nicholls (C) was concerned that "any petty immigration officer [would have] power to decide as to which is a desirable alien immigrant and which is an undesirable one" (19 May 1919, 426). For his part, Hume Cronyn argued in the House that because immigration threatened Canadian standards of living, exclusion categories should be articulated explicitly in the act so that officials could act on them (29 April 1919, 1876-77). Liberal Nationalists ultimately found that they had less to worry about, however, as the new powers came to be used primarily for restriction.

There was also opposition to the proposed literacy test. If an immigrant "is unable to read, that is not his fault, but his misfortune," Jacobs argued, and this could be overcome through Canada's educational system (ibid., 1884). Moreover, those who could read were more likely to become dangerous agitators, George B. Nicholson (UP) warned (1 May 1919, 1962). Senator George McHugh (L) suggested that "literacy is not always a test of good citizenship" and thus would be of little help in the selection of good immigrants (19 May 1919, 421). Although the proposal was amended (at Jacobs's urging) to provide ministerial discretion, this hardly met the concerns of Liberal Internationalists.[7]

Another controversial subject involved "enemy aliens." In March 1919, the government passed an Order-in-Council to exclude people from Austria, Bulgaria, Germany, and Turkey. Henry Stevens (UP) then proposed to the House that such immigration should be prohibited for twenty years (24

March 1919, 769-73), while Senator George Bradbury (C) called for a ten-year moratorium that included Russian immigrants as well (16 May 1919, 401-3).[8] MP Donald Sutherland (UP) wanted those interned during the war removed "just as soon as it is possible for us to get them out, and I hope they will be kept out for the rest of their lives" (29 April 1919, 1886). In contrast, Jacobs argued that "so soon as peace has been signed we have no longer any quarrel with these people and we cannot, on the ground that they have been alien enemies in the past, refuse to allow them into this country or bar their entrance" (ibid., 1881).[9] Similarly, Senator William Roche (L) proposed that "we must discriminate between the governments of the countries and those who will not agree to the laws of those countries" (19 May 1919, 417).

Pacifist religious groups were also singled out for discrimination. In May 1919, Doukhobor, Hutterite,[10] and Mennonite immigration were outlawed by Order-in-Council. John Edwards questioned whether the principles of such groups during the war had been more than a front to mask a desire to benefit economically while others fought overseas.[11] Such immigrants were also criticized because they would not kill at the command of the state: "Embedded in the very heart of those religious views there is a false political philosophy, a false conception of their relation to the state, which makes it impossible for them to become other than a people in Canada," Howard Whidden (UP) warned (30 April 1919, 1923). Moreover, these pacifists, who lived and worked communally, were now viewed through the prism of anti-communism.

Fear of communism and socialism came to the fore during the May 1919 Winnipeg General Strike. With increasing union membership and similar labour/management crises occurring in other liberal democracies, those on both sides of the picket line saw "the strike as part of a broader radical wave sweeping over western civilization" (Bothwell et al. 1987, 166). Even before Black Saturday brought an end to the strike, Calder, with the unanimous consent of the House, introduced amendments to his immigration proposals[12] on 6 June 1919 that would see Section 41 of the 1910 *Immigration Act* allow the government to deport anyone who "defends or suggests the unlawful destruction of property," "who without lawful authority assumes any powers of government in Canada," or "who is a member of or affiliated with any organization entertaining or teaching disbelief in or opposition to organized government," among other transgressions (Section 1). The government would further be empowered to deport anyone who was not a Canadian citizen, including British-born immigrants who had not yet received Canadian citizenship.[13] The bill passed all three readings, Senator George Bradbury later recalled, in about ten minutes, and took less than eight in the Senate (27 May 1920, 421).[14] This small amendment was a focal point for debates over control and the rights of non-citizens for almost ten years, bringing greater attention to due process rights within British liberalism and initiating a new round of rights-based politics in Canada.

The government soon determined that it had been hasty. In 1920, Senator Gideon D. Robertson (C) sought to amend the 1910 *Immigration Act* on the government's behalf so that British subjects in residence for five years would, for the purposes of immigration, be treated on an equal footing with the Canadian-born. Moreover, British subjects would have full recourse to the judicial system if ordered deported under the 1919 changes. Opinion was growing, Robertson said, that the "Star Chamber trial" (9 June 1920, 509) allowed under the Section 41 changes "was contrary to British customs and British institutions, and what we ordinarily term British liberty" (27 May 1920, 417).[15] In opposition, Bradbury warned that Robertson's proposals would tell "the red element of Canada: 'Agitate; create all the trouble you like; destroy property, cause loss of life; the Government will not deport you'" (ibid., 421). He preferred that the state keep its "big stick" to threaten people: "Behave yourselves, or this stick will fall, and we will get rid of you and send you out of the country" (ibid., 422). "If you are going to try these men," Edward L. Girroir argued, "you are simply going to aid them in the dissemination and distribution of the doctrines which they advocate" (ibid., 424). John G. Turiff (L) also expressed satisfaction that the minister would be fair in reviewing cases, making unnecessary any access to the courts.[16] Furthermore, Liberal Nationalists maintained that such immigrants deserved little sympathy.[17]

Although Robertson's amendments were rejected, they extended the debate begun during the war concerning the due process rights of non-citizens. Against complaints that trials were too expensive, Senator James J. Donnelly (C) remarked: "If we were guided entirely by the question of cost in giving a fair trial to all those who come before the courts – if we carried that argument to its logical conclusion, we would adopt lynch law in this country" (27 May 1920, 426). "I do maintain," Senator William H. Bennett (C) said, "that there should be in Canada henceforth at least a chance for any man to meet his accuser face to face when any charge is preferred against him" (ibid., 433). Without legal protections, Senator Lawrence Power (L) argued, the law "practically places the liberties of a very large proportion of our people in the hands of any government understrapper who may be actuated by vindictiveness or some other unworthy motive" (ibid., 430). Thus, while not always extended to all non-citizens, the Liberal Internationalist case was firmly rooted in two basic notions of British liberalism: equality before the law and the right to a fair trial. These ideals, however, continued to meet with stiff opposition in the Senate, which turned back a second effort to undo the 1919 changes in 1921.[18]

This was consistent with a generally weak commitment to immigration during this period. Although the postwar recession caused a decline in people wanting to come to Canada, the government renewed limitations on the admission of workers at west coast seaports and instituted monetary requirements for most categories of immigrants ($250 per adult and $125 per child). Nonetheless, there were continued concerns over the lack of any effective screening procedure overseas,[19] and the government still generally met particular business demands for foreign labour. Thus, even as the Conservatives pursued a somewhat more rigorous selection policy than their Liberal predecessors, they continued to rely on the private sector and on chance. This began to change when the Liberals returned to power.

European Immigration and Rights-Based Politics (1921-39)

Elected in 1921, the Mackenzie King government soon adopted a mix of expansionist and restrictionist policies that broadened the definition of who was undesirable while admitting many of them. On the expansionist side, the monetary requirement was lifted for non-Asian immigrants and the ban on Hutterite and Mennonite immigration was rescinded in 1922 (the Doukhobors had to wait until 1926). In 1923, restrictions on German and other "enemy alien" immigration were abandoned, and by the mid-1920s, a four-pronged selection approach had been established:

> British and American citizens were permitted to enter Canada relatively freely, provided they either had employment or could support themselves, and were not black. Immigrants from the preferred countries of northern Europe and Scandinavia could enter Canada provided they had valid passports, were sponsored by Canadian relatives, or had an occupation of which Canada was in need. Immigrants from the non-preferred countries of Eastern and southern Europe were admitted through special permits, and those from Asia and Africa were virtually excluded. (Kelley and Trebilcock 1998, 189)

The government also gave the Canadian National Railway and the Canadian Pacific Railway virtually a free hand in recruiting agricultural workers from non-preferred European countries. Although Canadian officials undertook medical examinations and passport checks before departure, recruitment and occupational certification were carried out by the transport companies. In response, J.S. Woodsworth (Labour) blasted the government for having "practically abdicated" immigration control (29 January 1926, 567).[20] The oft-criticized agreement with the railway companies was terminated in 1930 by newly elected Prime Minister Richard B. Bennett (C), who had campaigned against it.

In a restrictionist vein, Mackenzie King's government shored up the state's capacity to screen arrivals soon after it came to power.[21] It instituted more systematic pre-departure medical inspections and required passports for all non-citizens except Americans and specified British subjects, while implementing a visa policy for all but the United States and Britain. The government also promoted, through Empire Settlement Agreements, British agricultural immigration. Despite increasing success in excluding non-white immigration, however, the proportion of non-British European arrivals remained high from the 1920s until the Second World War.

This frustrated Liberal Nationalists. "It is a notorious fact," Alan Neill (P) declared in the House, "that nations in the northern part of Europe, brought up in a hard climate and under severe conditions, are of a more virile type than the peoples of southern Europe" (15 March 1923, 1191). The latter, Neill feared, undermined the strength of the Canadian nation. This view was shared by Liberal Immigration and Colonization Ministers Robert Forke (6 February 1928, 187) and Charles A. Stewart (7 June 1928, 3918). Moreover, when the Standing Committee turned in 1928 to examine Canadian immigration policy, it strongly recommended concentrating on attracting British migrants. Noting its "doubt as to the desirability of giving to the Railways special authority to recruit immigrants," it called for more restrictive terms (Canada 1928, x). As Richard Bennett stated in the House, Canada could only "maintain [our British] institutions ... by continuing to bring to this country a proper modicum of settlers who understand and appreciate them" (7 June 1928, 3925). British civilization was the standard to which all immigrants must conform: "We desire to assimilate those whom we bring to this country to that civilization, that standard of living, that regard for morality and law and the institutions of the country and to the ordered and regulated development of the country" (ibid., 3926). Minister Forke agreed: "There are backward and forward people and backward and forward nations ... Some nationalities ... are much more easily absorbed than others, and we have to take that into consideration in considering this question of immigration" (15 March 1929, 985).

This ideal of British (or Canadian) civilization did not go unchallenged, however. For example, Milton Campbell (P) said of the Doukhobors: "They learned some of the habits of Canadian boys, such as playing poker, drinking whisky and smoking tobacco. Some of them are quite Canadianized now" (8 June 1828, 3960). More generally, Michael Luchkovich (United Farmers of Alberta), Canada's first MP of Ukrainian origin, dismissed the supposed difficulties in assimilating other groups: "Measured by any standard whatever, I fail to see wherein and how it takes longer to make a desirable Canadian citizen of the central European than is the case with any other European" (28 May 1929, 2903). He challenged the preferred/non-preferred distinction: such a "stupid classification ... differentiates; it discriminates; it prejudices; it provokes and, in a word, it tends to stimulate a bitter antagonism among the newcomers to Canada" (ibid., 2904). This, he maintained, "can do nothing to bring about that unity without which no country can become really secure and great" (ibid.).[22] Samuel Jacobs maintained that "the test of a man's ability to make good in this country is not the country from which he comes; it is the character of the man" (1 March 1927, 776).[23] "After all," he said, "what is the British race but a conglomerate mixture? ... That is what has made the British people great; it is a mixture of all these races" (7 June 1928, 3897).

In early 1922, Woodsworth proposed to return Canada closer to its British liberal roots by overcoming the "reversion ... to the condition of affairs which prevailed before the time of the Magna Charta" that the 1919 changes had caused (3 May 1922, 1388).[24] Tasks such as deciding whether someone disbelieved in government or was opposed to it were better left to the courts than immigration officials, he felt. Canada would "be in keeping with the very best British practice if we condemned men only when they committed some overt act and not for merely thinking this or the other thing" (ibid., 1390). Arresting and deporting people without warrant or offering reasons why was "an intolerable situation," he argued (ibid.). The government, however, sidetracked his amendments into a committee, where they re-emerged within a more general call for legislative revision at some future session of Parliament.

In May 1923, Immigration and Colonization Minister Charles Stewart introduced amendments to return Section 41 to its pre-1919 wording, arguing that it "does seem to give rather drastic power to the minister, a power that I think in most cases could very well be exercised by the courts" (3 May 1923, 2428). In the House, the proposal garnered support from both Liberal Nationalists and Liberal Internationalists. John Baxter (C) declared that he "should like to see an opportunity given every man to be heard in his own behalf before sentence of deportation is pronounced against him" (ibid., 2436), while Woodsworth noted that "the time when we most need the safeguards of the law is when there is some extraordinary excitement" that might provoke hasty punitive measures (ibid., 2433). Stewart captured the general tone of the debate in stating that "there is no honesty taking hold of an individual and bundling him out of the country" (ibid., 2436). Woodsworth wanted to ensure that the changes would not simply apply to British-born immigrants but Stewart refused, maintaining that Canada should "decide for herself who shall become citizens of this country" (ibid., 2435). Although it passed the House easily, Senator Lougheed expressed the view commonly held in the Senate that "this Bill does not represent the sentiments of that House, and it certainly does not represent the attitude of the Parliament" (16 May 1923, 556),[25] and the proposed changes were rejected in that chamber.[26]

In 1924, the issue was debated again as part of a package of changes to grant the department greater discretion in landing or deporting individuals. Although the minister could already permit people to enter under the law, this would be joined with an authority to allow those already in Canada to remain. For Neill, this raised the possibility that the government would "allow any man, black, brown, white or yellow, to come into this country and stay for any unlimited period" (3 July 1924, 4018). It was "a very wide and a very drastic power to put into the hands of any minister," he warned (ibid.). Greater attention, however, fell on provisions concerning the rights of non-citizens prior to deportation.

Woodsworth again objected that people could be deported "by common repute" under the proposals: "A man ought to be proved guilty of any crime" (ibid., 4004). He argued that someone "should not be declared guilty simply because some official suspects him of belonging to an illegal organization ... we should have something more than suspicion on which to convict him" (ibid.). Moreover, such protections should extend to all immigrants. Woodsworth also complained that the language of the proposed Section 41 replacement, "so loosely drawn, lends itself to broad interpretations under which almost anyone might be convicted" (ibid., 4005). Although he agreed with barring undesirables, "when a man comes into this country, when he lives for a time here, when he commits or is suspected of committing a crime against the country, his trial ought to be, not a mere departmental inquiry, but a trial before a judge and jury. We owe him that" (ibid.). In support, Andrew R. McMaster (L) maintained "that it is un-British, un-Canadian and unfair to turn a man out of this country because he may have a common repute of being undesirable" (ibid.).[27]

Many MPs, however, wanted the government to have the tools to remove those engaging (or suspected of engaging) in labour strife. Future Prime Minister Arthur Meighen (C) argued that deportation was not a punitive measure but "simply a power, one of many, exercisable for the purpose of selecting the immigrants who come to Canada" (ibid., 4007). Non-citizens, he maintained, did not possess the same rights as citizens: "To suggest that we must give a man a trial by jury before we decide whether he has a right to come to Canada and stay here after he has arrived is to my mind absurd" (ibid., 4008). Acting Immigration and Colonization Minister James A. Robb (L) argued that rights restrictions were a legitimate means "to protect the people of Canada and I am going to see to it that they get that protection" (ibid., 4029). This did little to meet McMaster's basic objection "that if you have a law that is wrong in principle you are likely to have injustice arise from it" (ibid.). Although the government's proposals once again passed in the House, the Section 41 change – "which has always been a storm centre in this Chamber," Lougheed noted (14 July 1924, 748) – was rejected by the Senate.

It was not until 1928 (after further unsuccessful efforts in 1926 and 1927) that the government was able to restore the pre-1919 wording of Section 41. Liberal Nationalists like Richard Bennett still maintained that such restrictive provisions were necessary, even if rarely used:

Legislation which it is said takes away the right of a man to trial by jury and matters of that kind is legislation that sometimes has to be used in all countries for the preservation of law and order, and that is far more important than the possible chance of its application to individuals perhaps once in a hundred years. (7 April 1927, 2097)

There were, then, times when the government had to act in an arbitrary or capricious manner in the name of national security.[28] Bennett maintained that "deportation is not punishment" (8 April 1927, 2104) and that non-citizens (at least those neither British nor white) could not claim many rights in the country.[29] Lucien Cannon (L) supported the more restrictive wording because, with deportation, "the immigration authorities still maintain control over [the immigrant] after he has entered" (ibid., 2120). Moreover, Senator James H. Ross (L) argued, "there is not the slightest chance of any honest, law-abiding man who comes into this country being in any way molested under this provision" (15 June 1926, 244). The threat against Canada, Senator Lendrum McMeans (C) warned, was very real: "We know that to-day the country is honeycombed with people who are preaching [communism], even in the Sunday schools" (ibid., 245). Senator James Calder, who as minister had introduced the 1919 changes, maintained that "the Government must be in a position to deal with certain deportable cases without recourse to the courts" (ibid., 247).

In contrast, Liberal Internationalists like Woodsworth argued in the House, "most emphatically, that the worst man in this country ought to have a fair trial by jury" (8 April 1927, 2107). This should apply, he maintained, to all non-citizens, otherwise how could newcomers learn to respect British institutions if non-British immigrants were granted fewer rights than the British?[30] For Railways and Canals Minister Charles A. Dunning (L), "the principle gets down to the very roots of our freedom, as to whether men who are charged with crime shall be equal before the law, shall all be treated before the same courts in the same way, or whether there shall be an arbitrary authority set up" (30 April 1928, 2507). Stewart (again serving as minister) simply said: "Do not ask the minister to decide upon the worthiness or unworthiness of the person concerned; let the court decide that, and afterwards we will perform the duty of getting him out of the country" (7 June 1926, 4112). Senator Raoul Dandurand (L) felt that while ministers would usually seek to exercise due caution, "in times of stress and difficulty you could possibly project into this matter the political action of the Minister" at the expense of justice (15 June 1926, 241). The law, he said, "savors of autocracy, and in a free country under British institutions that condition should not prevail" (ibid., 243). Although expeditious, deportation without trial was not "an argument that will stand in a free country like Canada" (3 May 1928, 417).[31]

Senator Allen Aylesworth (L), who had voted for the 1919 amendment with reservations, examined the issue from "the standpoint of the man who is innocent and who is either suspected or charged as guilty of an offence under the legislation as it now stands" (15 June 1926, 248). Canada owed this person a certain degree of justice: "Is not every man who sets foot upon British soil entitled to a trial?" (ibid.). If an innocent person was deported, he reasoned, this involved not simply a "restraint upon individual liberty, but it is extending that imprisonment beyond the territorial limits of this country; it is sending the man into some other country, in which he does not wish to be" (ibid.). This was incompatible with a society governed by law, "for what end, other than to protect the innocent and to secure the punishment of the guilty, have all our laws been passed? To what other end do we owe it that we to-day enjoy the rights and privileges we have as British subjects under Magna Charta [sic] and under that other great protective charter of British liberty, the Habeas Corpus Act?" (ibid.). Against the claims of Bennett and Meighen, he maintained that deportation was not simply an administrative action but was "actual punishment" for a crime that may never have been committed (ibid.).

As a refinement to the Liberal Internationalist position, Senator Napoléon A. Belcourt (L) sought to distance state sovereignty arguments from due process protections. "I am not for one moment questioning the right of any nation to say who shall be allowed to come into its country to stay," he began, but upon admittance "there has been a sort of agreement, a sort of contract between the Canadian state and that person" (ibid., 249). The immigrant has "acquired some rights" (ibid., 250). As it stood, the law was "arbitrary, extremely draconian and violates every principle of justice, of fair play, and even of law. The means adopted are inhuman and cruel" (9 May 1928, 518). It was not enough, he warned, to trust in the goodwill of officials, who might make mistakes or have ulterior motives. "To exile a man without giving him a chance of defending himself," he concluded, "is revolting to every principle of law and justice that I know" (ibid., 521).

The basic contours of a new phase in the rights-based politics of control, then, were being set, as concerns over the equality rights of a broader range of non-citizens were joined to an interest in ensuring their due process protections. Although the 1928 amendment made Canadian immigration law less rights-restrictive, it did little to improve the due process protections of the foreign-born, as the pre-1919 wording was itself fairly restrictive. Moreover, the government still removed people quickly and quietly, which often prevented its actions from being scrutinized by the courts.[32] Indeed, by the 1930s it was engaged in a twin attack on labour activists and those seeking state welfare assistance during the Great Depression (Roberts 1988). By the beginning of that decade, the department was "shovelling out" thousands of immigrants each year with little opposition in Parliament (ibid.,

Chapter 8).[33] It was not until 1934 that deportation levels began to drop, and not only as a result of an improved economic climate: "it was the changes in the political culture that were crucial" (ibid., 160), including shifts in the understanding of the rights of non-citizens vis-à-vis the state.

As the Great Depression unfolded, the deportation of long-term immigrants was repeatedly raised in the House as a question of justice. In 1931, Woodsworth proposed legislation to prevent the government from removing those who had been in the country for ten years or more.[34] "Surely," he stated, "anybody who has been in Canada for fifteen years has acquired some rights" (10 July 1931, 3646). In support, Abraham A. Heaps (Labour) contended that "we have in this country sufficient of the milk of human kindness to allow people to remain here when they become sick and infirm after they have probably given their best to Canada" (2 June 1931, 2246).[35] Immigration and Colonization Minister Wesley A. Gordon (C) argued, however, that there was no legal right to remain and that to give immigrants one would undermine a core control objective, "the supreme importance of seeing that the population of this country is kept clean" (ibid., 2249). If he had to err, he would do so on behalf of Canadians, as non-Canadians were the responsibility of another government (10 July 1931, 3650).

The issue came to a head when eleven labour activists were arrested on May Day in 1932 and sent secretly to Halifax for deportation. "It may be that the procedure adopted is in harmony with the immigration law," John L. Brown (Liberal-Progressive) protested, "but it certainly is not in harmony with what we understand to be the principle of British justice" (6 May 1932, 2685).[36] "If this is the kind of thing that is going to be done in the name of democracy, you have no real democracy at all; you are vitiating it and destroying the very principle on which this house was established," E.J. Garland (P) reflected (ibid., 2688). The government responded that it was a convenient way to deal with cases about which officials had no doubts and that few complained about the practice. Gordon declared that the method employed, "of necessity, has to be pursued if law is to be enforced and those responsible for the invocation of the law are to do their duty" (23 May 1932, 3249). As this was simply an administrative review of their status, such non-citizens did not need access to the courts, he said.[37] Moreover, such procedures served the national interest by allowing the government to remove "undesirable" immigrants so that Canadians would remain welcoming towards others.

By the mid-1930s, the general public was increasingly ill at ease with the government's deportation practices, and various municipalities as well as the British government had lodged complaints. It was not until Thomas Crerar (L) became Immigration and Colonization Minister in 1935, however, that the policy was significantly changed. By this time, very few immigrants – or refugees – were able to enter the country anyway.

Restricting European Refugees (1914-39)

The refugee issue arose in several new and complicated ways between the two world wars. For example, in 1931, Alexandra Tolstoy (Leo Tolstoy's daughter) wanted to visit the Doukhobors in Canada, as her father had been very concerned with their plight. The Canadian government was reluctant to admit her because she was a refugee and it was therefore unclear to what country she could be deported if she refused to leave Canada (22 April 1931, 809-10). During the interwar years, Canada's refugee policy was not motivated primarily by compassion or shared international responsibility. Rather, it reflected an inward-looking appreciation of the national interest characteristic of Liberal Nationalism, and this was particularly evident in Canada's response to specific groups such as Armenians and Jews. The techniques and justifications employed were very much akin to the restrictions established for Asian immigrants during this period. As a result, Canada isolated itself from European efforts to forge an international refugee regime among liberal democracies.

Although refugee policy was rarely debated in the House, it was primarily Liberal Internationalists who voiced support for refugees. In 1921, Immigration and Colonization Minister Calder reaffirmed the accepted view that "the real problem ... is not simply to get people; we must get the right kind of people ... to shut out certain classes of people from Canada" (26 April 1921, 2572). Among those to be shut out were the "hundreds of thousands of people" in Europe, including the "the war refugees," many of whom "have lost everything they had in the world, and are looking out over the world to find a new country in which they can make a home" (ibid., 2579). In "an endeavour to hold back that flood," he said, the government was using the $250 monetary qualification and the continuous journey requirement (ibid.). This restrictive approach was supported by the majority of MPs who responded, such as Howard Whidden, who argued against "making Canada an asylum, a place of refuge, for all who desire to come here. That may be good church policy; it is not the way to built [sic] a nation" (30 April 1919, 1923).

This approach was criticized by two MPs whose religious backgrounds were the same as some of those being shut out – Samuel Jacobs (Jewish) and William Euler (Mennonite). Jacobs raised the case of a family from Romania that had escaped to Britain and now wanted to come to Canada but would be excluded under the continuous journey requirement (26 April 1921, 2586). The really dangerous people, he concluded, would find a way to circumvent these restrictions, so why obstruct those who might become good citizens? Euler warned that discretion in applying the monetary qualification sometimes hid the real grounds for exclusion: "If it is desired to keep certain people out of the country for reasons other than poverty, those reasons should be stated and no one should be kept out for some reason that is after all only an excuse for excluding him" (ibid., 2591). He spoke of Russian refugees who had fled to Poland on the way to Canada and who were admitted only because of his direct interventions with the department.

One legacy of the First World War was a much more tightly controlled system of border control among liberal-democratic states, both in North America and in Europe (Marrus 1985). With fewer countries willing to welcome them, refugees became stateless persons, unable or unwilling to return to their countries of origin and often at best tolerated wherever they sought refuge in Europe. Millions had fled from the after-effects of the revolution in Russia and the breakdown of the Ottoman Empire after the war, and hundreds of thousands sought to escape persecution in the years leading up to the Second World War, such as German Jews and Spanish leftists. These refugee movements gave European states little choice but to seek a coordinated and institutionalized response to promote regional security. Thus, during the 1920 and 1930s, the scope of European agreement expanded through a series of international meetings that resulted in the creation of the 1933 League of Nations Convention Relating to the International Status of Refugees to govern state behaviour (Hathaway 1984; Skran 1995). In this context, refugees were increasingly differentiated from other international migrants, and the responsibilities of states towards them were defined with greater precision.

Canada's participation in this process was deliberately slight, and its outlook negative. As Europe created a special passport to provide status for stateless persons and thereby facilitate efforts to provide safe haven, Canada refused to take part, arguing that such people would not be deportable. At an international conference in 1926, Canada made it clear that it would "not accept the Nansen passport so long as it remains a one-way document" (quoted in Kaprielian-Churchill 1994, 285). This "negate[d] the very spirit and purpose of the Nansen Passport" (ibid., 288). Canada subsequently declined to participate in conferences held in 1928 and 1933 or sign the agreements that these meetings produced. For years, immigration officials argued that if European countries would not accept the return of those deemed by the department to be "misfits," then Canada would not resettle any refugees. This was consistent with the Liberal Nationalist understanding of state sovereignty that justified discrimination on ethnoracial grounds and defined the national interest in narrow, inward-looking terms. "By taking this hard line, Canada rejected the humanitarian and internationalist principles advocated by the League of Nations and opted instead for a utilitarian and isolationist approach to the refugee problem" (Avery 1995, 90). While some refugees could still reach Canada due to the lack of government oversight of departures from Europe, and while the presence of active constituencies working on behalf of certain refugee groups facilitated some entries (especially Mennonites; see Epp 1982), most refugees, particularly those facing genocidal persecution, were denied admittance.

For example, thousands of Armenians fled the genocidal policies of first the Ottoman Empire and then the Turkish Republic between 1915 and 1923. Their situation was something of a *cause célèbre* in postwar Canada, with the Toronto *Globe* undertaking a front-page campaign to raise funds alongside the Armenian Relief Association of Canada. Between 1919 and 1930, however, the control regime constructed during the preceding twenty years was fully utilized against these refugees, who were to be admitted only

> if they complied "in the fullest possible way" with existing regulations governing all immigrants – notably the passport regulation, Asian classification, money qualification, continuous journey ruling, labour qualification, and family reunification. As an additional precaution, instructions from the departmental deputy minister discouraged "any special privileges for the refugees." (Kaprielian-Churchill 1990, 88)

Thus, although just over 1,200 Armenians arrived between 1920 and 1930, other non-preferred peoples (for example, around 39,000 Jews and some 1,650 Syrians) were more likely to be allowed to resettle, whereas the United States accepted some 23,000 Armenians and France admitted around 80,000 (ibid., 81).

Assistant Deputy Minister Frederick C. Blair argued plainly in the 1920s that Canada could not accept Armenian refugees because they were poor and would, as a result, become public charges: "If Canada offered an open door, we would have all who have money to move, and our cities would be literally overrun with these unfortunates" (quoted in ibid., 86). Since their classification as Asians rendered them subject to stricter selection criteria, Armenians in Canada sought unsuccessfully to have this changed. Departmental officials simply countered that this would mean having to do so for other groups, such as Syrians.[38] Aside from official biases, Armenian community advocacy was further hampered by the fact that there were so very few Armenians in Canada.

This was no longer true of the Jewish community, although its success in overcoming official restrictionism was only slightly greater and only for a limited time. With the postwar return to a policy of settling farmers with "preferred" origins, Jews were at a double disadvantage. This was compounded by the continuous journey and monetary regulations, the passport requirement as well as the nativist and anti-Semitic climate in Canada. In response, Jacobs and other Jewish community leaders "went to Ottawa and made the rounds of Cabinet ministers, influential MPs and senators, and department officials" (Tulchinsky 1998, 39). This succeeded occasionally, as when arrangements were made to resettle 200 Jewish orphans from Eastern Europe in 1921 and 5,000 Jewish refugees in 1923 (although fewer actually arrived than planned; see ibid., 40-54). Such efforts helped to bring more than 44,000 Jews to Canada between 1920-21 and 1929-30, representing about 3.5 percent of immigration totals during that decade (Department of Mines and Resources 1946, 241-43, Tables 4 and 5).

From the mid-1920s onward, however, it became increasingly difficult to arrange admission to Canada, especially after Immigration and Colonization Minister James Robb and Deputy Minister William J. Black (both reportedly less antagonistic towards Jewish immigration) were succeeded by ministers with less interest and restrictionist officials such as Frederick Blair and William Egan. Indeed, "by 1925 officials had stiffened their resolve against Jewish immigration, and by 1926 restrictionist bureaucrats determined to keep all non-British immigration to a minimum" (Tulchinsky 1998, 54). By the 1930s, Jewish refugee resettlement supporters pursued a strategy of quiet diplomacy, as "Canadian Jews understood very well that any outburst could be used against them. The community would be branded as disloyal and some might even be deported" (Abella 1990, 201). Prominent Canadian church representatives, especially Protestants, also tried to mobilize support, notably through the Canadian League of Nations Society, later the Canadian National Committee on Refugees and Victims of Political Persecution (CNCR). Such efforts, hampered by fears of provoking anti-Semitism,[39] "found no echo of Canadian public opinion in favour of refugee admissions" (Tulchinsky 1998, 59). The presence of a more sympathetic voice in Cabinet with the appointment of Thomas Crerar as minister in 1935 produced few tangible results. The "rabid anti-semite" Blair now declared that while "pressure on the part of the Jewish people has never been greater than it is now ... it has never been so well controlled. Fewer Jews are coming in than ever before" (quoted in Abella 1990, 200). Indeed, from 1933 to the founding of the state of Israel in 1948, Canada admitted 13,000 Jews, "arguably the worst [record] of all possible refugee-receiving states" (Abella and Troper 1991, xxii).

The government, stated Immigration and Colonization Minister Gordon in 1931, was focused on the national interest: "As long as conditions in this country are as they are to-day there need be no fear that the bars will be let down to immigrants" (24 June 1931, 3012). That same year, the government enacted a new regulation (PC 695) that limited immigration to British and American citizens, agriculturalists with funds to farm in Canada, and the wife and children under 18 of any Canadian citizen or legal resident who was able to support them. By 1932, he could rightly claim "that as severe a restriction has been placed upon migrants coming to Canada as has ever been enforced by the department" (21 April 1932, 2256). The number of immigrants decreased from around 163,000 in 1929-30 to some 88,000 in 1930-31 and just above 11,000 in 1935-36, almost half of whom were American citizens (Department of Mines and Resources 1946, 243-44, Tables 5 and 6). Levels continued to fall until the end of the Second World War. Immigration had become so marginal that the folding of the department into a new Department of Mines and Resources in 1936 sparked little debate.

Closing the Doors to Asian Immigration (1914-39)

By the end of 1914, Canada had erected a fairly comprehensive system of control against Asian immigrants by limiting their due process and equality rights inside Canada, and preventing their arrival from outside. As levels of Asian migration dropped drastically during the First World War, the issue more or less disappeared from political discourse. Although concerns were occasionally voiced over the Chinese in Canada, there was some support in the House for exempting Chinese students from the Head Tax (see 8 June 1917, 2139-49). Moreover, Canada depended on the Japanese fleet to patrol the west coast against German ships.[40] After the war, however, the government faced criticism from opponents of its Asian immigration policies in Canada and abroad. Indeed, this subject was discussed during the Imperial War Conferences of 1917 and 1918 at India's request (see below). Canada also had to address a growing problem of illegal entries, as migrants sought to circumvent restrictive policies. In response to a rise in both Chinese and Japanese migration, Canada enacted the highly restrictive 1923 *Chinese Immigration Act* and arranged a new Gentlemen's Agreement with Japan. By the Second World War, however, the rights-based issues that had arisen in the context of European immigration during the interwar period were also being debated in the context of Asian migration, a development that in part grew out of the government's policies towards Jewish refugees abroad and people of Japanese origin in Canada.

Restrictions on East Indian Immigration

Despite the affirmation in 1917 of reciprocity between India and the other British Commonwealth territories on questions of immigration, it was agreed, Borden wrote in 1918, that "complete control of the composition of its own population by means of restriction on immigration from any of the other communities" was "an inherent function" of each self-governing Commonwealth member (Canada 1967, 352).[41] Although Canada accepted that "Indians already permanently domiciled [in Canada] should be allowed to bring in their wives and minor children," subject to identification (ibid., 353), annual intake remained small throughout the interwar period. On average, 37 East Indians officially arrived each year, for a total of 734 (see Department of Mines and Resources 1946, 240-45, Tables 3 through 6), as new provisions were added to the continuous journey, monetary, and labour restrictions in place since 1908.

Aside from new passport requirements, the government made it harder for East Indians who had left Canada to return, demanding an exit registration certificate even though issuance of the certificate had never been anything more than an ad hoc procedure, and setting a three-year time limit that left many unable to return, given transportation difficulties during and after the war (Buchignani et al. 1985, 72). An almost wholesale ban was then placed on Asian immigration in 1930 through an Order-in-Council, PC 2115, which prohibited "the landing in Canada of any immigrant of Asian race" except "the wife or unmarried child under 18 years of age, of any Canadian citizen legally admitted to and resident in Canada, who is in a position to receive and care for his dependents" (Sampat-Mehta 1972, 115). Facing such barriers, "South Asian Canadians used their carefully delimited freedom to consolidate their familial, economic, and community organizations ... No substantial attack on either the immigration ban or discriminatory British Columbia legislation was to develop again until the late 1930's [sic]" (Buchignani et al. 1985, 71).

At the same time, restrictions became "a licence for prospective South Asian immigrants to try to beat the system" (ibid., 91). Some were brought in as "relatives" of those already in Canada, while others were moved surreptitiously across the US border. Thus, in the face of restrictions, community members

> devised several strategies to enable family members to migrate. On return visits, immigrants suggested to adult ... family members that they should try to reach Canada by alternate routes through other countries. Younger members of the [extended family] were sometimes taken to Canada under a false identity, showing them as sons of different fathers and sometimes as different sons of the same father. Immigrants made deliberate efforts to evade authorities in both Canada and India, and their kin ... cooperated in the process. (Verma 2002, 207-8)

In 1937 and 1939, community representatives went to Ottawa on behalf of such illegal migrants, securing special programs that saw a few hundred given legal status. Ottawa also came under increased pressure from East Indians in Canada and officials in India to help overcome franchise restrictions in British Columbia, with support coming from the Co-operative Commonwealth Federation (CCF) and some labour organizations. This rights-based battle was eventually won in 1947 (for the Chinese as well; the Japanese had to wait until 1949). The size of the East Indian community in Canada was, however, quite small, and thus its ability to pursue rights-based politics was fairly limited.

Restrictions on Chinese Immigration

In the 1920s, the issue of Chinese migration came to prominence again when it was determined that British officials overseas were approving Chinese merchant applications for entry too liberally. In response, the Conservative government of Arthur Meighen introduced *An Act to amend the Chinese Immigration Act* in 1921 to make the Controller of Chinese Immigration in Canada, rather than a British official in China, responsible for recognizing Chinese merchants (Section 1.1). The old identification certificates would be abolished and migrants would have to demonstrate their bona fides to the Controller's satisfaction, while questions of the legal status of Chinese migrants would be determined by a board of inquiry rather than the courts (Section 2).[42] The government also extended the time that a Chinese resident could remain outside Canada before having to pay the Head Tax again from one to two years (Section 4.1). Although Rodolphe Lemieux (L) expressed concerns in the House that possible injustices might be committed against legitimate Chinese migrants because the terms of admission were so vague (23 May 1921, 3828), the bill passed with little debate.

After the Liberals returned to power in 1921, William G. McQuarrie (C) moved that the government "take immediate action with a view to securing the exclusion of future [Asian] immigration" (8 May 1922, 1509). In a lengthy attack on "the wily Chinese," he observed that "it has been found that no matter how restrictive our regulations were, no matter how well they had been thought out and carefully planned, and no matter how stringently worded they were, the Chinese still kept coming into the country" (ibid., 1510). Canada should therefore implement more restrictive policies with respect to the Chinese and remove itself from the terms of the 1908 Gentlemen's Agreement to halt Japanese arrivals. Among many justifications, he cited his belief that Asians would never assimilate.[43] This was, many argued, a question of national survival. "A few years ago," Alfred Stork (L) stated, "the Japanese were regarded as a simple, childlike and interesting people; but experience has shown us that they are the very incarnation of commercial aggressiveness" (ibid., 1518). Successive speakers, such as E.J. McMurray (L), warned that "a rock washed by the waves, of the ocean, if it is not composed of one element, sooner or later will disintegrate. And so it is with the nations; if a nation is not built of one stock and woven together into a national fabricate, it will sooner or later crumble" (ibid., 1527).[44] Some recommended the expropriation of property held by Asians followed by their forced deportation. The core issue for MPs like Henry Stevens was the preservation of a white Canada: "Which [civilization] shall prevail, ours, or theirs?" (ibid., 1548).

Only Woodsworth stood apart from the anti-Asian attitude demonstrated in this debate, observing that "a good deal has been said that showed racial prejudice and an appeal made to racial bigotry" (ibid., 1571). Canada could not, he argued, cut itself off from other countries with an exclusionist policy. Asian immigration was primarily a product of big business demands for cheap labour, and thus the best strategy was to increase the standard of living for all, making it unprofitable to admit those willing to work for low wages. Like many Liberal Internationalists, Woodsworth was not opposed in principle to decreasing Asian immigration, but resisted efforts to demonize such immigrants.

The Chinese community itself was not inactive on the question of restriction (Con et al. 1982, Chapters 7-10; Mar 2010). By the early 1920s, Chinese organizations existed across the country, and dynamic leadership was emerging from a steadily increasing Canadian-born Chinese population alongside a growing number of students arriving from China. Moreover, the participation of Chinese Canadians in the Canadian military during the war had renewed a demand for the franchise when Canada's election law was reviewed in 1919.[45] A new assertiveness could also be seen in the rise of workplace actions by Chinese labour after the war. Members of the Chinese community also continued to press for fair treatment through the courts, and some law firms engaged Chinese employees to assist in such cases. Although a number of legal challenges were successful, many rulings were upheld even as they clarified the authority of the state with respect to restrictive border control.[46]

In 1923, the government entered into talks with Chinese Consul-General Chilien Tsur to explore the possibility of crafting an agreement to regulate Chinese migration. This led Tsur to solicit input from Chinese organizations, which produced a twelve-point proposal that, among other features, focused on the equality rights of Chinese already in Canada. The government had already decided against a bilateral agreement, however, on the grounds that China did not possess effective control over its territories. Instead, Canada moved to replace the 1885 *Chinese Immigration Act* with an even more restrictive law.

Alan Neill had already introduced legislation to provide "a simple and yet complete and unassailable method by which the people of Canada can exclude any form of undesirable immigration that they desire without at the same time becoming involved in any dispute with any foreign nation or government whatsoever" (6 February 1923, 74).[47] He proposed that all immigrants should have to secure permission to enter Canada before arrival and that the minister be granted authority to "arbitrarily and without question decide whether or not that particular immigrant shall be admitted" without being required to provide any explanation (ibid.). This would confirm Parliament's "absolute right to control and regulate immigration into this country of whatever source or origin" (21 February 1923, 497). The proposal was abandoned, however, after the government introduced its own restrictive legislation.

Prime Minister Mackenzie King argued that outright exclusion would transgress "the conception of British freedom as I understand it; I have never known a time when the British flag has stood for inflicting anything in the nature of an indignity upon the people of any country in the world" (30 April 1923, 2313). Nonetheless, "British justice and fair play, and fair dealings with the peoples of other parts of the world," might still produce effective exclusion of Chinese immigration (ibid.). He proposed that Canada should maintain trade and cultural relations with China while establishing, without being explicit, the means to exclude the Chinese. Although Chinese labour would be completely inadmissible under the new law, Mackenzie King maintained that admitting select merchants (and their families) would be beneficial for all.

An Act respecting Chinese Immigration would remove the Head Tax and replace it with a system of external control. Only representatives of the Chinese government and their staff, Canadian-born children of Chinese parents in Canada, merchants, and students could enter, and the latter two categories had to possess a passport issued by Canadian officials overseas (Section 5).[48] In Canada, the Controller of Chinese Immigration would have discretionary power "to determine whether an immigrant, passenger or other person seeking to enter or land in Canada or detained for any cause under this Act is of Chinese origin or descent and whether ... [they] shall be allowed to enter, land or remain in Canada or shall be rejected and deported" (Section 10.1). An appeal to the minister would be available if lodged within forty-eight hours, but the appellant would be detained while awaiting a response (Sections 12-13) unless a "deposit of money to an amount and under conditions specified by the ... Controller" was made (Section 14). The courts were denied any role in overseeing the work of officials (Section 38). The law also provided for the mandatory registration of all Chinese living in Canada (Section 18). Furthermore, Masters of Vessels would be limited to carrying one Chinese passenger per 250 tons, who could not disembark before a full identity and medical inspection had been completed (Sections 19-20). Any person of Chinese origin who wished to leave the country would have to register upon departure and return within two years (Sections 23-24).

Parliamentary critics of the proposed law were few and their interventions generally concerned judicial review. Richard B. Hanson (C) sought clarification on Section 38 to ensure that "the court of record would have the right to have the King's writ run" (30 April 1923, 2337). In reply, Immigration and Colonization Minister Charles Stewart claimed that if cases were tied up in the courts, then abuse of the law was encouraged, and that this had often led to Chinese immigrants being kept in the country in "a sort of slavery" by their compatriots. He suggested that denying the right to be heard before the courts "would be very much to the advantage of the nationals of China themselves" (ibid.). Woodsworth disagreed with placing the minister in a position of absolute arbitrary authority ... [or the] placing any one official in such a position that the public generally have no opportunity of taking active steps or appealing against his decision. It seems to me that the action of any minister ought to be subject to review by a court, or by some other body in this country. (Ibid., 2338)

While still not averse to preventing Asian immigration, he criticized policies that prevented family reunification and spoke of the need to "very definitely and consciously attempt to overcome the prejudices which we have against men of other races and other colours than our own" (4 May 1923, 2485). The voices for restriction were dominant, however, and amid calls from Liberal Nationalists such as Simon F. Tolmie (C) "to preserve this country to the white man" (30 April 1923, 2317), the legislation passed easily in the House.

For its part, the Chinese community undertook an unsuccessful attempt to mitigate the law's restrictive features. The editor of one Chinese-language paper argued that

it was up to the Chinese in Canada to make their case clear to Members of Parliament and the newspapers, representatives of possibly sympathetic groups, and Canadian society in general. Meanwhile, telegrams should be sent to influential groups in industry, commerce, and education in China and to Overseas Chinese in countries other than Canada, pointing out that the proposed legislation was insulting to China. Wires should also be sent to the British government and to British diplomats in China, stressing the point that this legislation was unreasonable and contrary to principles of international good will. (Con et al. 1982, 142)

The Toronto-based Chinese Association of Canada organized a one-thousand-strong meeting in late April and sent a delegation to the Senate as it discussed the bill.[49] These efforts produced only modest changes (see the comments in the House by Stewart in 28 June 1923, 4536-38), however, and on 1 July 1924, the 1923 *Chinese Immigration Act* came into effect.[50] Between 1924-25 and 1938-39, only eight Chinese immigrants were officially landed in Canada, an average of fewer than one every two years (Department of Mines and Resources 1946, 241-44, Tables 4 through 6).

Despite the resultant decrease in the Chinese population in Canada during the interwar period, there was significant growth in its associational life, stimulated in part by the various forms of discrimination faced by the community (Wickberg 1980).[51] Since so few Chinese migrants arrived after 1923, an ever-increasing proportion of the Chinese population in Canada was Canadian-born.[52] As the community spread out across the country, and as many members converted to Christianity and became employed in non-traditional areas, "the Chinese population was becoming more associated with Canada" (Con et al. 1982, 150). Canada's rights-restrictive approach was increasingly debated, both inside and outside the Chinese community, in terms of equality and due process rights. Aside from organizing annual boycotts and demonstrations against the 1923 law, Chinese Consolidated Benevolent Associations across Canada protested other restrictive legislation at all levels of government. Furthermore, in a bid to circumvent restrictive legislation, "there occurred efforts to by-pass the regulations and to enter Canada illegally" (ibid., 213).[53]

Restrictions on Japanese Immigration

After the First World War, the Canadian government wanted to reduce Japanese immigration through a new Gentlemen's Agreement but Tokyo was not easily persuaded. Japan had been at the table in Paris in 1919 to negotiate the creation of the League of Nations, advocating the inclusion of a racial equality clause in the founding Covenant. Perceiving the growth of anti-Asian sentiments in British Columbia and Parliament, Mackenzie King repeatedly pressed Tokyo to negotiate. It eventually agreed to do so but insisted that any outcome must be "consistent with a sense of justice and a regard for fair human rights" (Canada 1970, 706). In 1923, Mackenzie King revealed that Japan would reduce the annual number of labour migrants to 150 (down from 400), with wives continuing to fall outside the quota.

This did little to diminish the increasing view that Japan constituted a national security threat, that, Thomas G. McBride (P) claimed in the House, the Japanese wanted "to get control of the Pacific coast, including all British Columbia" (30 April 1923, 2326).[54] In 1925, this argument was fully aired when amendments were introduced to the 1920 *Dominion Elections Act*. Neill sought to undo 1919 changes that allowed Asians who had served in the armed forces to vote in federal elections even if they were not allowed to vote at the provincial level. He argued that "if these men are allowed to vote it will be said by-and-bye, why not their sons, their brothers and so on" (25 June 1925, 4906). In response, Woodsworth opposed "taking from members of any one race their innate rights as human beings to direct their own affairs" (19 June 1925, 4581). Without the right to vote, he maintained, "British citizenship becomes an absolutely empty thing" (25 June 1925, 4907). Indeed, he called for all Canadian citizens of Asian descent to be enfranchised. William Irvine (L) agreed, stating that "we cannot hope to solve the oriental problem by imposing restrictions and seeking to oppress these people" within the country (19 June 1925, 4582). Others simply could not countenance the denial of the franchise to those who had fought for the country during the last war. It would be, Soldiers' Civil Re-establishment Minister Henri S. Beland (L) commented, "a slur upon the men who ... were found good enough to go to the front and expose their lives for the sake of the country" (25 June 1925, 4906). Neill's proposal was, said Lucien Cannon, based on "a principle which to my mind is altogether illiberal" (ibid., 4911).

Amid continued pressure and evidence that Japanese migrants were entering the country illegally, Mackenzie King sought to restrict the terms of the Gentlemen's Agreement further. In 1928, it was agreed that only 150 Japanese immigrants would be authorized to enter each year (including women and children) and passports would now be processed by Canadian officials in Japan (Pringsheim 1983, 23). Although levels were often well below 150 by the 1930s, the incidence of Japanese people smuggling grew. For example, in early 1931 a smuggling ring responsible for an estimated 2,500 entries was uncovered by the Royal Canadian Mounted Police (RCMP) (Adachi 1976, 180).

Few in Canada advocated on behalf of the Japanese and "their disparate voices were clearly insufficient to counterbalance the larger and much more vociferous group who sought to limit those rights" (ibid., 179). With the creation of the CCF in 1932, however, there was one political party that supported their rights-based claims. In its founding manifesto, the party "called for the 'equal treatment before the law of all residents of Canada irrespective of race, nationality or religious or political beliefs'" (Melnyk 1989, 104). For its part, the Japanese Canadian Citizens' League (JCCL) addressed a Special Committee on Elections and Franchise Acts of the House of Commons in May 1936 and made rights-based claims against franchise restrictions (Canada 1936). With Japanese military actions in Manchuria and elsewhere in China during the 1930s, however, it became even more difficult to mobilize support. As relations between Japan and the West deteriorated, stories of Japanese spies preparing the ground for an invasion of Canada circulated, and anti-Japanese sentiment spread.

During this time, several important shifts were occurring within the Japanese Canadian community. As with the Chinese, first-generation settlers (the *Issei*) became outnumbered by Canadian-born Japanese (the *Nisei*). Moreover, increasing numbers within the community were converting to Christianity and taking up employment in new areas, although they were less likely than the Chinese to leave British Columbia (Adachi 1976, Chapters 5-7). Exclusion from mainstream society fostered associational activities covering every major aspect of their lives, including mobilizing against rights-restrictive policies. The *Nisei* in particular focused attention on the denial of equality rights: "To be told that, because of their racial origin, they might never be able to vote was humiliating to a group brought up in the belief that the ideals of 'democracy' and 'fair play' were real and universally valid" (ibid., 158). This commitment was seen in the creation of the JCCL in 1936 and an English language weekly, *The New Canadian*, in 1938. The call for equality rights served as a unifying force in the community and opened up possibilities for links with groups and individuals interested in the broader question of a bill of rights in Canada. It would not prove effective against a rising tide of restriction against Japanese immigrants in the late 1930s, however, as Liberal Nationalists such as Neill warned MPs of a time when the Japanese would be so numerous that "they must be given the vote and all the privileges our own citizens possess, the opportunity to become lawyers, doctors and all the rest of it" (10 May 1938, 2743).

By the Second World War, then, the politics of control surrounding Asian (especially Japanese) immigration had become more fractious, even as government control policies had become more effective. There were nonetheless important differences from the time of the First World War. First, the Chinese, East Indian, and Japanese communities in Canada consisted more and more of those who had been born in the country or who had become naturalized Canadians, and so the restriction of their rights was more difficult to justify through simple references to state sovereignty. Second, these Canadians were at the forefront in ensuring that their communities organized around rights-based concerns. Third, circumvention now regularly occurred in all three communities in response to restrictive government policies. Finally, all three found new allies within mainstream society, especially in the churches, the CCF, and the nascent civil liberties movement, and even in British Columbia "many newspaper editors, in some cases inspired by humanitarian and civil libertarian motives, urged greater toleration for Asians already in the province" (Roy 2003, 131).

The Apex of Liberal Nationalism (1939-45)
The groups that suffered most from the government's rights-restrictive approach to control during the Second World War were Jewish refugees seeking sanctuary within Canada's borders and the Japanese already within them. Their treatment serves as a benchmark for tracing developments in the post–Second World War period concerning the rights of non-citizens in Canada. The war years were also a time when important links, intellectual and political, continued to be made between the rights of non-citizens and immigrants, on the one hand, and British liberalism and the concept of human rights, on the other. This contributed to the resurgence of Liberal Internationalism after the war, and it is difficult to appreciate the nature of rights-based politics to the present without understanding these changes. During and immediately after the war, however, Canada's actions towards Jews overseas and the Japanese at home were embedded within Liberal Nationalism, premised on the notion that state sovereignty sanctioned racial discrimination as a legitimate means of pursuing the perceived national interest. While some decision makers did not hold or wish to promote racist views, government policies generally reflected and played to the concerns of those who did, and they continued to do so well into the postwar period.

For its part, Liberal Internationalism, although still a marginalized force in the politics of control, experienced continued renewal and extension as events unfolded.

Rejecting Jewish Refugees

In the run-up to and onset of the war, immigration officials maintained a restrictive response towards Jewish refugees. When considering resettlement proposals, officials took so long to deliberate and act that it was often impossible to do anything even if, on rare occasions, a positive decision was reached. While Jewish MPs such as Jacobs, Abraham Heaps (CCF), and Samuel Factor (L) as well as the CNCR pressed for a more humane policy, both Crerar and Blair told Jewish community leaders that if they tried to get around the department by lobbying MPs and Cabinet, they might find that those few Jewish refugees accepted would not gain admittance (Abella and Troper 1991, 92). When the community approached the department, however, almost every request was refused on the grounds that restrictive rules could not be bent lest a precedent be set that could inhibit future restrictive policy options. Perceiving an increase in anti-Jewish feeling in Canada, Jewish leaders generally felt that they could not take too strong a public stand: "Seeking what they thought was reasonable and just, they went quietly and unobtrusively [to Ottawa and] ... returned with empty promises" (Draper 1988, 152). At the international level, Canada continued to avoid commitments. When it agreed to participate in an Inter-Governmental Committee on Refugees from 1938 onward, it anticipated, Under-Secretary of State for External Affairs Norman Robertson noted, that nothing much would come of it but that it might "be a useful step in placating the opinion which takes the vein that Canada should be a more active participant in refugee matters" (quoted in Abella and Troper 1991, 182).

A more public debate arose in the case of the *St. Louis* in 1938 (ibid., 63-64). Sailing from Hamburg with 907 Jewish refugees aboard, the ship was destined for Cuba but was denied entry even though the passengers possessed valid visas. Jewish groups abroad sought another place where the refugees could disembark, unsuccessfully approaching Argentina, Panama, Paraguay, and Uruguay. As the ship travelled north, an American gunboat accompanied it to prevent it from landing in the United States. While influential Canadians petitioned Ottawa to permit the refugees to come to Canada, Minister of Justice Ernest Lapointe (L) expressed outright opposition, and Blair listed various ways that the refugees did not meet Canada's restrictive admissions criteria and argued, moreover, that no country could "open its doors wide enough to take in the hundreds of thousands of Jewish people who want to leave Europe: the line must be drawn somewhere" (quoted in ibid., 64). With this final rejection by Canada, the ship returned to Europe, where many of those on board perished in the Holocaust.

Although Jews in Canada recognized that the government "lacked the conscience to which they appealed so eloquently," they never switched to a more forceful rights-based approach (Draper 1988, 152). Despite the support of a few MPs, few parliamentarians were willing to engage in such a politically unpopular issue. John R. MacNicol (National Government) raised a rare voice when he expressed his hope to the House "that the department may view with the greatest compassion the plight of some of these people who are asking to be permitted to come into this country" (14 June 1941, 4027). It was not really until the final years of the war that MPs began to criticize the government's approach. For example, when Mackenzie King spoke favourably of Canada's refugee record, M.J. Coldwell (CCF) replied that he "was glad to hear the expressions of sympathy for the refugees ... but I believe we might have initiated some conferences or made some attempts to solve this problem in a way which I might term more Christian" (9 July 1943, 4569). Stanley H. Knowles (CCF) urged that since public opinion did not seem to support a humanitarian response to "the terrible plight of the people of the Jewish race ... a lead should be given to our people" by Parliament (ibid., 4605). He admonished the government, saying that "waiting to help these people in the best way that we can later on is ... really not good enough in view of the fact that many of them – thousands, perhaps millions – will not be there to help" (ibid., 4608).

> Many of them we could not help, no matter how much initiative the government or the people of this country might display. But it does seem to me, that as human beings we should do our best to provide as much sanctuary as we can for those people who can get away. I say we should do that because these people are human and deserve that consideration, and because we are human and ought to act in that way. (Ibid.)[55]

Such comments were few and far between, however.[56] In the Senate, Cairine Wilson (L) was one of the few who spoke against restriction, quoting: "He who watches murder without making any kind of attempt to save the victims cannot avoid sharing to some degree the guilt involved" (18 May 1943, 243).[57]

Against admitting Jewish refugees, however, Liguori Lacombe (Independent Liberal) demanded: "Will the government understand where lay the interests most dear to our people, or will it give in to national and international conspiracies hatched in secrecy and all of them detrimental to Canada?" (1 February 1944, 92). "The arrival of refugees will not add to [Canada's] wealth," Pierre Gauthier (Bloc populaire canadien) argued. "If other nations ... wish to be charitable, let them indulge their whim at their own expense" (2 February 1944, 130). Jean-François Pouliot (L) warned that "we must look after our own people in the first place, and then we must be very careful that we are not ruled by the bold refugees who come here from outside to take hold of this country, or then we shall be slaves in our own country" (30 March 1944, 2005).[58] Frédéric Dorion (I) claimed that Jewish refugees already had too many privileges extended to them, "so much so that, at times, we are wondering whether or not we were engaged in this war for the sole purpose of saving or helping out the Jews all over the world" (29 June 1944, 4370). As the reality of the Holocaust spread, such language virtually disappeared from Parliament, although restrictive policies towards Jews did not, at least not until 1948 (Abella and Troper 1991). Jewish leaders in Canada would draw from these experiences several lessons that would shape their engagement in rights-based politics after the war, and they would find common cause with other groups, such as the Chinese and Japanese.

Removing Japanese and Japanese Canadians from Canada

The wartime experiences of the Japanese community in Canada included its forced displacement from coastal British Columbia, the internment of hundreds of its members, and the attempt to remove as many of the 22,500-strong population as possible to Japan after the war. The treatment of the Japanese was more extreme than that of German or Italian "enemy alien" populations at the time. When Defence of Canada Regulations (DOCR) were passed under the authority of the 1914 *War Measures Act* in early 1940, Justice Minister Ernest Lapointe declared that "any persecution of racial minorities in this country is unworthy of our people, and foreign to our traditions and our national spirit" (23 May 1940, 146),[59] while Mackenzie King stated that "freedom must be restricted wherever restriction is essential to winning the war; but we must remember that we are fighting to preserve freedom, not to suppress it" (11 June 1940, 662). In contrast to the previous war, many protested against the arbitrary and excessive nature of the government's actions with respect to European "enemy aliens," but not until after the war was an effective campaign mounted against the treatment of the Japanese.

As civil liberties associations monitored the government's actions from the outside, the CCF was active on a parliamentary committee established to study the application of the regulations. Thus, Tommy Douglas (CCF) pressed for changes to ensure that they "should be so clear and so specific that they cannot lend themselves to the persecution of any individuals or any groups of people in Canada" (13 June 1940, 752).[60] There were protests over the suspension of important due process protections,[61] especially from those on the political left who worried that representatives of labour organizations were being targeted.[62] Although civil liberties associations succeeded in decreasing the severity with which these were implemented in some instances, numerous due process and freedom of expression principles deeply anchored in British liberalism were abrogated (Lambertson 2005, Chapter

2). Overall, some 2,500 European "enemy aliens" were interned, mostly of German or Italian background (Kelley and Trebilcock 1998, 275). Along with government policies towards the Japanese, the DOCR experience revealed that, "in the end, the traditional concepts of civil liberties protection under the British parliamentary system had been shown wanting, at best" (MacLennan 2003, 31).

Meanwhile, heightened fear over the "yellow peril" – the idea that Japanese living along the coast of British Columbia were a threat to national security – was a reality by the late 1930s. Despite little evidence of espionage, Canadian fears grew, especially after Japan entered the Tripartite Pact with Germany and Italy in 1940 (Roy et al. 1990, 31-40). With the outbreak of war with Germany in 1939, prominent voices in the Japanese Canadian community, such as the JCCL and *The New Canadian,* pledged loyalty to Canada and raised funds for the war effort, while community members sought to enlist (Adachi 1976, 188-93). In the complex political environment of the day, defined by a lack of cultural understanding, decades of racist policies, security fears, a vocal public demand for more restrictive actions, economic opportunism, and concerns over the safety of the Japanese, the government acted. After a series of consultations and reports initiated in the late 1930s, it undertook a registration of all people of Japanese descent in Canada, noting those to be arrested in the event of war with Japan. Meanwhile, Japanese community representatives, reflected here in a quote from *The New Canadian,* reasserted the "need now to place our assurance in the inherent tolerance, good sense and decency of our Canadian neighbours and the democratic way of life" (quoted in ibid., 198).

Pressure for stronger measures was building in Parliament, however. On the grounds of "once a Jap always a Jap," Neill argued that if the government would "take a bold stand ... it will stand us in good stead not only with the Japanese but with every native race in the world" (25 February 1941, 1017, 1022).[63] This left Angus MacInnis (CCF) a lone voice of support for the Japanese for much of the war, "wondering what we are fighting for in Europe today" (ibid.). "I am satisfied," he said, "that if we treat the Japanese and our other oriental citizens aright, we shall get their loyalty ... We will secure their loyalty by fairness and kindness" (ibid., 1020). Moreover, he reminded MPs, "a great many of these people are Canadian citizens no matter what the colour of their skins may be, and they are entitled to the treatment that would be accorded to a Canadian citizen whose skin is white" (2 July 1942, 3878).

After the attack on Pearl Harbor in December 1941, the RCMP arrested a few dozen Japanese on national security grounds, and more than a thousand fishing boats of Japanese nationals were seized. Amid rising fears of fifth-column activities, expressed more by those outside than those inside government, a new policy was unveiled on 14 January 1942:

The government announced the immobilization of the Japanese fishing fleet, restrictions on the purchase of gasoline and explosives and the use of radios and cameras, and plans to organize a Civilian Corps and to provide employment for male enemy aliens. Buried in the announcement was the news that steps were being taken to remove enemy aliens without RCMP permits from [a] protected area which was yet to be defined. (Roy et al. 1990, 84)

After a series of Japanese military victories in Asia, demands for full implementation of this policy grew, especially from British Columbia MPs.[64] Meanwhile, Japanese workers were being fired in that province, and Japanese-owned establishments were threatened with violence. In response, the government empowered itself by an Order-in-Council to "evacuate" all Japanese persons from the protected area (defined as one hundred miles inland from the coast).

By 1943, around 21,000 people, most of whom were said to be Canadian citizens by birth or naturalization (Roy 2007, 59), had been removed to various camps. Several hundred were interned (some until after the war), either as security threats or for resisting relocation. Property that evacuees could not take with them was held by the state and much of it was later sold without their agreement. After relocation, the government turned its attention to ensuring that Japanese immigrants did not return to the west coast after the war. Against those who spoke of the rights of the Japanese in Canada, Neill fumed: "It is apt to make one spit when one hears people use these fulsome terms of hypocritical affection towards these 'brown brothers' ... Let us at least take advantage of this one opportunity to correct our error and make for all time a white British Columbia and a civilized, Christian Canada" (1 March 1943, 798).[65]

The government devised a "voluntary departure" proposal, which, however, was not enough for those like Neill, who wished to remove completely from "within our body politic a cancer composed of these unassimilable people" (30 June 1943, 4209). By the time that Japan had surrendered in September 1945, more than 10,000 people had signed up (some 43 percent of the target population), but the first ships did not depart until May 1946 (Roy et al. 1990, 166).[66] Thousands soon asked to cancel their agreements, however, particularly those who were Canadian citizens. While considering its options, the government was confronted with growing public protests over its rights-restrictive approach.

It is not surprising that there was little objection during the war years to the treatment of the Japanese in Canada, "particularly when the war was proceeding so disastrously for the Allies. People were fearful, worried, and unready to trust the actions of those living among them who spoke a different language or merely looked different" (ibid., 42). Indeed, "the fact that a group of people was expelled from a large area of the country, without hearings or trials and merely on the grounds of racial ancestry, and that all rights of citizenship had been abrogated, excited little comment across the country" (Adachi 1976, 218). The people who most consistently "emphasized that protecting the rights of the individual was a part of the inherited traditions of 'British fair play and justice' and hence part of the Canadian national ethos, and that arbitrary and unreasonable interference with those rights were repugnant to national instincts," were the Japanese themselves, especially those who were Canadian citizens (ibid., 221).

Alongside individual petitions protesting the sale of confiscated property, the separation of families, and "voluntary" male labour to construct roads in the interior, new forms of collective action emerged within the Japanese community.[67] With forced removals from their homes, it was difficult to maintain old organizations (such as the Canadian Japanese Association and the JCCL) but new groups emerged from different segments of the community to press for change, such as the Japanese Canadian Committee for Democracy and the Co-operative Committee for Japanese Canadians. These and other organizations faced difficulties due to the government's powers to relocate and even intern individuals, and they often battled among themselves to represent Japanese Canadians (Bangarth 2008, 116-19). For a long time, their efforts received little support from mainstream society, but this began to change in 1944.

For example, when the government passed legislation in 1944 to ensure that relocated Japanese could not vote in the next federal election, various church organizations protested.[68] Besides the National Inter-Church Advisory Committee, "approximately sixty persons and organizations" wrote to the Prime Minister in protest, including "several branches of the YMCA, Women's Auxiliaries of the Anglican and United Churches, and some United and Anglican Church leaders" (ibid., 80). It was only after the implications of the "voluntary departure" policy became clear, however, that the rights of Japanese Canadians were discussed more widely in Canada. As the number wishing to cancel their agreements grew, the CCF and the major churches took up the cause, as did the Canadian Jewish Congress, among other organizations. Their campaign – which featured many who would play a major part in the debate over the rights of immigrants and refugees in Canada after the war, such as Bernard Sandwell (the editor of *Saturday Night* magazine), Arthur Roebuck, and Cairine Wilson – was framed in terms of the civil liberties and human rights of Japanese Canadians.

After an unsuccessful attempt to authorize its deportations policy in October-November,[69] the government sought to implement the "voluntary departures" policy through orders-in-council passed under the expanded authority provided under the 1914 *War Measures Act* in December. As newspapers that "objected to policies based on race" criticized the government, other opponents "passed resolutions, wrote letters, distributed leaflets, and circulated petitions" (Roy et al. 1990, 175; see also Roy 2007, 197-200). In the House, Alistair Stewart (CCF) declared that the government's actions were "a direct negation of Liberalism and of decent, elemental fundamental democracy" (17 December 1945, 3704). Lawyer Andrew Brewin, who later emerged as a stalwart Liberal Internationalist MP but who was then advising the Japanese Canadian Committee for Democracy on legal strategies, tested the validity of the orders-in-council before the Supreme Court, which handed down a split decision that led to an appeal to the Judicial Committee of the Privy Council in London, which confirmed in December 1946 that the regulations were not *ultra vires*, and that Canada could deport Canadian-born citizens on racial grounds (see Adachi 1976, Chapter 13).

In the meantime, political pressure was maintained by those supporting the rights of Japanese Canadians. For example, the Co-operative Committee for Japanese Canadians argued that even if it was legal, the government's policy was not necessarily moral, and maintained that to deport people on racial grounds transgressed basic human rights. After the Judicial Committee's ruling, protests grew as the policy sat uncomfortably with several other government initiatives, such as creating a new Canadian citizenship and promoting international human rights in the construction of a postwar international order. Eventually, Mackenzie King convinced Cabinet early in 1946 to reduce the policy to one of removing only those who wished to return to Japan. After some four thousand had left, the Prime Minister announced on 24 January 1947 that the other deportation orders would be cancelled. Other wartime race-based controls over the lives of the Japanese in Canada would remain until early 1949. By then the mood in the country, even in British Columbia, had changed, perhaps best seen in the unanimous decision of the provincial legislature to enfranchise the Japanese. This was probably facilitated by the fact that, whereas British Columbia had once contained the overwhelming majority of the Japanese-origin population in Canada, the figure now stood at about 33 percent of a much smaller total population (Adachi 1976, 335).

Conclusion

"I am glad the Prime Minister takes the ground that we have a right to do as we please here in Canada" concerning immigration control, Woodsworth (now leader of the CCF) said in 1936. "The question is: What is right for us to do?" (20 February 1936, 389). Successive Canadian governments, with at least the tacit approval of most Canadians, answered this question by embarking between the wars upon the most restrictive period of control in the country's history. Not only did arrivals decrease dramatically but the rights of non-citizens were increasingly circumscribed. This was true of both immigrants and refugees (indeed, special attention was often paid to preventing the arrival of the latter), and was premised not only on ethnoracial considerations but also on a variety of socio-political criteria. Moreover, through numerous deportations, including efforts to remove thousands of Japanese Canadians at the end of the Second World War, the government pushed its concept of control further than ever before to include Canadian-born children of immigrants. As in the past, the country's rights-restrictive approach both gave rise to rights-based politics and encouraged circumvention.

By the end of the Second World War, an expanding human rights discourse concerning the rights of non-citizens had joined the older discourse centred on British liberalism within Liberal Internationalist circles in Canada. Its most forceful promoters were often those whose rights were in question, such as Japanese Canadians, rather than members of the majority Canadian population. The only MP to voice such sentiments throughout the war was Angus MacInnis, who in late 1945 concluded that the country's treatment of the Japanese had "violated every democratic tradition and every Christian principle," and lamented that "while the finest of our young men were fighting to destroy the concept of building a world order based on race hatred and the master race, we were dealing with this problem solely on the basis of race" (21 November 1945, 2385-86). By the end of the war, however, a broader coalition had emerged in support of the Japanese, and it undertook a campaign of rights-based politics pursued through public education, demonstrations, direct interventions in Ottawa, and efforts to secure their aims through the courts. This resurgence in Liberal Internationalism would find a much more receptive audience in the postwar political period.

5
A New Era of Human Rights
(1945-52)

The question of the rights of non-citizens in both its due process and equality dimensions has long been central to the politics of control in Canada. From the late nineteenth century to the end of the Second World War, the state established and pursued increasingly restrictive measures to regulate who could enter into and remain in the country based on the claim that state sovereignty trumped the due process and equality rights that could be claimed by non-citizens. Although many essential elements in this approach to control were maintained well into the 1960s, Liberal Internationalist criticisms began to carry more weight after the war, as the concepts of international human rights and procedural fairness reinvigorated British liberal ideas in Canada. For their part, despite having resisted change successfully for many years, Liberal Nationalists had to respond to increasingly accepted international and national ideas about appropriate state behaviour towards citizens and non-citizens alike. It would continue to define Canadian control policies for some time yet, but its place in the universe of political discourse was less secure than in the previous half-century, and Liberal Internationalism was clearly in the ascendant.

In tracing these shifts, this chapter begins with a brief overview of the migration challenges that existed in Europe at the end of the war and explores the discursive and political changes that occurred with the rapid development and institutionalization of the concept of human rights within the new United Nations system. This discourse was quickly taken up in Canada, though not without concerns on the part of Liberal Nationalists. Canadian control policies between 1945 and 1949 are then examined, especially with regard to the "displaced persons" of Europe. Although Canada eventually opened its doors to European immigration, it maintained a restrictive approach to control through its decision not to sign the 1951 United Nations Convention Relating to the Status of Refugees and through the passage of the 1952 *Immigration Act*. Even as Liberal Nationalism continued to dominate the practice of control, however, it became ever more difficult to ignore the challenge of a resurgent Liberal Internationalism. This set the stage for a transformation of the politics of control in the 1960s.

International Migrants and Human Rights after the Second World War

The end of the Second World War ushered in a new era of European migration, producing another massive population movement both within Europe and outward to traditional destinations such as Australia, Canada, and the United States. Although many of the estimated 30 million displaced persons had no homes to return to, and others were too traumatized to go back, millions were eventually resettled where they had lived before the war (Marrus 1985, 297).[1] Between the middle of 1947 and the end of 1951, more than 1 million Europeans were resettled in other countries, 170,000 of them remaining in Europe and 634,000 going to Australia, Canada, and the United States (ibid., 344-45). At the same time, important conceptual shifts were occurring with respect to human rights, and these significantly influenced the politics of control in liberal democracies such as Canada.

Although the protection of rights and freedoms served as a major rhetorical and political anchor in the conduct of the war, the Holocaust ensured that it persisted well after the peace was settled.[2] This occurred in response not simply to the genocide itself but also to the West's reluctant response to those who had sought to escape. Thus, whereas the Covenant of the League of Nations had been silent on human rights, the Preamble to the Charter of the United Nations served "to reaffirm faith in fundamental human rights, in the dignity and worth of the human person." The Universal Declaration of Human Rights (UDHR), adopted by the UN General Assembly in 1948, identified several rights related to international migration, such as the individual's "right to leave any country, including his own, and to return to his country" (Article 13.2) and the individual's "right to seek and to enjoy in other countries asylum from persecution" (Article 14.1). Recognizing the importance of human rights was different, however, from determining how best to protect them.

As a language "of the oppressed or dispossessed ... [used principally] to challenge or seek to alter national legal or political practices," human rights have come to embody "a moral standard of national political legitimacy" (Donnelly 1993, 20-21). They constitute at least a normative tool that can be used to challenge the idea of the absolute sovereignty of states. Their legitimacy stems partly from their independence of any particular territorial unit, even though their practical import is primarily realized within the nation-state. Thus, although the formal institutional mechanisms of international human rights are generally acknowledged to be quite weak, their normative stature has been difficult to challenge, especially in the liberal West. This was recognized by the Canadian participants in the creation of the UDHR. In response to suggestions that the document had little value without an implementation mechanism, Escott Reid, who served on Canada's delegation to the 1945 San Francisco conference at which the UN Charter was signed, replied:

> This argument runs counter to British traditions and experience since it has proved useful in the development of liberties in England to secure agreement on bills of rights even before it was possible to ensure that they would be implemented. The bill of rights becomes a goal which is eventually achieved. When a government departs from the principles of the bill its opponents can appeal to them. (Canada 1977, 887)[3]

As such, rights can appropriately be understood as being the product of continued political debate and struggle: "Human rights did not just happen, they had to be invented; and their proponents had constantly to defend them against the view that they were chimerical" (Vincent 1986, 19). This can certainly be seen in the case of Canada.

Although a Canadian, John P. Humphrey, wrote the first draft of the UDHR (Hobbins 1989), the government was not actively engaged in this process (Holmes 1979, 290-95). Moreover, the final version was initially "greeted with considerable hostility by the majority of mainstream forces in Canada," including many in government (Hobbins 1998, 325).[4] Nonetheless, Canada eventually made at least a formal and rhetorical commitment to human rights and this affected rights-based politics at the domestic level. Indeed, Canada's support of human rights at the international level was often used by Liberal Internationalists to promote a less restrictive approach to control. More generally, the new language and institutions of human rights extended easily from the rights-based politics generated within the context of British liberalism.

Canada struggled to secure a position that matched its own ideas of the role it should play within the postwar international order. The government, particularly the Department of External Affairs, wanted to establish Canada as a "middle power" to ensure that the United Nations would not simply be dominated by Britain, China, the United States, and the Soviet Union. Thus, it advanced a functional principle whereby "in those areas where a smaller state had both interest and expertise ... it should be regarded as a major power and given the right to be represented on the decision-making bodies in those areas" (Nossal 1997, 54). In reality, however, this often meant siding with Britain and the United States to reinforce the stability and success of the new system (Mackenzie 2007). Even before the end of the war, Canada "had already determined that it could best protect its interests in a recon-structed world through commitment to a new collective security organiza-tion" alongside its Atlantic partners (Nolan 1991, 281). Unlike during the interwar period, participation in international affairs would be promoted as a way to achieve national security through global security. Canada therefore initially focused more on security debates and arrangements and less on human rights.[5] This lack of attention persisted until the San Francisco conference, where the government promoted the sanctity of state sovereignty vis-à-vis human rights in international affairs.[6]

Although Commonwealth countries of immigration such as Australia, New Zealand, and South Africa were concerned that human rights features in the proposed United Nations Charter might undermine their sovereign control over immigration, Canadian officials were more sanguine, arguing that the language would be primarily declaratory (ibid., 287).[7] Although suspicious of documents that attempted to define rights in concrete terms (which was not part of the British common law tradition), the government eventually supported the inclusion of a commitment to rights on pragmatic political grounds – not, however, before first being the only liberal democracy not to vote in support of the draft of the UDHR in 1948 (Holmes 1979, 292-94). Eventually, the diplomatic need to be seen to support the new UN initiative overcame internal misgivings and outright opposition to the new rights focus.[8] In the process, the government, Secretary of State Lester B. Pearson noted, would show that it did not "intend to depart from the procedures by which we have built up our own code under our own federal constitution for the protection of human rights" (quoted in Nolan 1991, 292). Nonetheless, officials anticipated that the new international human rights instruments would be used at the domestic level in the pursuit of rights-based claims (MacLennan 2003, 79).

Indeed, as work on the UDHR progressed, "Canadian civil libertarian leaders and groups mobilized to support this venture and to press the federal government to give domestic protection to human rights by means of a Canadian bill of rights" (Egerton 2004, 457). With roots in the interwar period, this movement had been renewed by the principles of freedom advanced during the war and the specific struggles against both the Defence of Canada Regulations under the 1914 *War Measures Act* and the government's policies towards the Japanese. Indeed, the postwar period saw a surge in the number of rights-based organizations advocating a Canadian bill of rights, and a continued shift from a traditional commitment to British liberalism to incorporate universal human rights: "Taking their cue in part from the efforts of the UN and in part from a deep concern for the status of individual rights and freedoms at home, parliamentarians and professors, unionized workers and lawyers, ethnic associations and women's organizations all challenged the various governments in Canada to better ensure the human rights of citizens" (MacLennan 2003, 3; see also Lambertson 2005).

In response, the government convened a Special Joint Parliamentary Committee in the late 1940s to investigate human rights protections in

Canada. Long-standing Liberal Internationalists such as Stanley Knowles and Alistair Stewart were joined by John Diefenbaker (who would, some thirteen years later, see his idea of a bill of rights enshrined in a federal statute) in calling for more formal rights protection in Canada. In the end, the committee recommended against a domestic bill of rights while accepting international declarations that had a moral rather than a statutory foundation (ibid., 88-89).

The centrality of rights was also seen in the context of the government's efforts to establish a new foundation for Canadian national identity through the adoption of a distinctly Canadian flag and uniquely Canadian citizenship. In introducing the 1946 *Canadian Citizenship Act*, Secretary of State Paul Martin (L) stressed that the latter would foster a better understanding of "the great traditions of constitutional liberty and even justice that are the root and source of our individual liberty," of how "every new citizen becomes a doughty champion of the democratic way of life" (22 October 1945, 1337). As for border control, Liberal Internationalists would often draw on the new language and institutions of human rights in pressing for reform.

A Cautious Welcome (1945-49)
The early period of postwar Canadian immigration policy has been described as "unimaginative, plodding, and inadequate" (Dirks 1977, 148). In general, the government's approach continued to reflect the restrictive outlook that had characterized it since the turn of the century. The most important exception was that Canada began, with considerable hesitation, to open its doors to European migrants, including those displaced by the war. On the surface, then, little had changed in the politics of control, but at a deeper level more significant shifts were occurring. In particular, Liberal Internationalism was now a regular and prominent feature of parliamentary debate about control. Grounded in British liberalism and drawing on the new discourse of international human rights, it offered a much more extensive critique of Liberal Nationalism, which, for the first time in over half a century, found itself on the defensive in Canada. The resurgence of Liberal Internationalism can be seen in the context of how Canada responded and defended its response to the humanitarian crisis in postwar Europe, as well as in the government's decision to repeal the 1923 *Chinese Immigration Act* in 1947 (although "Asian" immigrants continued to face a number of barriers until the late 1960s).

Early Indications (1945-47)
In response to criticisms that the government had no clear postwar direction for immigration policy, Mackenzie King himself delivered a key speech to the House in 1947 that, while it claimed to map out both short- and long-term plans, was fairly devoid of substance: "It laid down smooth-sounding principles of delightful rotundity, and gave hardly any indication how they

were to be applied" (Barkway 1957, 4). Immigrants would be welcomed as long as they could "advantageously be absorbed in our national economy," the Prime Minister stated, but there would be no "fundamental alteration in the character of our population" (1 May 1947, 2644, 2646). Overall, the statement revealed little enthusiasm for immigration, fitting securely within the hesitant and inward-looking Liberal Nationalist outlook that had been dominant since early in the century.[9]

Nonetheless, there were indications that the doors might be opened wider than previously, even to "persons who are displaced and homeless, as an aftermath of the world conflict" (ibid., 2644). Indeed, Mackenzie King noted that narrow self-interest would not suffice:

> Canada is not obliged, as a result of membership in the united nations [sic] or under the constitution of the international refugee organization, to accept any specific number of refugees or displaced persons. We have, nevertheless, a moral obligation to assist in meeting the problem, and this obligation we are prepared to recognize. (Ibid., 2645)

Canada was a sovereign state entitled to determine its own course, but that course was, in part, shaped by an obligation to assist those forced to flee from their homes.[10] This basic idea had been expressed much earlier by Liberal Internationalists in their battles against the 1885 *Chinese Immigration Act,* drawing upon the country's British liberal traditions. Now it also reflected Canada's new commitment to international stability in the postwar era. As for ethnoracial discrimination, Mackenzie King similarly tried to contain a tension between core Liberal Internationalist and Liberal Nationalist perspectives, between international human rights and state sovereignty:

> Canada is perfectly within her rights in selecting the persons whom we regard as desirable future citizens. It is not a "fundamental human right" of any alien to enter Canada. It is a privilege. It is a matter of domestic policy. Immigration is subject to the control of the parliament of Canada. This does not mean, however, that we should not seek to remove from our legislation what may appear to be objectionable discrimination. (Ibid., 2646)

While the tension remained unresolved, it reflected the difficulties that arose after the war in squaring sovereignty with rights.

Although the Prime Minister's statement sparked some debate in the House, the Senate took the lead on the question of Canadian policies towards immigrants and refugees after the war, establishing a Standing Committee to investigate the subject in April 1946. Senator Arthur Roebuck (L) sang the praises of immigrants past, detailed how the country was ripe with opportunities for all if enough labour could be found, and argued that if Canada was "to become one of the most pregnant and powerful of nations" then it would need to undertake a more expansive immigration policy (4 April 1946, 103). On the basis of the near unanimity of opinion received, the Standing Committee recommended "a well-considered and sustained policy of immigration, selective in character and pursued by Canadian authorities with initiative and enterprise" (Canada 1946, No. 11, 315). For admissions, it was proposed that

> any suggestion of discrimination based upon either race or religion should be scrupulously avoided both in the act and in its administration ... Unnecessary and technical restrictions such as the requirement of direct travel from the country of origin, the possession of funds when support is made available from others, and mere degrees of consanguinity or relationship, should be cleared away, leaving to those in charge the freest exercise in discretion in the choice of those desirable. (Ibid., 310)[11]

The 1910 *Immigration Act,* Senators complained, was "a non-immigration act" and its "main purpose seems to be exclusion" (ibid.). Although familiar cautionary control tools were to be maintained (for example, immigrants had to be screened to ensure their mental and physical health, and intake levels should be consistent with Canada's "absorptive capacity"), the predominantly positive chord struck by the Standing Committee was clear. A few Senators, such as Thomas Vien (L), worried about those who could not be "assimilated into the structure of our nation and become true Canadians" (4 April 1946, 107-8), but the majority appeared to side with Cairine Wilson (L), who warned that a lack of immigration would leave Canada like the old elm tree in her garden, "strangling itself with its own roots" (15 April 1946, 665).

In the House, David A. Croll (L) reflected a broad consensus in arguing that "there are no groups, or no organization or representative bodies, in fact very few individuals in this country, who do not think we need more people" (27 August 1946, 5492). Few supported non-discrimination, however. For example, John R. MacNicol (PC) declared that he favoured the immigration of qualified people of whatever background as long as they were predominantly British and certainly European (28 August 1946, 5505-6). Still, it was already evident that the war had fundamentally changed how ethnoracial questions would be discussed in Parliament. When John H. Blackmore (SC) complained that too many people with non-British names lived in Canada's rural areas,[12] and expressed suspicions about government plans to resettle four thousand Allied Polish soldiers, demanding to know their religion,[13] he was taken to task by Mines and Resources Minister James Glen. Blackmore's defensive response – "My questions were not implying anything. I was asking ordinary questions that the ordinary person using common sense is asking, on the street" (ibid., 5517) – signalled that discriminatory declamations would no longer pass unchallenged in the House.[14]

Despite what appeared to be broadly based support for a more expansion- ist immigration program,[15] restrictive laws and policies remained largely unchanged for the first few years after the war. As hostilities in Europe drew to a close, the Chinese were essentially barred under the 1923 *Chinese Immigration Act,* while "Asiatics" were still generally excluded through PC 2115. The only people who could readily resettle in Canada – mostly Americans and Britons – continued to be defined by PC 695. The problematic relationship between such discrimination and the conflict just concluded in Europe was evident to many MPs. "It seems strange," W. Ross Thatcher (CCF) observed, "that during the recent war, at the very time Canadians were being urged to enlist to help in eradicating racial intolerance abroad, our own nation was practising similar intolerance at home in selecting its immigrants" (3 April 1946, 525).

The government passed numerous orders-in-council between 1945 and 1948 that formally made it easier for Europeans to resettle in Canada, but argued (at least until 1947) that it could not act on them, claiming that transatlantic transport was being used to bring home armed forces personnel and their dependents, and that overseas inspection facilities shut down during the war had yet to be reopened. Scholars have subsequently identified three further factors: a deeply ingrained tradition of restriction within the department, the relatively marginal position of immigration within the sprawling Department of Mines and Resources, and a weak minister in the person of James Glen (Hawkins 1972, Chapters 3 and 4; Margolian 2000, Chapter 4). Critics attacked the government for a lack of initiative, noting that Argentina, Australia, Brazil, New Zealand, and the United States were moving much faster (see, for example, Canada 1946, No. 1). Although Canada eventually implemented one of the most expansive (in per capita terms) postwar resettlement programs among countries of immigration, it gave little indication during these early years that this was in the cards.

As for racial discrimination, the first notable change came in 1947, when the government repealed the 1923 *Chinese Immigration Act.* Henceforth, a male Canadian citizen of Chinese origin could apply to have his wife and unmarried children eighteen years or younger living overseas join him. The Chinese would continue to be governed by PC 2115, however. In support of this move, Glen observed that many had argued that it was "detrimental to the interests of the Chinese in Canada, and that in view of our position in the united nations [sic] and the democratic way in which we live, we are not justified in maintaining it" (11 February 1947, 308).

Support for repealing the law had been building for some time, both inside and outside the state. As early as 1942, Mines and Resources Minister Thomas

Crerar advocated repeal, arguing that "when the war is over, and the Axis powers are defeated, China will be one of the countries where great development will take place, in the material sense, and, when that time comes, it will be worth much to Canada to have goodwill in that country" (Canada 1980, 1793). In December 1943, officials noted that "through the whole country east of the Rockies there is a rising resentment on the part of all people of the old-time liberal faith against the government's policy which is likely to break loose in a national political issue of an unpleasant type unless something is done soon" (quoted in ibid., 1814). In March 1944, they observed that "our immigration laws and regulations ... have become a symbol of racial discrimination" (ibid., 1817).

Criticisms also came from an expanding human rights community and represented "an example of early postwar human rights efforts in Canada" (Bangarth 2003, 395). In 1946, in continuation of their work during the war, Chinese Canadian community organizations and their non-Chinese allies formed the Committee for the Repeal of the Chinese Immigration Act, which included both religious and secular figures (Con et al. 1982, 205-6).[16] In a brief to Glen, the committee argued that the 1923 law was inconsistent with the United Nations Charter as well as the values that underpinned Canadian democracy (ibid., 206). By 1947, numerous major newspapers, labour organizations, Catholic and Protestant religious bodies, the Council of Women, and Liberal, Conservative, and CCF MPs were calling for repeal. The move also found support in public opinion polling undertaken at the time (Roy 2008, 161).

Many of the arguments presented by Liberal Nationalists and Liberal Internationalists in this debate followed traditional lines. In opposition, the former asserted Canada's right to remain British and white,[17] voiced fears that thousands of Chinese would come,[18] claimed that the Chinese did not assimilate,[19] and suggested that Asians could threaten national security in the future.[20] In support, the latter expressed dissatisfaction that discrimination would remain under PC 2115, which contradicted a statement made by the Prime Minister some weeks earlier,[21] and admonished the government for continuing to discriminate when, as Diefenbaker put it, "we could easily do the right thing and do it graciously and generously" (11 February 1947, 325).[22] The 1923 *Chinese Immigration Act* was, Thatcher claimed, "an insulting and unwarranted slur against a fine race of people, people, moreover, who were our allies in the recent war" (ibid., 313). Moreover, for Liberal Internationalists, the principles being pursued in the construction of the United Nations provided an opening to link their views on the rights of immigrants with the national interest.

It was Diefenbaker who made the strongest link to the UN Charter. Although it could not dictate policy, he noted that "we in this parliament accepted the united nations charter [sic] and passed it" (ibid., 319).[23] He specifically referred to the Preamble, which declares that all nations are determined "to reaffirm faith in fundamental human rights, in the dignity and worth of the human person, in the equal rights of men and women and of nations large and small." He also raised Article 1, which calls for states to work together "in promoting and encouraging respect for human rights and for fundamental freedoms for all, without distinction as to race, sex, language or religion." In short, Canada had "accepted responsibility that no legislation would be passed by our parliament which would discriminate against any person on the basis of race, sex, language or religion" (ibid., 320).[24] David Croll agreed, asking: "How do we justify our requiring these people to live an abnormal and unnatural life? ... What right have we to mess up their lives?" (ibid., 324). Canada, continued M.J. Coldwell, would "be looked upon as something of a hypocrite in international affairs" (ibid., 331). Again, Angus MacInnis (CCF) reminded the House, Canada still possessed the right to control who could cross the border, but this authority had to be pursued on the basis of non-discrimination in accordance with the UN Charter (ibid., 337).

Thus, Liberal Internationalists began to tie together arguments in favour of expanded immigration, respect for human rights, and the national interest. Diefenbaker argued that "this country is great on the basis of the number of her races and the diversity of her religions. Canada can never achieve greatness on the basis of intolerance. Mutual respect, forbearance, and strict adherence to the principles and ideals of the united nations [sic] are necessary" (ibid., 321). On a more practical level, MacInnis predicted that Asian countries would soon be powerful actors in global affairs and that "it would be just as well if we tried now to make amends for our arrogance, failures and insults of the past" (ibid., 338). For William Irvine, the national interest involved even more fundamental considerations: "It is because we want to guard against any infringement of our own accepted principles of freedom that [the government should ensure] the complete removal of discrimination against any class of Canadian citizens" (2 May 1947, 2705).[25] The question was not the number of Chinese who might arrive but the values that lay behind Canadian policies, which should be consistent with Canadian liberal democracy.[26] "If we are to build a democratic society in Canada," Joseph W. Noseworthy (CCF) would later advise, "then we can ill afford to shut out from our country immigrants purely on the basis of their colour, creed or race" (15 February 1955, 1171). Indeed, Walter G. Dinsdale (PC) argued, in addressing the supposed superiority of one race over another, "these ideas are tending to disappear under the pressure of circumstances as we are forced to rub shoulders more closely with the representatives of the various nations of the world" (26 June 1954, 6812).

Many Liberal Nationalists were not prepared to back down, however. Blackmore suggested that an expansionist agenda was being fostered "to satisfy certain pressure groups working for certain ulterior objectives, regardless of whether those objectives will contribute to the greater prosperity, unity and happiness of Canada" (11 February 1947, 341). Pierre Gauthier (L) argued against "the mass immigration advocated by some people interested in the setting up of powerful associations whose purpose is to promote extensive migrations" (2 May 1947, 2728). Liberal Nationalists also feared the potential influence of the United Nations. Blackmore warned that "the whole charter of the united nations [sic] has been worded in a dangerously vague and general way, so that almost any expression in the charter is susceptible of several interpretations which can be made by interested parties who may wish to accomplish their own private ends" (11 February 1947, 344). Some MPs could not understand how they could be accused of racism for wanting to ensure that Canada remained British and French. "I actually believe," Frederick D. Shaw (SC) complained, "that some in this country are using the expression 'racial discrimination' indiscreetly and indiscriminately ... and are deliberately creating difficulties among the people in their relationship one with the other" (2 May 1947, 2711).

Indeed, Liberal Nationalists denied that their policies were discriminatory. For example, when Alistair Stewart criticized "the wretched discriminatory basis which is contained in the regulations of the immigration branch" that divided the world into preferred and non-preferred countries (4 February 1947, 114), citing in particular its negative effects on Polish and Ukrainian immigrants, Glen denied that any group was singled out: "Until I heard the hon. member speak last night I did not know that there was any discrimination against either Ukrainians or Poles ... and when I inquired of the officers of the department they assured me that there is no such discrimination" (5 February 1947, 151). For Glen, a policy that treated a broad category of people, such as Eastern Europeans or the Chinese, differently from the British simply reflected the encouragement of the immigration of those deemed to be most likely to assimilate. In this vein, Senator Thomas Crerar noted that he had "no hesitation in saying that I am opposed to [Oriental immigration], but I want my opposition to be on a basis that will not offend countries like India, China, and – when she regains her sovereignty – Japan" (9 May 1947, 341).

This attitude was carried for quite some time by successive ministers responsible for immigration. In 1950, Walter Harris (L) argued that no discrimination was practised against the Chinese because they were "covered by the same P. C. as other Asiatic peoples" (15 June 1950, 3694). Jack Pickersgill (L) said in the mid-1950s that he did "not understand there is any real difference between the words selection and discrimination" (17

February 1955, 1248), and that the dissimilar criteria established for regions of the world were based on administrative and not ethnoracial considerations (8 August 1956, 7205-6).[27] He also declared that the issue of low levels of immigration from Asia was not a question of discrimination but sovereignty. In the 1960s, Ellen Fairclough (PC) would deny that there was racial discrimination in her government's immigration policies, just before she sought to take credit for introducing changes to reduce it.

Beyond Parliament, members of the Chinese community openly attacked PC 2115, which, representatives of the Committee for the Repeal of the Chinese Immigration Act told the Senate Standing Committee, "subjected the Chinese in Canada to discrimination and the status of an inferior people under Canadian immigration law" (Canada 1948, No. 4, 96).[28] This transgressed the principles of equality and freedom at the heart of a liberal-democratic state: "We must treat all races alike or frankly admit that though we preach democracy, where our immigration laws are concerned, we do not practise it" (ibid.). Moreover, it contradicted the commitments that Canada had made in supporting the UN Charter. Their presentation convinced the committee, which recommended that PC 2115 be scrapped. Around the same time, the Vancouver Khalsa Diwan Society petitioned the minister against continued discrimination, similarly arguing that it went against the UN Charter (Buchignani et al. 1985, 104). It would be some years, however, before officials began to admit that Canadian policies were discriminatory, and PC 2115 remained in force until broader regulatory changes were enacted in 1956. As a result, although the number of "Asian" immigrants rose somewhat after the war, Canadian policy remained fairly restrictive for such migrants until the late 1960s.

Responding to Refugees in Europe (1945-49)

After the war, few questioned the conclusion drawn by E.B. McKay (CCF) that "the world is faced with the problem of finding homes for refugees created as a result of militarism and anti-race prejudice run wild" (2 May 1947, 2732), but not many were prepared to respond with a refugee policy based on non-discrimination. For some MPs, Canada had done too little both before and during the war to help refugees, particularly European Jews. "Thousands of persons who have sought sanctuary in Canada over the past fifteen years are today dead because that sanctuary was not granted," lamented Thatcher (11 February 1947, 315). In the Senate, Roebuck recounted Canada's weak record during the war (4 April 1946, 105), concluding that the country had not learned the lesson evident in British history as to the positive contribution that refugees could make to the economic development of receiving countries. After the war, however, few wanted to recognize the country's poor record. Even Roebuck seemed at pains to ensure that representatives of the Canadian Jewish Congress declare that anti-Semitism had played no part in Canada's policies with respect to Jewish refugees, although they clearly knew otherwise (see Canada 1947, No. 6, 156).

Indeed, when Saul Hayes and Louis Rosenberg appeared before the Senate Standing Committee in 1946, they argued that "our dominion has not done its humane duty to the persecuted Jewish people during their worst time even within the limits of the written immigration law" (Canada 1946, No. 6, 171).[29] To prevent this from happening again, they called for immigration laws and policies free of racial and religious discrimination,[30] and advocated against the continuous journey rule, underlining that "very large numbers of refugees by the very fact that they are displaced persons cannot come from their country of origin" (ibid., 175). They also suggested that the focus of immigration move beyond agriculturalists and that a policy of assisted passage be instituted to help those who, having lost everything during the war, could not afford to travel. More generally, they reiterated the oft-made point that "transportation is not the key that is failing to unlock the door" but rather the lack of government initiative to formulate an immigration policy to address the postwar situation in Canada and Europe (ibid., 182).

The committee also heard from the CNCR. On behalf of the group, Senator Wilson stressed that by supporting a more expansionist approach, Canadians "might show our sympathy and support of democratic principles and aid those who were suffering for their religion, their political faith or their race" (Canada 1946, No. 9, 227). Bernard Sandwell emphasized that Canada's refugee policies needed a distinct statutory foundation that struck a balance between national security and the nation's responsibilities towards the persecuted:

> The obligation to grant sanctuary is not, and never was, unlimited. The nation has the right to protect itself against excessive influx of population, against disease, against ethical and political ideologies hostile to its own. But the obligation to grant sanctuary still exists, the need for sanctuary is greater than ever before in history, and the nation which ignores this obligation will suffer as all nations ultimately do which ignore the fundamental moral obligation, the debt which man and nations owe to the human being at their gates simply because he is a human being. (Ibid., 239)

It was precisely because Canada was a country of immigration, he maintained, that it had a special obligation to take a leadership role in resettling the refugees of Europe.[31]

The CNCR recommended that Canada move quickly to place immigration officials in Europe (especially in the refugee camps), expand the grounds for admission by including a wider range of family relationships and even people without family in Canada, and notify refugees that they would be admitted once shipping became available. Moreover, Canadian law should be changed to include

> special provisions whereby persons falling under the definition of "refugee" as established by the International Refugee Organization of the United Nations shall be exempted from the ordinary restrictions on immigration into Canada, and shall be subject only to whatever special restrictions may be considered by Parliament to be necessary and justifiable in face of the moral claim of the refugees to the right of sanctuary. (Ibid., 240)

As an indication of the expanding scope of Liberal Internationalism, A.R. Mosher of the Canadian Congress of Labour argued that "the admission of refugees, though it has, of course, economic aspects, is primarily a humanitarian question. Canada is under an obligation to humanity to admit her due share of refugees even if it costs her something. It may actually bring her important economic benefits" (Canada 1946, No. 8, 208).[32]

The Senate provided only modest support for refugee resettlement, recommending the admission of refugees "who are bona fide immigrants, and thus intend to make Canada their permanent home" (Canada 1946, No. 11, 314), but a more humanitarian outlook was apparent in the House. In their replies to the 1945 Speech from the Throne, both Frederick S. Zaplinty (CCF) and Anthony Hlynka (SC) called on the government to give special humanitarian consideration to European refugees (11 September 1945, 80; 24 September 1945, 385-87). In 1946, Hlynka raised "the long-established practice of international law under which protection and asylum have always been extended to refugees in the past" (25 March 1946, 224).[33] Such a commitment was, Thatcher suggested, a question of meeting "the interests of justice and humanity" (3 April 1946, 525). Indeed, "a readiness to help out people who have become political or religious refugees" was, Zaplinty said, an essential part of Canada's British heritage (28 March 1946, 352). Croll tied assisting refugees to the national interest, declaring that they would strengthen Canada: "We shall find that they are among our most loyal and zealous citizens, remembering that they came from lands of misery and oppression" (3 April 1946, 529).[34]

Senators heard repeatedly that Canada was not living up to its obligations in this respect, and that culpability lay with the government. A former Canadian UN refugee worker, Ian MacKay, reflected that Canadians "ought to be thoroughly ashamed of ourselves in this great dominion of ours. We like to call ourselves great, but we forget that with greatness goes responsibility" (Canada 1947, No. 3, 77). Restrictionism was becoming more difficult to maintain, however, as Western states began to question repatriation behind the Iron Curtain. Indeed, arguing against forced repatriation meant that Canada had to establish a new refugee policy, Constance Hayward of the CNCR pointed out: "I do not see how we could take any other stand and be consistent with our democracy ... these people are then non-repatriable if they refuse to go back; and in taking that stand we acknowledge the responsibility to assist them in finding other homes, places of resettlement" (Canada 1947, No. 10, 263). Officials still maintained, however, that the best course was to integrate refugees into a revived European economy (Dirks 1977, 121).

Since there was no distinction in Canadian law between immigrants and refugees, the latter were initially subject to the same restrictions imposed upon the former. "Time and again," Thatcher complained to the House, "the government has expressed concern about refugees and displaced persons in Europe. Yet the words of the cabinet ministers and the actions of the immigration branch are strangely contradictory" (11 February 1947, 315). This discrepancy led Leslie A. Mutch (L) to conclude that "the department has been instinctively inclined to feel that its mission was to exclude those who sought to come here," a problem so ingrained that it would require the department "to be born again" (5 May 1947, 2750). Even if the government could not resettle the refugees for logistical reasons, some suggested, it could provide visas for their admission and assurances to relatives in Canada in anticipation that this difficulty would be overcome, and then act swiftly when the time came.

Some MPs felt, however, that Canada should not be too generous in resettling refugees. "I am convinced that among them must be many who have no appreciation whatsoever of what democracy means," warned Frederick Shaw (2 May 1947, 2711). "The fact that a man or woman is a refugee," Jean-François Pouliot (L) maintained, "is not a qualification for admittance to Canada; not at all" (5 May 1947, 2761). Those who opposed large-scale resettlement programs had difficulty addressing the powerful moral arguments raised, however. For example, no one challenged Hlynka, who, upon returning from Europe, reminded MPs that "there are in those camps persons who have written numbers of books and persons who can make the most remarkable things out of practically nothing. If any of us found ourselves in a camp, what could we do? What would our talents be?" (2 May 1947, 2736). It was only in April 1947, however, that the first refugees from the camps began to arrive in Canada.

Responding to Asylum Seekers from Europe (1947-50)

Besides overseas refugees, the issue of asylum seekers arose in surprising ways that could not be ignored after the war, although it could be and was contained. It is important to study the government's response not only because it produced a rights-restrictive approach consistent with Liberal Nationalism but because it reveals the persistence of difficulties that decision makers have in balancing control and rights in handling claims for protection against persecution.

After the war, the issue of asylum seekers first arose in the context of Nazi war criminals and collaborators who had entered the country,[35] especially the high-profile case of Count Jacques de Bernonville, who had been a member of the Vichy government in France and who had subsequently been found guilty in absentia of war crimes. On the run from French authorities, de Bernonville arrived illegally in Canada via the United States in late 1946 and lived quietly in Quebec as Jacques Benoit (Lavertu 1995). A chance encounter with a former member of the French Resistance led de Bernonville to seek legal status for himself and his family in early 1948. Canadian officials instead ruled that he was inadmissible and ordered him deported; subsequently, he and his family were detained. Friends of de Bernonville, particularly those who formed the Committee for the Defence of French Refugees, helped him challenge the deportation order before a Quebec Superior Court judge, who ruled in early 1949 that the move against de Bernonville was illegal. In response, the government constituted another board of inquiry and in early 1950 de Bernonville was again ordered deported. After continued wrangling between his supporters and the government, de Bernonville finally left Canada for Brazil in 1951.

The Liberals, fearing that the issue might mobilize Quebec nationalists, proceeded cautiously, while Alistair Stewart kept the question on the political agenda. Replying to the 1949 Speech from the Throne, he alleged that people had been admitted to Canada who had "willingly supported nazism to the detriment of the allied [sic] cause" (22 February 1949, 791). He contrasted the case of de Bernonville with that of seven Jews who had recently been ordered deported for having entered the country illegally. In refusing to allow the latter to stay, Stewart recounted, the minister had stated that he did not want to set a precedent by sanctioning illegal entries. If that was the case, then why was the government moving so slowly in deporting Nazi supporters like de Bernonville?[36] The new Minister of Mines and Resources, Colin Gibson, responded vaguely that the government "had decided that some of the men who had been able to satisfy the authorities would be permitted to remain in the country, and those who had not would be deported (9 December 1949, 3039). He would not (for reasons of confidentiality) discuss the information used to make these decisions or reveal how many had been deported.

On the other side, a few Quebec MPs (including some Liberals) took a vocal stand against de Bernonville's deportation. Frédéric Dorion, who was also de Bernonville's solicitor, portrayed the issue as one of ethnicity and religion: "Why make it a crime for a French Catholic to seek refuge in this country," he asked, "when no one dares to say a word about the Jews who are in the same situation" (24 February 1949, 877). Dorion made reference to Article 14.1 of the UDHR, which affirms that "everyone has the right to seek and to enjoy in other countries asylum from persecution," and claimed that, "contending as I do that he is a political refugee, I say to the government that it is their duty to give to him shelter in our country because the right of asylum is a sacred right which has always been recognized by all civilized countries of the world" (ibid., 881).[37] Bona Arsenault (L) recalled that Canada had provided sanctuary to a former president of Cuba, Gerardo Machado, as well as an unspecified ousted president of a nation in the West Indies (2 March 1950, 399).[38] It is likely that his support for de Bernonville's cause led Arsenault to introduce a Private Member's Bill to have Canada become a signatory to the 1951 Refugee Convention.[39]

The asylum seeker issue also arose with the arrival of "boat people" on the Atlantic coast between 1947 and 1950. At the end of the war, tens of thousands from the Baltic region, including Estonians, Latvians, and Lithuanians, remained in Sweden, having fled their homelands in the face of German and Soviet aggression (Aun 1985, 25-28). The refugees felt insecure in Sweden because its government had recognized the Soviet occupation of their homelands in 1940, the Soviet Union was pressuring Sweden to repatriate them, and Sweden was outside the non-repatriation consensus among Western states as it had not joined the International Refugee Organization (the precursor to the Office of United Nations High Commissioner for Refugees). In response, many refugees bought and provisioned some forty-six boats and set out for the Americas and Britain. Two of the vessels reportedly sank, two disappeared, and ten arrived in Canada.

The first to arrive in North America landed in the United States in mid-1947, carrying twenty-four people. The Americans would not let the asylum seekers remain but granted them time to find somewhere else to resettle. At the behest of the Canadian Lutheran World Relief organization, Ottawa became involved and the asylum seekers were soon allowed to land (authorized by Order-in-Council) to avoid any adverse "political fallout" (Margolian 2000, 128). As support for Baltic immigration in Canada grew among some ethnic organizations and the railway companies, the government sent officials to Sweden in mid-1948 to investigate resettlement possibilities. Finding Swedish authorities amenable but concerned lest the Soviet Union object, Canada agreed to send a screening team disguised as diplomatic staff. By September 1948, the details had been worked out and approved by Cabinet but little progress had been made. As a result, only 115 visas had been approved by February 1949.[40]

Meanwhile, Baltic refugees continued to set out in boats, and by late 1949 some 1,000 asylum seekers had reached Canada's shores. They were inadmissible under the 1910 *Immigration Act,* but the government decided to land them by order-in-council following an inland screening. In order to regain control, officials recommended that Canada prosecute those who piloted the ships and even send back some asylum seekers as a deterrent to others (ibid., 130-31). The government accepted the first recommendation but rejected the second. All told, along with several hundred others who were admitted after landing in the United States, 1,593 Baltic "boat people" arrived in Canada between 1948 and 1950, with only 12 being rejected and deported. This process was facilitated by the sponsorship offered by the Lutheran Church of Canada, which helped to defray the financial costs of resettlement, and the generally positive reputation that Baltic immigrants had in Canada.

The de Bernonville and Baltic "boat people" cases possess some notable features. First, they confirm that Canadian border control policy after the war remained predominantly reactive. Thus, once it learned how de Bernonville (and others) had entered the country – using a visa for the United States to gain entry to Canada as a tourist – the government tightened the rules governing admissions (ibid., 68). As for the Baltic asylum seekers, by 1949 the government was seeking to deter additional refugees from setting out for Canada. Although Canada had long resisted establishing mandatory overseas screening procedures, this quickly became the norm after the war. Second, the government learned that the arrival of asylum seekers, either as individuals or in groups, often raised difficult political questions. In both cases, it worried that its response would provoke negative political reactions within the country. Thus, rather than creating a more principled framework for responding to asylum seekers, it reacted in an ad hoc manner based on the perceived political imperatives of the moment. Finally, the cases again brought the question of control to the fore – how were the demands of control and the rights (or at least humanitarian needs) of non-citizens to be combined? Although the government, Croll noted, had "placed humanity above regulations" for the Baltic asylum seekers (9 December 1949, 3036), would it be willing to do so for those still in camps in Europe? Would it open its doors to other asylum seekers? While the answer to the former would be a contingent "yes," the answer to the latter was a decided "no." This position was consistent with Liberal Nationalism's inward-looking appreciation of the national interest.

Repeat Restrictionism (1947-52)

During the early postwar period, a resurgent Liberal Internationalism was reflected to a degree in two policy decisions: the repeal of the 1923 *Chinese Immigration Act* and the admission of thousands of displaced persons and others (including Baltic asylum seekers) from Europe. These initiatives were still consistent with Liberal Nationalism, however. Chinese immigration remained limited by PC 2115 and European immigrants were selected as much for Canada's labour needs as on the basis of the humanitarian claims of non-citizens. Even as the breadth, precision, and strength of the Liberal

Internationalist critique continued to grow, the continued dominance of Liberal Nationalism was demonstrated by a number of important policy and legislative decisions through the early 1950s, including Canada's decision not to sign the 1951 Refugee Convention, the establishment of a new Immigration Department in 1951, and the passage of a new *Immigration Act* in 1952.

The 1951 Convention Relating to the Status of Refugees (1949-51)

The traditional tale told in the literature is that Canada did not sign the 1951 Refugee Convention until 1969 because of concerns that this might prevent the deportation of bona fide refugees who were perceived to threaten national security (Dirks 1977, 180; Kelley and Trebilcock 1998, 339; Whitaker 1987, 54). While not an inaccurate historical reading, it does not sufficiently identify the sources of Canada's unwillingness. Indeed, Cabinet and External Affairs documents indicate that security was but one aspect of a much broader concern – namely, that non-citizens might gain rights in Canada that could be used to challenge government border control policy. Immigration officials had long ago recognized the utility of limiting the rights of foreigners and had, in the early part of the century, built an extensive and effective system of control based on this idea. The decision not to sign the Refugee Convention was consistent with this outlook.

Initially, the Mackenzie King government supported the development of a draft convention on refugees. Although it would continue seeking to avoid equal burden sharing among Western states, Canada increasingly acknowledged that refugees constituted an international problem requiring a coordinated international effort. In August 1946, Glen reported to the House that Canada would be asked to take in refugees after a series of discussions on the situation in Europe at the United Nations (27 August 1946, 5496). Canadian representatives subsequently became very active in the various agencies established to address the needs of European refugees, especially with respect to the drafting of the Refugee Convention.

By 1949, it was clear that a permanent agency was needed to deal with the ongoing refugee problem in Europe, where hundreds of thousands still required resettlement, and elsewhere, as major refugee populations resulted from the partition of India and Pakistan as well as the creation of the state of Israel. Since the International Refugee Organization had been created as a temporary measure, it was decided to establish a High Commissioner for Refugees, a semi-autonomous body with a mandate to assist refugees, which was accomplished by 1950. Meanwhile, work began on a convention to govern refugee/state relations.

It was a Canadian, Leslie Chance, who served as chair of the ad hoc committee of the UN Economic and Social Council (ECOSOC) that drafted the document in 1950, and Cabinet instructed its representatives at the ECOSOC to declare Canada's general approval of the text the same year. As the process edged towards completion in July 1951, when states would be asked to indicate their willingness to become parties to a convention at a Conference of Plenipotentiaries, External Affairs Secretary of State Lester B. Pearson advised Cabinet in a 14 June memorandum that, with a minor adjustment to account for the country's federal system and a clarification concerning the grounds on which a refugee might be deported, Canada should add its signature (Canada 1996, 425-26). On 26 June, however, Minister of Citizenship and Immigration Walter Harris informed Cabinet that he had not yet read the draft convention and requested time to do so before the government's position was determined (ibid., 428).

Three days later, Harris detailed a number of concerns with respect to Articles 26, 27, and 28, which altogether "prescribed certain automatic rights which were to be granted to refugees, legally or illegally admitted, and also prohibited the expulsion to territories where the life or freedom of refugees was threatened on grounds of race, religion, nationality or political opinion" (ibid., 429). To consider these points more fully, Cabinet agreed to postpone its decision, and Pearson instructed Chance that he "should not give any indication that Canada will sign the Convention" (ibid., 430). Chance took his name out of the running to chair the final meeting and wrote Pearson of his hopes that he might soon be instructed to sign subject to amendment or reservation. "Any turning back on our part now," he cautioned, "might create [a] very unhappy situation. We have been regarded throughout as taking [a] forward attitude, somewhat in contrast to that of the United States" (ibid.).

While Chance tried to explain Canada's new hesitancy to his counterparts in Europe, objections around the Cabinet table solidified. Harris worried that the convention might result in non-citizens gaining rights against the Canadian state: "As it stood, the Convention was between countries that were parties and did not confer any rights on individuals. There would, however, almost certainly be a general feeling that it did confer individual rights or, alternatively, that legislation should be passed giving parallel individual rights under domestic law" (ibid., 433). The Prime Minister was concerned that it might prevent the deportation of communists.[41] There were fears, then, that adding Canada's signature would not only have an immediate effect on state practice but also fundamentally alter the legal relationship between the state and non-citizens within the country. After much debate, Cabinet agreed that Chance should communicate Canada's objections but on no account take any initiative to negotiate changes. "I judge [the] attitude of Cabinet to be that [the] convention is not particularly important from the Canadian standpoint," Chance wrote Pearson. "They might even prefer not to become party to any convention of this nature" (ibid., 436). As a result, Canada was not among the twelve states that signed the final text on 28 July 1951.

In his final report to Ottawa on the Conference of Plenipotentiaries, Chance stressed his embarrassment when after more than a year and a half of expressing Canada's support for – indeed, embodying its leadership concerning – the convention, he suddenly had to withdraw, for all intents and purposes, from discussions. He detailed various ways in which most of Cabinet's stated concerns had been addressed during the course of the conference; in other areas, he stressed the difficulty in reaching a satisfactory outcome when he could not be an active participant. He concluded by recommending that an interdepartmental committee be formed among the relevant ministries to study the document and report to Cabinet on the advisability of attaching Canada's signature.

Security concerns clearly constituted an important stumbling block to Canada's signing of the convention. In particular, de Bernonville and the case of four communists from the United States who were thought to be in the country were raised in Cabinet. It is important, however, to identify the nature of this concern more precisely. Certainly, the Cold War context of the day was important. Since the Igor Gouzenko affair in 1946, there had been a heightened fear of the presence of communists in Canada in general and foreign communists in particular (Whitaker and Marcuse 1994). With the advent of the Korean War and the continued deterioration of relations between Canada and the Soviet Union, such concerns only grew (Bothwell 1998). Indeed, throughout this period the ability of Canada to screen non-citizens on security grounds was a prominent issue and a core feature of Canadian immigrant selection policies overseas.[42]

This was, however, but one aspect of a more specific concern that as a result of signing the convention the government might not be able to limit the rights-based claims that non-citizens could make against the state. In writing to Chance, Pearson relayed Cabinet's fear that a refugee might gain "the right to be represented in the hearing of his appeal against deportation" (Canada 1996, 435). In particular, there was concern that the convention would "grant rights to communists or to other persons who believe in the destruction of fundamental human rights and freedoms" (ibid., 432). This would challenge the Liberal Nationalist approach that had dominated policy thinking for almost half a century.

External Affairs returned several times to the question of the 1951 Refugee Convention. In 1957, it was stonewalled by immigration officials, who replied that the minister "had many other urgent problems to attend to and as the possibility of Canada's accession to the 1951 Convention was not necessarily urgent, consideration so far of this matter has been deferred" (quoted in Dirks 1977, 181). In 1960, immigration officials concluded that the convention was not compatible with Canadian immigration law. It was only after the entire organization of the department and its policies were reviewed in a 1966 white paper that the issue was again studied, and not until 1969 that Canada added its signature. By then, the country had gone through almost two decades of serious debate over the rights of non-citizens following the passage of the 1952 *Immigration Act*.

The Department of Citizenship and Immigration (1949-52)

Since 1946, many had proposed that responsibility for immigration be removed from the sprawling Department of Mines and Resources and given its own department and minister. In 1949, Prime Minister Louis St. Laurent introduced legislation to create a new Department of Citizenship and Immigration. That its establishment would not lead to any substantial reorientation of Canadian policy was confirmed by Walter Harris, its inaugural minister. The aim of the department, he said, paraphrasing Mackenzie King's 1947 statement, was "to promote an increase in the population of Canada of carefully selected, readily assimilable immigrants within the absorptive capacity of the country" (21 April 1950, 1763). In doing so, he assured Canadians, "the basic races of Canada [would remain] French and Anglo-Saxon" (ibid.).[43]

This was reflected in the regulations governing admissions published in 1950 (PC 2856), "prohibiting the landing in Canada of immigrants of all classes and occupations" except for certain specified categories. Aside from British subjects and Irish citizens coming directly from the United Kingdom, Ireland, Australia, New Zealand, South Africa, and the United States, only American and French citizens were to be admitted, provided they had sufficient funds. Otherwise, a person had to satisfy the minister that

> he is (a) a suitable immigrant having regard to the climatic, social, educational, industrial, labour, or other conditions or requirements of Canada; and (b) is not undesirable owing to peculiar customs, habits, modes of life, methods of holding property, or because of his probable inability to become readily adapted and integrated into the life of a Canadian community and to assume the duties of Canadian citizenship within a reasonable time after his entry.

Asian immigrants were still assessed under PC 2115, which was amended in 1951 to allow those applying to have their wife, husband, or unmarried children under the age of twenty-one admitted to Canada. Faced with this discriminatory approach, MPs from all parties pushed for change. Leon D. Crestohl (L) declared that "we are rapidly coming to the realization that an effective immigration policy is a *sine qua non* for the industrial, commercial and defensive future of our country. Implementing it satisfactorily will make of Canada that great democracy that it is destined to be in the future" (17 April 1951, 2128). The problem, opined David Croll, was that on this file the government "hesitates, falters and stumbles. When it speaks now on immigration it has a hollow sound because its policy at present time is an echo of the past" (13 June 1950, 3585). The postwar situation demanded a new and proactive approach to immigration, he said.

In January 1951, the government announced that it had reached agreements with India, Pakistan, and Ceylon to allow 150, 100, and 50 immigrants, respectively, to resettle in Canada on an annual basis (on top of those allowed under PC 2115). In the postwar context of international human rights and decolonization, however, it was hard to justify such discrimination, and Canada's policies were challenged on the international stage, especially by Indian officials (see Canada 1980, 1082). The Canadian government had great difficulty responding to charges of discrimination because very little had changed in its overall approach since the beginning of the century, when its "interest in India was first aroused by the desire to keep Indians out of Canada" (Eayrs 1972, 226). At the 1945 British Commonwealth Relations Conference, Indian delegates requested that Canada enter into a bilateral agreement to remove any discrimination (ibid., 242). By 1948, John D. Kearney, Canada's first High Commissioner in India, had negotiated an informal arrangement with Indian officials to establish an annual quota of 100 immigrants, all of whom would be hand-picked by the Indian government to ensure that they "would be people of education and means, and constitute a valuable though unofficial group of ambassadors for India in Canada" (quoted in ibid.). The quota system dampened Indian complaints, but the government had more difficulty escaping criticism in Parliament.

"As long as we continue to exercise any discrimination against persons of origins within other commonwealth countries so long shall we be endangering that association," M.J. Coldwell cautioned, as this fostered antagonisms between peoples and undermined political cooperation (4 July 1952, 4261). Moreover, he reasoned, in the Cold War context the need for established democracies to lead by example was even more important: "We are living in a world today when we are on trial as democratic countries and our opponents in their propaganda use every possible means to show that we are giving lip service to freedom, equality and democracy but that we are not fulfilling our obligations in those respects within the borders of our own countries" (ibid.). If developing countries were not treated on the basis of equality, they might fall into the Soviet sphere of influence. E. Davie Fulton (PC) complained that many Asian immigrants

came here in some cases up to 30 or 40 years ago. Many of them were born here, have been Canadian citizens for all that length of time, yet they cannot bring in their brothers, cousins, or nephews except in extremely limited circumstances ... whereas others who have come to Canada in the last five years ... have acquired Canadian citizenship and are allowed to bring in their relatives as of right. (23 April 1953, 4324)[44]

Such discrimination, he felt, did not reflect well on Canada.

The 1952 Immigration Act

The need to replace the 1910 *Immigration Act* had been identified as early as the 1946 Senate committee hearings, and the government's decision to introduce *An Act respecting Immigration* in 1952 was warmly welcomed, even if several provisions sparked considerably less enthusiasm. This "poor and illiberal piece of legislation" (Hawkins 1972, 118) concentrated almost exclusively on keeping people out, reflecting the continued commitment to restrictionism among decision makers. "There would seem to be words in the bill before us which suggest to me that the concept of exclusion still lingers in the minds of those in charge of the department," Alistair Stewart observed in the House (10 June 1952, 3079). The law introduced changes to deportation and the discretionary powers of immigration officials that engendered sharp debates over the rights of non-citizens and mobilized members of the legal community in particular to be more active in challenging state actions in this policy area.

The restrictive purpose of the bill was evident in a number of ways. More emphasis was placed on distinguishing who had a right to enter (Canadian citizens and those with Canadian domicile) and who did not. The bill identified the circumstances under which people might be prohibited from entering, removed after having entered, or refused re-entry. When officials were unsure, cases were to be forwarded to a Special Inquiry Officer (SIO), who was armed with a wide range of "dreadful powers" (Corbett 1957, 74) to "inquire into and determine whether any person shall be allowed to come into Canada or to remain in Canada or shall be deported" (Section 11.3). Immigrants could be detained at the pleasure of an SIO (Section 18), the minister or the deputy minister (Section 15). The government was granted considerable discretion to make regulations to govern entry under a wide range of circumstances (Section 61.g), such as a person's:

(i)　nationality, citizenship, ethnic group, occupation, class or geographical area of origin,

(ii)　peculiar customs, habits, modes of life or methods of holding property,

(iii)　unsuitability having regard to the climatic, economic, social, industrial, educational, labour, health or other conditions or requirements existing temporarily or otherwise, in Canada or in the area or country from or through which such persons come to Canada, or

(iv) probable inability to become readily assimilated or to assume the duties and responsibilities of Canadian citizenship within a reasonable time after their admission.

One of the few non-restrictive features involved the creation of the Minister's Permit, whereby individuals could be admitted despite being inadmissible (Section 8). The minister could also land prospective immigrants under certain circumstances (Section 9). Although nominally expansionist, these features increased the amount of discretion exercised by the government, and thus offered little protection against continued ethnoracial discrimination or the denial of due process.

The bill was subjected to considerable scrutiny by a Special Committee of the House of Commons. Much debate revolved around the government's expanded powers to detain and deport immigrants, and the limited recourse that individuals would have to appeal adverse decisions. Deportations had been a central control technique since the beginning of the twentieth century, and this continued as the government adapted immigration policies to the new Cold War climate.[45] One of the main purposes behind efforts to "modernize" immigration law, Harris observed, was to speed up the process "so that we will not have as much delay in the transactions with persons who are either ordered deported or allowed to land" (2 June 1952, 2800). This would be achieved by spelling out in greater detail the deportation process and continuing to limit judicial oversight of control.

MPs raised concerns over both the grounds on which people could be deported and the fairness of the process. While no one disagreed with the principle of ensuring administrative efficiency, some did not want to see the already limited rights of non-citizens further reduced. "Anything that will contribute to expeditious handling of these appeals is naturally desirable," Donald M. Fleming (PC) argued, "provided that nothing is done to subtract anything from the rights of those concerned" (10 June 1952, 3078). Others worried that those who had contracted a disease while being out of the country temporarily could subsequently be refused admission, even after having lived in Canada for several years. Such a person, E. Davie Fulton argued, "showed all the prospects of becoming a good and valuable citizen" and therefore it was against the country's best interests to have them deported (Canada 1952, No. 1, 38). MPs also complained that an immigrant could be deported for falling ill in Canada after having already been admitted by immigration officials with a clean bill of health. In these and other cases, they argued, Canada was neglecting its responsibilities towards those who had been admitted and who had come in good faith.

For Harris, however, a line had to be drawn between the rights of the state and those of non-citizens. To provide immigrants with a full range of enforceable appeal rights "has never been part of the immigration law of Canada," he said, and would be "contrary to all the concepts up to the present time" (ibid., 76). Furthermore,

> if you attempt to place in the hands of the courts decisions about deporta-
> tion, you will ultimately obtain a rigidity in your law and precedent ... It is
> a matter of opinion, I suppose, as to how many rights a landed immigrant
> acquires on the first day, or the second day or the third day after landing;
> generally the Act says that he does not acquire many of these rights until
> he is here five years. That may be wrong in principle, but that is the principle
> on which the Act is based, and it is the basis on which most immigration
> Acts are written. (Ibid., 112, 38)

Until an immigrant had gained domicile by remaining within the country for five years, he stated, "there is no right in any non-Canadian to come to Canada" (ibid., 62). In his view, not only could the state prevent specific categories of people from entering but it could also remove people years after they had legally arrived if they had become prohibited persons. Because Harris held this to be a fundamental state prerogative, he maintained that such immigrants had no right to test before the courts the fairness or justice with which the state had administered the law.

To achieve this end, the government proposed in Section 39 to continue to limit the jurisdiction of the courts.[46] Except in certain cases where people had been refused entry on medical grounds or had been convicted under the 1929 *Opium and Narcotic Drug Act,* all persons ordered deported could appeal an SIO decision only to the minister, who had complete discretion in rendering a final decision. Originally, those arriving at the border were granted no right to appeal the decision of an immigration official who had turned them away on the grounds that they were unable to be examined due to incoherence. David Croll protested:

> I think in every conceivable circumstance a man must have the right to
> appeal under the Immigration Act ... I object to these words "no appeal." I
> think they are the most unliberal words I can think of and I do not think
> they become us. It is hard for me to swallow that language; it does not previ-
> ously appear in the Act, I have not come across it and I do not recall it in
> any other similar legislation. (Ibid., 64, 65)

While the offending section was ultimately removed, the question of an appeal came in for further scrutiny in the case of those whose applications for landing as immigrants had been rejected. Leon Crestohl argued that "we should allow the man who feels aggrieved by the decision which the minister or the department or the board of inquiry might make, to be permitted to have his day in court; and I think we should work out some machinery to allow a person ordered deported to address himself to the courts" (ibid., 75-76).[47] It also arose in situations in which a board of inquiry (which would henceforth consist of one person rather than three) found someone guilty of subversive activities: they did not have to have been convicted in court and they had no recourse to the courts, only an appeal to the minister. As Donald Fleming put it: "I am completely in sympathy with the idea of dealing rigorously with persons who are engaging in subversive activities, but I want to be very sure that they get the full benefit of our rules of law and of our judicial processes before it is found conclusively that they have engaged in subversive activity, when these serious consequences flow from such a finding" (ibid., 127).

As for refugees, the issue arose only when the government sought to give itself the power to pass regulations "prohibiting or limiting of admission of persons who are nationals or citizens of a country that refuses to readmit any of its nationals or citizens who are ordered deported" (Section 61.f). Crestohl suggested that victims of political persecution should be exempted but Harris considered this unnecessary as the section merely empowered the government to create regulations and did not necessarily define their content (Canada 1952, No. 1, 156-57). The admission of refugees continued, therefore, to be governed by criteria established for immigrants. This was made clear in a subsequent discussion on the admission of East German refugees, when Harris informed the House that "if the refugees can meet the requirements of the Immigration Act and our regulations, then they may be admitted to Canada in due course" (6 March 1953, 2685).

Although the core objective behind the 1952 *Immigration Act* was to increase control, one of its major results was to hamper it instead by complicating the administration of immigration policy in Canada. The broad discretionary powers granted the minister resulted in officials being overwhelmed by requests for exceptions to be made in particular cases. In 1955, Jack Pickersgill claimed that he spent about 90 percent of his time on questions of ministerial discretion (Canada 1955, 49). Until the Immigration Appeal Boards were given greater authority in 1967, this was a constant complaint of successive immigration ministers. It was widely recognized that their ability to pursue reforms in the system was undermined by their need to spend so much time on individual cases. Another significant effect of the law was that it provided a ready target for Liberal Internationalists in their efforts to bring the country's immigration policies more into line with certain basic principles of liberal-democratic governance as well as the evolving language of international human rights.

Indeed, the rights-restrictive approach embedded in the 1952 *Immigration Act* caused considerable discontent among many non-state actors involved in this policy area, especially within the legal profession. MPs on both sides of the House also became frustrated with constantly being called upon to tackle the immigration bureaucracy on behalf of non-citizens and their relatives in Canada. This bred a more knowledgeable set of critics both inside and outside the House (Hawkins 1972, 106-7). Because the legislation was, in the words of a senior immigration official, "extremely restrictive and control-oriented" (Manion 1993, 53),[48] it offended core principles of fundamental justice in a liberal democracy such as Canada. As Corbett (1957, 66) wrote in the mid-1950s:

> The administration of immigration policy contains a potential danger in that officials with power to keep immigrants out of the country may be tempted to lord it over the applicants who come before them. It becomes important to finds means to suppress autocratic tendencies and maintain humility and civility at all levels in the immigration service.

This would require immigration ministers and officials alike to move away from the Liberal Nationalist perspective that considered due process and equality concerns to be subservient to the state's sovereign right to control its borders.

Conclusion

At a rhetorical level, and in some instances in a practical vein, the Canadian government embraced the new rights-based discourse that emerged after the war, and committed itself to upholding this regime by adding its signature to the Universal Declaration of Human Rights. This, however, did not extend to Canada's approach to control, which continued to be based on the idea that state sovereignty took precedence over the rights of non-citizens. Thus, rather than ensuring that immigration laws and policies more closely reflected the human rights standards that they supported in other forums, the Liberals chose to re-entrench a rights-restrictive approach based on ethnoracial discrimination and an absence of key due process protections.

As before, this gave rise to rights-based politics, but now Liberal Nationalists found themselves much more on the defensive as their long-standing association of state sovereignty with ethnoracial discrimination came into conflict with new international norms and commitments. Their policy preferences continued to prevail, but it was increasingly difficult to justify them in the face of an emboldened Liberal Internationalist critique. Moreover, in providing for ministerial discretion to overcome the injustices that the system was bound to create, the government created long-term administrative problems: cases were forwarded to the minister for ultimate resolution, which interfered with the regular work of the department. Finally, non-citizens – especially Asian migrants – continued to circumvent Canada's restrictive policies. Thus, a rights-restrictive approach continued to open up avenues along which state authority and capacity could be challenged effectively. This became even more prominent as Canada's centenary-year celebrations drew closer.

6
The Return of Liberal Internationalism in Canada (1952-67)

Despite Liberal Nationalism's continued dominance, Liberal Internationalism had become a prominent part of political discourse regarding border control by the 1950s. From this time forward, extensive and serious debates unfolded concerning the grounds on which Canada should allow noncitizens to enter the country and remain within its borders. These important developments have long been overlooked in the Canadian literature on control. For example, Kelley and Trebilcock (1998, 311, 314) argue that there was "a relative absence of controversy over immigration issues" prior to the early 1960s and that "immigration policy rarely attracted serious parliamentary debate." Similarly, Hawkins (1972, 351) states that "one of the most striking facts which emerges from a study of Hansard from 1946 onwards is the infrequency of debates on immigration and the small number of M.P.s who participate in them." As described below, however, the expansion of rights-based discourse and politics during the immediate postwar period continued right through to Canada's centenary year. Moreover, the critiques concerning the discrimination and unfairness embedded in the system led to significant changes in policy and law that constituted a decided shift to a more Liberal Internationalist approach. It is important to understand this history because without it the emergence of a stronger rights-based tradition in Canada – and the transformation of Canadian society that it brought about and reflected – appears more a spontaneous and particular development than one that is deeply rooted in the country's past.

Liberal Internationalist criticisms of the 1952 *Immigration Act* appeared immediately after its enactment and were repeated and expanded time and again. Although successive governments were reluctant to replace the law (which would stand until the passage of the 1976 *Immigration Act*), the need to alter, if not remove, core restrictive features was broadly accepted in Parliament by the early 1960s, albeit not without considerable and sometimes rancorous debate. This process led to a new consensus that largely reflected

Liberal Internationalist concerns, as key restrictive features employed by Canada since the early 1900s were dismantled. By 1967, the government had institutionalized a commitment to formal non-discrimination and expanded due process protections for non-citizens, anchoring a new era in Canadian control policy. Nonetheless, although Liberal Internationalist ideas and policies had come to dominate political discourse, Liberal Nationalist perspectives did not disappear but began to adapt to their more marginal position. By the end of the twentieth century, such perspectives were able to once again challenge Liberal Internationalism, and shift the policies and politics of control anew.

The Liberal Internationalist Advance (1952-63)

Although the Liberal Party would eventually come to present itself as "the party of immigration" in Canada, this claim does not find firm support for much of the country's history covered in this book. For example, between the 1906 *Immigration Act* and its 1952 successor, the Liberals held power for all but about fifteen years, and almost every border control policy initiative that they instituted placed significant limitations on judicial or parliamentary oversight of executive and administrative authority and practice in this area. During the 1950s, the Liberals resisted growing calls for changes to the system to promote due process and equality for non-citizens, staunchly defending the status quo. Instead, it was a Conservative government that initiated a more Liberal Internationalist approach in 1962 when it reduced (but did not eliminate) ethnoracial discrimination in the immigrant selection process and increased (albeit ineffectively) due process protections for those in the immigration process. Five years later, these measures were extended by the Liberals with little controversy.

The Rights of Non-Citizens (1952-56)

The difficulty in defending the Liberal Nationalist approach embedded in the 1952 *Immigration Act* became clear when Joseph Noseworthy (CCF) challenged Citizenship and Immigration Minister Walter Harris's claim that the weather could be used to assess resettlement potential. In correspondence regarding the government's refusal to admit a Canadian citizen's granddaughter from Barbados for a visit, Harris had claimed that

> in the light of experience it would be unrealistic to say that immigrants who have spent the greater part of their life in tropical or sub-tropical countries become readily adapted to the Canadian mode of life which, to no small extent, is determined by climatic conditions. It is a matter of record ... that natives of such countries are more apt to break down in health than immigrants from countries where the climate is more akin to that of Canada.

It is equally true that, generally speaking, persons from tropical or sub-tropical countries find it more difficult to succeed in the highly competitive Canadian economy. (Quoted in 24 April 1953, 4351-52)

When asked to prove that this was "a matter of record," the department could produce no evidence. Noseworthy concluded that officials were "judging the case on the basis of some theory that has probably been laid down by the department of immigration for some time rather than by any actual statistics or records" (ibid., 4352). According to the president of the Brotherhood of Sleeping Car Porters, Stanley G. Grizzle, the letter reflected an opinion that was "illogical, unsound, undemocratic and un-Christian" (quoted in Corbett 1957, 53).[1] Not long thereafter, the admissions regulations were revised and the climatic restriction removed.

Noseworthy's challenge was part of a broader set of rights-based criticisms advanced during this period (see Walker 1997, 274-85). In the early 1950s, the Negro Citizenship Association and the Khalsa Diwan Society protested against regulations that prevented non-white Commonwealth citizens from immigrating to Canada. Their efforts were supported by the CCF, several churches, and many labour organizations. The Toronto Labour Committee for Human Rights (TLC) took a lead role, "posting bonds for jailed deportees, making individual inquiries to officials and to the minister," and helping non-citizens take the government to court (ibid., 275). Notably, the TLC and lawyer Andrew Brewin helped Trinidad-born Harry and Mearl Narine-Singh contest the department's decision to deport them for being of the Asian "race," and the case was heard by the Supreme Court.[2] Officials also came under pressure from other departments as well as both British and Caribbean officials (Schultz 1988). In response, the government introduced minor policy changes without altering its discriminatory approach. For example, a new program was instituted in 1955 to allow a hundred Barbadian and Jamaican women to come as domestic servants each year; this was increased to around three hundred in 1960. As well, more West Indian and African students were admitted to study in Canada.

The Vancouver Chinese Benevolent Association made annual treks to Ottawa to protest continued restrictions on Chinese immigration,[3] while representatives of the Chinese Community Centre (founded in 1945) and other local Chinese organizations in Toronto became leaders in opposing discrimination in the immigration system (Con et al. 1982, Chapters 15 and 16). Jewish organizations took an even more proactive approach, challenging discriminatory legislation before the courts and promoting legal protections for minority groups across the country (Patrias and Frager 2001; Walker 2002). Such efforts were bolstered by the United Nations' focus on the need to protect human rights through legislative means (Walker 2002, 6). This work was often undertaken alongside the Association for Civil Liberties

(created in 1949), whose membership included such Liberal Internationalists as Andrew Brewin, Bernard Sandwell, and David Croll. Some of the
major churches in Canada (such as the Anglican Church and United Church)
also began to take a stronger stand against racial discrimination in Canadian
immigration policies.

It continued to be difficult to challenge the government's rights-restrictive
policies through the courts, however, because of the statutory restriction on
judicial oversight.[4] Even when defeated in the courts, the government was
often able to maintain those policies. For example, after officials refused to
admit Canadian Leong Hung Hing's son, Leong Ba Chai, in 1951 because he
was born of his father's second wife while his father was still married to the
first, and was therefore deemed illegitimate and inadmissible, three judicial
rulings determined that the government had no authority under the law to
render such a decision (see Walker 1997, 283-84). Despite being reprimanded
by the Supreme Court, the government stalled, using various administrative
means until late 1954, when the father died and the son's application was
rejected because there was no one in Canada to sponsor him.[5]

The government also made it difficult to challenge its control policies in
Parliament by regularly leaving the examination of department estimates to
the very end of the parliamentary term.[6] Nonetheless, E. Davie Fulton (PC)
initiated an important discussion of the rights of non-citizens in 1954. He
began by expressing his dissatisfaction with the standard of justice enshrined
in immigration law for those trying to come to or remain in the country.
While accepting that national security could legitimately trump the individual's right to know the reasons for a refusal of admission, he argued that
people should be told whether they had been rejected on such grounds, and
that in all other cases the details ought to be disclosed. Otherwise, questions
of justice as well as administrative efficiency were raised, as the practice led
people to petition the state to find out why they had been refused and
whether the reasons were accurate.[7] Walter Dinsdale (PC) agreed that officials
had too much discretionary power over deportations, that they, "without
recourse to the normal channels of justice, can arbitrarily deport immigrants
from this country" (26 June 1954, 6813).

Roland Michener (PC) recommended a more formal method as "what is
in issue in these proceedings is of equal importance to the issues in criminal
prosecutions or civil suits involving personal and property rights, and it
warrants the same sort of treatment as a Canadian or foreign citizen can get
under the judicial process" (ibid., 6817). He suggested a process wherein
applicants would know the criteria in place, have right of counsel, and be
informed of the reasons behind decisions "so that the whole matter be dealt
with as far as possible in a judicial manner" (ibid.). Instead, under the 1952
Immigration Act, William M. Hamilton (PC) concluded that, "this almost star
chamber attitude ... means that a person has no opportunity whatsoever to

go to the minister and his department and give them information in order to pursue the matter further and perhaps correct any errors which may have crept into the information they have" (ibid., 6835).[8]

Harris replied that the consensus position in the House in 1952 had been that "we did not want to get into the system which obtains in some other countries whereby we would try to define in a law those persons who could be admitted to Canada, so that one could approach the courts in this country and have a judge decide in an action at law whether an applicant came within the terms of the law" (ibid., 6832). Rather, ministerial responsibility allowed Parliament to oppose any actions of which it disapproved on a political level. Moreover, if applicants were provided with reasons for rejection, Harris claimed, they might manufacture evidence to gain acceptance.[9] In conclusion, he suggested that people could have confidence in the department because officials looked at cases several times and were always willing to reconsider evidence. This reflected the Liberal Nationalist position that the state's sovereign right to control its borders should remain an almost unchallenged prerogative of the executive and that judicial oversight of its actions was unnecessary or even harmful.

In 1955, Fulton became more aggressive, moving that "in the opinion of this house, the immigration policy of the government is not clear, consistent or co-ordinated; it is not in conformity with the needs or responsibilities of Canada; and in its administration denies simple justice to Canadians and non-Canadians alike" (15 February 1955, 1158). Although the debate ranged widely, the charge that "the practices of the government in administering that department ... create injustices, hardship, and inequities" was central (ibid.). In supporting this censure motion, MPs signalled their rejection of the government's claim that

> with respect to those applying for admission to Canada, or who are applied for by Canadians in Canada, there are not legal rights; that the whole thing is a matter of discretion. Such a decision is a denial of the rights of Canadians and can only make, as it has done, for administrative chaos amounting in fact by its nature and extent to inevitable administrative lawlessness. (Ibid., 1164)

In particular, Fulton criticized the degree of discretion granted to officials: "It is as a result of that type of regulation, leaving the whole thing to discretion and to the exercise of arbitrary decisions, not subject to appeal or to any process of law or semi-judicial process, which has resulted in the injustices of which we complain" (ibid.). Canadians, he argued, had the right to know why their relatives had been refused admission and had rights of appeal against departmental actions; these were not rights enshrined in the

1952 *Immigration Act* but were derived from the principles of justice found in British and Canadian legal and political history.

"We proceed on the basis that a Canadian citizen has rights, one of them being access to the courts. Unless they are taken away from him by statute those rights exist and are capable of enforcement in the courts," he declared (ibid., 1165). Because the government had established certain admission criteria under which Canadians could apply to have relatives admitted, British justice – with roots stretching back to the Magna Carta[10] – required some mechanism whereby departmental actions could be judged fairly when it was felt that officials had committed an injustice towards an applicant. Such rights, Fulton suggested, extended to landed immigrants, those ordered deported, and those applying to become Canadian citizens: "Our feeling is that some amendments should be made to the act so that the right of appeal is recognized, and the discretionary and arbitrary practices which amount to a denial of rights can be dealt with on a legal and orderly basis and so that the rights inherent in Canadian citizenship can be protected and asserted" (ibid.). In a system based on departmental discretion, he warned, "error, corruption, favouritism and injustice are invited and rights and liberties are denied in principle as well as in fact" (ibid.).

In support of his case, he referred to a subcommittee of the Committee on Civil Liberties of the Canadian Bar Association, which had recently presented findings along these lines to that organization's annual general meeting. The subcommittee had recommended:

(a) Possible codification of regulations issued by your department.
(b) Publication of intra departmental directives – particularly instructions to field officers as to the application or interpretation of the act.
(c) The implementation of proper and legal appeal procedures as contemplated in the act ...
(d) The possibility of making departmental files available to applicants and their attorneys [barring certain confidential materials].
(e) The recognition of the role of barristers and solicitors in immigration law.
(f) The establishment of a procedure setting forth reasons for rejection in each case, in such a way as to give the rejected party or the applicant concerned an opportunity of overcoming the department's objection. (Quoted in ibid., 1165-66)

The report, Fulton claimed, had generated too much political heat and was sent back for further study and review, but the findings were of a sufficiently serious nature as to render it incumbent upon the minister to respond.[11]

The censure motion gained vocal support from a number of MPs, not all of whom were Liberal Internationalists. For example, Frederick Shaw (SC), who could in the same breath argue for and against racial discrimination in immigration,[12] nonetheless held that reasons should be given: "If a person is a communist, tell him so; that is my view. Tell him we do not want him. If it is something else, tell him in straightforward language. This may have legal implications, but on the other hand it would be the decent way of dealing with him" (ibid., 1173). As for security screening, Noseworthy complained that "immigrants are tried and condemned without even knowing that their trial is taking place," which cut against core liberal-democratic values (ibid., 1170). Similarly, Harold E. Winch (CCF) objected that "if a person has no chance whatever either of knowing the charge or of pleading innocent I do not think it is following out the meaning of democracy as we have come to understand it in this dominion and the meaning of justice of which we boast in this dominion" (17 February 1955, 1292). In this Liberal Internationalist vein, the fact that Canada had a liberal-democratic political system set limits on the approach to control that it should pursue.

In response, Citizenship and Immigration Minister Pickersgill called into question the subcommittee report, focusing on how it came into being rather than on its substance. He cast doubt on its worth since it had not been adopted by the Canadian Bar Association. As for the recommendations themselves, he simply observed that he did "not think they could be carried out by any responsible person administering the act" (ibid., 1242). He dismissed out of hand the criticisms raised by one member of the subcommittee, John R. Taylor, alleging that "Taylor had been acting as an advocate before the department for a number of clients, that he had not been uniformly successful in his advocacy, and he did not like it" (ibid.).

For Pickersgill, the legal rights involved were clearly circumscribed in the law – a Canadian citizen had the right "to apply and to have that application decided by the minister in the final analysis, or by someone under the minister's control; and it is no more than that" (ibid., 1247). Even if it were a good idea in principle, he maintained that it was not fiscally prudent to allow for an appeal to the courts. As for disclosure, confidentiality limited the information that could be provided to solicitors or relatives in Canada.[13] Moreover, if people were supplied with the reasons in all but security cases, then it would be clear who had been refused on security grounds, which would put Canada's access to information from other countries at risk. Finally, the department had only so much money to spend and, "after all, the purpose of our Immigration Act is to get good immigrants into Canada and not to enter into complicated consideration of marginal cases" (ibid., 1248). He concluded in Liberal Nationalist fashion by stating that being admitted to Canada was a privilege and that people therefore had no claim on the government with respect to how it administered the law.

Diefenbaker was scathing in his attack against Pickersgill, declaring: "He places himself on a pedestal and says that the decisions that he in his omnipotence makes shall be unchallenged" (ibid., 1256).[14] Diefenbaker argued:

When there is no recourse to the courts the power of discrimination becomes intensified ... Is there anyone in this house who will tell me that when the minister is despotic and highhanded, when he rides roughshod over the statute, when he substitutes the caprice of a minister for the will of parliament, the courts of this country should not have the right to say: You shall not do that. (Ibid.)

To place the Minister "in a position where in his unchallengeable power, in the secrecy of his own office, he can determine my rights is something that shocks the sensibilities of those who believe that the courts of the land are standing guard over the rights of the people" (ibid., 1260). It was necessary, Diefenbaker maintained, to ensure that the department conformed to "those principles that British justice has shown through the generations are necessary for the preservation of the fundamental freedoms of the individual" (29 April 1955, 3321). Although Fulton's motion was defeated, the Opposition returned to this theme during the Standing Committee on the Estimates and the debates following that committee's report.

Liberal Nationalists like Pickersgill castigated opponents as those who thought "that the right to migrate from one country to another is one of the rights recognized in the universal declaration of human rights" (quoted in 17 February 1955, 1254).[15] Such allegations were made despite repeated declarations by those who supported Fulton's motion that Canada had a sovereign right to control its borders but that this must be done in conformity with certain principles of (British) justice. Against this more complex reading of the nature of state authority over borders, those in favour of the status quo put forward an either/or situation in which the government could exert control as it saw fit or have no control at all. Thus, Harris closed the discussion by warning that Canada could allow the courts to decide who should come in or it could allow the department to do it, but should not mix the two (ibid., 1297-98).

The courts, however, were becoming more interested in the Section 39 restriction in the 1952 *Immigration Act,* as can be seen in the case of Shirley Kathleen Brent, an American ordered deported on the grounds that she was inadmissible under a broadly construed section of the regulations. Technically, the case turned on "whether or not the applicant had [had] a hearing as required by law" and whether the government had to provide reasons to those who had been refused entry (*Ex parte Brent* [1954], 708). Judge John L. Wilson of the High Court of Ontario determined that at no time was [Brent] even given any indication of the grounds upon which she was to be deported or to be refused landing in Canada. None can be deduced from her evidence. No such information was given to her on her appeal [to the minister]. So far as the material discloses, she was given no opportunity on the appeal to meet objections to her entry or landing. (Ibid., 709)

For a proper inquiry to take place, he concluded, "there must be some intelligible definition of the grounds for excluding the applicant" (ibid., 710). The deportation order was therefore quashed. On appeal, the government lost at both the Ontario Court of Appeal and the Supreme Court of Canada.

On Brent's behalf, lawyer Andrew Brewin argued that "where a tribunal is set up to determine rights there are essential elements of justice, one of which is that the person affected shall know the nature of the allegations against him, and that these essentials must be observed" (*Ex parte Brent* [1955], 484). The Court of Appeal agreed[16] and ruled that the immigration regulations were *ultra vires* of the 1952 *Immigration Act* because they cast categories of inadmissibility in much too general terms.

In short, those limited powers of legislation, wide though the limits of the subject-matter may be, which Parliament has delegated to His Excellency in council have not been exercised by the delegate at all, but, on the contrary, by him have been redelegated bodily, for exercise not merely by some one other individual but, respectively and independently of each other, by every special inquiry officer who sees fit to invoke them and according to "the opinion" of each such sub-delegate. (Ibid., 490)

When the Supreme Court upheld this decision in 1956, the government had to rewrite its regulations, which it did that same year through PC 785.

In doing so, the government also responded to such recent court cases as *Leong Ba Chai* and *Narine-Singh*. With respect to the former, the new regulations defined a child as being "the issue of lawful wedlock and who would possess the status of legitimacy if his father had been domiciled in Canada at the time of his birth." In terms of the latter, the regulations completely removed the language of race and ethnicity and established a hierarchy of countries of citizenship for immigration purposes, one that still permitted racial discrimination by geographical preference. In response to *Brent*, a new provision required all but British, French, and American citizens to acquire a visa and medical certificate abroad before being allowed to land. Thus, people could still be rejected without ever knowing the reasons if a visa was not granted or if a medical appointment was not made by immigration officials. "All the information you are given or are entitled to receive is information to the effect that you do not meet the requirements of the

Immigration Act," Brewin later complained as an elected MP (16 April 1964, 2254).[17] Although the Supreme Court subsequently upheld this practice,[18] Brewin argued that this did not make it right and that it went against Section 2 of the 1960 *Canadian Bill of Rights*.[19]

Meanwhile, the rights of non-citizens dominated the debate over the department's estimates in August 1956. In July, East Indian community representatives had contacted MPs to solicit support for removing continued discriminatory practices (especially concerning family reunification), and had lobbied Pickersgill himself. If they could not be treated on conditions of equality with other Commonwealth immigrants, they wrote, then they wanted to "be treated no worse than Latin Americans and Levantines, and ... be given the same rights that they are given as to bringing in relatives" (quoted in 8 August 1956, 7203). Their campaign succeeded in that British Columbia MPs from both sides of the House now spoke unanimously in support of East Indian immigration. For his part, Pickersgill claimed that "there was no intention to discriminate in these matters in the sense of saying that some people are better than others. It is just an administrative device" (ibid., 7206).[20]

At the same time, Pickersgill announced that family reunification cases involving Chinese immigrants would now be reviewed only once because too much time was being spent looking at the same cases over and over. Since immigrants overseas had no right to come to Canada, he reasoned, "there is no question of justice or injustice at all in this matter. It is purely a matter of administration" (ibid., 7211).[21] This decision provoked considerable outrage as many MPs had long been arguing for a more humanitarian policy towards the Chinese. Harold Winch felt that the government had simply abandoned its responsibilities: "If you have not sufficient staff, you should get more staff; if you have not the trained staff you should train the number required. Why throw completely overboard every principle of British justice for the reasons outlined?" (ibid., 7210). Fulton agreed – "Certainly there are administrative difficulties involved in every department. That is why ministers are paid" (ibid., 7212) – and again raised the relationship between departmental practice, racial discrimination, the rights of non-citizens, and the courts.

As administrative law, immigration regulations had the force of law and therefore the question of rights and the relationship of such law to the courts had to be addressed. "If it is a part of the law," he asked, "does the minister argue that there are no rights under the law except those which he cares to confer? ... I disagree because there is such a thing as the rule of law ... Under our law, which includes that field known as administrative law, once regulations are passed by order in council they have the force of law, and then the minister cannot or should not disregard them" (ibid.). In administrative law, he argued, consistent decision making across cases through the development of precedents was needed to guide decision makers and those whose cases were being decided, rather than having "each case being decided upon a principle which rests somewhere in the mind of the minister" (ibid., 7215). To ensure the fair application of the rules, an appeal to an impartial observer was also required, as occurred, for example, with pensions. If applicants could not know whether they were being treated fairly, if the minister "played ducks and drakes" with the law as he saw fit, Fulton said, then injustice was bound to occur (ibid.).

Moreover, the workload of the minister and the department might be considerably lessened if Immigration Appeal Boards (IAB) were appointed, as had been authorized under the 1952 *Immigration Act*. The reluctance to do so appeared to stem from a fear within the department that "once an Appeal Board comes into operation the government loses control" (Corbett 1957, 86). In response, Pickersgill created a new four-person IAB in January 1956 and published regulations concerning its functions (see ibid., 82-83). Persons ordered deported would state in their notice of appeal whether they wished the IAB or the minister to hear their case (the minister could still ask the IAB to review any given case). Appellants would also state whether they wished to make a written submission or to have an oral hearing. If the IAB was chosen, its decision, rendered in writing, would be final, although by law the minister had the right to overturn any conclusion reached by the IAB.

Although Pickersgill's actions demonstrated a growing acceptance of Liberal Internationalist critiques, Fulton was not satisfied with the new arrangements: "If the minister had wanted to create an appeal board that would really give the right to an impartial hearing in accordance with the generally accepted principles of justice, could he not have arranged to set up a board with less than three out of four of the personnel from the department whose decision is under appeal?" (7 March 1956, 1885). Pickersgill replied that civil servants could be trusted to act in a conscientious and impartial manner. In an effort to increase fairness in the system, Fulton introduced a Private Member's Bill to provide for a uniform appeal process in cases of rejection, one that would publish its proceedings to develop a body of consistent and public practices (4 March 1957, 1823).[22] The legislation failed to make it past First Reading but the question remained part of parliamentary debate until it was resolved through the 1967 *Immigration Appeal Board Act*.

During the 1950s, Canadian refugee policy appeared occasionally but with some regularity on the parliamentary agenda before rising to prominence with the refugee crisis in Hungary in late 1956 (Keyserlingk 1993), and the question of discrimination was debated as it became clear that postwar refugees would not be simply a European phenomenon. Thus, when the 1949 Chinese Revolution caused hundreds of thousands to flee to Hong

Kong, many Chinese Canadians sought to resettle relatives in Canada. As well, the creation of Israel and the violence that subsequently beset the region led to a significant refugee population.[23] Jewish community advocacy was able to secure the resettlement of four hundred Jewish refugees living in Egypt during the 1956 Suez Canal war (Whitaker 1987, 67-68). In such cases, the department continued to respond to refugees within its discriminatory admissions criteria, drawing sharp criticism in the House.[24] Although no meaningful shift from this approach took place until the Conservatives returned to power, the government's relatively rapid response to the Hungarian refugee crisis is generally credited with demonstrating to officials and politicians that a less restrictive approach did not necessarily lead to a decrease in control (Dirks 1977, Chapter 9; Hawkins 1972, 114-17).

Another Conservative Interlude (1957-63)

Despite having expressed a serious interest in immigration while in opposition, incoming Prime Minister Diefenbaker did not appoint a full-time Citizenship and Immigration Minister until 1958.[25] Neither did he provide much leadership on immigration in Cabinet.[26] Instead, he first appointed Fulton – already serving as Justice Minister – as Acting Minister. Early on, Fulton reversed Pickersgill's policy on reviews of Chinese family sponsorship cases. The government also broadened sponsorship possibilities for Asians in Canada so that applicants did not have to wait until they became Canadian citizens (at least five years after landing) to sponsor family members, but could, like other immigrants, do so upon demonstration of their ability to support them.

Several MPs, including Pickersgill, questioned Fulton closely on the rights of non-citizens.[27] In response, he announced an internal review of the disclosure question and anticipated that the problems involved would not be insurmountable. As for appeals, he envisioned a procedure whereby the applicant or the sponsor could "bring before the appeal board all the information he has been able to gather to counter the reasons for rejection" (30 January 1958, 4058). The new system would see "a volume of precedents built up for the guidance of officials and of the public and of those who represent the applicants" (ibid., 4059).[28] Once a basic framework had been developed, Fulton said, interested non-state actors involved in immigration would be consulted.

Little was accomplished, however, before Ellen Fairclough became Citizenship and Immigration Minister in 1958. She felt that those for and against increased immigration were about equal in the Canadian population, but "those opposed always seemed to be most vocal. Horror stories were quickly picked up by the media, and my office had to handle the 'damage control'" (1995, 111). Indeed, her days in office were marked by numerous controversies, some raising questions of control and the rights of non-citizens.

In response to restrictive policies in North America since the late nineteenth century, and the difficulties that many Chinese migrants had in providing documentation of family relationships to immigration officials after the Chinese Revolution, sophisticated smuggling organizations had developed. By 1960, the RCMP and Hong Kong police had uncovered sufficient evidence to confirm "the existence of a very large and well-established illegal immigration movement from Hong Kong to Canada" (Hawkins 1972, 132). Amid RCMP raids across the country and the RCMP Commissioner's talk of 11,000 of the 23,000 Chinese who had come into the country since 1946 being illegal immigrants, a climate of fear spread throughout the Chinese Canadian community (Avery 1995, 213-14).[29] The government's response was markedly Liberal Internationalist. Fairclough stressed "that there is no intention to prosecute those people who are, let us say, the victims of these transactions. The intention is rather to curb the activities of the racketeers" (9 June 1960, 4722). She proposed that "any of those who care to come forward can be assured that we will do everything in our power to have their status in Canada regularized and their true identity established" (ibid., 4724). A special amnesty policy was soon established for those who had arrived before 1 July 1960.

A Liberal Internationalist outlook also defined parliamentary discussions on this issue. Canada's first MP of Chinese ancestry, Douglas Jung (PC), argued that "it would be very difficult to make out a moral case against the majority of these Chinese, because the Immigration Act, as it stands, was, and is, unduly restrictive" (25 May 1961, 5390). His reasoning was supported by many MPs, including Pickersgill.[30] For its part, a Chinese Canadian delegation came to Ottawa to meet with the Prime Minister, Fairclough, and Fulton. Wong Foon Sien, a community leader, showed Diefenbaker various ways in which the RCMP raids had violated the proposed bill of rights, noting that "the situation resembles a country under martial law" (quoted in Con et al. 1982, 216). In 1962, the RCMP investigation was halted and fifteen people of Chinese descent in Canada were either fined and/or given prison sentences of six months or less, and the amnesty remained operational until 1973, landing over twelve thousand Chinese immigrants (ibid., 217). Not for the first time, rights-restrictive policies had created an environment in which circumvention had been seen to be justified by those who sought to enter Canada on conditions of equality with other migrants.

This issue and its associated control problems further underlined the need to replace the 1952 *Immigration Act*. As early as 1955, Noseworthy had complained that "the department of immigration has become, over the years, nothing but a jungle of overgrowth and undergrowth composed of orders in council, rules and regulations and red tape to such an extent that it has become impossible for any hon. gentleman effectively to administer that department" (15 February 1955, 1168-69). Fairclough agreed and the government promised on almost a yearly basis to introduce legislation for Parliament's consideration, but without sufficient support in Cabinet little progress was made.

To provoke a response, Leon D. Crestohl (L) introduced an amendment in 1959 to secure for all non-citizens ordered deported access to an appeal before the judiciary. He called specific attention to Section 39 of the 1952 *Immigration Act*: "To deny a human being justice if a minor immigration official should make a mistake by not permitting a right of appeal certainly is beyond every concept of justice as we understand it in Canada" (5 May 1959, 3347). Since he first criticized Section 39 in 1952, Crestohl had been unable to elicit a clear justification for the denial of an appeal.[31] In areas such as tariff policies, he observed, individuals could lodge multiple appeals if aggrieved:

> One is really shocked and appalled to find that when dealing with matters of dollars and cents ... there are four stages of appeal in order to seek redress and justice but under the Immigration Act, which deals with human liberty and human rights, there is no right of appeal. It is really incongruous. (Ibid.)

In support, Pickersgill said that he now realized that this would help restore the actual as well as perceived integrity of the immigration system.[32] Against those who argued that Section 39 already allowed for recourse to the courts through writs of certiorari, prohibition, and habeas corpus, he countered that much depended on the skill of the lawyer involved and the sympathies of the judge hearing the case, noting that there could be great variation in both respects. Although Crestohl's proposal failed, it was followed over the next few years by similar efforts.

The sentiments underpinning such dissatisfaction continued to revolve principally around concerns over the lack of adequate due process protections and the practice of ethnoracial discrimination as both separate and related issues (for example, it was argued that an appeal was needed because ethnoracial discrimination could so easily occur due to the amount of discretion granted officials). In 1958, John R. Taylor (PC), who had been involved in the Canadian Bar Association report reviewed earlier, complained that "skilled legal talent has difficulty understanding the procedural mysteries of the immigration department. Even with the best administrative radar equipment it is difficult to tell who is admissible to this country and who is not" (29 May 1958, 647). He noted the absence of guidebooks based on reported cases to assist in understanding the law, which perpetuated "a lack of uniformity" (ibid.).[33] Instead, decision making was shrouded in secrecy, based on a "paternalistic" system of ministerial discretion, one that had "provoked sharp criticism from the bench and bar, from the press and from the general public alike" (ibid.).

A year later, Crestohl complained about the extensive use of regulations to define who should be admissible to Canada, and the lack parliamentary oversight that this involved: "All these prohibitions and all these permissions are contained in the regulations which parliament never saw. The regulations were prepared by the government or by departmental officials and were enacted by order in council" (5 March 1959, 1632). In 1960, Taylor observed that while both federal and provincial governments had moved "to provide adequate machinery for the hearing and appealing of applications, ministerial orders and the like" in many spheres of government action during the postwar period, immigration remained "an outstanding exception to this general tendency" (9 June 1960, 4735). This was because the government still stressed that immigration was a privilege, and did not recognize that the rights of non-citizens were not wholly subsumed within the prerogatives of control. This was about to change, however.

A Break with the Past (1962-63)

The first decided policy break with Liberal Nationalism came in the last months of Fairclough's tenure. Initially, she had maintained that racial discrimination did not exist in Canadian policy. Answering Winch's charge that "Canada, even within the commonwealth of nations, maintains a colour bar" (4 March 1959, 1617),[34] she asserted that people from the West Indies, for example, were mainly turned away because "they have not the skill or the financial resources to maintain themselves in this country for long enough to settle in" (5 March 1959, 1652). There was, she claimed, no colour bar but rather simply the administration of the law. Three years later, however, she stressed that a new set of regulatory changes constituted "a substantial advance over the former regulations in that the selection of [skilled] immigrants ... will [now] be done without discrimination of any kind" (19 January 1962, 9).

Discrimination also continued to enter into discussions with respect to refugees, a subject that arose in diverse ways during the Conservative years. For example, MPs queried the restrictive features of immigration policies towards Hong Kong and the Middle East (15 July 1960, 6388). Inquiries were made concerning the willingness of the government to consider resettling black South Africans facing oppression (5 April 1960, 2907-8). Crestohl made a specific plea on behalf of Iraqi, Lebanese, and other Middle Eastern tourists and students in Canada: "If these people are forced to return to these countries some of them will not go back because it means certain death" (9 June 1960, 4733).[35] In response to such questions, Fairclough revealed that admissions standards were sometimes suspended on compassionate grounds, including cases involving refugees (ibid.).[36] Overall, however, Canada remained reluctant to take a more proactive approach to refugee resettlement. Thus, External Affairs noted in 1962 that "at this stage it would seem unrealistic to us to consider taking in African and Asian refugees at least until such time as the necessity for such efforts is apparent and other countries have begun to share our concern" (quoted in Dirks 1977, 225).

That same year, Fairclough announced two historic changes in Canadian control policy that prepared the ground for Liberal Internationalist developments in the late 1960s and beyond. First, racial discrimination in Canadian admissions policies was reduced by placing "primary stress on education, training and skills as the main condition of admissibility regardless of the country of origin of the applicant" (19 January 1962, 9).[37] This made for a more level playing field between potential white and non-white immigrants,[38] but although the range of family members that could be sponsored was expanded for persons who had been discriminated against in the past, there was still preferential treatment for certain countries of origin.[39] Nonetheless, the minister could claim that "the general effect of section 31, taken as a whole, is to improve the position of nationals of all countries, without weakening the position of any" (ibid., 10).[40] Certainly, the move stood out in comparison with countries of immigration such as Australia (with its White Australia policy) and the United States (with its restrictive quota system).

Second, Fairclough changed the IAB process. Henceforth, all deportation appeals would be handled by the boards, a move that she felt would ensure that they were heard "in the most impartial manner possible" (ibid.). The procedures were given greater specificity and were designed, Fairclough said, to "follow the principles of natural justice and are in line with the spirit of the bill of rights" (ibid.). The IABs were not empowered to hear appeals from rejected sponsorship cases, however, and decisions were still subject to ministerial review. Although the changes did not go as far as critics such as Crestohl and Taylor wanted, they provided a more impartial body to which non-citizens could turn on points of law. The Opposition initially welcomed these developments because they brought Canadian immigration policy more closely in line with liberal-democratic values.[41] However, after having received assurances since 1958 that revision of the 1952 *Immigration Act* was a priority, some MPs took umbrage that the government had instead chosen to pursue reform by revising the regulations. This was, Crestohl complained, "an invasion of the rights of parliament and an abuse of authority which reflects on the very basis of our method of enacting laws in this House of Commons" (27 February 1962, 1326-27).[42] The changes were of such a fundamental nature, he argued, that they required a renewed legislative foundation.

Fairclough never had a chance to develop her ideas on control further. In late 1962, she became Postmaster General and Richard Bell was given the immigration portfolio. Although he would become an active participant in control debates during the late 1960s, he had only eight months to act before the 1963 general election. According to Hawkins (1972, 135-36), "he [had] found the state of morale in the Department at this point very low indeed. There was a policy of 'drift' ... The resources of the Department were very limited and officials felt that they had no political backing whatsoever." Many of the organizational and policy changes that he felt were needed would instead come from the Liberals, who returned to power in 1963.

A New Liberal Internationalist Approach (1963-67)

The 1963 Speech from the Throne of Lester B. Pearson's minority government promised an overhaul of the 1952 *Immigration Act*. Although this did not occur until the passage of the 1976 *Immigration Act*, Canada's approach to control had been altered radically by 1967. At first, the Liberals concentrated on organizational reforms, such as replacing the Department of Citizenship and Immigration with a Department of Manpower and Immigration. This reflected the government's desire to align immigration with broader economic and labour market objectives. Meanwhile, many control issues arose in the years leading up to Canada's centenary, most controversially with respect to ship deserters who wished to claim political asylum in Canada. This fed into an ongoing review of Canadian immigration and refugee policy, which led to the publication of a government white paper in 1966. Core proposals in this document drew Liberal Internationalist criticism, which generated further support for two major policy developments regarding the due process and equality rights of non-citizens. These established new benchmarks for policy debates and developments before, during, and after the passage of the 1976 *Immigration Act*.

Continuing Criticisms (1963-65)

In early 1963, a Canadian-born citizen of Chinese origin, Wayson S. Choy, was refused an immigrant work visa by the United States on account of his ethnoracial background. Prime Minister Pearson responded that "as for Canadian law and policy, the present government ... is firmly opposed in principle and in practice to racial discrimination" (18 October 1963, 3738). Similarly, Citizenship and Immigration Minister Guy Favreau (L) affirmed that "true Canadianism permits no discrimination" (quoted in 14 December 1963, 5885).[43] If these two statements embodied an official position, Andrew Brewin (NDP) proposed, the government should move quickly to remove the remaining sources of official ethnoracial discrimination in Canadian immigration policy and practice. Brewin returned repeatedly to this theme over the next few years, complaining that Canada discriminated against the majority of the world's population by treating applicants from Africa and Asia differently from those coming from Europe (14 August 1964, 6831).

The need to stop this practice, he declared, was underlined by Canada's decision to support the adoption of the United Nations Declaration on the Elimination of All Forms of Racial Discrimination in 1963.[44] He even introduced a Private Member's Bill "to eliminate racial discrimination from the immigration laws of Canada" (12 March 1965, 12318).[45]

Critics often focused on the case of the West Indies. In 1963, the premier of Barbados, Errol Barrow, complained in a speech in Canada that "there is either tacitly or explicitly some element of discrimination against the West Indian immigrant" in Canadian policy (quoted in 25 September 1964, 8438). Less than two years later, President Eric Williams of Trinidad and Tobago observed that "the world has worked out the curious hybrid of juridical equality of states and racial inequality of peoples," as evidenced in the immigration policies of Canada, among others (quoted in 7 March 1966, 2319). "I think the people of Canada and the government of Canada owe it to the people of the West Indies," David Orlikow (NDP) commented, "if the commonwealth concept means anything, if the democratic concept of equality of all people regardless of race, religion and colour means anything, to either correct this situation" or to explain its necessity (25 September 1964, 8438). Reg Cantelon (PC) argued that there were no such reasons:

> In most cases West Indians speak at least one of our two official languages. They have the same ethical standards as ourselves, though I am free to admit they do not always observe them any better than we do; and, of course, they are members of the commonwealth. These ought to be sufficient reasons for us to remove restrictions on West Indian immigration. (Ibid., 8443)[46]

Orlikow warned that "if this world is going to remain free, if this world is going to remain democratic, we must convince those people who are not white, who after all far outnumber those who are white, that we in fact believe them to be the equals of the white peoples" (7 March 1966, 2319).

In response to such concerns, Citizenship and Immigration Minister René Tremblay (L) simply declared that "there is no discrimination against the British West Indies" and asserted that low admissions reflected the lack of skills that applicants possessed (25 September 1964, 8457).[47] Parliamentary Secretary Hubert Badanai (L) said that there was no racial discrimination within any one (geographically defined) nationality group: thus, "all citizens of France are treated alike, regardless of whether they are Chinese, Negro or of any other origin" (12 March 1965, 12321).[48] Such denials were the norm until Manpower and Immigration Minister Jean Marchand (L) admitted in 1966 that "undoubtedly, discriminatory provisions remain in the act, and I believe there will shortly be means to eliminate such discrimination in a democratic country like ours" (7 March 1966, 2327).[49] This was accomplished the following year by Marchand himself.

As for procedural justice, Brewin called attention to discrepancies between the 1960 Bill of Rights and Canadian control policy. It was against the national interest to refuse either to tell people why they had been rejected or to allow an appeal: "Any unfairness applied to people who seek to come into Canada creates a bitterness that does damage to Canada and to Canada's reputation throughout the world, and in the world of today we cannot afford not to live up to the principles which we expound so eloquently from time to time" (14 December 1963, 5887). He suggested that the IAB ought to have at least one member trained in law and to assess cases not merely on their legal aspects but also "on compassionate grounds" (ibid., 5888). At that time, the IAB could address only a limited range of appeals, was staffed primarily by people connected to the immigration bureacracy, and was not required to give reasons for its decisions.

The continued political saliency of these issues was demonstrated during the 1964-65 parliamentary session, when the conditions under which ship deserters were detained prior to deportation came under attack. By the session's end, the government had employed a well-known Toronto barrister, Joseph Sedgwick, to review the department's actions and propose reforms. There had been a marked increase in such deserters, including those coming from behind the Iron Curtain, and many of them appeared to disappear sometime after their arrival. For example, of 904 known deserters in 1965, 355 had been ordered deported but the other 549 could not be located (29 August 1966, 7758-59). The minister argued that most of the deserters simply wanted to get around the rules governing immigration to Canada by asking for landed immigrant status after having entered the country illegally. Thus, the issue was primarily one of abuse. For many MPs, however, Canada risked sending back refugees to face persecution in their countries of origin.

Under heightened parliamentary and media attention, Citizenship and Immigration Minister René Tremblay responded to charges that people were not being brought before the courts to confirm their detention at regular intervals (as required by law), that they were not being advised of their right to legal counsel, and that some were being kept in detention for very long periods (in one case, an individual was kept in jail for over ninety days without being charged). He began by reasserting that immigration was a privilege and not a right, and that "if we do not want chaos to prevail in matters of immigration, Canada must apply the control measures required to deport persons who, somehow, entered our country illegally" (22 June 1964, 4555). Although he would not elaborate, he alleged that criminal organizations were involved in smuggling people into the country. He maintained that immigration officials had adhered to the law[50] and that some delays came from the need to process each case carefully or to consider additional information that might benefit the detainee.[51]

Hearing the casual manner in which concerns were brushed aside, Terry Nugent (PC) complained that Tremblay "did not seem to understand the seriousness of the allegations made ... where the rights of individuals can be so easily tampered with and where there can be so much hardship caused by the ordinary routines of the department" (23 June 1964, 4610). It was insufficient to tell people they could get counsel if they needed help, Orlikow observed, if they did not have the money to do so, if they could not speak English or French well, and if they had no friends to turn to for advice. Holding deserters in prison made it appear as though "it is assumed they are already guilty, although the trial has not yet been held and very often not even an inquiry has been held," he said (22 June 1964, 4583). Among other restrictions, detainees could not receive visitors except at prescribed times, and their access to mail was restricted. There were also claims that people had been told that it would do no good to get a lawyer, that they should plead guilty, and that they should turn in anyone they knew who was in the country illegally if they did not want to serve time before being deported. A more positive policy had the potential to promote abroad the political values on which the country was based, Orlikow argued: "Let us see if we cannot give a demonstration of the height to which Canadian democracy can grow" (25 September 1964, 8448).

A more fundamental problem stemmed from the 1952 *Immigration Act* and its regulations, "which [have] become so involved and so obviously discriminatory that it is impossible for the affairs of the department to be conducted without criticism being forthcoming," according to Orlikow (22 June 1964, 4581). To remedy this situation, Brewin introduced two Private Member's Bills to provide for a fair hearing in all cases of deportation and (as noted earlier) to remove the last vestiges of discrimination in immigration law, respectively. Brewin concluded that it was "perfectly obvious that the intention was that parliament desired to provide a full and fair hearing for those who sought admission to the country" (16 April 1964, 2252). As well, "the courts have also made it clear that a fair hearing requires the person who is threatened with deportation to be furnished with particulars of the objections to his admission, so that he can make an appropriate answer to those objections" (ibid., 2252-53). "The fundamental right to a fair hearing is contained in thousands of cases. The sort of practice we now have and which we are now discussing is a cloak behind which people can be refused admission on any discriminatory ground that the official sees fit to employ" (ibid., 2254). Even Adam and Eve, he recalled, were given a chance to explain themselves to God before being expelled from Eden. National security was not a sufficient justification, for in the absence of a more transparent process, the government could use security as an excuse for keeping people out on other grounds. Eldon M. Woolliams (PC) supported Brewin in the hope that it might counter "a terrible usurpation of natural justice" (ibid., 2255), noting that the same issue arose in cases of applications for Canadian citizenship, when people were rejected without being told why.[52] In a fair immigration policy, John J. Greene (L) maintained, the rules "are up above the table, instead of down below somewhere, where we have to crawl on our hands and knees to find among the dust why people have been precluded from entering the country" (ibid., 2260).[53]

In his reply, Hubert Badanai focused on whether immigrants had a right to enter Canada, skirting the substance of Brewin's amendments, which called for "reasonable restrictions" (ibid., 2252) combined with a recognition of the right of people to be treated fairly as Canada pursued its sovereign right to control its borders. Badanai asserted that without the current policy, Canada would lose control over its borders, and that if reasons were disclosed, then evidence of an embarrassing "social disease" or a criminal conviction might be revealed, causing that person discomfort (ibid., 2259). Moreover, "hon. members may take it as a matter of record that a very exhaustive examination of the circumstances is undertaken before a decision is reached" (ibid.) and that the minister could be trusted to produce a fair decision. Non-citizens who objected to this system, he implied, were just trying to circumvent the rules.

Critics were not convinced. Brewin cautioned that unfair rules led people to enter the country illegally. Moreover, Terry Nugent argued, "merely be-cause an individual may be in the country illegally, or that he may happen to be a lawbreaker to some extent, does not excuse any government officials or anyone else taking away his legal rights" (23 June 1964, 4610). It was not enough, Gordon Fairweather (PC) suggested, for those responsible to parrot the words of Mackenzie King concerning the privilege of coming to Canada to forestall criticisms of the department.[54] What was needed, Brewin pro-posed, was "that we recognize that these people who come from various parts of the world are human beings who are entitled to be treated with dignity as human beings" (ibid., 4606). This was not possible if immigration was understood simply as a privilege. On a more practical level, Canada needed to change its policies to attract the immigrants needed for its own prosperity. "We shall be forced to reconsider this present policy which, as everyone knows, discriminates," William A. Peters (CCF) observed (25 September 1964, 8452).

As the issue gained damaging political momentum, the government re-tained Sedgwick to investigate the cases in question and suggest improve-ments to policies for dealing with illegal arrivals. Following further criticism of the exercise of ministerial discretion, Sedgwick's inquiry was expanded to address larger questions of immigration law and policy. His recommenda-tions were eventually discussed by a Special Joint Committee of Parliament in 1966 (see below). His first report was tabled in the House of Commons at 2:00 AM as the parliamentary session was being prorogued. For Tremblay, this was unfortunate as it essentially cleared the department of any wrongdoing, although Sedgwick's second report would call for substantial reforms to how the government detained and deported people.

Although Sedgwick was respected on both sides of the House, Brewin complained that "we have absolutely no need of an eminent lawyer to discover that a hearing without disclosure of the real grounds for rejection is practically meaningless; it is not, in fact, a fair hearing" (23 June 1964, 4604).[55] Tremblay asked for patience, as he was close to being able to assign priorities for future studies as to possible changes that might be made.[56] "Surely," Brewin replied, "... we do not need to worry about assigning priorities when the courts of this country as well as members of this house have again and again expressed, in the most clearcut terms ... that there are basic deficiencies in the present administration" (14 August 1964, 6832). For his part, Fairweather could not "understand this worship at the altar of the sanctity of a statute" (ibid., 6851). As the government continued to hesitate, support for reform continued to build.

On the Road to Reform (1965-67)
The first indication that change was afoot was Pearson's unexpected announcement that the Department of Citizenship and Immigration would be disbanded and its core responsibilities for immigration transferred to a new Department of Manpower ("and Immigration" was appended following criticism). At the same time, Jean Marchand was appointed minister and long-time Liberal insider Tom Kent became deputy minister.

Ever since watching Favreau struggle through immigration files because "his great humanitarianism made him acutely conscious that a scribbled decision on a buff file could make a vast difference to the lives of a family," Kent (1988, 243) had considered immigration an area in need of substantial reform. First, he sought to improve lines of decision making within the department: "The basic reason why the administration of immigration was overcentralized [why so many decisions came before the minister] was that the policy was obscure" (ibid., 406-7). The rules did not express "the purpose of the program being administered [but were simply] procedures, made necessary by the lack of definite policies" (ibid., 407). Because so much was left to discretion, applicants were often dissatisfied and bureaucrats sent difficult cases up the administrative ladder because there were no clear guidelines. In such a condition of complexity without clarity, "the selection procedures, for all their elaboration, were by no means the determinant of how many people came to Canada and who they were. The equally important control was, simply, administrative delay" (ibid., 409). Since immigration work was coming under increasing public scrutiny amid calls for greater judicial oversight, the system required reform.

Commenting on the number of people who sought landed status from within the country (as allowed for under law), Marchand began by warning that "Canada is in danger of losing control over its immigration policy. We will need a better control than in the past ... as things are now, we do not know where we are going and have not known for many years" (7 March 1966, 2328). Without changes, he said, criminals and other undesirable people might become established in Canada. Against this backdrop, he announced a new status adjustment program in July 1966 for non-citizens who were in the country illegally. The department had some twenty thousand inland applications for landed immigrant status on file, and many more visitors would probably like to apply. "This situation," he said, "amounts to a wholesale circumvention of our normal system of immigrant selection and control" (8 July 1966, 7376). In addition, the number of people who could enter without being screened had grown since Canada had waived visa requirements for many (primarily European) countries in 1961.

Under the new policy, those in Canada as of 8 July who had already applied for landing or who did so before 25 July would be granted permanent resident status if they met relaxed immigration criteria; somewhat narrower provisions were established for those who did not meet this deadline or who arrived in the future, but they would be denied permanent resident status for one year to encourage people to apply from abroad. In either case, those rejected would be allowed to leave voluntarily before being ordered deported. The policy was generally welcomed by parliamentarians. It was the last time Marchand would find such support while he was minister.[57]

After Joseph Sedgwick's second report was tabled in March 1966, and the government's often-promised and long-awaited *White Paper on Immigration* (DMI 1966) was published in October,[58] Richard Bell suggested that a joint parliamentary committee examine both documents, and a Special Joint Committee on Immigration (SJCI) was duly appointed. While Hawkins (1972, 161) holds that its work was "undistinguished," with no "collective vision and purpose," Kent (1988, 429-30) maintains that participants "were closely interested in the subject and fully aware that the differences about it did not run on party lines," concluding that it "had a considerable influence on policy." It certainly provides a vital window into the politics of Canadian border control policy at the country's centenary.

Sedgwick proposed many changes to improve the due process protections of non-citizens in the immigration system. In his opinion, "an appeal should lie in all cases from the making of an Order of Deportation" (1966, 3). The grounds on which people could be prohibited or made subject to deportation also required revision since they were, in his view, far too broad and unfair.[59] As for the IAB, he argued that its decisions should be final (not open to ministerial review) and subject to an appeal to the courts, which would necessitate that Section 39 be struck from the 1952 *Immigration Act*. Moreover, the IAB should be allowed to hear appeals on points of law and fact and to permit people to remain on a discretionary basis. This would include appeals from non-immigrants (such as visitors) who wished to remain in Canada, especially "persons in respect of whom there are reasonable grounds to believe that they would be subject to political persecution or suffer extreme hardship if required to return to their country of origin" (ibid., 8). Sedgwick also suggested that the IAB should be allowed to hear appeals by people in Canada whose applications to sponsor close relatives from abroad had been rejected. Furthermore, the board could be made responsible for assessing the weight to be given to security information provided by the state in a particular case, even if it would not always be able to reveal the information to the person in question. The creation of such a truly independent IAB would relieve the minister of much work and produce a more impartial set of guidelines and rules for the interpretation of immigration law, he reasoned.

Finally, Sedgwick called for an assertion in the law that "admission to Canada, either as an immigrant or non-immigrant, is a privilege and is not to be construed as a right" (ibid., 20). He wanted to ensure that "coming and then staying here illegally should not confer ... any *rights,* no matter how long [a person] has been here" (ibid., 21; emphasis in original). He later tempered this Liberal Nationalist position, agreeing that non-citizens had rights that had been conferred by statute, and that they had basic procedural rights, that non-citizens – in Brewin's terms – "have the right to a fair judicial hearing as to whether [they] fall within these classes, the prohibited or the admissible" (Canada 1966-67, No. 14, 920).[60] Although Sedgwick's report "did not produce many new thoughts ... it did produce some authoritative opinions which helped to establish certain clear priorities" (Hawkins 1972, 149). In doing so, it consolidated core features of the Liberal Internationalist critique of Canada's Liberal Nationalist approach. Within two years, many of these would provide a new foundation for Canadian border control policy.

A New Liberal Internationalist Foundation (1966-67)

As he released the white paper, Marchand announced that the government would institute an expansionist and non-discriminatory immigration policy rooted in a higher standard of due process protections for those affected by departmental decisions. Repeated incremental alterations, he said, had left the law "complicated, confused, uncertain, even contradictory" (14 October 1966, 8651). His initial proposals were criticized for being too restrictive, however, and he altered them to reflect the Liberal Internationalist outlook prevailing in Parliament. Although still present, Liberal Nationalism had become a much more marginal force in the universe of political discourse surrounding Canadian control policies.

The *White Paper on Immigration* proclaimed that Canadian policy should "as a matter of principle ... involve no discrimination by reason of race, colour or religion" (DMI 1966, 6), which drew no negative reaction from parliamentarians. The same cannot be said for the government's announcement that it would strike "a new balance between the claims of family relationship and the economic interest of Canadians as a whole, which is that immigrants should generally be the well qualified people for whom employment opportunities are increasing" (14 October 1966, 8651-52).[61] It proposed that immigration be "planned as a steady policy of recruitment based on long-term considerations of economic growth," which were, in turn, dependent upon the arrival of "people who will, by their skill and adaptability, complement, in the most productive way possible, the training, employment and movement of workers who are already here" (DMI 1966, 12, 9).

The reaction in Parliament combined disappointment with hostility. Although parliamentarians endorsed the move to a fully non-discriminatory approach, Marchand's claim that he was introducing an expansionist policy was rejected. A broader range of people could now apply, but the family class would be diminished significantly, and this would affect people from some regions more than others, Richard Bell said: "the full potential of this nation will be built upon the strength of immigrant peoples; and for all of them, from whatever shore they come, there must be full and absolute equality as Canadian citizens, not some secondary status which is subordinate to people of other origins" (14 October 1966, 8653). In arguing against continued discrimination through such administrative categorization, Brewin highlighted the need to "make sure that the procedures coincide with the basic principles of elementary justice" (ibid., 8654).

In response, immigration officials reconsidered the whole question and returned, some months later, with the notion of a points system, whereby immigrants would be selected from abroad against a universal set of criteria relating to such factors as age, education and training, employment offer, and English and French language capability, most of which could be quantified in fairly objective terms. One area of discretionary decision making would remain: the immigration officer's assessment of the person's potential to adapt to life in Canada. A reduced set of criteria would be used for sponsored immigrants. It would thus be possible to remove the last vestiges of formal racial discrimination from the regulations governing admission while maintaining control over sponsored immigration. "For the first time," Marchand declared, "the rules governing the selection of immigrants are spelled out in detail for all to see," which "should provide an objectivity and a humanity which it has not in the past been able to ensure" (26 October 1967, 3505-6). It was not long before the characteristics of immigration to Canada took on a much less European orientation. Thus, although elements of discrimination remained (see Arat-Koc 1999), a historic transformation of Canadian immigration policy had occurred.

Although the white paper was generally uncritical of Canadian refugee policy, it expressed a more Liberal Internationalist approach towards refugees who had previously been considered hard to resettle, such as "the sick and the handicapped" (DMI 1966, 17). It recommended that "there should be provision ... for the movement to Canada of persons deserving of permanent admission for compassionate or humanitarian reasons irrespective of their personal abilities" (ibid., 5). This would give substance to "the humanitarian instinct of Canadians to be of assistance to people of other lands who need a place of refuge and a chance to rebuild their lives" (ibid., 7). The government also signalled its intention to sign the 1951 Refugee Convention and noted that it might "be desirable to establish a Refugee Eligibility Commission, with authority to decide whether an individual applying for asylum is entitled to refugee status" (ibid., 23). E.P. Beasley, director of the Policy and Planning Directorate, later stated before the SJCI that "there is a tendency of late for Canada to become a country of first asylum" and that "the time may have come to set forth in legislation machinery and a methodology for determining these individual [inland refugee] cases more precisely and more fairly" (Canada 1966-67, No. 4, 149). Possible models existed in Europe, where such commissions were "charged with the responsibility of determining whether the person is in fact a bona fide refugee within the definition of that term under the international convention" (ibid.). The establishment of such an independent inland refugee determination process in Canada would take more than another two decades.

As for due process, Marchand told the House "that to the best of our ability immigration must be administered in accordance with the basic principles of justice and humanity which Canadians demand in their national endeavours" (3 June 1966, 5940). The white paper promised that "no immigrant will be deportable for a cause beyond his own control" (DMI 1966, 33), and procedural changes within a new IAB structure were recommended, including the establishment of a more public setting during inquiries, a broader definition of counsel, an improvement in the competency of interpreters, and the possibility of employing lawyers instead of immigration officials to conduct inquiries, all of which would help ensure that deportation was "subject to a fair hearing and the right of appeal" (ibid., 35). "For justice to be done," the white paper declared, "... it must be seen to be done" (ibid., 33-34). This idea, which had underwritten the mid-1950s Canadian Bar Association proposals that were reviewed earlier, was now, in July 1966, reflected in legislation to change the nature of the IAB, the *Immigration Appeal Board Act.*

Parliamentary Secretary John C. Munro observed that "in no other area is equality and consistency so hard to achieve as it is in immigration matters" (20 February 1967, 13267). Balancing control with fairness required that the government possess considerable discretion in the law's administration. Such latitude, however, would result in mistakes as officials sought to perform their "onerous responsibility," and some mechanism was therefore needed "to assure that the proper concepts of the rights of the individual are applied to our immigration procedures" (ibid., 13267, 13269). It was "self-evident," Munro stated, that "the minister should not have the final say in cases where the individual has claim to rights in Canada or as a Canadian" (ibid., 13268), as this would raise questions of fairness and justice even as it created an administrative nightmare if people pursued favourable decisions through ministerial intervention.[62]

Under the proposed legislation, the Governor-in-Council would be authorized to appoint between seven and nine people to sit on the IAB, with the chair and at least two others being from the legal profession (Section 3). The IAB would hear all deportation cases, appeals of certain categories of rejected sponsorship applications made by relatives in Canada,[63] and disputes over detention pending an appeal (Sections 11-18). The one exception involved criminal and security cases, when a legal deportation order was accompanied by a certificate signed by the Solicitor General and the Immigration Minister (Section 21). IAB decisions would be final, subject to an appeal (by the individual or the department) by leave on points of law to the Supreme Court (Section 23). Moreover, Munro announced, the board would "be able to bring the humanitarian and other non-legal aspects of a particular case fully into consideration" in reaching decisions (20 February 1967, 13268). This included "the existence of reasonable grounds for believing that if execution of the order is carried out the person concerned will be punished for activities of a political character or will suffer unusual hardship" (Section 15.1.b.i). The IAB would operate as a court of record and set precedents on points of law through its decisions (Section 7). The new system would, Munro hoped, "assure the individual not only that justice will be done but that it will be seen to be done, and to be done with humanity and compassion" (20 February 1967, 13269). Although this initiative received support from all parties,[64] several concerns were raised. In the end, three significant changes were accepted by the government, while two were rejected.

The most straightforward change, suggested by Kenneth H. More (PC), was to allow the IAB to travel across the country to hear cases. It would cause many appellants considerable hardship, he noted, to have to go to Ottawa in pursuit of a fair hearing (21 February 1967, 13308). The government was also called on to clarify the IAB's scope to admit people on humanitarian and compassionate grounds. It was important, Bell said, for IAB members to "bring warm hearted, human understanding to the cold print of the immigration laws" to ensure that the human dimensions were not caught within rigid administrative practices (ibid., 13282). This was especially the case, Stanley Haidasz (L) observed, for ship deserters and asylum seekers (ibid., 13299). Until Canada ratified the relevant UN agreements on refugees[65] (it would do so in 1969), he urged that decisions be guided by their principles regarding the protection of those fearing or escaping from persecution. Marchand amended the bill to empower the board to set aside a deportation order on what it felt to be "humanitarian and compassionate grounds."[66]

Finally, MPs complained that the department was not required to provide reasons for a rejection, making it hard for people to prepare an effective appeal. David Lewis (NDP) stated: "It is simply nonsense to tell me that I can appeal to the appeal tribunal, if I do not know ahead of time what I am appealing against. I should not have to guess it" (ibid., 13317-18). Marchand eventually agreed to make it the minister's responsibility to provide reasons to appellants. Brewin also moved that the IAB be required to give reasons for its decisions (either orally or in writing) when requested to do so by either party to the case. Although Marchand suggested that the board would do this as a matter of course, Brewin reminded him that it frequently did not do so at present: "The result of this is not only a feeling of injustice by the aggrieved party, but the failure to build up a system of jurisprudence as it were, a system of principle, upon which decisions of this tribunal are based" (22 February 1967, 13350).[67] In providing reasons, substance would be given to any subsequent appeal to the Supreme Court. With a further alteration by Bell, who wished to ensure that the IAB could provide reasons on its own initiative, the amendment was accepted by Marchand.

The minister would not, however, expand the range of people who could appeal a rejected application to immigrate to Canada. Under the new law, only Canadian citizens could access the IAB when their applications to sponsor a relative had been refused. Critics found this distinction between citizens and non-citizens in Canada – both of whom could legally sponsor relatives – arbitrary and discriminatory. According to Bell, "if they are legitimate appeals and if their number is likely to swamp the board, the board should be expanded so that it is able to deal with all the appeals which will be forthcoming" (21 February 1967, 13313). Ian G. Wahn (L) also wanted to grant an appeal to those who had applied to remain in Canada and been refused (ibid., 13323). Marchand argued that the appeal was limited to citizens because "we must recognize, according to the Canadian law, that only Canadian citizens have rights; the others do not have rights" (ibid., 13325). He quickly acknowledged that non-citizens in Canada had rights but sought to keep the debate focused on non-citizens outside the country and not those already within.[68] He retreated, first, into the argument that as the change was experimental it was better to move slowly,[69] suggesting that the government wanted to ensure that "Canadian citizens have more rights than landed immigrants" (ibid., 13326). He agreed, however, to leave to the Governor-in-Council the question of which persons in Canada would be allowed an appeal rather than to define it in law. Among other critics,[70] Brewin maintained that it produced a "monstrous anomaly" (22 February 1967, 13362) to provide for a general right of appeal and then to assign to the Governor-in-Council the authority to decide who should be able to avail themselves of that right.[71] This opened the door – David Lewis maintained – to "a kind of arbitrary, bureaucratic discrimination" (1 March, 1967, 13627).

Security was another major area of concern. Lewis challenged the "undemocratic and indefensible" provision that denied people who were deemed to be a risk to national security the right of an appeal (23 February 1967, 13380). He compared this unfavourably to when internees during the Second World War had been able to hear the charges (if not the sources of those charges) against them and to respond during tribunal hearings. Gerald W. Baldwin (PC) agreed, arguing that "to leave this discretion to ministers of the crown is simply repeating the mistakes of the past" (21 February 1967, 13298).[72] The procedure did "not conform to what I believe," Bell complained, "to be natural justice" (ibid., 13313). It created, Brewin said, "a grave and gaping hole in this admirable principle" that all people should be able to appeal a deportation order:

> There is no point in beating our breasts about human rights in theory and then denying them in practice. Reasons of security of state are always used in an effort to excuse breaches or denials of rights acknowledged in theory. Admittedly there may be occasions when genuine reasons of state may require the suspension of normal rights, but this is not such an occasion. (1 March 1967, 13635-36)

Moreover, it did not conform to Sedgwick's recommendations. Marchand argued, however, that "as soon as we would make use of that information in public, its source would dry up overnight. Such is our problem" (21 February 1967, 13311). As well, if partial evidence was revealed, people would demand all of it (22 February, 1967, 13367). The fact that two ministers had to sign the certificate ensured that the rights of those involved would be protected, he concluded, as these two were responsible to Parliament for their actions.

It was not necessary, Lewis said in rebuttal, to provide precise information and sources to give people a chance to respond; instead, the person could, in camera, "be given in general terms the particulars of the grounds on which the action against him had been taken" and an opportunity to address them if desired (ibid., 13317). This would protect national security while allowing the accused as fair a process as possible. "I do not understand the minister's logic," Lewis lamented, "when he says over and over again that it is right, proper and not frustrating to give the appellant no information at all but there is something vicious about giving him part of the information" (23 February 1967, 13378).[73]

Although particular due process complaints remained,[74] MPs recognized that the *Immigration Appeal Board Act* would have a profound impact on Canadian control policy. Indeed, not long after it came into effect, Hawkins (1972, 166) wrote that "the advent of an independent Immigration Appeal Board with substantial powers can hardly fail to have a significant effect on immigration policy and procedure if only because it introduces a new element in decision-making in relation to the admission of certain classes of immigrants." In doing so, however, it was not so much creating a new situation in Canada as it was reverting back to the situation at the beginning of the century, before a decision was made to severely curtail the role of the courts in this policy area.

The decision to undo the rights-restrictive approach that had isolated departmental decisions from judicial scrutiny since the 1910 *Immigration Act* was essentially uncontroversial.[75] Although the desire for continued ministerial discretion remained in some quarters, no one publicly supported Liberal Nationalist comments such as those made by Joseph.-A. Mongrain (I), who compared immigrants to adopted children who have no right "to force anything on me ... I think the government should give the benefit of the doubt to the Canadian nation rather than to the immigrant who wants to come and live in our country" (1 March 1967, 13631-32). Indeed, most MPs, including Marchand, aligned themselves with Brewin when he declared:

> Fundamental rights are not for the majority alone. They are not for the popular. They are not for the accepted. Fundamental rights are for minorities, for unpopular minorities. They are for harried, would-be immigrants who are seeking admission to this country. It is important in the interests of Canada, not just of the immigrants, that our immigration procedures should be fair and in accordance with the best of our traditions. (Ibid., 13636)

Although the meaning of these traditions continued to be debated and contested, and to evolve, the Liberal Internationalist approach that had been so prominent in the universe of political discourse during the early post-Confederation years had returned to the fore again as Canada reached its first centenary.

Conclusion

The formal removal of ethnoracial considerations from immigrant selection and the reintegration of the courts into the control process were two fundamental steps in the dismantling of the Liberal Nationalist approach that had been dominant since the early twentieth century. This did not occur evenly across all categories of non-citizens, however. For example, the state's relationship with asylum seekers was not fully integrated into the Liberal Internationalist consensus that had come to prominence in Canadian control politics. Thus, even as significant strides had been made in removing the ethnoracial considerations from Canadian overseas refugee resettlement policies by the mid-1970s, serious limits on the due process protections recognized for refugee claimants in Canada remained for many years (see Anderson 2010). Nonetheless, the decision in 1969 to add Canada's signature to the 1951 Refugee Convention marked an important turning point, as it drew major international norms directly into the heart of the politics of control. More generally, it is important to observe that the developments traced in this chapter occurred almost exclusively in the legislative domain, which suggests that analyses that focus primarily on judicial activism and interest groups tell only part of the tale. Rather, these changes were more a reflection of the consolidation of a new consensus (as reflected through parliamentary institutions) concerning the rights of non-citizens, one that stemmed from traditional Liberal Internationalist concerns that can be traced back through debates over the meaning of being a British/Canadian liberal country. Although the courts clearly now play a much more prominent role in control politics in Canada and elsewhere, it is important to approach this phenomenon with a broader analytical perspective than just rights-based politics and control policy failures.

Liberal Nationalism did not disappear with the return to dominance of Liberal Internationalism; rather, it evolved, and continues to evolve, in response to changes in Canadian political culture and practice as well as international migration patterns. Thus, from at least the 1980s onward, Liberal Nationalists moved away from direct discriminatory arguments concerning the assimilability of newcomers and instead focused on such issues as the presumed dangers of ethnocultural diversity for social cohesion and, increasingly, the extent to which non-citizens abuse Canada's generosity by seeking to circumvent its control policies. From the 1970s onward, increased attention was paid to policies of "remote control" that could be used to prevent non-citizens from arriving in Canada in the first place. In this way, Canada could seek to avoid the issues of fundamental rights and fairness that, Brewin suggests in the last quote offered above, help shape what it means to be Canadian. Thus, while Canada entered an expansionist period of immigration in many respects from the late 1960s onward, debates over the due process and equality rights of non-citizens continued to define control politics, as they had since the first rights-restrictive policies were instituted in the late nineteenth century. An overemphasis on rights expansion and control policy failure, however, has distracted attention from the continued rights-based nature of state policies, to the detriment of a more complete and complex understanding of the control/rights nexus today.

7
Contemporary Canadian and Comparative Concerns

During its second century, the understanding of Canada as a country of immigration – as a country whose past, present, and future are inseparable from immigration – has become deeply embedded within its national identity. Indeed, soon after 1967, immigration became conjoined with the idea of multiculturalism as an essential part of what it means to be Canadian. When Prime Minister Pierre Elliott Trudeau (L) announced a policy of "multiculturalism within a bicultural framework" to the House of Commons in 1971, he made just such a connection, observing that this policy

> should help to break down discriminatory attitudes and cultural jealousies. National unity if it is to mean anything in the deeply personal sense, must be founded on confidence in one's own individual identity; out of this can grow respect for that of others and a willingness to share ideas, attitudes and assumptions. A vigorous policy of multiculturalism will help create this initial confidence. It can form the base of a society which is based on fair play for all. (8 October 1971, 8545)

Forty years later, this idea has grown from being seen as a means of fostering national unity to being considered a basic reflection of Canadian reality. Thus, the Department of Canadian Heritage (2012) states:

> Canada's experience with diversity distinguishes it from most other countries. Its 32 million inhabitants reflect a cultural, ethnic and linguistic makeup found nowhere else on earth. Approximately 200,000 immigrants a year from all parts of the globe continue to choose Canada, drawn by its quality of life and its reputation as an open, peaceful and caring society that welcomes newcomers and values diversity.

Aside from constituting a core feature of national self-understanding, Canada's status as a multicultural country of immigration has also become a prominent part of how it promotes itself abroad (Kymlicka 2004).[1]

This does not mean that Canadian immigration and refugee policies have been uncontroversial since 1967, or that the return to prominence of Liberal Internationalism precluded considerable debate over the meaning and practice of liberal-democratic control. Indeed, while "immigration and diversity are a source of pride for Canadians ... the policy architecture, policy goals, and measures of policy success are frequently contested" (Biles et al. 2008, 3). Although the debates that surrounded the passage of the 1976 *Immigration Act* strongly reflected the basic Liberal Internationalist consensus that had taken hold by 1967, especially in terms of an acceptance of the relevance of the principles of due process and equality for non-citizens along important dimensions, the precise manner in which these features of control have been interpreted and understood has continued to evolve. Indeed, Liberal Nationalism has experienced resurgence in recent decades and once again occupies a prominent place in the politics of control. By outlining some of the ways in which these issues have been debated since 1967, this chapter provides an opportunity for reflection upon the meaning of the findings presented in this book for the study of border control in Canada and other liberal-democratic states. In particular, it questions the conclusion found in the control literature that "democracy once installed tends to develop an expansionary logic of its own so that when rights are recognized for one group the pressure to extend the same rights to those not yet under their cover intensifies" (Freeman 2005, 3). It also suggests some directions for future research.

The shift to a formal policy of non-discrimination was quickly completed with the adoption of the points system in 1967. The effects of this policy change were soon reflected in the composition of annual intake levels. In particular, there was a substantial growth in immigration from Asia, the West Indies, and, to a lesser but still significant degree, Latin America (during the 1970s and 1980s) and Africa (in the 1990s) (see Li 2003b). Moreover, a formal commitment to equality was made with the passage of the 1976 *Immigration Act,* which declared that a core objective of Canadian policy was "to ensure that any person who seeks admission to Canada on either a permanent or temporary basis is subject to standards of admission that do not discriminate on grounds of race, national or ethnic origin, colour, religion or sex" (Section 3.f). This was renewed when the law was replaced with the 2001 *Immigration and Refugee Protection Act.*[2] As for refugees selected overseas, whereas Canada had traditionally resettled such migrants in larger groups from European countries (for example, Hungary in 1956 and Czechoslovakia in 1968), in the 1970s major refugee movements were accepted from Africa (Asian Ugandans), Latin America (Chileans), and Southeast Asia (Vietnamese), and a similar diversity was soon reflected in the source countries of asylum seekers accepted in Canada (see Kelley and Trebilcock 1998, Chapters 8 to 10).

Despite an official policy of non-discrimination, questions have been raised concerning how far this principle has been put into practice. Even as the 1976 law was being debated, critics noted that barriers to equality among immigrant applicants would remain. "It may be true," David Macdonald (PC) observed, "that we do not have any particular discrimination against people from any particular origin, but it is true that we locate our offices and the processing of those who apply for immigration very much with a view to origin and geographic location" (16 March 1977, 4056).[3] This remains a matter of concern (see, for example, National Anti-Racism Council of Canada 2002). As well, the process of immigrant selection has often been criticized for its discriminatory features, especially in gender and ethnoracial terms (Arat-Koc 1999; Jakubowski 1997; Li 2003a; Thobani 2000). For example, "while the adoption of the point system putatively introduces an objective, neutral test linked with seemingly value-free economic considerations, the requirements are not value-free. The so-called indicators of worth are socially constructed and reflect the prevailing Canadian political and economic power structure" (Abu-Laban 1998a, 76).

Discrimination, especially for visible-minority immigrants and even into the second generation, still exists within Canadian society and its labour market (Reitz 2007). Criticism has also been levelled against the country's temporary labour migration programs, "document[ing] the centrality of racism and processes of racialization in the recruitment and allocation of non-citizen foreign workers" (Prebisch and Binford 2007, 8; see also Boyd and Pikkow 2008; Stasiulis and Bakan 2005). Concerns have been raised that recent efforts to integrate migration policies in North America will produce not "a smooth and seamless regional space but one that is hierarchically differentiated," where the "marginalized, the dispossessed, and the unemployed have no opportunities for mobility, and are to remain very much fixed in place where they are" (Gilbert 2007, 90, 93).

Differential treatment in the context of a formally neutral approach has also been observed with respect to Canadian policies towards refugees and asylum seekers. It has long been argued that the source countries for refugees selected overseas bear too little resemblance to actual resettlement needs, in particular that Canadian policy has been "biased ... against regions of the world with large refugee populations (principally Africa, the Middle East, and West Asia)" (Nash 1994, 120; see also Basok and Simmons 1993). As for asylum seekers, a wide range of equality issues have been raised over the years. For example, in the mid-1980s the Canadian government quickly imposed a visa requirement on visitors from the Dominican Republic after some 300 asylum claims were made by citizens from that country, but waited until over 4,000 claims had been made by Portuguese citizens before acting.[4] A racial dimension has also been seen by some in the treatment of exceptional refugee arrivals, such as the 174 Sikhs who arrived by boat off the

Eastern coast in the summer of 1987. In both official and unofficial circles, "the discourse on the 'refugee crisis' ... focused almost exclusively on non-European migrants, whether from refugee-producing countries or not, while ignoring or expressing sympathy for some European groups using the refugee system to bypass regular immigration channels" (Creese 1992, 124). More generally, critics have questioned the move by Canada and other liberal-democratic states to limit access to their inland refugee systems in the post-Cold War era, replacing a relatively expansive response to European refugees with a more restrictive one for those from Africa, Asia, and Latin America (Richmond 1994).

Since 11 September 2001, as questions of security and migration have become even more intertwined, ethnoracial discrimination has continued to be a widely debated feature of the politics of control. Indeed, "an overtly racialized discourse, not tolerated in polite public spaces following the liberalization of the 1960s, can now be heard articulated unchecked" (Thobani 2007, 235; see also Razack 2008). At a policy level, the issue of racial profiling as a counter-terrorism tool quickly rose to prominence, with the debate shifting from whether it occurred to the terms under which it could be acceptable (Bahdi 2003; C. Smith 2007; Tator and Henry 2006). As the government unveiled its legislative responses to 9/11, critics noted the unevenness of the effects that it would have across communities, especially the born-in-Canada/born-abroad divide – "the fact that laws can be applied only to those born outside the country exemplifies systemic racism: legislation appears racist-free on the surface, but in reality it has differential results" (Wilkinson 2008, 119-20; see also Daniels et al. 2001; Ibrahim 2005). Such concerns also arose when Canada sought to enact legislative changes that would allow the government to revoke a naturalized individual's Canadian citizenship up to five years after it had been granted, with limited judicial oversight (Anderson 2008). As has frequently been the case in the history of Canadian control policy, these and other concerns about the equality of non-citizens (and increasingly the foreign-born in general) have overlapped with debates over due process.

With the 1967 *Immigration Appeal Board Act,* the judiciary once again had a more direct role to play in Canadian control policy. This was consolidated with the passage of the 1976 *Immigration Act,* as Manpower and Immigration Minister Bud Cullen (L) declared that the new law was "sensitive to the need to safeguard the civil rights of those who are subject to immigration proceedings" (10 March 1977, 3863). Parliamentary Secretary (Solicitor General) Art Lee (L), after noting that his great-grandfather had worked on the Canadian Pacific Railway as a Chinese migrant in the late 1800s, observed "how far we have come in Canada in buttressing and developing the rights of all peoples" in the country (11 March 1977, 3901).[5] Thus, while the law contained the usual list of "Inadmissible Classes" (Section 19), it also provided non-citizens with a wide range of procedural protections and generally ensured access to judicial review for those in Canada.[6] Although amended often and the object of considerable criticism over the years,[7] the 1976 *Immigration Act* was widely held to constitute a significant liberalization of policy.[8] A similar commitment to the due process rights of non-citizens was articulated with respect to the 2001 *Immigration and Refugee Protection Act.* As she introduced the legislation, Citizenship and Immigration Minister Elinor Caplan (L) declared that

> we do believe in due process, and in Canada we're proud of our Charter of Rights and Freedoms, which gives people a fair opportunity to have their say ... We are determined, as a government, to respect the Charter of Rights and Freedoms, and to see that it applies to everyone in Canada all the time – not just some people, selectively. We do not support changes that would uni-laterally strip rights away from people in Canada. (Canada 2001, 935, 950)

The government also created the independent and quasi-judicial Immigra-tion and Refugee Board (IRB) in 1989 to provide greater due process protec-tion for immigrants and refugees in Canada. As with equality, however, the meaning of this principle has continued to be contested during Canada's second century.

This can be seen in part in the large number of immigration and refugee cases in the Canadian court system. For example, during the last quarter of 2011, the Federal Court of Canada had 3,892 immigration cases pending, including 2,230 relating to refugee matters and 1,662 relating to immigra-tion.[9] This is not simply a reflection of the renewed involvement of the courts since 1967 but is also due to the fact that control measures are enacted within a much more extensive system of rights-based law: "Over the past decades, constitutional, regional and universal standards dedicated to the protection and promotion of rights and freedoms of all in general, and of migrants in particular, have become more sophisticated, and implementa-tion mechanisms are more effective than before" (Crépeau et al. 2007, 313).

These have been important developments during the post-Second World War period, with significant antecedents in the prewar period, that need to be assessed. Unfortunately, it is a subject that has received little systematic treatment in the Canadian literature, and thus the actual role of the judiciary in control politics and policies remains unclear.[10] The two areas that have perhaps had the most exposure have concerned refugees and, more recently, state security.

Questions of due process have been central to the consideration of refu-gees and, to a greater degree, asylum seekers in the politics of control. Since the 1970s, when Canada began to pursue a more active and extensive policy of overseas refugee resettlement, the government has been criticized for providing no mechanism whereby decisions made by officials abroad can be reviewed to ensure that candidates have been assessed fairly (Treviranus and Casasola 2003). As for asylum seekers, although the 1976 *Immigration Act* established the country's first formal procedure for inland refugee status determination, it lacked numerous due process protections, such as an oral hearing before a decision was rendered.[11] Concerns grew throughout the 1980s and 1990s as the government enacted several major and often restrictive changes to the inland process (Dirks 1995, Chapter 7; Matas and Simon 1989). In an expansionary vein, it addressed a core due process issue (clarified through a Supreme Court ruling) by creating the IRB and ensuring that refugee claimants would receive an oral hearing during the determination process. At the same time, it sought to restrict access to the inland system through various policies of interdiction (or "remote control") that prevent claimants from reaching Canada in the first place (Crépeau 2003; Kernerman 2008). With the passage of the 2001 *Immigration and Refugee Protection Act,* one of the most controversial due process debates revolved around the failure to implement a promised Refugee Appeal Division (RAD), which would institute an internal review of negative decisions on points of merit (Saufert 2007). Although legislative amendments passed in 2010 (reviewed below) will finally establish the RAD, this is being done at the same time that a range of other rights-restrictive policies are being introduced.

As with equality, and in a related manner, the debate over due process protections for non-citizens, and even for naturalized Canadians, has continued in the post-9/11 period. In the same way that rights-restrictive measures during the Cold War led to debates over the meaning and status of civil and political rights (Lambertson 2005; Whitaker and Marcuse 1994), Canada's response to the attacks in the United States has resulted in a more extensive debate over the rights of citizens (including naturalized Canadians) and non-citizens alike (Roach 2003). Naturalized Canadians have been faced with the possibility of increased state powers of citizenship revocation, racial profiling, and security surveillance (Bhandar 2004; Lyon 2006; Pither 2008; Rollings-Magnusson 2008). In regard to non-citizens, the government has also enhanced security screening for visitors, immigrants, refugees, and asylum seekers; expanded its use of security certificates and detentions; and negotiated a Safe Third Country Agreement with the United States that restricts the ability of refugee claimants to enter Canada through that country (Diab 2008; Leddy 2010; Macklin 2005; Pratt 2005).

Although a significant strand of the critical literature in Canada reflects a Liberal Internationalist orientation (exemplified by many of the references provided in the preceding pages), Liberal Nationalist views have become prominent, especially since the 1990s. This is particularly true in three areas: asylum seekers, national security, and immigrant integration. Liberal Nationalists often argue that the Canadian inland refugee system "is racked by dysfunction, waste, and corruption" (Gallagher 2001, 1), that it is "liberal and porous," and that Canada requires a more restrictive approach to "reception, determination, removal, and citizenship policies" (Gallagher 2003, 29). More specifically, the government has been called upon to institute "manifestly unfounded" (that is, where the decision maker considers the claim to be fraudulent) and/or Safe Third Country screening policies for all claims, replace the independent IRB with a process staffed by civil servants, increase the use of detention for refugee claimants, and pursue a more stringent removal policy for unsuccessful refugee claimants (Bissett 2010a; Francis 2002; Stoffman 2002). Liberal Nationalist critics have also raised more general concerns about the extent to which immigrants are willing to become "Canadian" (Moens and Collacott 2008). This tendency has expanded in the post-9/11 period to include a growing focus on linkages between particular immigrant communities and terrorism (Bell 2005; Hamilton 2007). The government resists taking a more restrictive approach, Liberal Nationalists argue, because of the twin forces of the special (pro-migration) interests and the courts. As a result, "gradually, but inevitably, a rational immigration policy will become impossible, and Canadians will have lost their right to decide which of the growing millions of migrants in the world they wish to allow into their country and their society" (Bauer 1997, 679). Moreover, it is argued, government inaction in this policy area is increasing the risk of terrorist attacks.

The Liberal Nationalist perspective has found a more established institutional presence with the creation in September 2010 of a new think tank, the Centre for Immigration Policy Reform (CIPR), which promotes a restrictive approach to immigration and refugee policy. According to its website, the CIPR aims to "expose myths and reveal facts about Canadian immigration and refugee policies and provide authoritative research and data."[12] Besides high-profile advisory board members such as Derek Burney (former Canadian ambassador to the United States and chief of staff to Prime Minister Brian Mulroney) and Peter White (formerly of Hollinger Inc.), the CIPR provides a venue for long-standing Liberal Nationalist critics such as Martin Collacott and James Bissett, among others.

After the arrival of Tamil asylum seekers by boat in 2009 and 2010, CIPR members advocated a restrictionist response, reflected in Bissett's advice: "There is one solution to smuggling. That's to send them back. If you send one boat back you won't get another" (quoted in Greenaway 2010). Another proposed option was to process the claimants outside Canada, perhaps in a Central American country (see Collacott, in Canadian Broadcasting Corporation 2010), so that they could not access the inland system and thereby make rights-based claims against the Canadian state, or to at least keep them in detention and remove them as soon as possible. According to CIPR members, the driving force behind the Tamils' decision to come by boat was not persecution but the fact that it provided (for those who were not criminals or terrorists) a means of circumventing Canadian immigration selection criteria in order to resettle and then sponsor family members to join them. "Our attraction to asylum seekers in general is not only that we accept the claims of large numbers that no other country would consider to be genuine refugees," Collacott (2010a) maintains, "but that we provide the most generous system of benefits available anywhere for those making a refugee claim."

The Canadian government, CIPR members assert, hesitates to take a more restrictionist approach for three main reasons. First, there is an allegedly constrained discourse when it comes to immigration and refugees. "Nobody wants to talk about it," Burney claims; "it's not for polite company" (quoted in O'Neil 2010). Second, officials are unnecessarily hindered by activist courts. Third, politicians are beholden to "the powerful refugee lobby" – "our politicians seem only to listen to this self-serving group," Bissett (2010b) asserts.[13] Refugee advocates oppose restrictive measures, it is claimed, "because a wide open asylum system either gives them financial reward or satisfies a [mistaken] belief they are helping refugees" (ibid.). To solve this problem, it is argued that the government should largely ignore the concerns of refugee advocates, insulate decision makers more effectively from judicial oversight, and enact measures to decrease access to and fairness within the inland system so that Canada can "continue the tradition of resettling refugees from overseas but significantly reduce opportunities for people to make claims in Canada" (Collacott 2010b). This reflects a Liberal Nationalist approach that privileges a more insular interpretation of state sovereignty that supports a narrower range of rights that non-citizens can claim against the receiving state.

Of course, a Liberal Internationalist discourse also arose in response to the Tamil boat arrivals, and was most frequently advanced by the opposition parties in Parliament, the UNHCR, non-governmental organizations working with immigrants and refugees, ethnocultural groups, lawyers and migration experts, as well as many individual citizens. More generally, government polling in 2009 revealed that, while recognizing many problems with the inland system, "Canadians overwhelmingly support a fair system that provides asylum seekers benefit of the doubt" and "overwhelmingly believed in the idea of Canada being among the most open countries to refugees in the world" (Berthiaume 2010). Although a Liberal Internationalist outlook is often reflected in public debate, however, it appears to be increasingly marginalized and on the defensive in the universe of political discourse. This can be seen, for example, in Citizenship and Immigration Minister Jason Kenney's (C) dismissal of Amnesty International's concerns over rights-restrictive features of the government's response to the Tamil boat arrivals as as being "ideological" and therefore not constructive (Kenney 2010),[14] and the growing tendency to dismiss criticism of government control measures as a desire for the status quo.[15] Moreover, a Liberal Internationalist approach to asylum seekers, besides having a long history of being opposed by senior immigration officials (Anderson 2010), also appears to sit uncomfortably with the ideological stance and political interests of the Conservative government. As political columnist Don Martin (2010) put it following the arrival of the *MV Sun Sea:* "A frenzy of furious public opinion demanding a crackdown on refugee queue-jumpers is just what this law-and-order government needed to get back on message and ease a summer of voter discontent."

Indeed, the renewed prominence of Liberal Nationalism can be seen in the introduction of Bill C-49, the *Preventing Human Smugglers from Abusing Canada's Immigration System Act,* in October 2010, two months after the arrival of the *MV Sun Sea.* The proposed legislation was unveiled at a press conference held in front of the *MV Ocean Lady* (the boat that had arrived in 2009), effectively underlining themes of illegality and security. Government officials blurred the lines between refugees and people smugglers, and in doing so helped redirect public frustration over the latter towards the former. Thus, Minister of Public Safety Vic Toews (C) declared that "Canada opens its doors to those who work hard and play by the rules while cracking down on those who seek to take advantage of our generosity and abuse our fair and welcoming immigration system" (Public Safety Canada 2010b). Moreover, it was suggested that those who truly needed Canada's protection could find it overseas, and that those who made inland claims instead were acting in an unfair – if not abusive – fashion (Public Safety Canada 2010a). This focus on criminality and illegality, on the abuse of Canada's generosity, and on the presence of national security concerns was taken up and amplified in the media (on the 2009 arrivals, see Bradimore and Bauder 2011).

As an indication of the current prominence of Liberal Nationalism with respect to Canadian control policies, the government has introduced significant and extensive changes to the country's inland refugee status determination system since 2010 that reduce further the rights-based claims that asylum seekers can make against the state. Although it is not possible in this concluding chapter to provide a fuller account of the universe of political discourse within which these developments have occurred (some indication of which has been provided in the previous paragraphs), the snapshot provided here at least serves to underline the continued rights-based concerns that give definition to this policy area.

In introducing the 2010 *Balanced Refugee Reform Act* in the House of Commons, Kenney claimed that its provisions would "provide faster protection decisions for legitimate refugees while providing faster removals for the many who actually come here seeking to abuse Canada's generosity" (26 April 2010, 1945). Its restrictive elements included, among others (see Library of Parliament 2011):

- replacing Cabinet-appointed officials within the Refugee Protection Division (RPD) of the IRB with public servants[16]
- instituting a new interview stage to take place as early as fifteen days after an inland refugee claim has been made (previously claimants had twenty-eight days to fill out a Personal Information Form), during which the RPD official can question witnesses (previously this occurred at the actual hearing stage), with a failure to attend leading to a possible finding that the claim has been abandoned
- requiring that refugee determination hearings involve only one RPD member (previously the IRB chair could appoint three-member panels to address more complex cases)
- empowering the minister to assign "designated countries of origin" consisting of nationals of all or part of a country, or of a particular population within a country, and to allow for differential treatment of claims based on this categorization
- empowering RPD officials to declare that a claim has been rejected because it is considered to be "manifestly unfounded," which can also lead to differential treatment
- requiring that appeals to the Refugee Appeal Division (RAD) be filed completely within fifteen days of a negative RPD decision
- reducing the grounds on which Humanitarian and Compassionate applications (which allow some people to apply for permanent resident status in Canada when they do not meet the formal requirements) can be considered or accepted
- denying Pre-Removal Risk Assessments (PRRA, which allow some people to apply for protection before they are removed from Canada) for those whose refugee claims have been abandoned, rejected, or withdrawn during the previous twelve months
- denying temporary resident permits to refugee claimants until twelve months after their claims have been abandoned, rejected, or withdrawn
- implementing manu of the restrictive features of the law while delaying the few more rights-expansionist dimensions.

After considerable debate, the bill received Royal Assent on 29 June 2010. While certain Liberal Internationalist concerns were addressed in the legislation,[17] the overall direction suggested a Liberal Nationalist orientation.[18]

Although the proposed 2010 *Preventing Human Smugglers from Abusing Canada's Immigration System Act* died on the order paper when a federal election was called in early 2011, it was soon reintroduced as Bill C-4 when the Conservatives returned to power in June. Bill C-4 subsequently stalled at Second Reading, but many of its features reappeared in February 2012 when the government introduced Bill C-31, *Protecting Canada's Immigration System Act*. At Second Reading in the House, Kenney portrayed his proposals as sensible and necessary reforms in response to "human smugglers ... targeting Canada and treating this country like a doormat" and "false asylum claimants who seek to abuse our generosity" (6 March 2012, 5872). Among its various restrictive features, Bill C-31 (see Library of Parliament 2012):

- grants the minister discretionary power to declare groups as "irregular arrivals" that fall within a new "designated foreign national" category (this power is retroactive to May 2009, before the arrival of the *MV Ocean Lady*), rendering them subject to mandatory detention,[19] with less frequent detention reviews and more specific conditions for and after release[20]
- imposes a five-year period before those within the "designated foreign nationals" category who are granted refugee status by the RPD can apply for permanent residency and, subsequently, sponsor family members to join them,[21] and denies them for the same length of time access to travel documents to be issued to those with refugee status under the 1951 Refugee Convention
- provides for further differential treatment of claimants who fall within the "designated countries of origin," "manifestly unfounded," "no credible basis," and "designated foreign national" categories as well as those who apply for an exception under the Canada-US Safe Third Country Agreement, including barring them from access to the RAD and allowing for removal orders to be put into effect while Federal Court appeals are underway
- provides for differential treatment of those who apply at an immigration office in Canada as opposed to a port of entry
- reduces the "designated country of origin" category to countries only (no longer including regions within the country or targeted populations), allows more flexibility for the minister to designate such countries, and restricts the access of claimants within this category to the PRRA to thirty-six months after a negative RPD decision
- allows further time limits to be introduced by regulation for PRRA applications
- applies many of the new provisions to those within the determination system before the law comes into effect
- broadens the authority of immigration officers to detain people, including permanent residents of Canada, expands the definition of human smuggling, and expands the grounds on which refugees can have their refugee status subject to vacation or cessation.[22]

Unlike Bill C-11, which had been passed when the Conservatives held a minority government, Bill C-31 was subject to relatively few amendments from opposition MPs before it received Royal Assent on 29 June 2012.

As the bill made its way through the legislative process, however, it received numerous rights-based criticisms from Liberal Internationalists, reflecting their promotion of a strong positive link between the state and the rights of non-citizens, forged by liberal ideas of equality and freedom stemming from national and international laws and norms. The UNHCR (2012b) called attention to a wide range of concerns related to procedural fairness and emphasized the need to ensure non-discrimination, underlining "the problems associated with differentiated treatment of asylum-seekers and refugees, depending on the mode of arrival" (2012a, 1). Amnesty International (2012, 1) advised that many features of Bill C-31 contravened "binding international human rights treaties to which Canada is a party [including the 1951 Refugee Convention], and [that] it would likely result, if it were to be implemented in its current form, in serious violations of international refugee law, international human rights law and the Canadian Charter of Rights and Freedoms." Meanwhile, the National Immigration Law Section of the Canadian Bar Association (2012, 1) did "not believe that Bill C-31 in its current form will meet the objectives of faster processing and administrative efficiency while still ensuring fairness and accuracy." For its part, the Canadian Civil Liberties Association (2012, 10) concluded that it was "hard to reconcile [Canada's] humanitarian ideals ... with a Bill that penalizes innocents, discriminates, separates parents from children, and recklessly creates processes that could return individuals to persecution and torture." As for the Canadian Council for Refugees (2012, 1), it "called for the withdrawal of Bill C-31 because it provides for an unworkable process that will fail to respect the Canadian Charter of Rights and Freedoms and international obligations[,] ... will fail to give protection to refugees[, and] ... will be harmful to the successful settlement of refugees in Canada."

In keeping with the proposal made at the outset of this book, these and other criticisms of recent legislative and policy moves fit comfortably with the idea that the pursuit of an increasingly rights-restrictive approach to control (in this case with respect to asylum seekers) within a liberal democracy such as Canada can

> contribute to a decrease in control by creating opportunities for rights-based politics, encouraging circumvention of restrictive measures, and prompting additional decision-making stages that generate administrative inefficiencies. In other words, rights-restrictive policies can increase the risks of control failure when they open up avenues along which state authority and capacity can be challenged effectively. Furthermore, a loss of control may lead to additional restrictive measures, creating a negative feedback loop within the control/rights nexus ... wherein control failure prompts further rights-restrictive measures, which in turn result in failure, and so on, until a more serious or systematic loss of control occurs.

In the process, the country and citizenry's commitment to foundational political values such as liberty and equality – and thus its sense of what it means to "be Canadian" – is troubled if not undermined.

Canadian border control policy thus continues to operate within a universe of political discourse that can usefully be understood to be defined by Liberal Internationalist and Liberal Nationalist perspectives on the appropriate relationship between the rights of non-citizens (and, at times, even citizens) and the state. The rights-restrictive approach adopted over the course of several years now, especially with respect to asylum seekers, suggests that the findings presented in earlier chapters remain relevant. At the very least, the return to a more Liberal Nationalist approach calls for a much greater effort to determine whether the narrow interpretation of the control/rights nexus on which it is based – that the recent rise of rights-based politics undermines liberal-democratic state control – is an appropriate foundation on which to construct a sustainable and coherent political or policy response. This book has gone some way towards substantiating a more expansive interpretation, presented in Chapter 1, of how control and rights can intersect in liberal-democratic states, but much work remains to be done to fulfill its potential in both Canadian and comparative contexts.

Further research is needed to extend the utility of the expanded interpretation itself. For example, control policies could be more clearly distinguished according to the types of rights involved, the extent to which restrictive policies challenge how those rights are understood in legal and political terms, and their tendency to produce different forms of challenges to state authority and capacity. As well, there is a need for more structured and detailed accounts of how frequently rights-based politics arises and whether it bolsters or undermines state control. This will require a more substantial exploration of the role that the legal system (including the legal traditions, frameworks, courts, and lawyers) plays in control policy outcomes, and of the activities of immigrant and refugee communities as policy actors in their own right. In the absence of such investigations, general conclusions regarding the role of activist courts and interest groups must be considered to be but preliminary and partial. Moreover, such analyses will need to be conducted across policy periods, types of international migration, and liberal democracies. As is clear from the Canadian case, focusing on the rights-based nature of state control policies within the context of the liberal-democratic character of the political system can uncover previously unexplored dimensions of immigration and refugee history and shed new light on more familiar aspects. It can also provide legitimacy to a wider range of control policy options.

While control has been conceptualized here as regulating the conditions under which international migrants can enter into and/or remain within the territories under a state's authority, it will also be important to question further the expressed control objectives of the state itself. Control debates generally assume that states aim to restrict "unwanted immigration," but it cannot simply be assumed that a "failure" to limit international migration does not meet other economic and political objectives of the state (Andreas 2001; De Genova 2002). Both states and their interactions with non-state actors are extremely complex and thus it should be expected that policy goals in this field will be a reflection rather than a simplification of that condition. The model of the control/rights nexus used here provides two avenues along which such investigations could take place, assessing how both circumvention and administrative inefficiencies might mediate the relationship between rights-restrictive policies and control "failure." Finally, at the most critical level, the very foundations of liberal-democratic control need to be probed further. As an immanent rather than foundationalist analysis of state control (Carens 2003), this book does not challenge the state's right to regulate its borders, but such an approach constitutes an important analytical path that can provide many additional insights into the nature of control. In keeping with the approach taken in this book, it would help to problematize the role of the state, placing its actions at the centre of the analysis rather than – as the Canadian and comparative control literatures are often wont to do – leaving the state's authority to restrict the rights of non-citizens largely unquestioned. Such work would not only assist in developing a clearer understanding of the politics of control but would also contribute to a more refined understanding of the illiberal dimensions of liberal-democratic states.

In contrast, by focusing their analyses on rights-based politics, rights expansion, and policy failure, the Canadian and comparative literatures have not adequately probed the long-standing and continually unfolding debate between Liberal Internationalists and Liberal Nationalists on the politics of control. As a result, important policy dynamics and therefore essential policy lessons have been and continue to be overlooked. If it is true – and it would certainly seem to be true – that "in the liberal democracies today, rights are the key to regulating migration" (Hollifield et al. 2008, 8), then considerably more attention needs to be paid to how control and rights intersect. This suggests the need to take at least two important analytical steps. First, it is necessary to anchor the analysis in the rights-based nature of the policies that states pursue (or choose not to pursue). Second, contemporary developments need to be placed within a much more historically based context. In these ways, the ability to identify and explore broader patterns of continuity and change are increased significantly. Over the past twenty-five years, the literature has come a long way in identifying the liberalness of liberal-democratic states as an important factor in the politics of control. An unduly narrow conceptualization of the control/rights nexus, however, has caused the rights of the state to be privileged over those of non-citizens, and this has unnecessarily limited the range of explanations and policy options that are considered legitimate within control politics. The analysis presented here suggests that this is not an inevitable situation but requires policy analysts and practitioners alike to go further in challenging more conventional thinking about the nature of control and rights in liberal-democratic states.

Notes

Introduction: Reconsidering the Control/Rights Nexus

1   The bill died on the order paper when the 2011 general election was called. It was reintro-
    duced again in June of that year before being folded into Bill C-31, the *Protecting Canada's
    Immigration System Act,* which was passed by Parliament in June 2012. Both this bill and
    the 2010 *Balanced Refugee Reform Act* are discussed in Chapter 7.
2   A perspective that is not investigated in this book is the "open borders" stance, which
    questions the legitimacy and/or practicality of national borders. Instead, the analysis pre-
    sented here takes as given the state's right to regulate who enters into and remains within
    its sovereign territory. In a manner akin to Carens (2003, 95), this work seeks "to identify
    the norms and principles embedded in the immigration practices of liberal democratic
    states and reflect critically upon them. This is an immanent critique of immigration, rather
    than a foundationalist one."
3   For example, most discussions of the 1976 *Immigration Act* (such as Hawkins 1972; Kelley
    and Trebilcock 1998; and Knowles 1997) focus on how it constituted a break with the past
    (especially its predecessor, the 1952 *Immigration Act*) rather than a continuation of ideas
    that had long defined the politics of control in Canada.

Chapter 1: The Study of Liberal-Democratic Control over International Migration

1   A similar dynamic was apparent in the case of asylum seekers, Joppke (1997) argued, but
    here, states had acted more decisively to shore up state sovereignty in the face of rights-
    based claims.
2   Elsewhere, Canada is at best mentioned in passing, as in Freeman 1995.
3   It is not, of course, the only possible analytical point of departure. For example, alternative
    critical readings might involve questioning the intentions of the state in controlling its
    borders (De Genova 2002) or even the legitimacy of state control itself (Carens 1987; Sharma
    2006a). As noted in the Introduction, however, this book presents an immanent rather
    than a foundationalist analysis of state control (Carens 2003).
4   "Every paradigm contains a view of human nature, a definition of basic and proper forms
    of social relations among equals and among those in relationships of hierarchy, and speci-
    fication of relations among institutions as well as a stipulation of the role of such institu-
    tions," she writes (1989, 239).
5   It also reflects the binary structure of migration law itself, where "the principal distinction
    is between citizens and others, 'us' and 'them'" (Dauvergne 2005, 32).
6   In recent years, this idea has been explored within the context of cosmopolitanism (e.g.,
    Appiah 2006).
7   This is not the same as the concept of Liberal Nationalism that is advanced, for example,
    by Tamir (1993), which is separated from Ethnic Nationalism more clearly than is envisioned
    here.
8   Thus, Dauvergne (1999, 599) labels border control "an amoral arena" because it "is outside
    the reach of agreed versions of liberal morality, justice, and equality" that are rooted in the

206 Notes to pages 28-37

mutual obligation that defines relations between members of the national liberal political community.

9 "The voice of the people can be heard through the Senate, too, but the Senate ... is neither accountable to the people nor to any external body," he continues (D. Smith 2007, 4). Nonetheless, as will be seen, it does represent societal ideas and interests within Parliament.

10 More generally, D. Smith (ibid., 10) laments that "despite parliament's centrality, it is a subject of declining study." On the lack of attention paid to parliamentary committees, see Schofield and Fershau (2007).

Chapter 2: The Liberal Internationalist Foundations of Canadian Control (1867-87)

1 Significant non-European international migration had already occurred by the nineteenth century due to colonial practices of slavery and indentured servitude. For example, some 15 million slaves were transported to the Americas from Africa prior to 1850 (Castles and Miller 2003, 53).

2 "The francophone population had increased about threefold [to 1 million], almost entirely through natural increase, but the non-francophone population had increased tenfold, largely because of the massive influx of British emigrants" (Buckner 1997, 17-18).

3 Canada also had a history of creating refugee movements. Perhaps some eight thousand Acadians (of an estimated ten to twelve thousand) were forcibly removed from their homes between 1755 and 1762 (Griffiths 1992). Many political exiles fled during the rebellions in Lower and Upper Canada in the mid-nineteenth century – that is, if they were not caught, convicted, and then executed, imprisoned, or shipped to Australia (Cahill 1998). In addition, many Aboriginal peoples were forced to move from their traditional lands (Royal Commission on Aboriginal Peoples 1996).

4 For example, the government reported in 1872 that aside from its established immigration agencies in Britain and France, it would also send out "a number of agents to the rural parts of England, Scotland, Ireland, and parts of the continent, particularly Alsace and Lorraine, to the contiguous parts of Germany and France, and to the Scandinavian Kingdoms" to attract settlers (Canada 1872, 13).

5 "One of the most fundamental underlying perceptions of Britain during the nineteenth century focused upon the idea of the country as a cradle of liberty in comparison with the intolerant and unstable regimes which existed in other European states" (Panayi 1994, 41).

6 "Even before 1870 ... aliens were absolutely tolerated as *visitors,* which made Britain ... one of the *most* hospitable countries of Europe. As well as the same laws as Britons they were subject to the same processes of law, with the added privilege, until 1870, of being able to be tried by a 'mixed' jury of half foreigners if they so elected. They could not be prevented from coming in to Britain, or expelled for doing anything in Britain. After 1836, they did not even have to notify anyone they had come or were there. For the best part of the nineteenth century, therefore, the British government deliberately denied itself any control over immigration, and appeared indeed for the most part to take no interest in it" (J. Porter 1979, 4; emphasis in original).

7 As well, the British state conducted surveillance on some non-citizens on account of their politics (B. Porter 1984).

8 "Everyone in the union would be equally subject to Parliament's laws; every individual would be equally entitled to the benefits of 'peace, order and good government'" (Ajzenstat 2007, 8). As McKay (2000, 626) notes, "the 'individuals' at [liberalism's] conceptual nucleus are not to be confused with actual living beings." Thus, it was possible to treat broad categories of people (women, Aboriginal peoples, non-Europeans, etc.) differently while still adhering to a liberal position, which illustrates the illiberal/liberal terrain upon which control politics unfolds.

9 Most European states, however, had established systems to control the movement of foreigners (and sometimes citizens) *within* their borders (Fahrmeir 2000). States also sought to restrict particular migrant groups on occasion (Moch 1992).

10 Immigration control was instead carried out at the state level. Most immigrants disembarked in New York, where, beginning in 1847, they were met by members of the State Board of

Commissioners of Immigration, who "made every effort to assist the newly arrived foreigners" (Dinnerstein and Reimers 1999, 31).

11 "In each Province the Legislature may make Laws in relation to Agriculture in the Province, and to Immigration into the Province; and it is hereby declared that the Parliament of Canada may from Time to Time make Laws in relation to Agriculture in all or any of the Provinces, and to Immigration into all or any of the Provinces; and any Law of the Legislature of a Province relative to Agriculture or to Immigration shall have effect in and for the Province as long and as far only as it is not repugnant to any Act of the Parliament of Canada."

12 Hereafter referred as to the Standing Committee; the committee tasked with discussing immigration policy changed several times over the years, as can be seen in the relevant references listed in the bibliography.

13 Within twenty-four hours of arrival at their final destination in Canada, the Masters of Vessels were required to submit a manifest documenting the particulars of every passenger on board at the time of disembarkation, identifying those passengers who were "lunatic, idiotic, deaf or dumb, blind or inform" for officials (Section 9.1). The Medical Superintendents, for their part, had to determine whether such individuals were "likely to become permanently a public charge" (Section 11.2). On various ways in which Masters of Vessels might be held accountable, see Sections 8-15.

14 In 1874, he again summarized their role for the Committee: "On arriving in Canada, the immigrants are received by the Dominion agents, who give them information, counsel, and in nearly every case a free passage to their place of destination and, in case of want or illness, an asylum and help" (Canada 1874b, 14).

15 "Intending emigrants who have been pauperized, or who are tainted with crime, or who do not possess thoroughly satisfactory characteristics, and a capacity for hard work will not receive any encouragement," he nonetheless promised, "but decided discouragement from the officers of your Department" (Canada 1888a, 241).

16 For example, in 1885 Tupper rejected an appeal "to establish a colony of deaf and dumb persons in the North-West Territories" (Canada 1885b, 155-56).

17 "Nothing in this Act shall prevent the Master of any Vessel from permitting any Passenger to leave the Vessel at the request of such Passenger before the arrival of the Vessel at her final Port of destination" (Section 6). The law was rewritten in 1906 so that passengers could do so only outside Canada.

18 As late as 1908, Superintendent of Immigration William D. Scott reported that "first class passengers speaking English are not examined by immigration officers" (Canada 1908a, 344). It was left to a ship's crew to report those who needed to be examined.

19 Some immigrants were inspected by an office of the British government – the Boards of Trades – in England, while all passengers were ostensibly assessed by sight on board by a doctor hired by the ship's owners. However, a description of these medical professionals offered by Canada's Medical Superintendent of Immigration P.H. Bryce in 1908 cannot have offered much reassurance to the members of the Standing Committee, to whom it was directed: "I have known of young men a little anemic or a little tubercular, who have gone on board as ship's surgeon, because they are delicate in health. Once in a while you will find an old soaker, but not many in recent years I am glad to say. Then there is a class of bright young fellows who want to get a little pocket money and experience of the world" (ibid., 392).

20 It temporarily abandoned the practice several times during this period when it was felt that the private agents were sending too many paupers to Canada.

21 Although the government sent its own agents overseas to recruit immigrants, Macdonald (1966, 41-42) notes that they were "largely political appointees, favourites or nominees of government and of its friends, and rewarded by some form of political appointment for work done for the cause. Many of them were sent abroad on a holiday at public expense. Motives were therefore questionable, the cost excessive, the results insignificant. Fortunately their appointments were usually for short periods ... Of their reports to the Minister of Agriculture it was said that nothing in fiction or romance, in sensational or humorous literature could be more ridiculous."

22 When responsibility for immigration was transferred to the Department of the Interior in 1892, Deputy Minister A.M. Burgess (Canada 1893, 154) observed that "to try to keep track of those coming in and those going out would, to my mind, be practically like trying to count the sands of the sea," and thus he ordered that no record be kept, a practice that seems to have persisted until 1898.

23 "The class of simply poor persons has in the great majority of cases proved to be the best for settlement in this country, that is to say, a man having no means but his strength and energy would be more likely to succeed in this country than a man who simply comes with money, and without having in the same degree these other qualifications," he later said (Canada 1889, 45).

24 For example, in 1888, a lengthy Supply Debate was initiated in the House by Richard Cartwright (L) concerning the level of "necessitous and unfit persons coming to this country" (2 May 1888, 1155). Agriculture Minister John Carling (C) denied that there was any great problem. The subject also received in-depth treatment before the Standing Committee, which found complaints to lack "definiteness, no precise information as to numbers being given, and no attempt being made to discriminate between the ordinary poor, always found in large cities, and immigrants of that class" (Canada 1888b, 3). The government nonetheless decided to suspend its assisted passage scheme that same year, a move usually tailored to reduce pauper immigration.

25 "The rule of the Department is that immigrants who have not been over one year in the country, are, in some measure, under the care of the Department; and if it has been found, after they have come to the country, that, from illness or bodily infirmity, they have been unable to get their living, they have been sent back, as the simplest and cheapest mode of dealing with them" (Lowe, in Canada 1879b, 40).

26 "Although they did not hesitate to repress indigenous revolutionaries, the governments of the liberal states were generally tolerant of the exiles, who made few demands on them beyond asylum itself, as long as they stayed out of domestic politics and their presence was compatible with foreign policy" (Zolberg et al. 1989, 10-11).

27 Dirks (1977, 29) offers a figure of about nine thousand. There would be other small movements of Mennonites to Canada after this time, until their entry was prohibited following the First World War, on account of their beliefs (see Epp 1982).

28 The Agriculture Department declared in its 1873 annual report that "every effort has been made that could be made to invite the Mennonites to settle in Canada" (Canada 1874a, xii). The Standing Committee recommended that all sixty thousand Mennonites in southern Russia be resettled in Canada (Macdonald 1966, 201).

29 These "privileges" are enumerated in a copy of a letter sent to the Mennonites, dated 26 July 1873 (see Canada 1874a, xiii). Interpretive disputes over these privileges led to fractious relations between the Mennonite community and both federal and provincial governments, which in turn fed a growing unease in Canada over the admission of immigrants from non-northern European countries (see Janzen 1990).

30 By way of comparison, the terms of group settlement offered at about the same time to Germans, Icelanders, Scandinavians, and others provided fewer special provisions (Macdonald 1966).

31 "After years of ill-concealed hostility of the Rothschilds against Canada," he wrote to Galt, "you have made a great strike by taking up the old clo' cry, and going in for a Jew immigration into the Northwest ... [that might create] a link, a missing link ... between Canada and Sidonia [Jewish financiers]" (quoted in Tulchinsky 1992, 113-14). Not everyone was so opportunistic; for example, John Taylor, a Manitoba Immigration Agent, wrote that "providing new homes far removed from the cruelties and atrocities so shamefully perpetrated on this people in the name of religion ... would be a lasting credit to this country" (quoted in ibid., 114).

32 A Private Member's Bill was also introduced in the House by Gavin Fleming (L) to make the Masters of Vessels "responsible for pauper or destitute emigrants in the same manner as he is now held responsible with regard to those who may be lunatic, idiotic, deaf or dumb, blind or infirm" (5 March 1880, 453). It did not pass First Reading.

33 Roberts (1988, 53) notes that it is difficult to assess how immigration officials acted during these early years, as they often did so "informally and unofficially (and extra-legally)."

34 The *BNA Act* did "nothing to define the status of the new polity in the British Empire or the world ... [and] likewise had nothing to say about the conduct of foreign relations" (Stacey 1984, 1, 3). "For external affairs the imperial authority in Canada was more than a shadow. Executive government was explicitly vested in the queen, and in foreign or imperial affairs her representative, the governor general, was subject to instructions from London. Through him all dealings with foreign powers must be conducted, even between Ottawa and Washington" (Glazebrook 1966, 83).

35 While it is generally recognized that Canada's overseas diplomatic presence stemmed as much from the desire to promote immigration as it did from a wish to foster trade (Skilling 1945), the control dimension to the consolidation of Canadian sovereignty receives little comment in the literature.

36 Thus, in the Australian colonies, Canada, New Zealand, and the United States, "those defending the Chinese ... usually argued that the Chinese were peaceful, sober and industrious, and that restriction or discrimination was a denial of natural justice and a clear breach of British or American traditions and international agreements" (Price 1974, 104). Nonetheless, a certain Canadian exceptionalism has been noted: "Racism in British North America was less able to find expression in discriminatory laws and this legal situation may well have prevented in Canada some of the excesses of persecution that the Chinese suffered in California and other western states" (Con et al. 1982, 42).

37 Besides the estimated one thousand Chinese workers who died during railroad construction, many others eventually left for the United States or returned to China.

38 At that time, the Chinese were seen as being valuable workers and potential consumers but were not generally held to be good settlers (Ward 1990, 24-29).

39 From their first effort in 1878 onward, provincial politicians quickly learned that the federal government was able and willing to disallow legislation restricting Asian immigration that was felt to be *ultra vires* of Section 95 of the *BNA Act*, and would be upheld by the courts. Successive governments in Victoria passed such legislation well into the twentieth century to pressure Ottawa into adopting a more restrictive approach (see Ryder 1991).

40 Labelled by one Ottawa newspaper as a "great anti-pigtail champion," Bunster had previously and unsuccessfully sought as a provincial politician in British Columbia to have the Chinese pay a $5 tax for wearing a queue (see J. Morton 1974, 43-44). Before the province joined Confederation, he tried (also unsuccessfully) in 1871 to have a $50 poll tax levied on all people of Chinese descent working in British Columbia. He did succeed, however, in having the Chinese (along with Aboriginal peoples) excluded from provincial vital statistics surveys.

41 Underlining Mackenzie's Liberal Internationalist credentials, Thomson (1960, 242) quotes an 1875 speech in which the Prime Minister spoke of how British ideas of equality and freedom had been made manifest in the Dominion: "In our great colonies ... we take the ground simply and completely that every man stands equal in the eye of the law, and every man has the same opportunity by exercise of the talent with which God has blessed him to rise in the world, in the confidence of his fellow-citizens, the one quite as much as the other."

42 Not long thereafter, calls for the expulsion of those Chinese already in Canada were dropped from restrictionist discourse in the House. As Edgar C. Baker (C) later put it: "I do not ask for anything to expel the Chinaman from British Columbia, as we are satisfied they would soon die out, so that only their bones will have to be taken away" (30 April 1883, 906).

43 Mackenzie argued that "the principle that some classes of the human family were not fit to be residents in this Dominion would be dangerous and contrary to the law of nations and the policy which controlled Canada" (16 April 1879, 1262).

44 In 1290, King Edward I banished all Jews from his lands; this Edict of Expulsion was not formally rescinded until the 1650s.

45 After noting that "the Committee should be very impartial, in order to look at all phases of the question" (ibid., 1260), Macdonald ensured that it would not be by agreeing that de

Cosmos, a man with a long public record of anti-Chinese sentiments, should serve as chair. For example, as editor of the *Daily British Colonist,* de Cosmos wrote in 1862 of "their inferior civilization, their language, their religion, their habits of living – all so hostile to the customs and prejudices of the higher and dominant [white] race" (quoted in Ward 1990, 27).

46 "I share very much the feeling of the people of the United States and the Australian colonies," he said, "against a Mongolian or Chinese population in our country as permanent settlers. I believe they would not be a wholesome element for this country. I believe it is an alien race in every sense, that would not and could not be expected to assimilate with our Arian [sic] population; and, therefore, if the temporary necessity has been overcome, and the railway constructed across the continent, with the means of sending European settlers and laborers into British Columbia, then it would be quite right to join to a reasonable extent in preventing the permanent settlement in this country of Mongolian, Chinese or Japanese immigrants" (12 May 1882, 1477).

47 He warned, however, that Canadian commercial interests with China (and Japan) would limit the degree of restriction practised, once again demonstrating his pragmatic approach (2 April 1884, 1287).

48 In response to one MP who remained concerned about the Chinese queue, he proposed that "they have just as good a right to wear a pig tail as my hon. friend has to wear a bald head" (4 May 1885, 1585).

49 A year later, in response to Arthur Gillmor's observation that "the whole thing must be painful to him, because no man could have written and consented to the very humane and sympathetic report which he wrote, and yet bring in this legislation," Chapleau replied that "if it was a matter of personal feeling and opinion, I might not be altogether sympathetic with the legislation we passed" (12 May 1886, 1237).

50 Nonetheless, Chapleau operated from within a discriminatory outlook, declaring that "it is a natural and well-founded desire of British subjects, of the white population of this Dominion, who come from either Britain or the other European States and settle in this country, that their country should be spoken of abroad as being inhabited by a vigorous, energetic, white race of people" (2 July 1885, 3010). Earlier, he had supported the move to disallow the Chinese the right to vote, on the grounds that they did not want the franchise (see his comments at 4 May, 1885, 1590).

51 Those exempt from paying the tax were: "first: the members of the Diplomatic Corps, or other Government representatives and their suite and their servants, consuls and consular agents; and second: tourists, merchants, men of science and students, who are bearers of certificates of identity, specifying their occupation and their object in coming into Canada, or other similar documents issued by the Chinese Government or other Government whose subjects they are" (Section 4).

52 In its original form, the Head Tax was undetermined and the passenger restriction was one person per ten tons.

53 *An Act to amend "The Chinese Immigration Act"* included provisions to allow Chinese travellers in transit to pass through Canada without paying the Head Tax (Section 2), to permit the Chinese wife of a white man to enter without paying the tax (Section 1), and to ensure that the government of British Columbia received a portion of the tax (Section 3).

54 Many MPs said that it was not proper for them to comment on what was seen to be a regional concern, and British Columbia MPs often reminded eastern colleagues of this. For example, Arthur Bunster declared that "the people on the Pacific coast were better judges than gentlemen in the Eastern provinces of what the results of that great evil were likely to be upon the human family" (16 April 1879, 1260).

55 "The rule of the House is that a bill cannot take two stages in one day: that is, have two readings, but there is no reason why the House should not receive the report of a committee and, if there is no amendment, read the bill the third time at the same sitting – in fact it is usual practice," Alexander Campbell (C) said (18 July 1885, 1412).

56 Almon's frustration and firm conviction that it was a fundamentally illiberal piece of legislation is clear: "I think such legislation is a disgrace to humanity. I think it is rolling back civilization from the end to the beginning of the 19th century. The early part of this century

did away with the Slave trade, with the Test Act, and gave Catholic emancipation and abolished slavery in the West Indies. We now enact a law which is as vile as any of those to the repeal of which I have just alluded, and I think it will impress an indelible disgrace on this House and on the Dominion" (ibid., 1411).

57 Mackay (1963, 96) reports that about 1 percent of government bills from the House were rejected by the Senate between 1878 and 1896, a time when the Conservatives controlled both chambers.

58 For example, Scott declared that "the little tail that wags over in British Columbia on the Pacific Coast is not going to control the whole dominion – a fragment of the population not the size of the city of Ottawa – that you could hide away in one of the wards of the city – is not going to dictate to the 4,000,000 of this Dominion, and dictate to them on a subject that touches us in a tender part, our national honor as citizens of a free country" (26 May 1886, 747). For some Senators, the law would be more acceptable if it applied only to British Columbia, not because they agreed with the principles behind it but because they accepted that local government should have a significant say in local matters.

59 In later years, he recalled that "when the draft of the Bill was shown to me, it contained so many provisions that I strongly objected to, that I declined to take charge of it unless certain changes were made. These changes were assented to, and during the time the Bill was before this House other amendments were made in it ... but I cannot say that I felt altogether satisfied with the Bill itself, or with the principle involved in it" (29 June 1900, 852).

60 The Speaker based his ruling on Section 53 of the *BNA Act* ("Bills for appropriating any Part of the Public Revenue, or for imposing any Tax or Impost, shall originate in the House of Commons") and on the 47th Rule of the Senate according to *Bourinot* ("The Senate will not proceed upon a Bill appropriating public [money] that shall not within the knowledge of the Senate have been recommended by the Queen's representative") (quoted at 14 June 1887, 396). In response, Vidal argued: "I can easily understand that if we found the word 'Chinese' anywhere between cheese and cigars in the tariff bill that we could not touch it, but it is an extraordinary thing that we cannot amend a public Bill simply because there is a penalty attached from which the Government derive a revenue" (ibid.).

61 "The whole policy of this measure is to restrict the immigration of Chinese into British Columbia and into Canada," Prime Minister Macdonald pronounced in the House (31 May 1887, 642).

62 According to Vidal, for example, the "superior civilization" of the "Anglo-Saxon race" meant that whites should have no fear of being overpowered by the Chinese (13 July 1885, 1297).

Chapter 3: The Expansion of Liberal Nationalism in Canada (1887-1914)

1 Sifton's immigration policy was summarized by his friend and biographer John W. Dafoe (1931, 136): "If he was a white man, in both senses of that word, he could come from anywhere in the world and he was made welcome, and put to work with no questions asked as to his race, his religion, his language or his previous conditions of servitude."

2 For example, Deputy Minister James A. Smart (Canada 1902, 298) informed the Standing Committee that "the man who undertakes to carry on a propaganda openly in Germany, Sweden or some other European countries would be put in prison, so that everything has to be done quietly."

3 The specific arrangements changed over the course of four agreements, with later ones adding more restrictive elements to the selection process (see Skilling 1945, 22-25).

4 Between 1901 and 1906, an estimated 50,000 to 71,000 migrants arrived in this way (constituting between 6.5 and 9.5 percent of total admissions) at a cost of $250,000 to $350,000 (Kelley and Trebilcock 1998, 120, and fn. 37).

5 In 1907, however, a new bonus system was put in place for immigration from continental Europe.

6 See the extensive House (20 April to 1 May 1906) and Standing Committee (11 April to 8 June 1906) debates; the latter can be found in Canada 1906.

7 Petryshyn (1991, 28) concludes that "there is no evidence to support Sifton's contention that the NATC screened the immigrants to ensure quality."

8 He drew a sharp contrast between ethnic Germans and Slavic Galicians: "The German of Galicia is a German such as he is everywhere. He is a man of dominant race, of untiring energy, of great foresight; he is a man of sterling honesty and reliability ... He is a German, and a citizen of the highest character" (12 April 1901, 2934).

9 The spectre of a race war was raised by a number of MPs, including Thomas S. Sproule (C), who predicted that "there may be a fusion of races in the future, but they will assuredly drag down the Canadian race ... and I fear that there may be a time, it may not be in the near future, it may be in the distant future, when we shall be subjected to another such expense as we have had to incur in keeping the Boers under control in South Africa, and that will be for the purpose of taking care of and keeping in subjugation the undesirable class who are pouring into our country to-day" (9 July 1900, 9645-55).

10 "Out of 11,000 people, I suppose, it would be almost impossible to provide that some might not be of bad character," Sifton replied. However, "I venture to say that there are no 11,000 people in the Dominion who will show a smaller record of crimes committed during the last three years than these Galicians" (26 July 1899, 8506-07).

11 "The policy adopted of exciting racial prejudice is the most contemptible possible policy because it is one that does not depend upon reason. As you know you can excite the prejudice of one nationality against another by simply keeping up an agitation ... All you have to do is keep hammering away and appealing to their prejudices, and in the course of time you will work up an excitement, but a more ignorant and unpatriotic policy could not be imagined," he wrote in 1901 (quoted in Hall 1985, 70).

12 "The hon. member for Alberta and I have been friends for a good many years, I have known him for a long time," he told the House, "but I have never heard him express unqualified admiration for anything or any individual. There seems to be something about my hon. friend's constitution which, while it does not affect the keenness of his intellect, prevents him from expressing a favourable opinion about either men or things" (12 April 1901, 2974).

13 For example, Duncan Fraser "call[ed] upon the civilization of our country as represented by the government and upon the higher civilization of our country as represented by our societies and churches, to join in lifting these men up and making them good citizens of our great west" (ibid., 2942-43).

14 Soon, however, major conflicts emerged between the Canadian government and the Doukhobors concerning issues such as collective ownership of the land, public education, and exemption from military service (Janzen 1990; Woodcock and Avakumovic 1968). Much of the difficulty stemmed from an intolerance, especially in official circles, of the difference embodied in the Doukhobor belief system (Woodsworth 1999, 7). While change did not come easily to the Doukhobors, Janzen (1995) has shown how many community leaders sought to develop compromises to address state concerns.

15 "I have explained at least a dozen times that I don't want anything done to facilitate Italian immigration ... It seems to be difficult to get it through the heads of our officers" (quoted in Hall 1985, 68).

16 "Once Asian immigrants were excluded by law or prohibitive head taxes from entering North America, only Italians had the numbers to pose a threat to Anglo-saxon cultural and genetic domination of Canada" (Harney 1993, 53).

17 Arthur Baker of the Canadian Pacific Railway claimed in 1907 that it had "done more in the last two years with reference to encouraging the immigration along intelligent lines from the United States, Great Britain and Europe than the whole Dominion Department of Immigration" (quoted in Avery 1979, 23).

18 "There is such a large interchange of traffic ... [that] we make no effort to keep track of them all, it would be impossible," said Superintendent of Immigration William D. Scott (Canada 1904, 587).

19 "The result would be, that we place ourselves in antagonism with the steamship agents, and after an examination of the question I am satisfied, that would stop people from coming here at all," he said (14 June 1897, 4071).

20 "Up to the present time," he continued, "there has been no special occasion for drastic measures, and I would not propose drastic measures unless the indications were very strong that serious difficulty was likely to arise" (26 July 1899, 8515).

21 In March 1902, Frank Pedley informed the Standing Committee that "the regulations, generally speaking, are that any person afflicted with contagious or infectious disease is detained in quarantine ... and have to remain in quarantine until they are discharged by the officers, and after that they have a perfect right to land here" (Canada 1902, 405).

22 Although racial prejudice can be seen in his opinions on immigration, he shared the view of many in Canada that immigrants from Britain were especially problematic in this regard.

23 He was referring to those who were "paupers, crippled or insane, or have any dangerous disease, or are found to be criminals" (16 April 1902, 2962).

24 Stricter medical inspections were instituted on the west coast only in 1905; before then, it appears that the government did not count the number of immigrants arriving by sea in British Columbia, with the exception of Asians, especially the Chinese.

25 This had been suggested in the House some twenty years earlier (see 25 February 1880, 199).

26 "The few scores or few hundreds of infected people who come into this country are really, from the point of view of danger, a bagatelle compared with the amount of contagious disease which we, as a parliament and as a civilization, permit to stalk broadcast through the land ... we permit year after year loathsome and contagious diseases to be propagated in this country, and we have not the courage to take measures to prevent it," he said (21 July 1904, 7294-95). "I do not deny that there is danger, but I say that in our criticisms of the arrangements to prevent the importation of disease at these points, we are straining at a gnat and swallowing a camel" (ibid., 7317).

27 By 1903, Sifton "had come to regard immigration and settlement no longer as a challenge, but as an achievement," resulting in a "perceptible slackening of energy and interest in departmental detail" on his part (Hall 1985, 76).

28 This, Oliver noted, "is new and it is very drastic but the reason of its insertion is that there has been an immigration of gypsies lately and it is thought that such people are not desirable under any circumstances although they are physically and mentally fit, and that it would be quite proper to take power to say: You cannot come in" (13 June 1906, 5252-53).

29 "I think that is too wide a power, but it seems to be in unison with the trend in that department under the last minister, and the evil effects of which we have pretty well discussed in parliament," he observed (ibid., 5204-5).

30 "I have no desire to take undue power as a minister or place undue power in the hands of subordinates," Oliver said. "The object is to enable instantaneous and effective action to be taken. Possibly abuses may arise but the minister will be responsible, and I think, that that is really a sufficient safeguard" (ibid., 5213-14). "It is necessary to give the enlarged power asked for," he continued, "and to trust to the discretion of the government not to do injustice under the enlarged power" (ibid., 5256).

31 "If the House gives us that power it places a corresponding responsibility upon us; if it refuses to give us that power it relieves us of responsibility to that extent," he explained (ibid., 5216).

32 Aside from small changes noted above, there was an unsuccessful attempt in the Senate to ensure that deportations could be carried out only up to six months after entry, instead of two years. As well, a clause to deny an appeal to anyone fined under the law was amended to allow for an appeal in cases where the fine exceeded $100.

33 "We should scarcely take the right to ourselves to deport a man after so long a period as two years," agreed Senator Donald Ferguson (C), "merely for the fact for instance that he might have to take advantage of the hospital" (9 April 1907, 657).

34 Among various "sad and very pathetic" tales involving deportation, he invoked "the case of a man who has gathered his family and household goods together and spent a greater portion of his money to buy a passage out to Canada and for some reason, possibly illness in his family, the family has to go back to Europe, because it will happen that, if a child is ill the family cannot remain. The child cannot be abandoned. They go back, and the man is landed in the port from which he started. It may be in a country where he does not know the language. Nothing could be more sad. I am willing to believe that the immigration

officials do all in their power to soften their troubles, but I deplore these stringent laws" (15 April 1907, 729-30). Lougheed responded: "I suppose there is no law of this kind but will be evidenced by its hardships; at the same time one must take into consideration the more important element which have in view in thus excluding from our borders a most undesirable and criminal class of immigrants" (ibid., 730).

35 Many supported this view, such as Senator Robert Watson (C): "I certainly think that we cannot give too much power to the government to deport undesirable characters" (12 April 1907, 725).

36 Legislation had been introduced the previous session but was not dealt with before the House rose.

37 The power to appoint such boards had been introduced in the 1906 law but none appear to have been established.

38 The one exception involved the power to turn back tourists if they were deemed to possess insufficient funds; otherwise, MPs either approved or desired to increase the new restrictions. The same was largely true in the Senate, although Lougheed wondered whether some of the changes involved "rather a high-handed power for the government to take and exercise" (14 April 1910, 572). For his part, Senator Richard J. Cartwright (L) asked whether "in putting up those barriers for the purpose of excluding persons we do not want, we may exclude some people who would be valuable citizens" (ibid., 578).

39 A "part of our policy and administration," Oliver stated, was to "be lenient in the interpretation of our regulations as respects our kinsmen from the British islands," an approach that he said was "right and proper" (22 March 1910, 5860). Elsewhere, he noted that "we propose to give special consideration to English speaking immigrants. Next to those, the immigrants from the European countries adjoining the North Sea, namely, France, Belgium, Holland, Germany, Denmark, Norway, and Sweden. In regard to immigrants from other European countries the terms of the Act and regulations are to be applied stringently in all cases" (quoted in Sampat-Mehta 1972, 142).

40 The minister, Foster observed, had said "that he would go outside the law if he thought it best not to let a man in, but he would keep a good way inside the law if he thought the man should come in."

41 In another case, Superintendent of Immigration Scott had quickly taken action when informed that some twenty West Indians a month were being landed in the Maritimes, arguing that "Africans, no matter where they come from are not among the races sought, and hence, Africans no matter what country they come from are in common with other uninvited races, not admitted to Canada" (quoted in Schultz 1988, 260). To stop this movement, he prosecuted one of the ships involved on an unrelated technicality. When his assistant, L.M. Fortier, investigated the matter, he was surprised to find that local immigration officials thought that they should simply apply the law as it had been written and admit West Indians if they met the stated criteria. Fortier let them know that "it is the opinion of the Department that we don't want the West India nigger here" (quoted in ibid., 262).

42 In 1890, Chief Controller of Chinese Immigration W.S. Parmelee confirmed that "there has certainly been no increase in the number in the Dominion, but a steady decrease since 1886" (Canada 1890, 144).

43 "I need not tell this House that the Chinese are universally addicted to opium; that they are inveterate gamblers; that they are grossly immoral. These things are so well known and authenticated that I do not wish to dwell upon them in this Chamber ... We white people may not be perfect; I agree that we are not; but when you have a stream whose source is filth, and which flows over beds of long accumulated filth, flowing into the moral life of our people, it stands to common sense that our moral life will become more and more contaminated," he declared (9 September 1896, 897-98).

44 "Shall multitudes of depraved heathen with all the vices of heathendom be allowed to come into this country, to swarm, to overrun, to override the population that we must look to [i.e., the Anglo-Saxons] to make this Dominion a great country?" Charlton asked (16 September 1896, 1353).

45 "It is useless," he said, "to tell us that we can permit the importation of any kind of people into the country and that we are guilty of infraction of human rights if we impose any restrictions upon these immigrants" (ibid., 1352-53).

46 This was an extension of both his anti-protectionist economic views and his belief in converting the Chinese to Christianity.

47 Ward (1990, 59) observes that while Laurier did not think the Japanese could assimilate any more than the Chinese, "discriminatory legislation he regarded with distaste."

48 According to George Casey (L), "the Japanese are people who can be assimilated in Canada, and can become civilized in the proper sense of the word. They are not only a nation of clever mechanics and hard working people, but in their habits they are not so dissimilar from Europeans as the Chinese. When they come to Canada or to any European country, they live in a cleanly descent [sic], respectable manner, like other citizens" (25 June 1900, 8204).

49 As Richard Scott said in introducing the bill in the Senate, "Japan is a warm ally of Great Britain and there are Imperial interests which would prevent the Dominion of Canada from taking any legislative action that would ban the Japanese from coming to Canada" (28 June 1900, 832).

50 Miller (1993, 17) writes in his history of Canadian participation in the 1899-1902 Boer War that for many "the Boers stood for all that was exclusive, backward, 'medieval,' corrupt, and oppressive."

51 "The people do not desire to see the civilization they possess, the institutions they possess, in any way endangered by the influx of a great swarm of people who do not believe as they do, will not act as they do, but will subvert their civilization and will not subscribe to their religion and belief. That is the case in a nutshell," he said (25 June 1900, 8193).

52 Laurier received letters in opposition from some Presbyterians and Methodists from eastern Canada, who "complained that the tax violated liberty and would impair mission work in China" (Roy 1989, 156).

53 Liberal Internationalist concerns were raised by William Almon, Arthur Gillmor, William Macdonald, and Alexander Vidal, as well as Conservative newcomers such as Donald McMillan (C) ("I think it is contrary to British toleration and British freedom to put an embargo on any class of people" [28 June 1900, 835]), Francis Clemow (C) ("We profess to have our country open to men of all classes, of all nationalities, colours, and creeds, and I never could understand on what ground this tax was imposed" [ibid.]), Charles E.B. de Boucherville (C), and Andrew A. Macdonald (LCP) (although his concern may not have extended beyond being able to obtain quality house servants). Liberal Internationalist racism remained intact as well; thus, Gillmor argued that Canada need not have any fear of Chinese immigration because "white men are superior to Chinamen ... I believe that the white race is destined to rule the world and lead in civilization and everything that is great and good" (ibid., 838).

54 Almon felt that while most Senators opposed the 1885 *Chinese Immigration Act*, partisan considerations now dictated their votes (29 June 1900, 854). Three years later, former Prime Minister Mackenzie Bowell (C) claimed that "if they were free to do as their consciences would suggest, [many] would vote against the Bill imposing this high tax" (11 June 1903, 296). The force of partisan politics might also be seen in the shift by Scott to the restrictionist camp after he became a member of the Liberal government (serving as Secretary of State): "We all have to moderate our views as we grow older and we cannot carry out our old arbitrary convictions in the administration of public affairs" (ibid., 298).

55 Australia's restrictive 1901 immigration legislation may have encouraged East Indian migrants to travel to Canada instead. In addition, with growing restrictions on Chinese and Japanese migration, there was a demand for East Indian labour and, perhaps more importantly, passengers to fill berths on trans-Pacific steamships.

56 It has been estimated that "Sikhs made up more than 85 per cent of all East Indians migrating to Canada from 1900 to 1950" (Minhas 1994, 3).

57 The Sikhs, he told the Empire Club of Canada in 1912, "are British subjects; they have fought for the Empire; many of these men have war medals; but, in spite of this fact, they

are not allowed to have their families with them when they come to this country; in spite of their being British subjects, they are not allowed to have their wives here ... All we are asking of you is justice and fair play, because the Sikhs have believed in fair play, and have believed all the time that they will get justice; that ultimately they will get justice from the British people ... your laws cannot be one thing for one set and a different thing for the rest of us" (S. Singh 1913, 112-14).

58 While Asians constituted 11 percent of the population of British Columbia in 1901, their share had decreased to below 8 percent at the time of the next decennial census (Ward 1990, 54). Many Asian arrivals probably continued on to the US.

59 The crowd was said to have numbered between eight and nine thousand, many of whom attacked stores and houses in the Chinese and Japanese parts of Vancouver, causing a great deal of physical damage but no known fatalities.

60 Although Laurier initially thought it unnecessary to consider compensating the Chinese, he ultimately felt bound by Article I of the 1842 Treaty of Nanking between Britain and China – which provided the Chinese with "full security and protection for their persons and property" within the British Empire – after he received representations from the British government, which itself had set a precedent by seeking compensation for its own nationals harmed during the Boxer Rebellion of 1899-1901 (Sampat-Mehta 1972, 51-52).

61 Japan decided not to make the riots a major issue as it saw its own interests in a stable relationship with Canada and Britain (Iino 1983-84).

62 There was, however, no restriction on continued family migration. Thus, women still joined men already settled in Canada, which produced a natural population growth during subsequent years that stood in marked contrast to the Chinese community.

63 Although the question of immigration was not seen to be the deciding factor, it is thought to have helped sustain a sense of alienation from the Liberal Party on the part of much of the electorate in the province.

64 The 1908 *Act to amend the Chinese Immigration Act* provided Chinese students a Head Tax refund (Section 3), and clarified both penalties for evasion of the law (Section 5) and the process in deportation cases (Section 6).

65 Mackenzie King had first become aware of the opium trade in Canada when two Chinese importers requested compensation for damages resulting from the 1907 riots (he did not accept their claims). He subsequently wrote a report advocating suppression of the opium trade in Canada, participated in the 1909 international conference, and introduced the 1911 *Opium and Drug Act*. While aimed at those dealing in opium, it served as yet another tool to control Chinese migration (Bangarth 2002, 109-10).

66 "During the period 1911-14 the annual rate of Chinese immigration was higher than it had been at any time since 1904" (Con et al. 1982, 94).

67 "The difficulty is that a Japanese subject coming to Vancouver and Victoria and being confronted by the order in council will simply take the same course as was taken not long ago – apply to a solicitor and procure writ of habeas corpus, and the court will decide that the order in council has no application to him, and he therefore cannot be deported," he suggested to the House (8 April 1908, 6449).

68 It was put to the test in 1908, when the law was used successfully to challenge restrictive legislation passed by the government of British Columbia; see *In Re Nakane and Okazake*.

69 He worked for the British government in India as well as for the Americans (Johnston 1988).

70 In a dissenting opinion, Justice John Idington proposed that "it may well be argued that the highly prized gifts of equal freedom and equal opportunity before the law, are so characteristic of the tendency of all British modes of thinking and acting in relation thereto, that they are not to be impaired by the whims of a legislature; and that equality [not] taken away unless and until forfeited for causes which civilized men recognize as valid" (*Quong-Wing v. R.*, 452; see also Walker 1997, Chapter 2).

71 Thus, Vancouver press coverage at the time portrayed East Indians as "chaotic carriers of a dangerous and foreign culture who threatened the existence of [white] Vancouver" (Indra 1979, 168).

72 Another trip was arranged in 1913 and at least two voyages to London were made. At most, such activities generated sympathy in some quarters. For example, in 1913 the Senate discussed restrictions against East Indian immigration and several Senators criticized Canadian policies on the grounds that they were fundamentally unjust (see 2 June 1913, 930-38). Henry J. Cloran (L) took the opportunity to offer an extended criticism of the Chinese Head Tax.

73 As a reflection of the discretionary power that immigration officials possessed, Oliver noted to Superintendent of Immigration Scott: "This regulation is therefore intended as a means of excluding those whom it is the policy of the government to exclude, but not to exclude those whom the policy is to admit" (quoted in Sampat-Mehta 1972, 141).

74 In his introduction, Senator Scott stated that "substantially the object of the Bill" was to "prevent the influx of Hindoos who come from Hong Kong, and Japanese who come from the Sandwich Islands" (10 April 1908, 805).

75 One exception was John G. Haggart (C): "While it is right that we should protect ourselves against immigration that is detrimental to the interests of the country, when a man is a good subject of the empire in one part of it, he has the right to all the privileges as a subject of the empire on landing in this country" (8 April 1908, 6439).

76 There were also complaints that too much discretion was being given to front-line immigration officials.

77 Rahim continued to challenge the government's authority by repeatedly criticizing its discriminatory policies in both speeches and published articles. He also played a key role in coordinating a community response to the arrival of the *Komagata Maru*, discussed below.

78 For example, Bird argued that the continuous journey provision was unfair because it was not possible to arrive from India in such a manner, to which Hunter replied that in terms of the law governing control, "the Court is not concerned with questions of expediency or good faith, but only with their validity and interpretation" (*In Re Narain Singh et al.*, 509).

79 "In the face of the menace of Asian immigration, that the administration of the Government of Canada should be fully empowered, and should be absolutely responsible for protection against that menace, and that if the courts or any processes of law are allowed to interfere with the proper exercise of that authority in expressing the mind and the will of the people of Canada, then we are facing a condition that will require readjustment, and serious readjustment," he continued (2 March 1914, 1224).

80 "The difficulty is that the Hindus have got into the habit of going to our courts whenever any little minor dispute arises," he claimed (ibid., 1238).

81 Moreover, Stevens argued that since "Hindus do not exercise [democratic] rights in India ... they have no right to come and demand here a privilege that they do not exercise in their own country" (ibid., 1237).

82 He said that it was a matter of "injustice and shame" that East Indians were prevented from going to Canada (quoted in Josh 1975, 19). In an interview, Singh stated that "if we are admitted we will know that the Canadian government is just. If we are deported we will sue the government and if we cannot obtain redress we will go back and take up the matter with the Indian Government" (quoted in Johnston 1979, 30).

83 "If matter taken to court as lawyers advise from knowledge of situation and action of certain judges we will lose and not only this shipload but others will successfully land in Canada," he warned (Josh 1975, 35).

84 "They talk about socialists and anarchists," Bird later said. "There is no set of anarchists in Canada like the Immigration Officials who defy all law and order" (quoted in Johnston 1979, 49).

85 Because Asians within the British Empire were so different, he continued, "in their own interests, their proper place of residence is within the confines of their respective countries in the continent of Asia, not in Canada, where their customs are not in vogue and their adhesion to them here only give rise to disturbances destructive to the well-being of society and against the maintenance of peace, order and good government" (*Re Munshi Singh*, 291). He admitted that some might find his comments to be "extra-judicial" (ibid., 290).

86 Upon its arrival in Budge, India, on 29 September, the British sought to have the passengers immediately transported by train to the Punjab so that they could not arouse public sentiment. Some, however, decided to march directly to Calcutta to do just that. When the police attempted to stop them, violence ensued, resulting in twenty-six deaths, including twenty of the passengers. Gurdit Singh escaped and became a public figure in the independence movement (Johnston 1979, Chapters 9 through 11).

87 As the Supreme Court of Canada would not sit for several months, an appeal was deemed impractical.

88 See, for example, comments by MPs Daniel D. McKenzie (L) (19 January 1911, 2015) and Louis A. Lapointe (L) (12 January 1912, 1210), and a petition from Syrians in Cape Breton (31 May 1913, 11559-60).

Chapter 4: The Domination of Liberal Nationalism in Canada (1914-45)

1 "No person who is held for deportation under this Act or under any regulation made thereunder, or is under arrest or detention as an alien enemy, or upon suspicion that he is an alien enemy, or to prevent his departure from Canada, shall be released upon bail or otherwise discharged or tried, without the consent of the Minister of Justice" (Section 11).

2 "It takes away, with regard to persons who may come under its provisions, the right of every man to appeal to the courts, and to have those who are depriving him of his liberty compelled to show before a court or a judge the reason why he is being deprived of his liberty and is being kept in prison," he continued. "That is a pretty serious enactment to make, because there is no measure which English people regard with greater appreciation and of which they are more jealous and have been for centuries than the Habeas Corpus Act" (20 August 1914, 22).

3 "In all the camps, a total of six prisoners were killed by gunshot and four wounded in the course of their internment. More than 100 others were confined to mental institutions and another 100 died in confinement, mostly of tuberculosis and pneumonia" (Finkel and Conrad 2006, 194).

4 "We should be free to shut out any class of people that we do not think can be readily assimilated," he said. "If there are any peculiar peoples the world round whose customs and beliefs, whose ideals and modes of life are dissimilar to ours and who are not likely to become Canadian citizens, we have the right to put up the bars and keep them out" (29 April 1919, 1875). At the same time, he called for a more proactive approach to settlement support.

5 "Any lowering of the standard of civilization in Canada," he continued, "has been brought about by our lax immigration laws in permitting the entry of people who never should have been allowed to come here, people who have shown themselves to be absolutely unfit for the privileges and liberties they have enjoyed here" (30 April 1919, 1932).

6 Two years later, he criticized the government's policy for being one of "He is a stranger; heave half a brick at him" (3 March 1921, 508). Jacobs also had his prejudices, however, as he was "in favour of allowing into the country every healthy white person who is able to make a living" (23 April 1925, 2367).

7 Jacobs had wanted the clause struck from the bill. It is not clear whether the provision was ever used in any systematic manner. In 1962, Citizenship and Immigration Minister Ellen Fairclough informed the House that "the literacy test in the former regulations, which was not satisfactory and, in fact, rarely used, has been abolished" (19 January 1962, 10).

8 "The awful crimes for which the Germans, the Austrians, the Bulgars, and the Russians are responsible, stamp such classes as being absolutely undesirable. We have had a large number of these people living in the country, and it has been demonstrated beyond question that they have not been assimilated, and that it is actually impossible to assimilate a large portion of the enemy aliens who are now within our borders ... If we believe that these people ought not to be permitted to come into this country ... we are expected to say so in a manly, straightforward way, and not to shirk our duty and place the responsibility on the shoulders of the Government," he maintained (16 May 1919, 414-15).

9 He argued that "the alien of to-day will be the friendly alien of to-morrow and possibly the friendly alien of to-day may become the alien enemy of to-morrow" (29 April 1919, 1881).

10 The Hutterites (who stem from the same Anabaptist movement that produced the Mennonites during the Protestant Reformation) first arrived in Canada via the US as a result of anti-pacifist persecution after the latter country entered the First World War. Of the nineteen Hutterite communities in the US at that time, eighteen fled to Canada in 1918, resettling in Alberta and Manitoba (see Driedger 1999, 672-81).

11 "These people who would not lift a hand to save this country from being placed under the heel of the Hun, but were willing to let others go across the seas and fight and die for principles that we hold dear," he stated (30 April 1919, 1929). See Janzen 1990 (Chapter 8) on the experiences of the Doukhobor and Mennonite communities during the war and their respective contributions to the war effort.

12 *An Act to amend an Act of the present session entitled An Act to amend The Immigration Act.*

13 The government also introduced amendments to the country's naturalization law, authorizing itself to remove the Canadian citizenship of naturalized Canadians under certain conditions.

14 Although the government arrested and sought to deport many of the leaders of the Winnipeg General Strike using Section 41, only one was removed, under another section of the law; other labour activists who were non-citizens were denied a hearing (as Section 41 allowed) and quickly placed in an internment camp before being secretly removed from the country (Avery 1979, 82-86).

15 The deportation provisions were, he continued, "absolutely contrary to the spirit of the British constitution, and to that great bill of rights, the Magna Charta [sic], upon which it is founded ... [which provides that] no free man shall be outlawed or imprisoned, or have his property taken from him, except by the judgment of a lawful court composed of a jury of its own rank" (27 May 1920, 417-18).

16 "I have not the slightest fear," he stated, "that any man in Canada who would attain to the position of Minister of Immigration would be likely to deport a person without very fully inquiring into the case to determine whether he deserved deportation or not" (ibid., 420).

17 "The only treatment [communists] can understand is force – that is the thing they are advocating – and their own remedy should be applied to them to shut their blatant mouths," Senator George W. Fowler (C) later said (21 May 1923, 613).

18 The amendment would have ensured that British subjects who had been in the country for five years would not be subject to deportation without a trial, and had passed in the House. Robertson continued to argue in the Senate that "a British subject is entitled to a trial in accordance with British law and justice in any part of the British Empire ... If a man is once given naturalization papers in this country, surely, in the event of his being charged with an offence, he ought to be tried under the law of the land. He should not have his naturalization papers withdrawn and be kicked out without a trial" (1 June 1921, 725-26).

19 For example, in his 1923 report, Superintendent of Emigration for Canada in London J. Obed Smith wrote of the "many thousands of cosmopolitan and alien nationalities" outside of northern Europe who "for the most part not of the class Canada calls for" but coming nonetheless (Canada 1923, 21). Outside Britain, Canadian officials undertook unsystematic inspections only at Antwerp and Le Havre while "emigrants are passing out of Europe through a dozen other ports ... so that the whole question of inspection, etc., on the Continent is one that will have to be faced at an early date" (ibid., 22). An "inspection at only one or two ports will not provide much in the way of safeguards for Canada," he observed (ibid., 24).

20 "This may be a very excellent plan for the railway and steamship companies," Simon F. Tolmie (C) complained, "but what results can the country expect?" (15 February 1926, 999).

21 Comments made in departmental annual reports continued to be vague on the thoroughness or effectiveness of these efforts. For example, in his 1924-25 report, Deputy Minister W.J. Egan would only say that "on the Continent practically all immigrants are required to pass primary inspection at one or other of the six agencies" (Canada 1926, 7). Although people were clearly turned away at the ports, the system by which preferred and non-preferred immigrants were differentiated remained undisclosed.

22 "There is no question in my mind that the best way to deal with assimilation is to leave it alone ... The only method which should be followed is that of absolute fair play. Let us meet [the immigrant] half way and extend to him a helping hand and give him a square deal," he proposed (28 May 1929, 2904-5).

23 Under this policy, he continued, "the founder of Christianity would be debarred from coming into this country ... and none of the apostles could enter this country ... There are in the case of Jesus of Nazareth ... four orders in council which would prohibit him from coming in here. There would be first, the order relating to the non-agriculturalist class. Carpenters are not permitted to enter this country coming from that district. And then he would not have a proper passport; he would not be traveling by a continuous journey; and he would have no relatives in the country ... Michael Angelo [sic], although he built St. Peter's at Rome, could not enter this country ... If he came from Iceland and could build an icehouse, we could use him" (1 March 1927, 776).

24 In particular, see Section 29 of the 1297 version of the Magna Carta: "No Freeman shall be taken or imprisoned, or be disseised of his Freehold, or Liberties, or free Customs, or be outlawed, or exiled, or any other wise destroyed; nor will We not pass upon him, nor condemn him, but by lawful judgment of his Peers, or by the Law of the Land. We will sell to no man, we will not deny or defer to any man either Justice or Right."

25 "The small and irresponsible group in the Commons [behind the bill] would engraft upon the statute legislation which would permit of every license being exercised in the way of agitation and sedition, and it is for the Senate to prevent anything of that kind," he continued (16 May 1923, 556).

26 Not, however, without objections from a number of MPs, such as Neill, who demanded: "Is the minister going to take back-water from the Senate without any consideration at all?" (15 June 1923, 3981). Stewart responded that he did not want to risk losing other changes that were in the legislation.

27 "That a man should be liable to deportation, whether he is an alien or a British subject, just because he is suspected of entertaining certain undesirable beliefs, surely is very far from the ideals of justice and fair play," he explained (3 July 1924, 4005).

28 "There comes a time," Henry Stevens argued, "when by virtue of insurrection, rebellion, violence and seizing control of the machinery of government in a locality or in a country as a whole, or attempting to do so, the ordinary functions of the administration of law cannot be applied" (30 April 1928, 2501).

29 "It cannot interfere with liberty," Bennett maintained, "because it does not deal with British subjects, and since when did an alien have any right to protection in this country other than to be protected in his life and property, and be sent out of the country if he proved undesirable?" (8 April 1927, 2104).

30 Earlier he had argued that "you can fly the flag for a long time, but you are not going to make the foreign-born good Canadian citizens as long as there is gross injustice existing under that flag" (21 June 1922, 3283).

31 "I believe that it is repugnant to any human being to think that he can be so summarily and arbitrarily sent away from a country without a fair trial. I believe it is repugnant to the laws which have been enacted throughout the realm, which we have been in the habit of judging as the highest mark of civilization since the Habeas Corpus Act was proclaimed in Great Britain," he continued (3 May 1928, 417).

32 The reason that such deportations were done out of the public eye, Neill claimed in the House, was "only from a spirit of humanity" on the part of officials who "do not wish to inflict this greater publicity upon people who certainly are always deported for some cause" (2 June 1931, 2246).

33 "Like their counterparts in Cabinet, Senators were often little more than mouthpieces for the Department. Debates were focused on policy rather than practice, on legalisms rather than reality" (Roberts 1988, 197).

34 Woodsworth introduced additional legislation to curb government deportation powers in 1932 and 1934.

35 Similarly, William Euler called on the government to "apply the greatest judgment, generosity, fairness and justice to any proposal that they be deported" (21 April 1932, 2258).

36 If such actions were legal, Euler argued, then the law ought to be changed to make it conform with British traditions (6 May 1932, 2692).

37 In this rare instance, the matter ultimately went before the courts, as one of those seized was a Canadian citizen who subsequently sued the government over his treatment. Although the Supreme Court heard arguments on behalf of the ten non-citizens, it was difficult for any decision of a legally constituted board of inquiry to be challenged under the 1910 *Immigration Act*.

38 This classification was overturned in 1930, but by then, immigration to Canada had fallen dramatically due to the Great Depression and few refugees benefited. The Asian classification was reinstated a few months later and remained in place until 1952.

39 "From its inception," Craft (1987, 44) writes, "the CNCR wanted to be perceived, not as a typical anti-government lobby group, but as a collection of reasonable-minded citizens who could work with the Government." It was more effective during the Second World War in securing the release of refugees interned with the POWs from Britain and assisting those who remained in the camps.

40 As well, more than 150 Japanese-Canadians served in the armed forces, while many others trained in preparation for the possibility of overseas service and a few hundred Chinese also served overseas; see Roy 1978.

41 Borden commented that the "prime importance of this agreement from Canada's viewpoint is that we have secured formal and public acquiescence by [the] British Government and [the] Government of India in our view that we have absolute control of [the] composition of our population and their assent to such restrictions on immigration as we deem desirable" (Canada 1967, 353).

42 A negative decision could be appealed to the minister.

43 He listed seven additional reasons for exclusion, concluding that "it is desirable that we should have a white Canada and that we should not become a yellow or mongrel nation" (8 May 1922, 1516).

44 Similarly, George Black (C) lamented: "I have seen the white man retreat before the menace, as helpless to prevent it, or to hold it back, as he is to prevent the rising tide of the sea" (ibid., 1520).

45 The Conservatives' 1919 *By-Election Act* had, in theory, provided all citizens with the vote in federal elections; it was amended in 1920 so that only Asians who had served in the armed forces held the franchise at the federal level.

46 This is a subject that is sorely in need of dedicated research (see, however, Backhouse 1999; Walker 1997). A superficial read through *British Columbia Reports* during this period reveals numerous examples of such rulings, involving Chinese, Japanese, and East Indian immigrants.

47 "In the past the trouble has been that by endeavouring to exclude any particular race or body of people by name, you immediately involved yourself in objections raised on legal or treaty, or even sentimental grounds, by the government of the people you sought to exclude," he explained (6 February 1923, 74).

48 "One extremely important factor about setting up an office in China was the fact that Chinese refused entry could not bring their case into Canadian courts," regardless of their treatment (Sampat-Mehta 1972, 113).

49 There were also protests from some Protestant missionaries and the Chinese government itself.

50 In protest, many Chinese went on strike on that date, which was long thereafter recognized as Humiliation Day rather than celebrated as Dominion (later Canada) Day.

51 "The need for protection against Canadian discrimination was one reason behind the proliferation of Chinese organizations during this period" (Ng 1999, 14).

52 Foreign-born Chinese in Canada had a harder time becoming naturalized after the government passed a regulation (PC 1378) in 1931 that required them to secure a letter from the Minister of the Interior of China before being allowed to submit their application. The same Order-in-Council established a similar restriction for people of Japanese origin.

53 Illegal migration from China would become a major political issue in the late 1950s, as will be seen in Chapter 6.

54   McBride complained of the Japanese "forcing themselves" on Canada, something that no "self-respecting people" would do (2 April 1925, 1815).

55   "I believe it would increase our own sense of humanity, and increase our own consciousness of the fact that we are trying to establish a better world in which we will get rid of racial hatred, prejudice and antagonism ... I am satisfied that, despite the feelings that there may be among our own people toward this race, an effort of this kind would do us good," he continued (9 July 1943, 4608-9).

56   Thus, Arthur W. Roebuck (L) commented in the House in 1944 on the number of Jews admitted during 1941-42: "I draw attention to this figure of 111 persons out of the 1,500,000 scattered by Hitler ... Surely in Canada, with our great heritage of 3,500,000 square miles of territory, we have room for more than one or two hundred persecuted people fleeing for their lives from nazi [sic] butchers" (1 February 1944, 75). Likewise, to those who said that Canada had no room for the refugees, Fred Rose (Labour-Progressive) replied: "That is not humanity. That is cruelty" (11 February 1944, 4465).

57   Her comments were from a more general discussion on "Nazi crimes against humanity." While most Senators condemned Nazi actions in Europe (and the suffering of the Jewish people was mentioned by some), Wilson and Norman P. Lambert (L) felt that a critical eye should also be turned towards Canadian control policies.

58   In Liberal Nationalist fashion, he complained that "I know that by speaking like this I shall scandalize some virgin souls who do not like plain talk about these matters" (30 March 1944, 2006).

59   These measures "conferred upon the government enormous powers to restrict and control the rights and liberties of both Canadians and resident immigrants. Under these regulations, the government was given the authority to arrest without warrant and intern without trial persons suspected of subversive intent; to declare certain religious, political, and community organizations illegal; to censor the press; and to confiscate property" (Kelley and Trebilcock 1998, 274). "Enemy alien" immigrants and eventually some naturalized citizens had to report regularly to local police.

60   See also Angus MacInnis (CCF) and George H. Castleden (CCF) on the need for due process to prevail to the greatest extent possible (6 August 1940, 2566-67).

61   A major complaint was that people apprehended under the regulations had no right to access the courts or even to legal counsel. See, for example, the interventions of M.J. Coldwell (27 February 1941, 1068-69) and Tommy Douglas (3 March 1941, 1186-87). This concern transcended party lines (see 4 May 1942, 2079-101).

62   See, for example, the detailed complaint of Dorise W. Nielsen (United Progressive) (18 November 1940, 187-92).

63   He later argued that "the most fatal thing you can do with regard to an oriental native race is to lose face" (29 July 1942, 4939).

64   Escott Reid of the Department of External Affairs said of the west coast politicians: "I felt in that committee room the physical presence of evil" when they spoke of the Japanese "in the way that the Nazis would have spoken about Jewish Germans" (quoted in Adachi 1976, 204).

65   Resettling the Japanese across Canada would, he said, "start clusters, centres, cancers if you like, of this alien pagan race in every province, all reaching out and spreading out like some evil pool of poison" (5 May 1944, 2684).

66   It is unclear how voluntary this choice was; for example, more than 80 percent of those still in government-controlled camps opted to leave Canada, compared with only 15 percent of those who had already moved east (Adachi 1976, 301). Against charges of intimidation, Labour Minister Humphrey Mitchell (L) declared: "I would not stand for it for one minute, neither would the government nor the people; this is a free country" (quoted in ibid., 302). As Alistair M. Stewart (CCF) observed, however, "coercion is not [only] a matter of sticks or bludgeons or clubs" (17 December 1945, 3702).

67   Members of the Japanese community also challenged (unsuccessfully) the sale of their property in court during the war.

68   The legislation drew considerable criticism in the Senate from William A. Buchanan (L), William Euler, Norman Lambert, and Cairine Wilson, among others, on the grounds that

it was anti-democratic – that, as Lambert stated, it "represents the most hateful feature of Hitler's Nazi doctrine of racialism" (28 June 1944, 246). However, the views of Senators like William A. Griesbach (C) that the Japanese were "constitutionally unable to understand the principles of democratic government" and therefore should not vote prevailed (30 June 1944, 274). The House subsequently amended the bill to ensure that only Japanese Canadians who had been relocated from British Columbia would be denied the franchise.

69 In passing the 1945 *National Emergency Transition Powers Act,* the government sought to empower itself to control "entry into Canada, exclusion and deportation, and revocation of nationality" without effective oversight. At Second Reading, future Prime Minister John G. Diefenbaker (PC) blasted the Liberals: "This paragraph is a denial of the rights of British citizenship and it is asked for and placed in a measure introduced by a government which has said over and over again that irrespective of one's racial origin British citizenship means something. Instead of the government bringing in a bill to revoke British citizenship, it brings it in by the back door by giving power to the governor in council to deport anybody, no matter how many generations he may have lived in this country" (23 November 1945, 2455). The provision was eventually removed from the bill.

Chapter 5: A New Era of Human Rights (1945-52)

1 "Europe had never seen so many refugees. Among these was every possible kind of individual – Nazi collaborators and resistance sympathizers, hardened criminals and teenage innocents, entire family groups, clusters of political dissidents, shell-shocked wanderers, ex-Storm Troopers on the run, Communists, concentration camp guards, farm laborers, citizens of destroyed countries, and gangs of marauders. Every European nationality was present in both East and West. Some of the refugees remained shattered and bewildered by their experience, rooted to the soil where they were liberated. Others streamed in various directions, often without the slightest indication of what they would find at their destination" (Marrus 1985, 299).

2 "The catalyst that made human rights an issue in world politics was the Holocaust, the systematic murder of millions of innocent civilians by Germany during World War II," Donnelly writes (1993, 6). He also notes the importance of "the genocidal massacre of ... a half million Gypsies, and the deaths of tens of thousands of Communists, social democrats, homosexuals, church activists, and just ordinary decent people who refused complicity in the new politics and technology of barbarism" (ibid., 6-7).

3 "There's a good deal of difference between a national law and an international declaration in potential effectiveness," an anonymous hand protested in the margins of Reid's document (Canada 1977, 888, n1).

4 This opposition was rooted in "the political right, from the business community, and, especially, from the legal fraternity," primarily due to the inclusion of social and economic rights (Hobbins 1998, 326).

5 According to Holmes (1979, 290-91), "the Canadian government kept a low profile [on human rights]. It was the Americans, with their declaratory tradition, the Bill of Rights and all that, who pressed hard for strong or at least strong-sounding provisions about human rights."

6 A few Canadians looked for a stronger commitment to human rights, such as Escott Reid (1989, Chapter 14; see also Mackenzie 2004).

7 More pressing for Canada was the extent to which rights commitments might interfere with federal/provincial relations.

8 "Throughout the postwar period and into the 1950s Ottawa attempted to reconcile its public support for the UN's efforts to promote international human rights with a rather determined policy to avoid any commitment to their protection" (MacLennan 2003, 61).

9 It was "an unenthusiastic statement which did not appear to spring from, and was unlikely to generate, any excitement about a new and important area of Canadian development: the potential addition of several millions of people to the population of Canada" (Hawkins 1972, 93-94).

10 "Notice that he insists on Canada's sovereignty, yet acknowledges an obligation to humanity to help those in distress," Corbett observes (1957, 3). "One thing is carefully balanced against another."

11 That being said, the committee argued in favour of continued discrimination against Asian immigration, the justification being "based, of course, on problems of absorption" (Canada 1946, No. 11, 310).

12 "In whole areas of the country you can hardly find a name like Smith or Brown or Jones or McNab. They are all some sort of un-British name now," he lamented (28 August 1946, 5514).

13 "Are they Protestant, atheistic, Roman Catholic or Judaistic? I do not want to do anything I ought not to do but I believe every member of the house realizes that any preponderance of any one of these among new immigrants would certainly be creating a handicap to large bodies of the Canadian people," Blackmore explained (ibid., 5515).

14 Blackmore was aware of this change and he did not like it: "Of course, now it is popular to go clean crazy over internationalism, but by and by, unless we are careful, we shall wake up from the honeymoon phantasy we are in and begin to realize that in being too international we made a colossal mistake" (ibid.).

15 The basically positive outlook within elite circles has been identified by a number of authors (see, for example, Kelley and Trebilcock 1998, Chapter 8). As for public opinion, according to a Gallup Poll survey conducted in 1947, 51 percent of those who responded agreed that Canada needed immigrants (Tienhaara 1974, 18).

16 The authors report that 80 percent of the names on the organization's letterhead were non-Chinese.

17 "I believe that we are all brothers under the skin, but I should like to see us keep our places. I think people get along a good deal better with those who have the same colour of skin ... Has Canada no right to remain British?" Blackmore asked (11 February 1947, 342). Similarly, John L. Gibson (Independent Liberal) stated: "I feel that this is a white Canada that we have here, and we must definitely limit the number of Chinese we permit to come in" (ibid., 321). "Let us keep Canada British," suggested Thomas A. Kidd (PC) (2 May 1947, 2710).

18 For example, E. Davie Fulton (PC) worried that there would be an "influx of 22,000 wives and families into Canada and over 12,000 wives and families into one province alone, British Columbia (ibid., 2701). George R. Pearkes (PC) voiced his concern over the arrival of "a flood tide of these wives and children into the country" (ibid., 2716).

19 By assimilation, Liberal Nationalists such as James Sinclair (L) often appear to have meant little more than intermarriage with whites: "The fact that in twenty-three years so few of them have intermarried shows the difficulty of ordinary biological assimilation" (11 February 1947, 335). See also Blackmore's comments: "Canada wants people who are assimilable, people with whom Canadians can marry with desirable results. I emphasize 'desirable results'" (ibid., 341). Others made vague reference to an inability or unwillingness to participate in Canada's political and social institutions.

20 "I do not wish to say anything to occasion undue alarm, but a good many members of the house would appear to be taking the point of view that we are never going to face any further difficulty with people from the orient, and that the last war has been fought with people from the orient. I do not think people in our generation have a right to take that supine attitude," Blackmore maintained (5 May 1947, 2786).

21 The Prime Minister had said that "the effect of the repeal will be to remove all discrimination against the Chinese on account of race" (quoted by M.J. Coldwell (CCF) in 11 February 1947, 331).

22 As noted earlier, the Chinese also faced discrimination under PC 1378, which rendered their ability to become Canadian citizens subject to prior approval by the Chinese government. A few days after David Croll raised this in the House, the government announced that it would rescind this regulation.

23 "We accepted responsibilities under the united nations [sic]. We do not discharge them by lip service and then neglecting to act on its idealism. We do not practise its principles by intolerance" (ibid., 321). As Canada debated the Charter, Secretary of State for External Affairs Louis St. Laurent declared: "If war is to be abolished we must begin by respecting the rights of individual human beings. Hence the Canadian delegation welcomed and supported the decision to place in the charter ... the pledge to achieve international cooperation in promoting and encouraging respect for human rights and for the fundamental

freedoms of all, without distinction as to race, sex, language or religion" (16 October 1946, 1196). It was, he said three days later, a "solemn obligation" for Canada (19 October 1946, 1333).

24 At the first session of the General Assembly of the United Nations, the Canadian representative had stated that Article 1 was "an unqualified obligation which rests upon each member of the united nations [sic]" (quoted by Alexander M. Nicholson (CCF) in 5 May 1947, 2757).

25 Croll agreed: "We pledged ourselves to oppose discrimination not only in theory but in practice when we signed the united nations charter [sic], and unless we grant to these people a full measure of justice we shall have less reason to enjoy our own" (11 February 1947, 324).

26 Irvine did distinguish between equal treatment within Canada and the right to enter Canada, and stated that the country could justifiably deny entry to any group it wanted (2 May 1947, 2707). Liberal Internationalists still often accepted some forms of ethnoracial discrimination in determining the relationship between non-citizens and the state.

27 In contrast, Corbett (1957, 45) observed that "selection on geographic lines is only another way of selecting according to race and culture."

28 "If this is not discrimination against people on account of their race, then the word discrimination has no meaning," they stated (Canada 1948, No. 4, 96).

29 In testimony concerning the connection between Canadian policies and the Holocaust, Hayes declared: "It is my duty to say that the number of these victims could have been very much smaller and very many of their lives could have been saved if such countries as Canada would have paid due heed to the requests and pleas of their kin and of Jewish citizens to grant a refuge to some of them while there was still time. It is a simple and truthful fact that because the applications made to the Immigration Branch on behalf of many of them were not favourably acted upon, their ashes and bones to-day lie in Buchenweld [sic] and soap has been made of their bodies instead of their being free and useful citizens in Canada life to-day" (Canada 1947, No. 6, 177).

30 "The law should effectively protect the policy of the country and its present and prospective citizens from the caprices or the race or religious prejudice of any official," they recommended (ibid., 176).

31 The obligation to assist refugees did not stem from any agreement made at the United Nations but was, rather, the result of a more fundamental commitment, deeply rooted in Canadian history, to address the needs of the persecuted, Sandwell argued. Canada should therefore not wait for international negotiations to wrap up before acting (Canada 1946, No. 9, 238-42).

32 Corbett (1957, 7) noted that "labour's bias against immigration has been much less since the war," and that a noteworthy feature of "the change in labour's attitude is the remarkable decline in racial and national prejudice."

33 Similarly, Zaplinty held that "Canada has a definite responsibility to give sanctuary and help to refugees, regardless of whether they may be political, religious or any other sort of refugee. Aside from the more formal commitments we have made as a member of the united nations [sic] and as a participant in the international refugee organization [sic] we have a moral responsibility, which I think is set out very well in the draft declaration of human rights" (31 May 1948, 4588).

34 This sentiment was echoed by Walter A. Tucker (L): "If we take these people in we shall be taking in settlers who have already demonstrated their loyalty and devotion to the cause of freedom" (11 March 1947, 1259).

35 For an explanation of how some two thousand "Nazi war criminals and collaborators" entered Canada after the war, see Margolian 2000; for a look at later efforts to develop a policy to deal with the two hundred or so thought to be still living in Canada in the mid-1980s, see Matas with Charendoff 1987.

36 Stewart also wondered how de Bernonville and others had been able to come to Canada. "Is it possible," he asked, "that we have an underground railway into Canada by means of which these collaborators are being smuggled into this country?" (22 February 1949, 795). The existence of such "ratlines" in Canada is explored by Margolian (2000, Chapter 9), who concludes that until further state documents are declassified, the most that can be asserted

is that some ratlines did terminate in Canada and that there may have been some officials who knew about them.

37 He quoted Lord Palmerston, who had written in 1849 that "if there is today a rule which, more than any other, has been observed in modern times by all independent states, large or small, throughout the civilized world, it is the rule whereby a government should not hand over political refugees, unless some positive provisions of a treaty compel it to do so ... The rules of hospitality, the requirements of humanity, the feelings which are a natural attribute of man combine in ruling out such extraditions, and any independent government which of its own accord would grant one of such a nature would justly and universally be stigmatized as having disgraced itself" (24 February 1949, 881).

38 He noted that "if, during the uprisings of 1837, William Lyon Mackenzie had not found refuge in the United States, there would have been no Mackenzie King ... And if Louis-Joseph Papineau had not found sanctuary in France during the same period, we would have been deprived of Henri Bourassa" (2 March 1950, 399). Although Machado had greatly assisted the Royal Bank of Canada in Cuba during his dictatorship, he was allowed only temporary refuge in Canada on two occasions despite his desire to remain (Ogelsby 1976, 108-10).

39 Arsenault's bill would have seen Superior Court judges, like the one who had heard de Bernonville's case, empowered to decide whether the right of asylum should be granted in individual cases. It never made it past First Reading (20 February 1951, 495). Arsenault's interest in French-speaking refugees is evident in his six-volume study, *Histoire et généologie des Acadiens* (1965).

40 Some delays were due to currency restrictions in Sweden that made it impossible for many refugees to pay the funds required by Canadian immigration regulations; as well, many Estonians did not wish to leave their families behind to qualify under the Canada's Sponsored Labour Program (Dirks 1977, 166).

41 Mackenzie King made reference to four communists who had been sentenced to serve prison sentences in the United States and who were thought to have fled to Canada.

42 For example, in 1946, an Interdepartmental Security Panel recommended that the RCMP be involved in security screening with immigration officials overseas (Margolian 2000; Whitaker 1987).

43 Two years later, Harris said that immigrants would be admitted "in numbers not exceeding the absorptive capacity of our country and without altering the fundamental character of our people, such persons as are likely to contribute to our national life" (4 July 1952, 4263). "I am not sure that I know what is the fundamental character of any nation," Alistair Stewart later commented. "I only hope this is not a euphemism for skin pigmentation" (24 April 1953, 4346).

44 Nonetheless, he wished to "preserve the ethnic balance of our nation" (24 April 1953, 4338).

45 Government statistics continued to mask more than reveal the causes for removal from the country between 1947-48 and 1953-54, however. The reason for the deportation of about 2,000 of the more than 3,200 people removed was listed as "other civil reasons," which would "certainly include deportations for political reasons" (Whitaker 1987, 195). Thus, "Canada was still using deportation as a political weapon, perhaps not as much as it had before the war, but with a frequency that rivalled the American use of deportation" (ibid.). Fewer deportations in the US were likely to be successful, as the rights of non-citizens received greater protection in that country's constitutional system than in Canada, where administrative discretion combined with a lack of judicial oversight rendered the process essentially immune to outside scrutiny.

46 "No court and no judge or officer thereof has jurisdiction to review, quash, reverse, restrain or otherwise interfere with any proceeding, decision or order of the Minister, Deputy Minister, Director, Immigration Appeal Board, Special Inquiry Officer or immigration officer had, made or given under the authority and in accordance with the provisions of this Act relating to the detention or deportation of any person, upon any ground whatsoever, unless such person is a Canadian citizen or has Canadian domicile."

47 Despite his earlier comments quoted above, Croll now followed Harris's line, stating that "it would be a very dangerous principle to introduce" (Canada 1952, No. 1, 76). He did not

think that "you can divorce immigration from politics and from the House of Commons," and thus it was legitimate for the minister to have discretion in this instance (ibid.). Moreover, with an appeal the hopes of non-citizens would be drawn out, thus making any ultimate rejection more difficult to bear.

48 "God help those who had not followed due process or encountered one of the statutory prohibitions or were otherwise found wanting," John L. Manion (1993, 53), who served in the department at the time, later wrote.

Chapter 6: The Return of Liberal Internationalism in Canada (1952-67)

1 In *The Black Worker*, a March 1952 editorial fumed: "Here is a citizen of Canada who cannot even bring his granddaughter to Canada to see him. Why? Not because she is a communist or a subversive of any stripe, who might plot and conspire against the government; not because she is an indigent and may become a charge upon the government; not because she possesses some contaminating and contagious disease; but solely because she is a negro living in the West Indies" (quoted in Corbett 1957, 53).

2 Brewin argued against their deportation on the grounds that their exclusion had been based on "race" while the 1952 *Immigration Act* only used the term "ethnic group." The justices, referring to the *Oxford English Dictionary*, were not convinced and dismissed the appeal (see Walker 1997, Chapter 5). The Singhs were subsequently deported.

3 "These efforts yielded good results, even if, in some cases, only temporarily. Allowing children over the acceptable age to enter Canada on compassionate grounds, extending the right of sponsorship to landed immigrants who were not yet citizens, admitting parents over a certain age, and developing a special scheme for the immigration of Chinese brides are good examples of successes" (Ng 1999, 93).

4 For example, in 1955 the Supreme Court (specifically, Justice Robert Taschereau) dismissed one appeal on the grounds that "clearly, and the jurisprudence is unanimous on this point, [Section 39 of the 1952 *Immigration Act*] closes the door on the intervention of the courts" [author's translation: "Évidemment, et la jurisprudence est unanime sur ce point, cette disposition de la loi ferme la porte á l'intervention des tribunaux"] (*Masella v. Langlais*, 266).

5 In the House, E. Davie Fulton (PC) complained that "the government, which has embarked on the principle of arbitrary policies with respect to the administration of immigration, is stubbornly and arrogantly determined to adhere to that policy notwithstanding the findings of the court" (15 February 1955, 1168).

6 Fulton protested in 1954 that "since 1950 we have been able to discuss this department only on two days for about 3 hours each, one other full day, and one hour on another day" (26 June 1954, 6788).

7 "The reason they ask for the review is that they hope that in the course of the review some reason will be elicited, and the case against the application made clear to them, so that they will know what case they have to meet and whether in fact the reasons given by the department are reasons which in their opinion are valid, under the present immigration law, or whether they consider the department is misapplying or misinterpreting the present regulations," he explained (ibid., 6791).

8 Diefenbaker also had the Star Chamber in mind: "That was the attitude taken in the reign of Charles I by the then head of the Star Chamber when he once said: 'We administer justice; we need no lawyers, and whatever we do is right.' That was said in 1642, and [you] will recall that the person on behalf of whom that statement was made lost a head" (17 February 1955, 1255).

9 "We have people who come to our office and say, 'I am so and so; what do I have to tell you in order to get into Canada?'" he maintained (26 June 1954, 6833).

10 Citizenship and Immigration Minister Pickersgill was not convinced as to the validity of this linkage: "If the hon. member for Kamloops would like to edify the house by explaining the connection between Magna Carta and any possible legal rights an alien might have when entering Canada, I would be most interested to hear that piece of very original historical research" (17 February 1955, 1246). Diefenbaker replied: "What has the Magna Carta to do with it? Long years ago in 1215 Magna Carta made a declaration, and it has been of

the essence of the British peoples ever since: to no man will we deny, to no man will we delay, justice" (ibid., 1256).

11 To make such changes, he later argued, "would do nothing other than give recognition to the ordinary, simple concepts and principles of justice which should apply in [the] department as much as they should apply everywhere else in Canada" (8 August 1956, 7216).

12 If immigrants were barred "based only on a man's religion or even on his colour, then that would certainly be objectionable, and it would also be objectionable if it covered only racial origin ... [However,] I also agree that any mass immigration of persons which would change the fundamental complexion of Canada and its people should not be allowed," he said (15 February 1955, 1175).

13 Pickersgill later added that the department could not inform applicants overseas why their applications had been refused because this might leave officials open to being sued for libel or slander (Canada 1955, No. 2, 51).

14 The appeal contained in the 1952 *Immigration Act* was, he said, "an appeal to Caesar, to the minister himself. An appeal from the hired man to the hired man's boss" (15 February 1955, 1256).

15 See, for example, the comments of Auguste Maltais (L) (15 February 1955, 1187): "The hon. member for Kamloops [Fulton] this afternoon expressed the view that immigrants have a right to come to this country." Similar comments were made by Jean-François Pouliot (L) (17 February 1955, 1261-62).

16 "If the report to the special inquiry officer is to be of any assistance whatsoever to that officer when launching upon his inquiry, he should have before him the opinion of the immigration officer as to what particular provision would be infringed by admission into Canada of the person concerned; otherwise the special inquiry officer is left merely to grope in the dark and to speculate as to what motivated the immigration officer," Justice John B. Aylesworth wrote (*Ex parte Brent* [1955], 491).

17 Thus, he concluded, the procedure was now one "of refusing admission by reason of failure to have a document, which in turn is refused without any reason given" (16 April 1964, 2254).

18 In *Espillat-Rodriguez v. R.* (18), concerning the deportation of a citizen of the Dominican Republic who was in the country legally and wished to apply for landing, Justice John R. Cartwright offered a dissenting opinion: "In the case before us there is uncontradicted sworn testimony that the applicant is in perfect health and that he asked to be informed to whom he could submit himself for an examination. To deny him this information and a reasonable time in which to obtain a certificate would, in my opinion, be to deny him the sort of hearing to which under the Act and the common law he was entitled."

19 Section 2.e holds that "no law of Canada shall be construed or applied so as to ... deprive a person of the right to a fair hearing in accordance with the principles of fundamental justice for the determination of his rights and obligations."

20 He also argued that the East Indian community was so well respected in Canada because there were so few of them, implying that to increase their immigration would not be in their own interest.

21 "There are, as I have said over and over again, no rights involved at all. No person who is not a Canadian citizen has a right to immigrate to this country, and the purpose of our immigration department and the purpose of voting money to bring out immigrants into this country is to get the kind of people we want in this country to build up this country," he continued (8 August 1956, 7211).

22 His proposed reforms were similar to those of the Canadian Bar Association subcommittee, which could "be supported on the basis of a liberal internationalist political philosophy, and it is on this level that the government should be willing to defend itself ... even the stoutest supporter of the Cabinet system would hardly claim that the Cabinet should do the work of the courts as well as running the executive and administrative branches," Corbett (1957, 87) maintained at the time.

23 In 1956, some thirty-nine refugees and their dependents were selected from refugee camps in Jordan and Lebanon to resettle in Canada (Knowles 1997, 138-39).

24 Thus, Walter Dinsdale called upon the government in 1954 not to hold up the admission of Chinese refugees as it had those from Europe after the war, which had caused immense and unnecessary suffering in the process (26 June 1954, 6813). Erhart Regier (CCF) criticized the government for requiring that Arab refugees have knowledge of English or French and have a trade in order to be eligible for admission (25 January 1956, 540).

25 During the campaign, Diefenbaker had promised a more Liberal Internationalist immigration program: "We will overhaul the [immigration] act's administration to ensure that humanity will be considered and put an end to the bureaucratic interpretations which keep out from Canada many potentially good citizens" (quoted in Knowles 1997, 145).

26 According to Ellen Fairclough, who served as Citizenship and Immigration Minister under Diefenbaker, the Prime Minister "himself was not interested in immigration, although he paid lip service to it with the ethnic groups. Immigration simply did not excite his imagination at all. He was not concerned with it and did not support her efforts" (Hawkins 1972, 137). He was repeatedly criticized for inaction on this file. For example, Leon Crestohl observed that "with his sense of justice I feel that he could not fail to realize with regard to the Immigration Act, many sections of which he himself so vigorously criticized when he sat on this side of the house, that after three years in office with the power to alter those things which he criticized he has failed to take one single step to deal with those matters which he knows are faulty in the Immigration Act, and has so stated" (26 January 1960, 338).

27 See, for example, Winch's comments: "It has always been my understanding of British justice or Canadian justice that no individual can be charged without knowing the charge, that no individual can be tried without being heard, and that no individual in Canada can be found guilty without knowing the charge, without being heard or without knowing anything about it" (30 January 1958, 4039).

28 For practical reasons, he claimed, this would initially be limited to sponsored immigrants (i.e., those with a relative in Canada) and not to overseas applicants on the grounds that the latter would have difficulty in obtaining representation and petitioning the boards in Canada.

29 According to Con and colleagues (1982, 214), "it was one of the biggest [police] searches in Canada's history." While investigations took place in some sixteen cities across the country, "the offices of major Chinese organizations throughout Canada were raided, as well as many business premises and private residences of the leaders of the various Chinese communities. Documents were seized. The communities were in a state of shock." Some reportedly felt that it was a form of retribution for having pushed for more liberal immigration laws.

30 In 1963, Ian G. Wahn (L) introduced a Private Member's Bill to "grant amnesty to and confirm the rights of Asians, Africans and other persons subject to racial discrimination whose admission to Canada may have been irregular or illegal" (20 May 1963, 30). He later withdrew the bill at Second Reading as the government's Speech from the Throne indicated that a thorough review of immigration policy was forthcoming; this would not take place for another ten years.

31 The one reason that he had been given was that "it would introduce entirely new procedures into the immigration proceedings," which he found to be an insufficient concern in and of itself (5 May 1959, 3346).

32 Among other reforms he approved of now that he was no longer minister, he called for an appeal for those whose applications to sponsor relatives from overseas had been rejected (see 9 February 1961, 1914-17).

33 In contrast, he noted that such a reporting system existed in the United States.

34 As he later put it, "the policy of Canada is one of discrimination as between members of the commonwealth because in some countries they are black and in others they are yellow; therefore they are placed on a quota system" (9 June 1960, 4719).

35 The minister later responded that no one had been deported to Iraq during the previous three years (9 June 1960, 4761).

36 Crestohl later quoted a recent Conservative party convention that had resolved that "the immigration regulations be amended ... to redefine the term 'refugee' so as to widen and extend the qualifications for admissibility under this category" (9 February 1961, 1906).

37   "This means that any suitably qualified person from any part of the world can be considered for immigration to Canada entirely on his own merits without regard to his race, colour, national origin or the country from which he comes," she continued (19 January 1962, 9).

38   Then, as now, there were fewer Canadian immigration offices outside the United States and western Europe than within, making it much more difficult for non-whites to apply to come to Canada.

39   The discriminatory aspects of Section 31.d of the 1962 regulations (PC 1962-86) in force under the 1952 *Immigration Act* lay in the fact that it limited the admission of certain relatives to those related to "a person who is a citizen of any country of Europe, including Turkey; or of any country of North, Central or South America or islands adjacent thereto; of or Egypt, Israel or Lebanon, if such person is: (i) the son, daughter, brother or sister, as well as the husband or wife and the unmarried son or daughter under twenty-one years of age of any such son, daughter, brother or sister, as the case may be; or (ii) the unmarried orphan nephew or niece under twenty-one years of age, or fiancé of a Canadian citizen or of a person legally admitted to Canada for permanent residence, who is residing in Canada and who has applied for such person, and who is willing and able to provide care and maintenance for such person until he has established himself successfully in Canada." It is likely that Cabinet pressure kept this remaining discriminatory feature on the books (Hawkins 1972, 130-31).

40   The literacy test was also removed from the regulations at this time.

41   Harold Winch (NDP) said, for example, that they would "better demonstrate what democracy means to our country, our peoples, our governments and legislative bodies" (19 January 1962, 11). The CCF was folded into the New Democratic Party, a new political party, in 1961.

42   "Regulations have to be made for administrative purposes. But an abuse occurs when that authority is converted into the making of laws," he explained (27 February 1962, 1329).

43   Indeed, Favreau argued that immigration could help Canadians to overcome racial discrimination and religious intolerance in their own communities: "Through immigration we can do much to abolish antagonisms and to foster understanding" (14 December 1963, 5879).

44   He quoted in particular Articles 1 to 4 of the declaration, the last of which states: "All states shall take effective measures to revise governmental and other public policies and to rescind laws and regulations which have the effect of creating and perpetuating racial discrimination wherever it still exists" (12 March 1965, 12320).

45   The bill did not survive Second Reading.

46   Nonetheless, he advised that "it would be unwise to open the doors wide and let them all flood in, because they are not accustomed to our climate and I am afraid some of them could not adjust to our system of living" (25 September 1964, 8443).

47   He was more tactful than Pickersgill (1994, 428), who told the Jamaican Minister of Trade and Industry in 1955 that he "was not opposed to West Indians as immigrants, but [that he] was opposed to admitting immigrants from anywhere to populate the slums."

48   Officials had such wide discretion that they could easily, within the law, practice discrimination within countries.

49   "We in Canada should be in a position to accept immigrants whatever the colour of their skin, their religion[,] their race and their language," he continued. "That is basic" (7 March 1966, 2327).

50   "Let some member of the house, or counsel for one of the people who have been in trouble, suggest for a moment that possibly the interpreter who works part time for the department, I assume, may have left the wrong impression with one of the people involved, and the minister is immediately on his feet to tell us that neither the interpreter, any other member of the staff nor the deputy minister has ever made a mistake. He tells us that the department is perfect and always has been perfect ... there comes a time when any minister should go outside of his department so that he can get the whole story," David Orlikow complained (22 June 1964, 4581-82).

51   Nonetheless, the minister announced several changes to speed up the processing of detention cases (3 June 1964, 3898-99).

52 This was largely addressed with the creation of Citizenship Appeal Courts in 1967.

53 "I know that many ministers in good faith and with the best of intent have intended in the past to remedy this deplorable situation that has existed for so long; but somehow the weight of bureaucracy, of circumlocution of the department has been too much for their efforts," he observed (16 April 1964, 2260).

54 "The hungry and the wretched in the world are not impressed by Mr. Mackenzie King's narrow strictures," he advised (22 June 1964, 4565).

55 "No advice from a lawyer is going to substitute for the department itself deciding to go to the very root of the problem of immigration by deciding whether or not the would-be immigrant is, in fact, to have what parliament itself has said is required, namely a fair hearing under the act," he said (ibid., 4590).

56 Orlikow could not find it in himself to congratulate the minister "on the excellence of his speech ... because I have heard other ministers make the same kind of speech. The former minister made a wonderful speech last year. Ministers in earlier governments, both Liberal and Conservative, all made the same kind of speeches. I suppose they came out of the same file, because if one does not do anything to implement the speech that was made the previous year, there is not much point in writing a new speech" (14 August 1964, 6853).

57 Of the 31,107 people who applied under this program, 21,017 were landed (Department of Manpower and Immigration 1974, 48, Table 3.9).

58 In late 1964, Pearson announced that a white paper would be available in the spring. His immigration ministers, as a result, endured constant inquiries as to its whereabouts. When it was finally tabled, Richard Bell noted that it "has had a very difficult and very tardy birth. Conceived by the Prime Minister as long ago as December 1964 ... it has taken 21 months and three ministerial midwives to bring it to delivery today" (14 October 1966, 8652).

59 He was particularly concerned about prohibitions on medical grounds that ignored recent advances in science, and people ordered deported because they had become a public charge through no fault of their own.

60 Sedgwick came in for some criticism for having spoken with department officials and the RCMP but not immigrant groups. His protestation that "I did not know how to get in touch with them, because I do not know who they are," received little sympathy from John M. Roxburgh (L), who prompted Sedgwick into conceding that he "fell down on the job" (Canada 1966-67, No. 14, 928). He also admitted that many of his proposals were based on general statements he had received from the department rather than facts, a type of evidence that he confessed was not sufficient (ibid., 923).

61 Hawkins (1972, 160) suggests that "the major objective of the White Paper was the legitimate and long-standing one of achieving a reasonable control over the sponsored movement ... Exactly half the White Paper – twenty-one pages out of forty-two – is occupied with the development of arguments" to this end.

62 "In no department of government," Bell recalled, "is a minister subjected to so much paper work or called upon to exercise so many discretions or subjected to so many pressures – pressures from members of parliament, from candidates, from ethnic groups, from religious and philanthropic organizations and just about everyone conceivable" (21 February 1967, 13280).

63 As Munro informed the House, "for the first time sponsorship is recognized in effect as a legal right of the Canadian citizen" (20 February 1967, 13269).

64 "On all sides of the house there is unanimity of opinion that a new Immigration Appeal Board should be established. There is undoubtedly a desire that that board should be genuinely effective, and that in the administration of immigration procedures and law it act with that degree of human understanding and compassion which I think is essential," Bell noted (21 February 1967, 13312).

65 In particular, he was referring to the 1951 Refugee Convention and the 1957 Hague Agreement Relating to Refugee Seamen.

66 For the effects of this change on Canadian immigration law, see Janzen and Hunter 1973.

67 "I am not proposing something that is unique in this field of immigration. Those who have studied administrative tribunals and appeals therefrom in other fields are beginning to

insist that this be the practice in order to make the system work with justice and fairness and in a way which is consistent," he said (22 February 1967, 13350).

68 "If you refer to landed immigrants, of course they have rights here in Canada; but those who are not here in Canada do not have any rights according to the Canadian laws. Therefore, we are not depriving anybody of their rights," he claimed (21 February 1967, 13326).

69 "I believe we are conducting an experiment, not because we have been pushed to do so but because we wanted to try to give immigrants new rights," Marchand said (22 February 1967, 13358).

70 "It seems to me the minister is going right back to the kind of departmental authoritarianism which gives the department the right to do things without explanation, to which so many members on both sides of the house have objected in the past," Orlikow observed (ibid., 13359).

71 "It seems to me axiomatic that if you give a right of appeal to a class of person, every member of that class ought to have the opportunity of exercising it if he so wishes," Lewis said (1 March 1967, 13627).

72 Baldwin insisted that "surely it is not beyond the ingenuity of the government, its law officers and the civil servants to devise a means by which cases which are certified to involve security matters can be heard by this board or a special panel of the board sitting in camera if necessary" (21 February 1967, 13298). Security certificates continue to be controversial in Canada; for example, see Leddy 2010.

73 "What is the virtue of denying me all information and making me incapable of doing anything at all as against giving me some information on which I may be able to do something?" he asked (23 February 1967, 13397).

74 In addition, Herb Gray (L) reminded the minister, many of the problems encountered by the department were of its own making and "would be lessened to a great degree if there were sufficient highly trained and well paid staff in the field to administer a set of fair and reasonable rules" (21 February 1967, 13321-22).

75 A few, such as Gerald Baldwin, wanted to define more clearly (if not rein in specifically) the powers of the board: "Our experience is that whenever powers are given those powers will be used, even if they were not provided intentionally" (22 February 1967, 13348).

Chapter 7: Contemporary Canadian and Comparative Concerns

1 Of course, not all Canadians understand or view multiculturalism positively; for a reflection of some of the debates today, see Ryan 2010; Stein et al. 2007.

2 "This Act is to be construed and applied in a manner that ... ensures that decisions taken under this Act are consistent with the *Canadian Charter of Rights and Freedoms,* including its principles of equality and freedom from discrimination" (Section 3.3.d).

3 This concern cut across party lines. Similarly, Lincoln Alexander (PC) observed that "without relocation of officers, the small number of Canadian officers in third world countries compared with the number in the United States and Europe indicates a de facto policy of discrimination; there can be no doubt about that" (15 March 1977, 3994).

4 Both state and non-state actors agreed that Portuguese claims of persecution for being Jehovah's Witnesses were without foundation; see Malarek 1987, Chapter 9.

5 "A lot of the credit," he continued, "must go to those Chinese and other Asian immigrants who were pioneers in more than one sense of the word" (11 March 1977, 3901).

6 Thus, although the 1976 *Immigration Act* still had a restrictive orientation, it now had, unlike the 1952 *Immigration Act,* a rights-based orientation as well; see Grey 1984, 14-15.

7 As Galloway (1997, 311) notes, "Canada's immigration process is both complex and unwieldy, and is driven by a confusing array of principles and conflicting aims and values. The need for precise legal rules clashes with the need for flexibility; the need to promote economic growth conflicts with the need to fulfil international and humanitarian obligations and to promote family reunification; the need to maintain a process which is 'user-friendly' and compassionate and which facilitates the applicant's journey through the bureaucratic jungle conflicts with the need for a process which is able to identify, exclude, and remove illegal immigrants or those who do not fulfil the requirements of the law."

8 For example, Knowles (1997, 170) writes: "On balance, the Immigration Act, 1976 was a progressive statute that was generally regarded at the time of its baptism as the best legislation of its kind in the world."

9 Quarterly statistics are published at http://cas-ncr-nter03.cas-satj.gc.ca/portal/page/portal/fc_cf_en/Statistics.

10 For the most part, the relevant literature is defined by legal scholars and their works rarely (with a few exceptions, such as the work of Aiken and Macklin) draw on the work of political scientists in general or the control literature in particular. When the role of the courts is examined in any detail, it is usually in the context of a specific case or a few specific cases. There is especially a need to analyze developments concerning the rights of non-citizens in the context of the postwar expansion of administrative law in Canada. On the latter, see Girard (2007) and Taggart (2005).

11 This was well understood at the time of its passage; see Wydrzynski 1979 and Anderson 2010.

12 See "Overview" at http://www.immigrationreform.ca.

13 This includes "immigration lawyers, immigration consultants, the Canadian Council for Refugees, the Canadian Council of Churches, Amnesty International and a host of advocacy groups and NGOs" (Bissett 2010b).

14 Kenney has also criticized what he calls the "ideological bureaucrats" at the Canadian Conference of Catholic Bishops when they wrote a letter critical of Bill C-49 (Gyapong 2010) and taken the judiciary to task for overturning certain decisions by public servants enforcing Canadian immigration and refugee law (Friesen 2011).

15 This was a frequent device employed by Conservative MPs during recent parliamentary debates over proposed government legislation, which suggests that it was a coordinated effort. For example, in response to critics who praised some parts of the 2010 *Balanced Refugee Reform Act,* rejected others, and offered alternatives, Alice Wong (C) replied: "I was really disappointed that people are still happy with the present situation, whereby we have 18 months of wait time for genuine refugee claimants and we have people who have been here for ten years who still haven't got a final answer. I don't know why people still feel the present system is working" (Canada 2010, 22).

16 A major fairness issue debated in the 1970s and 1980s had been ensuring the independence of decision makers within the inland refugee determination system, and the IRB had been staffed by independent (Cabinet-appointed) adjudicators rather than public servants to address this concern.

17 Examples would include the commitment to create the RAD itself (after a decade of delay) and the move of PRRA decisions from CIC to the IRB. As of July 2012, however, these provisions had not yet come into force and now will do so (under Bill C-31; see below) at an unspecified time by order of Cabinet.

18 Because the Conservatives could not count on majority support in the House of Commons, significant changes were made to the proposed legislation between First Reading and Royal Assent, and some additional restrictive elements were removed as a result.

19 Unlike Bill C-4, Bill C-31 excluded mandatory detention for those under sixteen years of age.

20 The bill had originally called for no detention review before a twelve-month period but this was later changed to a first review after fourteen days followed by reviews every six months. Previously, such detainees would have received a review within forty-eight hours, followed by another within the next seven days and subsequent reviews every thirty days.

21 Generally, those who receive refugee status in Canada are to apply for permanent residence status within 180 days, and once it is granted they can apply to sponsor family members.

22 The law also allows for expanded collection of biometrics from foreign nationals and cooperation with both foreign governments and the Canada Border Services Agency (which is responsible for screening entries into Canada) in this respect.

Works Cited

Canadian Government Documents

Government of Canada
The following sources were systematically examined for relevant information within the 1867-1967 period: *Canada Gazette; House of Commons Debates; Senate Debates; Sessional Papers; Journals; Annual Reports* of the Department of Agriculture, Department of the Interior, Department of Immigration and Colonization, Department of Mines and Resources, Department of Manpower and Immigration, and Department of Citizenship and Immigration; *Proceedings of the [Senate] Standing Committee on Immigration and Labour* (1946-68); *Minutes of Proceedings and Evidence of the Special Joint Committee of the Senate and the House of Commons on Immigration* (1966-68).

Specific reference is made to the following sources in the text:

Canada. 1868. "Report of the Select Standing Committee on Immigration and Colonization [House of Commons]." *Journals.* Ottawa, Appendix No. 8.

–. 1869. "Immigration: Documents on the Subject of Immigration." *Sessional Papers.* Ottawa, No. 67.

–. 1870. "Report of the Minister of Agriculture of the Dominion of Canada for the Year 1869." *Sessional Papers.* Ottawa, No. 80.

–. 1871. "Report of the Minister of Agriculture for 1870." *Sessional Papers.* Ottawa, No. 64.

–. 1872. "Report of the Minister of Agriculture of the Dominion of Canada for the Calendar Year 1871." *Sessional Papers.* Ottawa, No. 2A.

–. 1873. *Census of Canada 1870-71, Volume 1.* Ottawa.

–. 1874a. "Report of the Minister of Agriculture of the Dominion of Canada for the Calendar Year 1873." *Sessional Papers.* Ottawa, No. 9.

–. 1874b. "Report of the Select Standing Committee on Immigration and Colonization [House of Commons]." *Journals.* Ottawa, Appendix No. 7.

–. 1875a. "Report of the Minister of Agriculture of the Dominion of Canada for the Calendar Year 1874." *Sessional Papers.* Ottawa, No. 40.

–. 1875b. "Report of the Select Committee on Immigration and Colonization [House of Commons]." *Journals.* Ottawa, Appendix No. 4.

–. 1878. "Report of the Minister of Agriculture of the Dominion of Canada for the Calendar Year 1877." *Sessional Papers.* Ottawa, No. 9.

–. 1879a. "Chinese Labor and Immigration: Report of the Select Committee on the Subject of Chinese Labor and Immigration affecting the Dominion." *Journals.* Ottawa, Appendix No. 4.

–. 1879b. "Report of the Select Standing Committee on Immigration and Colonization [House of Commons]." *Journals.* Ottawa, Appendix No. 1.

–. 1880. "Report of the Minister of Agriculture of the Dominion of Canada for the Calendar Year 1879." *Sessional Papers.* Ottawa, No. 10.

–. 1881. "Report of the Minister of Agriculture of the Dominion of Canada for the Calendar Year 1880." *Sessional Papers.* Ottawa, No. 12.

–. 1882a. *Census of Canada 1880-81, Volume 1.* Ottawa.

–. 1882b. "Report of the Minister of Agriculture of the Dominion of Canada for the Calendar Year 1881." *Sessional Papers.* Ottawa, No. 11.

–. 1883. "Report of the Select Standing Committee on Immigration and Colonization [House of Commons]." *Journals.* Ottawa, Appendix No. 6.

–. 1884. "Report of the Select Standing Committee on Immigration and Colonization [House of Commons]." *Journals.* Ottawa, Appendix No. 1.

–. 1885a. "The Honourable Commissioner Gray's Report Respecting Chinese Immigration in British Columbia." *Sessional Papers.* Ottawa, No. 54a.

–. 1885b. "Report of the Minister of Agriculture of the Dominion of Canada for the Calendar Year 1884." *Sessional Papers.* Ottawa, No. 8.

–. 1886. "Report of the Select Standing Committee on Immigration and Colonization [House of Commons]." *Journals.* Ottawa, Appendix No. 6.

–. 1887. "Report of the Minister of Agriculture of the Dominion of Canada for the Calendar Year 1886." *Sessional Papers.* Ottawa, No. 12.

–. 1888a. "Report of the Minister of Agriculture for the Dominion of Canada for the Calendar Year 1887." *Sessional Papers.* Ottawa, No. 4.

–. 1888b. "Report of the Select Standing Committee on Agriculture and Colonization [House of Commons]." *Journals.* Ottawa, Appendix No. 5.

–. 1889. "Report of the Select Standing Committee on Agriculture and Colonization [House of Commons]." *Journals.* Ottawa, Appendix No. 4.

–. 1890. "Report of the Minister of Agriculture for the Dominion of Canada for the Calendar Year 1889." *Sessional Papers.* Ottawa, No. 6.

–. 1893. "Report of the Select Standing Committee on Agriculture and Colonization [House of Commons]." *Journals.* Ottawa, Appendix No. 1.

–. 1898. "Report of the Select Standing Committee on Agriculture and Colonization [House of Commons]." *Journals.* Ottawa, Appendix No. 3, Part II.

–. 1899. "Report of the Select Standing Committee on Agriculture and Colonization [House of Commons]." *Journals.* Ottawa, Appendix No. 3, Part II.

–. 1900. "Report of the Select Standing Committee on Agriculture and Colonization [House of Commons]." *Journals.* Ottawa, Appendix No. 1, Part II.

–. 1902. "Report of the Select Standing Committee on Agriculture and Colonization [House of Commons]." *Journals.* Ottawa, Appendix No. 1, Part II.

–. 1903. "Report of the Select Standing Committee on Agriculture and Colonization [House of Commons]." *Journals.* Ottawa, Appendix No. 2, Part II.

–. 1904. "Report of the Select Standing Committee on Agriculture and Colonization [House of Commons]." *Journals.* Ottawa, Appendix No. 2, Part II.

–. 1906. "Report of the Select Standing Committee on Agriculture and Colonization [House of Commons]." *Journals.* Ottawa, Appendix No. 2, Part II.

–. 1908a. "Report of the Select Standing Committee on Agriculture and Colonization [House of Commons]." *Journals.* Ottawa, Appendix No. 2, Part II.

–. 1908b. "Report by W.L. Mackenzie King, C.M.G., Deputy Minister of Labour, on Mission to England to Confer with the British Authorities on the Subject of Immigration to Canada from the Orient and Immigration from India in Particular." *Sessional Papers.* Ottawa, No. 36a.

–. 1909. "Report of the Select Standing Committee on Agriculture and Colonization [House of Commons]." *Journals.* Ottawa, Appendix No. 2, Part II.

–. 1912. "Report of the Department of the Interior for the Fiscal Year Ending March 31, 1911." *Sessional Papers.* Ottawa, No. 25, Part II.

–. 1923. "Report of the Department of the Immigration and Colonization for the Fiscal Year Ended March 31, 1922." *Sessional Papers.* Ottawa, No. 13.

–. 1926. *Report of the Department of Immigration and Colonization for the Fiscal Year Ended March 31, 1925.* Ottawa.

–. 1928. *Report of the Select Standing Committee on Agriculture and Colonization.* Ottawa.

–. 1936. *Minutes of Proceedings and Evidence of the Special Committee on Elections and Franchise Acts* [House of Commons]. Ottawa, No. 10.

–. 1946-47. *Proceedings of the Standing Committee on Immigration and Labour* [Senate]. Ottawa.

–. 1952. *Minutes of Proceedings and Evidence of the Special Committee Appointed to Consider Bill No. 305, An Act Respecting Immigration* [House of Commons]. Ottawa.

–. 1955. *Minutes of Proceedings and Evidence of the Special Committee on Estimates: Department of Citizenship and Immigration* [House of Commons]. Ottawa, No. 2.

–. 1966-67. *Minutes of Proceedings and Evidence of the Special Joint Committee of the Senate and the House of Commons on Immigration.* Ottawa.

–. 1967. *Documents on Canadian External Relations, Volume 1, 1909-1918.* Ottawa.

–. 1970. *Documents on Canadian External Relations, Volume 3, 1919-1925.* Ottawa.

–. 1977. *Documents on Canadian External Relations, Volume 12, 1946.* Ottawa.

–. 1980. *Documents on Canadian External Relations, Volume 9, 1942-1943.* Ottawa.

–. 1996. *Documents on Canadian External Relations, Volume 17, 1951.* Ottawa.

–. 2001. *Minutes and Evidence of the Standing Committee on Citizenship and Immigration.* Ottawa, 1 March.

–. 2010. *Proceedings of the Standing Committee on Citizenship and Immigration.* Ottawa, No. 18.

Other Federal Government Documents

Canadian Heritage. 2012. "Canada's Commitment to Cultural Diversity." http://www.pch.gc.ca/pgm/.

Citizenship and Immigration Canada. 2003. *Facts and Figures 2002: Immigration Overview.* Ottawa.

Department of Manpower and Immigration. 1966. *White Paper on Immigration.* Ottawa.

–. 1974. *Annual Report.* Ottawa.

Library of Parliament. 2011. *Legislative Summary of Bill C-11: An Act to amend the Immigration and Refugee Protection Act and the Federal Courts Act (Balanced Refugee Reform Act)* [Publication No. 40-3-c11-e; Revised 12 January 2011]. Ottawa.

–. 2012. *Legislative Summary of Bill C-31: An Act to amend the Immigration and Refugee Protection Act, the Balanced Refugee Reform Act, the Marine Transportation Security Act and the Department of Citizenship and Immigration Act* [Publication Number 41-1-C31-E; Revised 4 June 2012]. Ottawa.

Public Safety Canada. 2010a. "Canada's Generous Program for Refugee Resettlement Is Undermined by Human Smugglers Who Abuse Canada's Immigration System." http://www.publicsafety.gc.ca/.

–. 2010b. "Harper Government Introduces Preventing Human Smugglers from Abusing Canada's Immigration System Act." http://www.publicsafety.gc.ca/.

Royal Commission on Aboriginal Peoples. 1996. *Report of the Royal Commission on Aboriginal Peoples.* Vol. 1, *Looking Forward, Looking Back.* Ottawa.

Sedgwick, Joseph. 1966. *Report on Immigration: Part II.* Ottawa, January.

Statutes of Canada

An Act to amend an Act of the present session entitled An Act to amend The Immigration Act, S.C. 1919, c. 26.

An Act to amend "The Chinese Immigration Act," S.C. 1887, c. 35.

An Act to amend the Chinese Immigration Act, S.C. 1908, c. 14.

An Act to amend the Chinese Immigration Act, S.C. 1921, c. 21.

An Act to amend the Immigration Act, S.C. 1902, c. 14.

An Act to amend the Immigration Act, S.C. 1907, c. 19.

An Act to amend the Immigration Act, S.C. 1919, c. 25.

An Act to amend the Immigration Act of 1869, S.C. 1872, c. 28.

Balanced Refugee Reform Act (An Act to amend the Immigration and Refugee Protection Act and the Federal Courts Act), S.C. 2010, c. 8.

British North America Act (An Act for the Union of Canada, Nova Scotia, and New Brunswick, and the Government thereof; and for Purposes connected therewith), 1867, 30-31 Vict., c. 3 (U.K.).

Canadian Bill of Rights (An Act for the Regulation and Protection of Human Rights and Fundamental Freedoms), S.C. 1960, c. 44.

Canadian Citizenship Act (An Act respecting Citizenship, Nationality, Naturalization and Status of Aliens), S.C. 1946, c. 15.

Chinese Immigration Act (An Act respecting Chinese Immigration), S.C. 1923, c. 38.

Chinese Immigration Act (An Act respecting and restricting Chinese Immigration), S.C. 1900, c. 32.

Chinese Immigration Act (An Act respecting and restricting Chinese immigration), S.C. 1903, c. 8.

Chinese Immigration Act (An Act to restrict and regulate Chinese immigration into Canada), S.C. 1885, c. 71.

Dominion By-Election Act (An Act to amend the Dominion Elections Act), S.C. 1919, c. 48.

Dominion Elections Act (An Act respecting the Election of Members of the House of Commons and the Electoral Franchise), S.C. 1919-20, c. 46.

Electoral Franchise Act (An Act respecting the Electoral Franchise), S.C. 1885, c. 40.

Immigration Act (An Act respecting Immigration), S.C. 1910, c. 27.

Immigration Act (An Act respecting Immigration), S.C. 1952, c. 42.

Immigration Act (An Act respecting Immigration and Immigrants), S.C. 1869, c. 10.

Immigration Act (An Act respecting Immigration and Immigrants), S.C. 1906, c. 19.

Immigration Act (An Act respecting immigration to Canada), S.C. 1976-77, c. 52.

Immigration and Refugee Protection Act (An Act respecting immigration to Canada and the granting of refugee protection to persons who are displaced, persecuted or in danger), S.C. 2001, c. 27.

Immigration Appeal Board Act (An Act to make provision for appeals to an Immigration Appeal Board in respect of certain matters relating to immigration), S.C. 1967, c. 90.

Japanese Treaty Act (An Act respecting a certain Treaty of Commerce and Navigation between His Majesty the King and His Majesty the Emperor of Japan), S.C. 1913, c. 27.

National Emergency Transition Powers Act (An Act to confer certain transitional powers upon the Governor in Council during the National Emergency arising out of War), S.C. 1945, c. 25.

Opium and Drug Act (An Act to prohibit the improper use of Opium and other Drugs), S.C. 1911, c. 17.

Opium and Narcotic Drug Act (An Act to amend and consolidate the Opium and Narcotic Drug Act), S.C. 1929, c. 49.

Protecting Canada's Immigration System Act (An Act to amend the Immigration and Refugee Protection Act, the Balanced Refugee Reform Act, the Marine Transportation Security Act and the Department of Citizenship and Immigration Act), S.C. 2012, c. 7.

Quarantine Act (An Act relating to Quarantine), S.C. 1872, c. 27.

War Measures Act (An Act to confer certain powers upon the Governor in Council and to amend the Immigration Act), S.C. 1914, c. 2.

War-Time Elections Act, S.C. 1917, c. 39.

Court Decisions

A selective survey of judicial decisions was made, drawing on *Canadian Reports – Appeal Cases*, *Supreme Court [of Canada] Reports* (S.C.R.), *Canada Federal Court Reports*, *British Columbia Reports* (B.C.R.), and *Ontario Reports* (O.R.).

Specific reference is made to the following decisions in the text:

Espillat-Rodriguez v. R., [1964] S.C.R. 3.

Ex parte Brent, [1954] O.R. 706.

Ex parte Brent, [1955] O.R. 480.

In Re Behari Lal et al., [1908] 13 B.C.R. 415.

In Re Nakane and Okazake, [1908] 13 B.C.R. 370.

In Re Narain Singh et al., [1913] 18 B.C.R. 506.

In Re Rahim, [1911] 16 B.C.R. 469.

In Re Rahim (No. 2), [1911] 16 B.C.R. 471.

Masella v. Langlais, [1955] S.C.R. 263.

Quong-Wing v. R., [1914] 49 S.C.R. 440.

Re Munshi Singh, [1915] 20 B.C.R. 242.
Tai Sing v. Maguire, [1878] 1 B.C.R. 101.

Secondary Sources

Abella, Irving. 1990. *A Coat of Many Colours: Two Centuries of Jewish Life in Canada.* Toronto: Lester and Orpen Dennys.

Abella, Irving, and Harold Troper. 1991. *None Is Too Many: Canada and the Jews of Europe, 1933-1948.* 3rd ed. Toronto: Lester Publishing.

Abu-Laban, Baha. 1980. *An Olive Branch on the Family Tree: The Arabs in Canada.* Toronto: McClelland and Stewart.

Abu-Laban, Yasmeen. 1998a. "Keeping 'em Out: Gender, Race, and Class in Canadian Immigration Policy." In *Painting the Maple: Essays on Race, Gender, and the Construction of Canada,* edited by V. Strong-Boag, S. Grace, A. Eisenberg, and J. Anderson, 69-82. Vancouver: UBC Press.

–. 1998b. "Welcome/STAY OUT: The Contradiction of Canadian Integration and Immigration Policies at the Millennium." *Canadian Ethnic Studies* 30 (3): 190-211.

Adachi, Ken. 1976. *The Enemy that Never Was.* Toronto: McClelland and Stewart.

Aiken, Sharryn J. 2007. "Risking Rights: An Assessment of Canadian Border Security Policies." In *Whose Canada? Continental Integration, Fortress North America and the Corporate Agenda,* edited by R. Grinspun and Y. Shamsie, 180-208. Montreal and Kingston: McGill-Queen's University Press.

Ajzenstat, Janet. 2007. *The Canadian Founding: John Locke and Parliament.* Montreal and Kingston: McGill-Queen's University Press.

Ajzenstat, Janet, and Peter J. Smith, eds. 1995. *Canada's Origins: Liberal, Tory, or Republican?* Ottawa: Carleton University Press.

Amnesty International Canada. 2010. "Fast and Efficient but Not Fair: Recommendations with respect to Bill C-11" (Brief to the House of Commons Standing Committee on Citizenship and Immigration). Ottawa, 11 May.

–. 2012. "Unbalanced Reforms: Recommendations with Respect to Bill C-31" (Brief to the House of Commons Standing Committee on Citizenship and Immigration). Toronto, 7 May.

Anderson, Christopher G. 2008. "A Long-Standing Canadian Tradition: Citizenship Revocation and Second-Class Citizenship under the Liberals, 1993-2006." *Journal of Canadian Studies* 42 (3): 80-105.

–. 2010. "Restricting Rights, Losing Control: The Politics of Control over Asylum Seekers in Liberal-Democratic States – Lessons from the Canadian Case, 1951-1989." *Canadian Journal of Political Science* 43 (4): 937-59.

–. 2011. "Immigration, Immigrants, and the Rights of Canadian Citizens in Historical Perspective" [Review Essay]. *International Journal of Canadian Studies* 43: 207-19.

Andreas, Peter. 2001. *Border Games: Policing the US-Mexico Divide.* Ithaca, NY: Cornell University Press.

–. 2005. "The Mexicanization of the US-Canada Border: Asymmetric Interdependence in a Changing Security Context." *International Journal* 60 (2): 449-62.

Andreas, Peter, and Timothy Snyder, eds. 2000. *The Wall around the West: State Borders and Immigration Controls in North America and Europe.* Lanham, MD: Rowman and Littlefield.

Appiah, Kwame Anthony. 2006. *Cosmopolitanism: Ethics in a World of Strangers.* New York: W.W. Norton.

Arat-Koc, Sedef. 1999. "Gender and Race in 'Non-Discriminatory' Immigration Policies in Canada: 1960s to the Present." In *Scratching the Surface: Canadian Anti-Racist Feminist Thought,* edited by E. Dua and A. Robertson, 207-33. Toronto: Women's Press, 1999.

Aun, Karl. 1985. *The Political Refugees: A History of the Estonians in Canada.* Toronto: McClelland and Stewart.

Avery, Donald. 1979. *"Dangerous Foreigners": European Immigrant Workers and Labour Radicalism in Canada, 1896-1932.* Toronto: McClelland and Stewart.

–. 1995. *Reluctant Host: Canada's Response to Immigrant Workers, 1896-1994.* Toronto: McClelland and Stewart.

Ayukawa, Midge M., and Patricia E. Roy. 1999. "Japanese." In *Encyclopedia of Canada's Peoples*, edited by P.R. Magocsi, 842-60. Toronto: University of Toronto Press.

Backhouse, Constance. 1999. *Colour-Coded: A Legal History of Racism in Canada, 1900-1950*. Toronto: University of Toronto Press.

Bahdi, Reem. 2003. "No Exit: Racial Profiling and Canada's War against Terrorism." *Osgoode Hall Law Journal* 41 (2-3): 294-316.

Bangarth, Stephanie. 2002. "Mackenzie King and Japanese Canadians." In *Mackenzie King: Citizenship and Community*, edited by J. English, K. McLaughlin, and P.W. Lackenbauer, 99-123. Toronto: Robin Brass Studio.

–. 2003. "'We Are Not Asking You to Open Wide the Gates for Chinese Immigration': The Committee for the Repeal of the Chinese Immigration Act and Early Human Rights Activism in Canada." *Canadian Historical Review* 84 (3): 395-422.

–. 2008. *Voices Raised in Protest: Defending North American Citizens of Japanese Ancestry, 1942-49*. Vancouver: UBC Press.

Barkway, Michael. 1957. "Turning Point for Immigration?" *Behind the Headlines* 17 (4).

Basok, Tanya. 2002. *Tortillas and Tomatoes: Transmigrant Mexican Harvesters in Canada*. Montreal and Kingston: McGill-Queen's University Press.

Basok, Tanya, and Alan Simmons. 1993. "A Review of the Politics of Canadian Refugee Selection." In *The International Refugee Crisis: British and Canadian Response*, edited by V. Robinson, 132-57. Oxford: Refugee Studies Programme.

Bauböck, Rainer, and Christian Joppke, eds. 2010. *How Liberal Are Citizenship Tests?* EUI Working Paper RSCAS 2010/41. Florence: Robert Schuman Centre for Advanced Studies, European University Institute.

Bauer, William. 1997. "Refugees, Victims, or Killers: The New Slave Trade?" *International Journal* 52 (4): 677-94.

Belkin, Simon. 1966. *Through Narrow Gates: A Review of Jewish Immigration, Colonization and Immigrant Aid Work in Canada, 1840-1940*. Montreal: Eagle Publishing.

Bell, Stewart. 2005. *Cold Terror: How Canada Nurtures and Exports Terrorism around the World*. Mississauga, ON: John Wiley and Sons Canada.

Berger, Carl. 1970. *The Sense of Power: Studies in the Ideas of Canadian Imperialism, 1867-1914*. Toronto: University of Toronto Press.

Berman, Sheri. 2001. "Ideas, Norms, and Culture in Political Analysis." *Comparative Politics* 33 (2): 231-50.

Berthiaume, Lee. 2010. "Government Prepares for Public Relations War over Refugees." *Embassy*, 17 March.

Berton, Pierre. 1997. *1967: The Last Good Year*. Toronto: Doubleday Canada.

Bhandar, Davina. 2004. "Renormalizing Citizenship and Life in Fortress North America." *Citizenship Studies* 8 (3): 261-78.

Bhatia, Vandna, and William D. Coleman. 2003. "Ideas and Discourse: Reform and Resistance in the Canadian and German Health Systems." *Canadian Journal of Political Science* 36 (4): 715-39.

Bigo, Didier, and Anastassia Tsoukala, eds. 2008. *Terror, Insecurity and Liberty: Illiberal Practices of Liberal Regimes after 9/11*. London: Routledge.

Biles, John, Meyer Burstein, and James Frideres. 2008. "Introduction." In *Immigration and Integration in Canada in the Twenty-First Century*, edited by J. Biles, M. Burstein, and J. Frideres, 3-18. Montreal and Kingston: McGill-Queen's University Press.

Birrell, Bob. 2001. "Immigration on the Rise: The 2001-2002 Immigration Program." *People and Place* 9 (2): 21-28.

Bissett, James. 2010a. *Abusing Canada's Generosity and Ignoring Genuine Refugees: An Analysis of Current and Still-Needed Reforms to Canada's Refugee and Immigration System*. Policy Series 96. Winnipeg: Frontier Centre for Public Policy.

–. 2010b. "Getting Tough on Human Smuggling." *Ottawa Citizen*, 27 October, A15.

Bogusz, Barbara, Ryszard Cholewinski, Adam Cygan, and Erika Szyszczak, eds. 2004. *Irregular Migration and Human Rights: Theoretical, European and International Perspectives*. Leiden, Netherlands: Martinus Nijhoff.

Bohmer, Carol, and Amy Shuman. 2008. *Rejecting Refugees: Political Asylum in the 21st Century*. London: Routledge.

Bonjour, Saskia. 2011. "The Power and Morals of Policy Makers: Reassessing the Control Gap Debate." *International Migration Review* 45 (1): 89-122.

Boswell, Christina. 2007. "Theorizing Migration Policy: Is There a Third Way?" *International Migration Review* 41 (1): 75-100.

Bothwell, Robert. 1998. *The Big Chill: Canada and the Cold War*. Toronto: Canadian Institute of International Affairs.

Bothwell, Robert, Ian Drummond, and John English. 1987. *Canada, 1900-1945*. Toronto: University of Toronto Press.

Boyd, Monica, and Deanna Pikkow. 2008. "Finding a Place in Stratified Structures: Migrant Women in North America." In *New Perspectives on Gender and Migration: Livelihood, Rights and Entitlements*, edited by N. Piper, 19-58. New York: Routledge.

Bradimore, Ashley, and Harald Bauder. 2011. *Mystery Ships and Risky Boat People: Tamil Refugee Migration in the Newsprint Media*. Working Paper Series No. 11-02. Vancouver: Metropolis British Columbia, Centre of Excellence for Research on Immigration and Diversity, January.

Brochmann, Grete, and Tomas Hammar, eds. 1999. *Mechanisms of Immigration Control: A Comparative Analysis of European Regulation Politics*. Oxford: Berg.

Broeders, Dennis, and Godfried Engbersen. 2007. "The Fight against Illegal Migration: Identification Policies and Immigrants' Counterstrategies." *American Behavioral Scientist* 50 (12): 1592-1609.

Brubaker, (William) Rogers. 1989. "Introduction." In *Immigration and the Politics of Citizenship in Europe and North America*, edited by W.R. Brubaker, 1-27. Lanham, MD: University Press of America.

–. 1995. "Comments on 'Modes of Immigration Politics in Liberal Democratic States.'" *International Migration Review* 29 (4): 903-8.

Buchignani, Norman, Doreen M. Indra, and Ram Srivastava. 1985. *Continuous Journey: A Social History of South Asians in Canada*. Toronto: McClelland and Stewart.

Buckner, P.A. 1997. "Making British North America British, 1815-1860." In *Kith and Kin: Canada, Britain and the United States from the Revolution to the Cold War*, edited by C.C. Eldridge, 11-44. Cardiff: University of Wales Press.

Burnet, Jean R., with Howard Palmer. 1988. *Coming Canadians: An Introduction to a History of Canada's Peoples*. Toronto: McClelland and Stewart.

Cahill, Jack. 1998. *Forgotten Patriots: Canadian Rebels on Australia's Convict Shores*. Toronto: R. Brass Studio.

Canadian Bar Association, National Immigration Law Section. 2012. "Bill C-31: *Protecting Canada's Immigration System Act*" (Submission to the House of Commons Standing Committee on Citizenship and Immigration). Ottawa, April.

Canadian Broadcasting Corporation. 2010. "Canada's Role with Refugees: A Debate." *The National*. Toronto, 21 August.

Canadian Civil Liberties Association. 2011. "Bill C-49 Punishes Asylum Seekers." http://ccla.org/our-work/focus-areas/bill-c-49/.

–. 2012. "Bill C-31: An Unjustified Assault on the Rights of People in Danger" (Submission to the House of Commons Standing Committee on Citizenship and Immigration). Montreal, April.

Canadian Council for Refugees. 2012. "Bill C31: Diminishing Refugee Protection" (Brief to the House of Commons Standing Committee on Citizenship and Immigration). Montreal, April.

Carens, Joseph H. 1987. "Aliens and Citizens: The Case for Open Borders." *Review of Politics* 49 (2): 251-73.

–. 2003. "Who Should Get in? The Ethics of Immigration Admissions." *Ethics and International Affairs* 17 (1): 95-110.

Carrothers, W.A. 1965. *Emigration from the British Isles*. London: Frank Cass (reprint of the 1929 edition).

Castles, Stephen. 2004. "The Factors that Make and Unmake Migration Policies." *International Migration Review* 38 (3): 852-84.

Castles, Stephen, and Mark J. Miller. 2003. *The Age of Migration: International Population Movements in the Modern World*. 3rd ed. New York: Guilford Press.

Castles, Stephen, Heaven Crawley, and Sean Loughna. 2003. *States of Conflict: Causes and Patterns of Forced Migration to the EU and Policy Responses*. London: Institute for Public Policy Research.

Chan, Wendy. 2006. "Crime, Deportation and the Regulation of Immigrants in Canada." *Crime, Law and Social Change* 44 (2): 153-80.

Cohen, Robin, ed. 1995. *The Cambridge Survey of World Migration*. Cambridge: Cambridge University Press.

Collacott, Martin. 2010a. "They Will Keep Coming." *Ottawa Citizen*, 11 October, A11.

–. 2010b. "Turning Away Visitors." *Ottawa Citizen*, 13 November, B7.

Con, Harry, Ronald J. Con, Graham Johnson, Edgar Wickberg, and William E. Willmott. 1982. *From China to Canada: A History of the Chinese Communities in Canada*. Toronto: McClelland and Stewart.

Corbett, David A. 1957. *Canada's Immigration Policy: A Critique*. Toronto: University of Toronto Press.

Cornelius, Wayne A., Philip L. Martin, and James F. Hollifield, eds. 1994a. *Controlling Immigration: A Global Perspective*. Stanford, CA: Stanford University Press.

–. 1994b. "Introduction: The Ambivalent Quest for Immigration Control." In *Controlling Immigration: A Global Perspective*, edited by W.A. Cornelius, P.L. Martin, and J.F. Hollifield, 3-41. Stanford, CA: Stanford University Press.

Cornelius, Wayne A., and Marc R. Rosenblum. 2005. "Immigration and Politics." *Annual Review of Political Science* 8: 99-119.

Cornelius, Wayne A., and Takeyuki Tsuda. 2004. "Controlling Immigration: The Limits of Government Intervention." In *Controlling Immigration: A Global Perspective*, 2nd ed., edited by W.A. Cornelius, T. Tsuda, P.L. Martin, and J.F. Hollifield, 3-48. Stanford, CA: Stanford University Press.

Cornelius, Wayne A., Takeyuki Tsuda, Philip L. Martin, and James F. Hollifield, eds. 2004. *Controlling Immigration: A Global Perspective*. 2nd ed. Stanford, CA: Stanford University Press.

Craft, Kenneth. 1987. "Canada's Righteous: A History of the Canadian National Committee on Refugees and Victims of Political Persecution." MA thesis, Carleton University.

Creese, Gillian. 1992. "The Politics of Refugees in Canada." In *Deconstructing A Nation: Immigration, Multiculturalism and Racism in '90s Canada*, edited by V. Satzewich, 123-43. Halifax: Fernwood Publishing.

Crépeau, François. 2003. "Overview of Interdiction by Sea, Land and Air." In *Interdiction and Refugee Protection: Bridging the Gap*. Workshop proceedings. Montreal: Canadian Council for Refugees.

Crépeau, François, Delphine Nakache, and Idil Atak. 2007. "International Migration: Security Concerns and Human Rights Standards." *Transcultural Psychiatry* 44 (3): 311-37.

Dafoe, John W. 1931. *Clifford Sifton in Relation to His Times*. Toronto: Macmillan Company of Canada.

Daniels, Roger. 2004. *Guarding the Golden Door: American Immigration Policy and Immigrants since 1882*. New York: Hill and Wang.

Daniels, Ronald J., Patrick Macklem, and Kent Roach, eds. 2001. *The Security of Freedom; Essays on Canada's Anti-Terrorism Bill*. Toronto: University of Toronto Press.

Dauvergne, Catherine. 1999. "Amorality and Humanitarianism in International Law." *Osgoode Hall Law Journal* 37 (3): 597-623.

–. 2005. *Humanitarianism, Identity, and Nation: Migration Laws in Canada and Australia*. Vancouver: UBC Press.

De Genova, Nicholas P. 2002. "Migrant 'Illegality' and Deportability in Everyday Life." *Annual Review of Anthropology* 31: 419-47.

Diab, Robert. 2008. *Guantánamo North: Terrorism and the Administration of Justice in Canada*. Black Point, NS: Fernwood Publishing.

Dinnerstein, Leonard, and David M. Reimers. 1999. *Ethnic Americans: A History of Immigration*. 4th ed. New York: Columbia University Press.

Dirks, Gerald E. 1977. *Canada's Refugee Policy: Indifference or Opportunism?* Montreal and Kingston: McGill-Queen's University Press.

–. 1995. *Controversy and Complexity: Canadian Immigration Policy during the 1980s.* Montreal and Kingston: McGill-Queen's University Press.

Docherty, David C. 2005. *Legislatures.* Vancouver: UBC Press.

Donnelly, Jack. 1993. *International Human Rights.* Boulder, CO: Westview Press.

Dowbiggin, Ian. 1995. "'Keeping This Young Country Sane': C.K. Clarke, Immigration Restriction, and Canadian Psychiatry, 1890-1925." *Canadian Historical Review* 76 (4): 598-627.

Dowty, Alan. 1987. *Closed Borders: The Contemporary Assault on Freedom of Movement.* New Haven, CT: Yale University Press.

Draper, Paula Jean. 1988. "Fragmented Loyalties: Canadian Jewry, the King Government and the Refugee Dilemma." In *On Guard for Thee: War, Ethnicity, and the Canadian State, 1939-1945,* edited by N. Hillmer, B. Kordan, and L. Luciuk, 151-77. Ottawa: Canadian Committee for the History of the Second World War.

Driedger, Leo. 1999. "Hutterites." In *Encyclopedia of Canada's Peoples,* edited by P.R. Magocsi, 672-81. Toronto: University of Toronto Press.

Dua, Enakshi. 1999. "Le passage de sujets à étrangers: Les immigrants indiens et la racialisation de la citoyenneté canadienne." *Sociologie et sociétés* 31 (2): 145-62.

Düvell, Franck. 2006. "Irregular Migration: A Global, Historical and Economic Perspective." In *Illegal Immigration in Europe: Beyond Control?* edited by F. Düvell, 14-39. Houndmills, Basingstoke, Hampshire: Palgrave Macmillan.

Eayrs, James. 1972. *In Defence of Canada: Peacemaking and Deterrence.* Toronto: University of Toronto Press.

Egerton, George. 2004. "Entering the Age of Human Rights: Religion, Politics, and Canadian Liberalism, 1945-50." *Canadian Historical Review* 85 (3): 451-79.

Epp, Frank H. 1974. *Mennonites in Canada, 1786-1920: The History of a Separate People.* Toronto: Macmillan of Canada.

–. 1982. *Mennonites in Canada, 1920-1940: A People's Struggle for Survival.* Toronto: Macmillan of Canada.

Fahrmeir, Andreas. 2000. *Citizens and Aliens: Foreigners and the Law in Britain and the German States, 1789-1870.* New York: Berghahn Books.

Fahrmeir, Andreas, Olivier Faron, and Peter Weil, eds. 2003. *Migration Control in the North Atlantic World: The Evolution of State Practices in Europe and the United States from the French Revolution to the Inter-War Period.* New York: Berghahn Books.

Fairclough, Ellen Louks. 1995. *Saturday's Child: Memoirs of Canada's First Female Cabinet Minister.* Toronto: University of Toronto Press.

Finkel, Alvin, and Margaret Conrad. 2006. *History of the Canadian Peoples: 1867 to the Present,* vol. 2. 4th ed. Toronto: Pearson Longman.

Francis, Diane. 2002. *Immigration: The Economic Case.* Toronto: Key Porter Books.

Franks, C.E.S. 1987. *The Parliament of Canada.* Toronto: University of Toronto Press.

Freeman, Gary P. 1995. "Modes of Immigration Politics in Liberal Democratic States." *International Migration Review* 29 (4): 881-902.

–. 1998. "The Decline of Sovereignty? Politics and Immigration Restriction in Liberal States." In *Challenge to the Nation-State: Immigration in Western Europe and the United States,* edited by C. Joppke, 86-108. Oxford: Oxford University Press.

–. 2005. "Political Science and Comparative Immigration Politics." In *International Migration Research: Constructions, Omissions and the Promises of Interdisciplinarity,* edited by M. Bommes and E. Morawska, 111-28. Aldershot, UK: Ashgate Publishing.

Friesen, Joe. 2011. "Minister Scolds Judges over Delays, Inconsistency in Refugee Cases." *Globe and Mail,* 11 February.

Gallagher, Stephen. 2001. "Canada's Dysfunctional Refugee Policy: A Realist Case for Reform." *Behind the Headlines* 58 (4).

–. 2003. *Canada's Dysfunctional Refugee Determination System: Canadian Asylum Policy from a Comparative Perspective.* Public Policy Sources No. 78. Vancouver: Fraser Institute.

Galloway, Donald, 1997. *Immigration Law.* Concord, ON: Irwin Law.

–. 2000. "The Dilemmas of Canadian Citizenship Law." In *From Migrants to Citizens: Membership in a Changing World,* edited by T.A. Aleinikoff and D. Klusmeyer, 82-118. Washington DC: Carnegie Endowment for International Peace.

García y Griego, Manuel. 1994. "Canada: Flexibility and Control in Immigration and Refugee Policy." In *Controlling Immigration: A Global Perspective*, edited by W.A. Cornelius, P.L. Martin, and J.F. Hollifield, 119-40. Stanford, CA: Stanford University Press.

Garrard, John A. 1971. *The English and Immigration, 1880-1910*. London: Oxford University Press.

Geddes, Andrew. 2003. *The Politics of Migration and Immigration in Europe*. London: Sage Publications.

Ghosh, Bimal. 1998. *Huddled Masses and Uncertain Shores: Insights into Irregular Migration*. The Hague: Martinus Nijhoff.

Gilbert, Emily. 2007. "Leaky Borders and Solid Citizens: Governing Security, Prosperity and Quality of Life in a North American Partnership." *Antipode* 39 (1): 77-98.

Girard, Philip. 2007. "Who's Afraid of Canadian Legal History?" *University of Toronto Law Journal* 57 (4): 727-53.

Glazebrook, G.P. de T. 1966. *A History of Canadian External Relations: The Formative Years to 1914*, vol. 1. Rev. ed. Toronto: McClelland and Stewart.

Godfrey, Sheldon J., and Judith C. Godfrey. 1995. *Search Out the Land: The Jews and the Growth of Equality in British Colonial America 1740-1867*. Montreal and Kingston: McGill-Queen's University Press.

Goslett, Henry M., and Barbara Jo Caruso, eds. 2010. *The 2011 Annotated Immigration and Refugee Protection Act of Canada*. Toronto: Carswell Legal Publications.

Goutor, David. 2007. *Guarding the Gates: The Canadian Labour Movement and Immigration, 1872-1934*. Vancouver: UBC Press.

Greenaway, Norma. 2010. "Send Migrants Back: Lobby Group." *Vancouver Sun*, 29 September, B2.

Grey, Julius H. 1984. *Immigration Law in Canada*. Toronto: Butterworths.

Griffiths, Naomi E.S. 1992. *The Contexts of Acadian History, 1686-1784*. Montreal and Kingston: McGill-Queen's University Press.

Guild, Elspeth. 2006. "The Europeanisation of Europe's Asylum Policy." *International Journal of Refugee Law* 18 (3-4): 630-51.

–. 2009. *Security and Migration in the 21st Century*. Cambridge: Polity.

Guiraudon, Virginie. 2001. "Denationalizing Control: Analyzing State Responses to Constraints on Migration Control." In *Controlling a New Migration World*, edited by V. Guiraudon and C. Joppke, 31-64. London: Routledge.

Guiraudon, Virginie, and Christian Joppke. 2001. "Controlling a New Migration World." In *Controlling a New Migration World*, edited by V. Guiraudon and C. Joppke, 1-27. London: Routledge.

Guiraudon, Virginie, and Gallya Lahav. 2000. "A Reappraisal of the State Sovereignty Debate: The Case of Migration Control." *Comparative Political Studies* 33 (2): 163-95.

Gyapong, Deborah. 2010. "Kenny Assails Bishops' Criticism of Anti-Human-Smuggling Bill." *BC Catholic Paper*, 2 December. http://www.bccatholic.ca/.

Hall, D.J. 1977. "Clifford Sifton: Immigration and Settlement Policy, 1896-1905." In *The Settlement of the West*, edited by H. Palmer, 60-85. Calgary: Comprint Publishing.

–. 1981. *Clifford Sifton: The Young Napoleon 1861-1900*, vol. 1. Vancouver: UBC Press.

–. 1985. *Clifford Sifton: A Lonely Eminence 1901-1929*, vol. 2. Vancouver: UBC Press.

Hamilton, Dwight. 2007. *Terror Threat: International and Homegrown Terrorists and Their Threat to Canada*. Toronto: Dundurn.

Hansen, Randall. 2002. "Globalization, Embedded Realism and Path Dependence: The Other Immigrants to Europe." *Comparative Political Studies* 35 (3): 259-83.

Hanson, Gordon H. 2007. *The Economic Logic of Illegal Immigration*. The Bernard and Irene Schwartz Series on American Competitiveness, Council on Foreign Relations, Council Special Report 26. New York: Council on Foreign Relations.

Harney, Robert F. 1993. "Italophobia: An English-speaking Malady?" In *From the Shores of Hardship: Italians in Canada [Essays by Robert F. Harney]*, edited by N.d.M. Harney, 29-74. Welland, ON: Éditions Soleil Publishing.

–. 1994. "The Padrone System and Sojourners in the Canadian North, 1885-1920." In *Immigration in Canada: Historical Perspectives*, edited by G. Tulchinsky, 249-64. Toronto: Copp Clark Longman.

Hathaway, James C. 1984. "The Evolution of Refugee Status in International Law: 1920-1950." *International and Comparative Law Quarterly* 33 (2): 348-80.

Hawkins, Freda. 1972. *Canada and Immigration: Public Policy and Public Concern.* Montreal and Kingston: McGill-Queen's University Press.

Higham, John. 1988. *Strangers in the Land: Patterns of American Nativism, 1860-1925.* 2nd ed. New Brunswick, NJ: Rutgers University Press.

Hindess, Barry. 2004. "Liberalism: What's in a Name?" In *Global Governmentality: Governing International Spaces,* edited by W. Larner and W. Walters, 23-39. New York: Routledge.

Hobbins, A.J. 1989. "René Cassin and the Daughter of Time: The First Draft of the Universal Declaration of Human Rights." *Fontanus* 2: 7-26.

–. 1998. "Eleanor Roosevelt, John Humphrey, and Canadian Opposition to the Universal Declaration of Human Rights: Looking Back on the 50th Anniversary of UNDHR." *International Journal* 53 (2): 325-42.

Hobsbawm, Eric J. 1992. *Nations and Nationalism since 1780: Programme, Myth, Reality.* Cambridge: Cambridge University Press.

Hodgetts, J.E. 1955. *Pioneer Public Service: An Administrative History of the United Canadas, 1841-1867.* Toronto: University of Toronto Press.

Hollifield, James F. 1992. *Immigrants, Markets, and States: The Political Economy of Postwar Europe.* Cambridge, MA: Harvard University Press.

–. 1999. "Ideas, Institutions, and Civil Society: On the Limits of Immigration Control in Liberal Democracies." *IMIS-Beitrage* 100: 57-90.

–. 2000. "The Politics of International Migration: How Can We 'Bring the State Back In'?" In *Migration Theory: Talking across Disciplines,* edited by C.B. Brettell and J.F. Hollifield, 137-85. New York: Routledge.

–. 2004a. "The Emerging Migration State." *International Migration Review* 38 (3): 885-912.

–. 2004b. "Migration and International Relations: The Liberal Paradox." In *Migration between States and Markets,* edited by H. Entzinger, M. Martiniello, and C. Wihtol de Wenden, 3-18. Aldershot, UK: Ashgate Publishing.

Hollifield, James F., Valerie F. Hunt, and Daniel J. Tichenor. 2008. "Immigrants, Markets, and Rights: The United States as an Emerging Migration State." *Washington University Journal of Law and Policy* 27: 6-44.

Holmes, Colin. 1988. *John Bull's Island: Immigration and British Society, 1871-1971.* Houndmills, Basingstoke, Hampshire: Macmillan Education.

Holmes, John W. 1979. *The Shaping of Peace: Canada and the Search for World Order, 1943-57.* Toronto: University of Toronto Press.

Huysmans, Jef. 2000. "The European Union and the Securitization of Migration." *Journal of Common Market Studies* 38 (5): 751-77.

Iacovetta, Franca. 1998. "Preface." In *A Nation of Immigrants: Women, Workers, and Communities in Canadian History, 1840s-1960s,* edited by F. Iacovetta with P. Draper and R. Ventresca, ix-xiv. Toronto: University of Toronto Press.

Ibrahim, Maggie. 2005. "The Securitization of Migration: A Racial Discourse." *International Migration* 43 (5): 163-86.

Iino, Masako. 1983-84. "Japan's Reaction to the Vancouver Riot of 1907." *BC Studies* 60: 28-47.

Indra, Doreen M. 1979. "South Asian Stereotypes in the Vancouver Press." *Ethnic and Racial Studies* 2 (2): 166-89.

IOM (International Organization for Migration). 2005. *World Migration Report 2005: Costs and Benefits of International Migration.* Geneva: IOM.

–. 2008. *World Migration Report 2008: Managing Labour Mobility in the Evolving Global Economy.* Geneva: IOM.

–. 2010. *World Migration Report 2010: The Future of Migration: Building Capacities for Change.* Geneva: IOM.

–. 2011. "International Cooperation." http://www.iom.int/jahia/Jahia/pid/268.

Irvine, J.A. Sandy. 2011. "Canadian Refugee Policy: Understanding the Role of International Bureaucratic Networks in Domestic Paradigm Change." In *Policy Paradigms, Transnationalism, and Domestic Politics,* edited by G. Skogstad, 171-201. Toronto: University of Toronto Press.

Jacobson, David. 1996. *Rights across Borders: Immigration and the Decline of Citizenship.* Baltimore: Johns Hopkins University Press.

Jacobson, David, and Galya Benarieh Ruffer. 2003. "Courts across Borders: The Implications of Judicial Agency for Human Rights and Democracy." *Human Rights Quarterly* 25 (1): 74-92.

Jakubowski, Lisa Marie. 1997. *Immigration and the Legalization of Racism.* Halifax: Fernwood Publishing.

Janzen, William. 1990. *Limits on Liberty: The Experience of Mennonite, Hutterite and Doukhobor Communities in Canada.* Toronto: University of Toronto Press.

–. 1995. "The Doukhobor Challenge to Canadian Liberties." In *Spirit Wrestlers: Centennial Papers in Honour of Canada's Doukhobor Heritage,* edited by K.J. Tarasoff and R.B. Klymasz, 167-82. Ottawa: Canadian Museum of Civilization.

Janzen, William, and Ian A. Hunter. 1973. "The Interpretation of Section 15 of the Immigration Appeal Board Act." *Alberta Law Review* 11: 260-78.

Jenson, Jane. 1989. "Paradigms and Political Discourse: Protective Legislation in France and the United States before 1914." *Canadian Journal of Political Science* 22 (2): 235-58.

Johnson, Stanley C. 1966. *A History of Emigration: From the United Kingdom to North America, 1763-1912.* London: Frank Cass (reprint of 1913 edition).

Johnston, Hugh. 1979. *The Voyage of the Komagata Maru: The Sikh Challenge to Canada's Colour Bar.* Delhi: Oxford University Press.

–. 1988. "The Surveillance of Indian Nationalists in North America, 1908-1918." *BC Studies* 78: 3-27.

Joppke, Christian. 1997. "Asylum and State Sovereignty: A Comparison of the United States, Germany, and Britain." *Comparative Political Studies* 30 (3): 259-98.

–. 1998a. "Immigration Challenges the Nation-State." In *Challenge to the Nation-State: Immigration in Western Europe and the United States,* edited by C. Joppke, 5-46. Oxford: Oxford University Press.

–. 1998b. "Why Liberal States Accept Unwanted Immigration." *World Politics* 50 (2): 266-93.

–. 1999. *Immigration and the Nation-State: The United States, Germany, and Great Britain.* Oxford: Oxford University Press.

–. 2001. "The Legal-Domestic Sources of Immigrant Rights: The United States, Germany, and the European Union." *Comparative Political Studies* 34 (4): 339-66.

–. 2005a. "Are 'Nondiscriminatory' Immigration Policies Reversible? Evidence from the United States and Australia." *Comparative Political Studies* 38 (1): 3-25.

–. 2005b. "Exclusion in the Liberal State: The Case of Immigration and Citizenship Policy." *European Journal of Social Theory* 8 (1): 43-61.

–. 2010. *Citizenship and Immigration.* Cambridge: Polity Press.

Joppke, Christian, and Elia Marzal. 2004. "Courts, the New Constitutionalism and Immigrant Rights: The Case of the French *Conseil Constitutionnel.*" *European Journal of Political Research* 43 (6): 823-44.

Josh, Sohan Singh. 1975. *Tragedy of the Komagata Maru.* New Delhi: People's Publishing House.

Jupp, James. 1998. *Immigration.* 2nd ed. Melbourne: Oxford University Press.

Kage, Joseph. 1962. *With Faith and Thanksgiving: The Story of Two Hundred Years of Jewish Immigration and Immigrant Aid Effort in Canada. 1760-1960.* Montreal: Eagle Publishing.

Kaprielian-Churchill, Isabel. 1990. "Armenian Refugees and Their Entry into Canada, 1919-30." *Canadian Historical Association* 71 (1): 80-108.

–. 1994. "Rejecting 'Misfits:' Canada and the Nansen Passport." *International Migration Review* 28 (2): 281-306.

–. 2005. *Like Our Mountains: A History of Armenians in Canada.* Montreal and Kingston: McGill-Queen's University Press.

Kelley, Ninette. 2007. "International Refugee Protection Challenges and Opportunities." *International Journal of Refugee Law* 19 (3): 401-39.

Kelley, Ninette, and Michael Trebilcock. 1998. *The Making of the Mosaic: A History of Canadian Immigration Policy.* Toronto: University of Toronto Press.

Kenney, Jason. 2010. "On the Record: Jason Kenney." *Globe and Mail*, 1 November.

Kent, Tom. 1988. *A Public Purpose: An Experience of Liberal Opposition and Canadian Government*. Montreal and Kingston: McGill-Queen's University Press.

Kernerman, Gerald. 2008. "Refugee Interdiction before Heaven's Gate." *Government and Opposition* 43 (2): 230-48.

Keyserlingk, R.H., ed. 1993. *Breaking Ground: The 1956 Hungarian Refugee Movement to Canada*. Toronto: York Lanes Press.

King, Desmond. 1999. *In the Name of Liberalism: Illiberal Social Policy in the United States and Britain*. Oxford: Oxford University Press.

Klein, Ruth, and Frank Dimant, eds. 2001. *From Immigration to Integration: The Canadian Jewish Experience – A Millennium Edition*. Toronto: Institute for International Affairs, B'nai Brith Canada.

Kneebone, Susan, and Sharon Pickering. 2007. "Australia, Indonesia and the Pacific Plan." In *New Regionalism and Asylum Seekers: Challenges Ahead*, edited by S. Kneebone and F. Rawlings-Sanaei, 167-87. New York: Berghahn Books.

Knowles, Valerie. 1997. *Strangers at Our Gates: Canadian Immigration and Immigration Policy, 1540-1997*. Rev. ed. Toronto: Dundurn Press.

Kraut, Alan M. 1982. *The Huddled Masses: The Immigrant in America Society, 1880-1921*. Arlington Heights, IL: Harlan Davidson.

Kymlicka, Will. 2004. "Marketing Canadian Pluralism in the International Arena." *International Journal* 59 (4): 829-52.

Lahav, Gallya, and Virginie Guiraudon. 2006. "Actors and Venues in Immigration Control: Closing the Gap between Political Demands and Policy Outcomes." *West European Politics* 29 (2): 201-23.

Lambertson, Ross. 2005. *Repression and Resistance: Canadian Human Rights Activists, 1930-1960*. Toronto: University of Toronto Press.

Lavertu, Yves. 1995. *The Bernonville Affair: A French War Criminal in Québec after World War II*, translated by George Tombs. Montreal: Robert Davies Publishing.

Leddy, Mary Jo. 2010. *Our Friendly Local Terrorist*. Toronto: Between the Lines Press.

Li, Peter S. 2003a. "Deconstructing Canada's Discourse of Immigrant Integration." *Journal of International Migration and Integration* 4 (3): 315-33.

–. 2003b. *Destination Canada: Immigration Debates and Issues*. Don Mills, ON: Oxford University Press.

Lipset, Seymour Martin. 1968. "Revolution and Counterrevolution: The United States and Canada." In *Revolution and Counterrevolution: Change and Persistence in Social Structures*, edited by S.M. Lipset, 31-63. New York: Basic Books.

Lyon, David. 2006. "Airport Screening, Surveillance, and Social Sorting: Canadian Responses to 9/11 in Context." *Canadian Journal of Criminology and Criminal Justice* 48 (3): 397-411.

Macdonagh, Oliver. 1961. *A Pattern of Government Growth, 1800-60: The Passenger Acts and Their Enforcement*. London: MacGibbon and Kee.

Macdonald, Norman. 1966. *Canada: Immigration and Colonization 1841-1903*. Toronto: Macmillan of Canada.

Mackay, Robert A. 1963. *The Unreformed Senate of Canada*. Rev. ed. Toronto: McClelland and Stewart.

Mackenzie, Hector. 2004. "'Writing Marginal Notes on the Pages of History'? Escott Reid and the Founding of the United Nations, 1945-46." In *Escott Reid: Diplomat and Scholar*, edited by G. Donaghy and S. Roussel, 23-43. Montreal and Kingston: McGill-Queen's University Press.

–. 2007. "Canada's Nationalist Internationalism: From the League of Nations to the United Nations." In *Canadas of the Mind: The Making and Unmaking of Canadian Nationalisms in the Twentieth Century*, edited by N. Hillmer and A. Chapnick, 89-109. Montreal and Kingston: McGill-Queen's University Press.

Macklin, Audrey. 2005. "Disappearing Refugees: Reflections on the Canada-US Safe Third Country Agreement." *Columbia Human Rights Law Review* 36: 365-426.

MacLennan, Christopher. 2003. *Toward the Charter: Canadians and the Demand for a National Bill of Rights, 1929-1960*. Montreal and Kingston: McGill-Queen's University Press.

Magocsi, Paul R., ed. 1999. *Encyclopedia of Canada's Peoples.* Toronto: University of Toronto Press.

Malarek, Victor. 1987. *Haven's Gate: Canada's Immigration Fiasco.* Toronto: Macmillan of Canada.

Manion, John L. 1993. "The Hungarian Refugee Movement: Implementing the Policy." In *Breaking Ground: The 1956 Hungarian Refugee Movement to Canada,* edited by R.H. Keyserlingk, 53-56. Toronto: York Lanes Press.

Mar, Lisa Rose. 2010. *Brokering Belonging: Chinese in Canada's Exclusion Era, 1885-1945.* Oxford: Oxford University Press.

Margolian, Howard. 2000. *Unauthorized Entry: The Truth about Nazi War Criminals in Canada, 1946-1956.* Toronto: University of Toronto Press.

Marrus, Michael R. 1985. *The Unwanted: European Refugees in the Twentieth Century.* New York: Oxford University Press.

Martin, Don. 2010. "Tories Milking Tamil Ship with Over-the-Top Dramatics." *Calgary Herald,* 14 August, A5.

Martynowych, Orest T. 1991. *Ukrainians in Canada: The Formative Period, 1891-1924.* Edmonton: Canadian Institute of Ukrainian Studies Press.

Massey, Douglas S. 1999. "International Migration at the Dawn of the Twenty-First Century: The Role of the State." *Population and Development Review* 25 (2): 303-22.

Matas, David, with Susan Charendoff. 1987. *Justice Delayed: Nazi War Criminals in Canada.* Toronto: Summerhill Press.

Matas, David, with Ilana Simon. 1989. *Closing the Doors: The Failure of Refugee Protection.* Toronto: Summerhill Press.

McKay, Ian. 2000. "The Liberal Order Framework: A Prospectus for a Reconnaissance of Canadian History." *Canadian Historical Review* 81 (4): 617-47.

McLaren, Angus. 1990. *Our Own Master Race: Eugenics in Canada, 1885-1945.* Toronto: McClelland and Stewart.

Melnycky, Peter. 1983. "The Internment of Ukrainians in Canada." In *Loyalties in Conflict: Ukrainians in Canada during the Great War,* edited by F. Swyripa and J.H. Thompson, 1-24. Edmonton: Canadian Institute of Ukrainian Studies, University of Alberta.

Melnyk, Olenka. 1989. *No Bankers in Heaven: Remembering the CCF.* Toronto: McGraw-Hill Ryerson.

Miller, Carman. 1993. *Painting the Map Red: Canada and the South African War, 1899-1902.* Montreal and Kingston: McGill-Queen's University Press.

Minenko, Mark. 1991. "Without Just Cause: Canada's First National Internment Operations." In *Canada's Ukrainians: Negotiating an Identity,* edited by L. Luciuk and S. Hryniuk. Toronto: University of Toronto Press.

Minhas, Manmohan Singh (Moni). 1994. *The Sikh Canadians.* Edmonton: Reidmore Books.

Moch, Leslie Page. 1992. *Moving Europeans: Migration in Western Europe since 1650.* Bloomington and Indianapolis: Indiana University Press.

Moens, Alexander, and Martin Collacott, eds. 2008. *Immigration Policy and the Terrorist Threat in Canada and the United States.* Vancouver: Fraser Institute.

Moore, Christopher. 1984. *The Loyalists: Revolution, Exile, Settlement.* Toronto: Macmillan of Canada.

–. 1997. *1867: How the Fathers Made a Deal.* Toronto: McClelland and Stewart.

Morton, Desmond. 1974. "Sir William Otter and Internment Operations in Canada during the First World War." *Canadian Historical Review* 55 (1): 32-58.

Morton, James. 1974. *In the Sea of Sterile Mountains: The Chinese in British Columbia.* Vancouver: J.J. Douglas.

Mountz, Alison. 2004. "Embodying the Nation-State: Canada's Response to Human Smuggling." *Political Geography* 23 (3): 323-45.

–. 2010. *Seeking Asylum: Human Smuggling and Bureaucracy and the Border.* Minneapolis: University of Minnesota Press.

Nash, Alan E. 1994. "The Development of Canadian Refugee Policy: The Empirical Data." In *Canadian Immigration and Refugee Policy and Practice,* edited by H. Adelman, 111-36. Berlin: Edition Parabolis.

National Anti-Racism Council of Canada. 2002. *Racial Discrimination in Canada: The Status of Compliance by the Canadian Government with the International Convention on the Elimination of All Forms of Racial Discrimination.* Toronto: National Anti-Racism Council of Canada.

Ng, Wing Chung. 1999. *The Chinese in Vancouver, 1945-80: The Pursuit of Identity and Power.* Vancouver: UBC Press.

Nolan, Cathal J. 1991. "Reluctant Liberal: Canada, Human Rights and the United Nations, 1944-65." *Diplomacy and Statecraft* 2 (3): 281-305.

Norrie, Kenneth, and Douglas Owram. 1996. *A History of the Canadian Economy.* 2nd ed. Toronto: Harcourt Brace Canada.

Nossal, Kim Richard. 1997. *The Politics of Canadian Foreign Policy.* 3rd ed. Scarborough, ON: Prentice Hall Canada.

OECD (Organisation for Economic Co-operation and Development). 2010. *International Migration Outlook.* Paris: OECD.

Ogelsby, J.C.M. 1976. *Gringos from the Far North: Essays in the History of Canadian–Latin American Relations, 1886-1968.* Toronto: Macmillan of Canada.

O'Neil, Peter. 2010. "Anti-Immigration Group Finds Powerful Ally." *Ottawa Citizen,* 27 September, A3.

Orsini, Michael, and Miriam Smith. 2007. "Critical Policy Studies." In *Critical Policy Studies,* edited by M. Orsini and M. Smith, 1-16. Vancouver: UBC Press.

Pal, Leslie A. 2006. *Beyond Policy Analysis: Public Issue Management in Turbulent Times.* 3rd ed. Toronto: Thomson-Nelson.

Panayi, Panikos. 1994. *Immigration, Ethnicity and Racism in Britain, 1815-1945.* Manchester: Manchester University Press.

Parias, Carmela, and Ruth A. Frager. 2001. "'This Is Our Country, These Are Our Rights': Minorities and the Origins of Ontario's Human Rights Campaigns." *Canadian Historical Review* 82 (1): 1-35.

Parry, Jonathan. 1993. *The Rise and Fall of Liberal Government in Victorian Britain.* New Haven, CT: Yale University Press.

Petryshyn, Jaroslav. 1991. "Sifton's Immigration Policy." In *Canada's Ukrainians: Negotiating an Identity,* edited by L. Luciuk and S. Hryniuk, 17-29. Toronto: University of Toronto Press.

Phillips, Susan D. 1996. "Discourse, Identity, and Voice: Feminist Contributions to Policy Studies." In *Policy Studies in Canada: The State of the Art,* edited by L. Dobuzinskis, M. Howlett, and D. Laycock, 242-65. Toronto: University of Toronto Press.

Pickersgill, J.W. 1994. *Seeing Canada Whole: A Memoir.* Toronto: Fitzhenry and Whiteside.

Pither, Kathy. 2008. *Dark Days: The Story of Four Canadians Tortured in the Name of Fighting Terror.* Toronto: Viking Canada.

Porter, Bernard. 1984. "The British Government and Political Refugees, c. 1880-1914." In *From the Other Shore: Russian Political Emigrants in Britain,* edited by J. Slatter, 23-45. London: Frank Cass and Company.

Porter, John. 1979. *The Refugee Question in Mid-Victorian Politics.* Cambridge: Cambridge University Press.

Portes, Alejandro. 1997. "Immigration Theory for a New Century: Some Problems and Opportunities." *International Migration Review* 31 (4): 799-825.

Pratt, Anna. 2005. *Securing Borders: Detention and Deportation in Canada.* Vancouver: UBC Press.

Pratt, Anna, and Sara K. Thompson. 2008. "Chivalry, 'Race' and Discretion at the Canadian Border." *British Journal of Criminology* 48 (5): 620-40.

Pratt, Cranford. 1989. "Humane Internationalism: Its Significance and Its Variants." In *Internationalism under Strain: The North-South Policies of Canada, the Netherlands, Norway, and Sweden,* edited by C. Pratt, 3-23. Toronto: University of Toronto Press.

Prebisch, Kerry, and Leigh Binford. 2007. "Interrogating Racialized Global Labour Supply: An Exploration of the Racial/National Replacement of Foreign Agricultural Workers in Canada." *Canadian Review of Sociology and Anthropology* 44 (1): 5-36.

Price, Charles A. 1974. *The Great White Walls Are Built: Restrictive Immigration to North America and Australasia, 1836-1888.* Canberra: Australian National University Press.

Pringsheim, Klaus H. 1983. *Neighbors across the Pacific: The Development of Economic and Political Relations between Canada and Japan.* Westport, CT: Greenwood Press.

Ramirez, Bruno. 1989. *The Italians in Canada*. Canada's Ethnic Groups Series 14. Ottawa: Canadian Historical Association.

Razack, Sherene H. 2008. *Casting Out: The Eviction of Muslims from Western Law and Politics*. Toronto: University of Toronto Press.

–. 2010. "Abandonment and the Dance of Race and Bureaucracy in Spaces of Exception." In *States of Race: Critical Race Feminism for the 21st Century*, edited by S. Razack, M. Smith, and S. Thobani, 87-107. Toronto: Between the Lines Press.

Reid, Escott. 1989. *Radical Mandarin: The Memoirs of Escott Reid*. Toronto: University of Toronto Press.

Reinemeyer, Gretchen, and Jeanne Batalova. 2007. "Spotlight on Legal Immigration to the United States." Migration Policy Institute. http://www.migrationinformation.org/usfocus/display.cfm?ID=651.

Reitz, Jeffrey G. 2004. "Canada: Immigration and Nation-Building in Transition to a Knowledge Economy." In *Controlling Immigration: A Global Perspective*, 2nd ed., edited by W.A. Cornelius, T. Tsuda, P.L. Martin, and J.F. Hollifield, 97-133. Stanford, CA: Stanford University Press.

–. 2007. "Immigrant Employment and Success in Canada" (Parts I and II). *Journal of International Migration and Integration* 8 (1): 11-62.

Richmond, Anthony H. 1994. *Global Apartheid: Refugees, Racism, and the New World Order*. Oxford: Oxford University Press.

Roach, Kent. 2003. *September 11: Consequences for Canada*. Montreal and Kingston: McGill-Queen's University Press.

Roberts, Barbara. 1986. "Doctors and Deports: The Role of the Medical Profession in Canadian Deportation, 1900-20." *Canadian Ethnic Studies* 18 (3): 17-36.

–. 1988. *Whence They Came: Deportation from Canada 1900-1935*. Ottawa: University of Ottawa Press.

Roche, T.W.E. 1969. *The Key in the Lock: A History of Immigration Control in England from 1066 to the Present Day*. London: John Murray.

Rollings-Magnusson, Sandra, ed. 2008. *Anti-Terrorism: Security and Insecurity after 9/11*. Black Point, NS: Fernwood Publishing.

Romney, Paul M. 1999. *Getting It Wrong: How Canadians Forgot Their Past and Imperilled Confederation*. Toronto: University of Toronto Press.

Roy, Patricia E. 1978. "The Soldiers Canada Didn't Want: Her Chinese and Japanese Citizens." *Canadian Historical Review* 59 (3): 341-58.

–. 1989. *A White Man's Province: British Columbia Politicians and Chinese and Japanese Immigrants, 1858-1914*. Vancouver: UBC Press.

–. 2003. *The Oriental Question: Consolidating a White Man's Province, 1914-41*. Vancouver: UBC Press.

–. 2008. *The Triumph of Citizenship: The Japanese and Chinese in Canada, 1941-67*. Vancouver: UBC Press.

Roy, Patricia E., J.L. Granatstein, Masako Iino, and Hiroko Takamura. 1990. *Mutual Hostages: Canadians and Japanese during the Second World War*. Toronto: University of Toronto Press.

Ruggiero, Guido de. 1981. *The History of European Liberalism*, translated by R.G. Collingwood. Gloucester, MA: Peter Smith.

Ryan, Phil. 2010. *Multicultiphobia*. Toronto: University of Toronto Press.

Ryder, Bruce. 1991. "Racism and the Constitution: The Constitutional Fate of British Columbia Anti-Asian Immigration Legislation, 1884-1909." *Osgoode Hall Law Journal* 29 (3): 619-76.

Sampat-Mehta, R. 1972. *International Barriers*. Ottawa: Harpell's Press.

Sarty, Roger. 1984. "'There Will Be Trouble in the North Pacific': The Defence of British Columbia in the Early Twentieth Century." *BC Studies* 61: 3-29.

Sassen, Saskia. 1996. *Losing Control? Sovereignty in an Age of Globalization*. New York: Columbia University Press.

–. 1998. "The *de facto* Transnationalization of Immigration Policy." In *Challenge to the Nation-State: Immigration in Western Europe and the United States*, edited by C. Joppke, 49-85. Oxford: Oxford University Press.

–. 1999. *Guests and Aliens*. New York: New Press.

Saufert, Stacey A. 2007. "Closing the Door to Refugees: The Denial of Due Process for Refugee Claimants in Canada." *Saskatchewan Law Review* 70: 27-51.

Schofield, Josie, and Jonathan Fershau. 2007. "Committees inside Canadian Legislatures." In *Policy Analysis in Canada: The State of the Art*, edited by L. Dobuzinskis, M. Howlett, and D. Laycock, 351-74. Toronto: University of Toronto Press.

Schultz, John. 1988. "White Man's Country: Canada and the West Indian Immigrant 1900-1965." In *Canada and the Commonwealth Caribbean*, edited by B.D. Tennyson, 257-77. Lanham, MD: University Press of America.

Schuster, Liza. 2002. "Asylum and the Lessons of History." *Race and Class* 44 (2): 40-56.

Scott, W.D. 1914. "Immigration and Population." In *Canada and Its Provinces: A History of the Canadian People and Their Institutions by One Hundred Associates*, vol. 7, edited by A. Shortt and A.G. Doughty, 517-90. Toronto: Glasgow, Brook and Company.

Sharma, Nandita. 2006a. *Home Economics: Nationalism and the Making of 'Migrant Workers' in Canada*. Toronto: University of Toronto Press.

–. 2006b. "White Nationalism, Illegality and Imperialism: Border Controls as Ideology." In *(En)Gendering the War on Terror: War Stories and Camouflaged Politics*, edited by K. Hunt and K. Rygiel, 121-44. Aldershot, UK: Ashgate Publishing.

Showler, Peter. 2010. "Tale of Two Refugees Shows Disturbing Inequality." *Edmonton Journal*, 28 October, A17.

Sifton, Clifford. 1922. "The Immigrants Canada Wants." *Maclean's*, 1 April, 16, 32-34.

Simeon, Richard. 1976. "Studying Public Policy." *Canadian Journal of Political Science* 9 (4): 548-80.

Singh, Narindar. 1994. *Canadian Sikhs: History, Religion, and Culture of Sikhs in North America*. Ottawa: Canadian Sikhs' Studies Institute.

Singh, Sunder. 1913. "The Sikhs in Canada." In *Empire Club of Canada*, edited by D.J. Goggin, 112-16. Toronto: Warwick Bro's and Rutter.

Skilling, H. Gordon. 1945. *Canadian Representation Abroad: From Agency to Embassy*. Toronto: Ryerson Press.

Skogstad, Grace. 2003. "Who Governs? Who Should Govern? Political Authority and Legitimacy in Canada in the Twenty-First Century." *Canadian Journal of Political Science* 36 (5): 955-73.

Skran, Claudena M. 1995. *Refugees in Inter-War Europe: The Emergence of a Regime*. Oxford: Clarendon Press.

Smith, Charles. 2007. *Conflict, Crisis, and Accountability: Racial Profiling and Law Enforcement in Canada*. Toronto: Canadian Centre for Policy Alternatives.

Smith, David E. 2007. *The People's House of Commons: Theories of Democracy in Contention*. Toronto: University of Toronto Press.

Smith, Peter J. 1987. "The Ideological Origins of Canadian Confederation." *Canadian Journal of Political Science* 20 (1): 3-29.

Soysal, Yasemin N. 1994. *Limits of Citizenship: Migrants and Postnational Membership in Europe*. Chicago: University of Chicago Press.

Spencer, Sarah, ed. 2003. *The Politics of Migration: Managing Opportunity, Conflict and Change*. Oxford: Blackwell Publishing.

Squire, Vicki. 2009. *The Exclusionary Politics of Asylum*. Houndmills, Basingstoke, Hampshire: Palgrave Macmillan.

Stacey, C.P. 1984. *Canada and the Age of Conflict: A History of Canadian External Policies, 1867-1921*, vol. 1. Toronto: University of Toronto Press.

Stasiulis, Daiva K., and Abigail B. Bakan. 2005. *Negotiating Citizenship: Migrant Women in Canada and the Global System*. Toronto: University of Toronto Press.

Stasiulis, Daiva, and Radha Jhappan. 1995. "The Fractious Politics of a Settler Society: Canada." In *Unsettling Settler Societies: Articulations of Gender, Race, Ethnicity and Class*, edited by D. Stasiulis and N. Yuval-Davis, 95-131. London: Sage Publications.

Stein, Janice Gross, David Robertson Cameron, John Ibbitson, Will Kymlicka, John Meisel, Haroon Siddiqui, and Michael Valpy. 2007. *Uneasy Partners: Multiculturalism and Rights in Canada*. Waterloo, ON: Wilfrid Laurier University Press.

Stevenson, Garth. 1993. *Ex Uno Plures: Federal-Provincial Relations in Canada, 1867-1896.* Montreal and Kingston: McGill-Queen's University Press.

Stoffman, Daniel. 2002. *Who Gets In: What's Wrong with Canada's Immigration Program – and How to Fix It.* Toronto: Macfarlane Walter and Ross.

Sugimoto, Howard H. 1978. *Japanese Immigration, the Vancouver Riots, and Canadian Diplomacy.* New York: Arno Press.

Swyripa, Frances. 1983. "The Ukrainian Image: Loyal Citizen or Disloyal Alien." In *Loyalties in Conflict: Ukrainians in Canada during the Great War,* edited by F. Swyripa and J.H. Thompson, 47-68. Edmonton: Canadian Institute of Ukrainian Studies, University of Alberta.

Taggart, Michael. 2005. "Prolegomenon to an Intellectual History of Administrative Law in the Twentieth Century: The Case of John Willis and Canadian Administrative Law." *Osgoode Hall Law Journal* 43 (3): 223-67.

Tamir, Yael. 1993. *Liberal Nationalism.* Princeton, NJ: Princeton University Press.

Tator, Carol, and Frances Henry. 2006. *Racial Profiling in Canada: Challenging the Myth of "a Few Bad Apples."* Toronto: University of Toronto Press.

Thobani, Sunera. 2000. "Closing Ranks: Racism and Sexism in Canada's Immigration Policy." *Race and Class* 42 (1): 35-55.

–. 2007. *Exalted Subjects: Studies in the Making of Race and Nation in Canada.* Toronto: University of Toronto Press.

Thomson, Dale C. 1960. *Alexander Mackenzie: Clear Grit.* Toronto: Macmillan Company of Canada.

Tienhaara, Nancy. 1974. *Canadian Views on Immigration and Population: An Analysis of Post-War Gallup Polls.* Ottawa: Department of Manpower and Immigration.

Treviranus, Barbara, and Michael Casasola. 2003. "Canada's Private Sponsorship of Refugees Program: A Practitioner's Perspective of Its Past and Future." *Journal of International Migration and Integration* 4 (2): 177-202.

Troper, Harold M. 1972. *Only Farmers Need Apply: Official Canadian Government Encouragement of Immigration from the United States, 1896-1911.* Toronto: Griffin House.

Trotter, Reginald George. 1971. *Canadian Federation: Its Origins and Achievement, a Study in Nation Building.* New York: Russell and Russell (reprint of the 1924 edition).

Tulchinsky, Gerald. 1992. *Taking Root: The Origins of the Canadian Jewish Community.* Toronto: Lester Publishing.

–. 1998. *Branching Out: The Transformation of the Canadian Jewish Community.* Toronto: Stoddart.

UN DESA (United Nations Department of Economic and Social Affairs). 2009. *Trends in Total Migrant Stock: The 2008 Revision* (POP/DB/MIG/Stock/Rev.2008). New York: United Nations.

–. 2010. *Population Facts* (No. 2010/6). New York: United Nations.

UNHCR (United Nations High Commissioner for Refugees). 2000. *The State of the World's Refugees: Fifty Years of Humanitarian Action.* Oxford: Oxford University Press.

–. 2001. "Comments on Bill C-11, 'An Act respecting immigration to Canada and the granting of refugee protection to persons who are displaced, persecuted or in danger'" (Submission to the House of Commons Standing Committee on Citizenship and Immigration). Ottawa, 5 March.

–. 2006. *The State of the World's Refugees 2006: Human Displacement in the New Millennium.* Oxford: Oxford University Press.

–. 2011. *Asylum Levels and Trends in Industrialized Countries 2010.* Geneva: UNHCR.

–. 2012a. "Statement Relating to Bill C-31, *Protecting Canada's Immigration System Act*" (Statement to the Senate Standing Committee on Social Affairs, Science and Technology). Ottawa, 18 June.

–. 2012b. "UNHCR Submission on Bill C-31, *Protecting Canada's Immigration System Act*" (Submission to the House of Commons Standing Committee on Citizenship and Immigration). Ottawa, May.

Verma, Archana B. 2002. *The Making of Little Punjab in Canada: Patterns of Immigration.* New Delhi: Sage Publications.

Vincent, R.J. 1986. *Human Rights and International Relations.* Cambridge: Cambridge University Press.

Vipond, Robert. 2008. "Introduction: The Comparative Turn in Canadian Political Science." In *The Comparative Turn in Canadian Political Science,* edited by L.A. White, R. Simeon, R. Vipond, and J. Wallner, 3-16. Vancouver: UBC Press.

Walker, James W. St. G. 1997. *"Race," Rights and the Law in the Supreme Court of Canada: Historical Case Studies.* Waterloo, ON: Wilfrid Laurier University Press.

–. 2002. "The 'Jewish Phase' in the Movement for Racial Equality in Canada." *Canadian Ethnic Studies* 34 (1): 1-29.

Ward, W. Peter. 1990. *White Canada Forever: Popular Attitudes and Public Policy toward Orientals in British Columbia.* 2nd ed. Montreal and Kingston: McGill-Queen's University Press.

Weiner, Myron. 1995. *The Global Migration Crisis: Challenge to States and to Human Rights.* New York: Longman.

Whitaker, Reg. 1987. *Double Standard: The Secret History of Canadian Immigration.* Toronto: Lester and Orpen Dennys.

Whitaker, Reg, and Gary Marcuse. 1994. *Cold War Canada: The Making of a National Insecurity State, 1945-1957.* Toronto: University of Toronto Press.

Wickberg, Edgar. 1980. "Chinese Associations in Canada, 1923-47." In *Visible Minorities and Multiculturalism: Asians in Canada,* edited by K.V. Ujimoto and G. Hirabayashi, 23-31. Toronto: Butterworths.

Widdis, Randy William. 1998. *With Scarcely a Ripple: Anglo-American Migration into the United States and Western Canada, 1880-1920.* Montreal and Kingston: McGill-Queen's University Press.

Wilkinson, Lori. 2008. "Are Human Rights Jeopardized in Twenty-First-Century Canada? An Examination of Immigration Policies Post-9/11." In *Anti-Terrorism: Security and Insecurity after 9/11,* edited by S. Rollings-Magnusson, 102-24. Black Point, NS: Fernwood Publishing.

Winks, Robin W. 1997. *The Blacks in Canada: A History.* 2nd ed. Montreal and Kingston: McGill-Queen's University Press.

Woodcock, George, and Ivan Avakumovic. 1968. *The Doukhobors.* London: Faber and Faber.

Woodsworth, John. 1999. "Russian Roots and Canadian Wings: An Introduction." In *Russian Roots and Canadian Wings: Russian Archival Documents on the Doukhobor Emigration to Canada,* edited by J. Woodsworth, 1-14. Toronto: Penumbra Press.

Wydrzynski, Christopher J. 1979. "Refugees and the Immigration Act." *McGill Law Journal* 25 (2): 154-92.

Zolberg, Aristide R. 1981. "International Migrations in Political Perspective." In *Global Trends in Migration: Theory and Research on International Population Movements,* edited by M.M. Kritz, C.B. Keely, and S.M. Tomasi, 3-27. New York: Center for Migration Studies.

–. 1997. "Global Movements, Global Walls: Responses to the First Immigration Crisis, 1885-1925." In *Global History and Migrations,* edited by W. Gungwu, 279-307. Boulder, CO: Westview Press.

–. 1999. "Matters of State: Theorizing Immigration Policy." In *The Handbook of International Migration: The American Experience,* edited by C. Hirschman, P. Kasinitz, and J. DeWind, 71-93. New York: Russell Sage Foundation.

Zolberg, Aristide R., Astri Suhrke, and Sergio Aguayo. 1989. *Escape from Violence: Conflict and the Refugee Crisis in the Developing World.* New York: Oxford University Press.

Index

Abbott, John J.C., 55
agriculturalists, recruitment of, 31, 37-38, 44, 56, 74, 98, 141; preferences in, 34, 60-61, 62, 96, 102, 110, 111; by railways, 101; under Sifton, 59-61, 62, 64
Alexander II, Czar, 43
Alexander, Lincoln, 232n3
Aliens Act (UK, 1905), 94
Aliens Restriction Acts (UK, 1914 and 1919), 94
Allan, George W., 54
Almon, William, 53, 210n56, 215nn53-54
Amnesty International, 1, 197, 201
Anglo-Japanese Alliance, 84
Anglo-Japanese Treaty of Commerce and Navigation, 80, 83-84
Armenian immigrants/refugees: as "Asian," 9, 92; and continuous journey regulation, 110; controls on, 75, 92, 108, 110; early exclusion of, 92
Armenian Relief Association of Canada, 110
Arsenault, Bona, 145, 226n39
Asian immigrants, 31, 42; assimilation of, 114, 210n46; ban on, 113, 136, 137, 139, 140, 146, 150-51; British Columbia and, 38, 80, 82-85, 113, 118, 209n39, 216n58; as British subjects, 81, 85, 88, 217n85; CCF support of, 113-20, 138; from Commonwealth, 112, 151, 160, 166, 167, 191, 227n2; and continuous journey regulation, 80-81, 82; control circumvention by, 9-10, 46, 82, 93, 112, 113, 128, 156-57, 196-97; controls on (1887-1908), 9, 58-59, 75-82, 92; controls on (1914-39), 9-10, 93-94, 108, 112-20; enfranchisement of, 118, 221n45; and family reunification, 117, 151-52, 167, 168-69, 170; in immediate postwar era (1945-52), 133, 136-40, 150-52, 156-57; King's involvement with, 80-82, 83; as perceived threats, 42, 46, 80, 91-92, 114, 137; as refugees, 168-69, 173, 192; and rights-based politics, 82, 84-85, 120; riots against, 80, 81, 83, 85, 216n65. *See also specific immigrant groups*
"Asians," 9-10, 133, 140; broad definition of, 9, 75, 92, 110, 221n38
"Asiatics," 49, 60, 72, 86, 91, 136, 139
assimilation, 74, 135, 220n22; of Asians, 114, 210n46; and British "standard," 102-3; of Chinese, 137, 224n19; of "enemy aliens," 218n8; of Galicians, 62; in *Immigration Act* (1952), 153; of Japanese, 125, 215nn47-48; need for, 78-79, 97, 139, 153, 218n4
Association for Civil Liberties, 161
asylum seekers: Britain as refuge for, 35-36, 49; Canadian literature on, 20, 21; Chinese, 1-2; later trends in acceptance of, 191-202; Pearson government and, 174, 183, 185, 188; from postwar Europe, 10, 129, 143-46; recent rights-restrictive approach to, 1-2, 3, 11, 13-17, 30, 190-204; ship deserters as, 174, 176-77, 185; Tamil, 1, 196-98; and Universal Declaration of Human Rights, 130. *See also* refugees
Australia, 13, 32, 37, 130, 136, 206n3, 209n36; immigrants from, 150; immigration controls in, 14, 15-16, 173, 215n55; and UN Charter, 132
Aylesworth, Allen, 106
Aylesworth, John B., 228n16

Badanai, Hubert, 175, 178

Baker, Edgar C., 50, 209*n*42
Balanced Refugee Reform Act (Bill C-11, 2010), 1, 11, 198-99, 233*n*15
Baldwin, Gerald W., 186, 232*n*72, 232*n*75
Baltic region, postwar refugees from, 145-46, 226*n*40
Barbados, 159-60, 175, 227*n*1
Barrow, Errol, 175
Baxter, John, 103
Beasley, E.P., 183
Beland, Henri S., 118
Belcourt, Napoléon A., 106
Bell, Richard, 180, 182, 185, 186, 231*n*58, 231*n*64; as immigration minister, 173-74, 231*n*62
Bennett, Richard B., 101, 102, 104-5, 106, 220*n*29
Bennett, William H., 100
Bernonville, Jacques de, 144-45, 146, 149, 225*n*36, 226*n*39
bill of rights, concept of, 10, 93, 119, 131, 132-33, 170. See also *Canadian Bill of Rights;* human rights
Bird, J. Edward, 87, 89-90, 217*n*78, 217*n*84
Bissett, James, 196, 197
Black, George, 221*n*44
Black, William J., 111
Black American immigrants/refugees, 33-34, 42, 60; as escaped slaves, 33-34, 43, 53; Oliver's attempts to bar, 72-73
Blackmore, John H., 135-36, 139, 224*nn*12-14, 224*n*17, 224*nn*19-20
Blair, Frederick C., 110, 111, 121
"boat people": Baltic refugees as, 145-46, 226*n*40; recent asylum seekers as, 1-2, 192-93, 196-98
Boers, 78, 212*n*9, 215*n*50
Borden, Robert, 83-84, 86, 90, 95, 112, 221*n*41; immigration control under, 73, 74-75
border/immigration control: in Confederation era (1867-87), 8-9, 31-57; early legality of, 37-39; early limitations of, 39-42, 43, 46, 56; in immediate postwar era (1945-52), 10, 129-57; in interwar period (1914-45), 9-10, 93-128; in later postwar era (1952-67), 10-11, 158-89; in post-Confederation era (1887-1914), 9, 58-92; recent trends in, 1-3, 8, 11, 13-17, 29-30, 190-204. *See also entries by time period*
border/immigration control, and liberal-democratic state, 12-30; Canadian literature on, 5-6, 12, 20-22, 195-97; comparative literature on, 4, 12, 16,

17-20; historical approach to study of, 19-20, 21-22, 23, 57; and "illiberal liberalism," 26-27, 203; in interwar period, 109; parliamentary debates on, 6-7, 10-11, 28-29; political discourse approach to study of, 7-11, 13, 24-29; in post-9/11 era, 3, 12, 14, 16, 193, 195, 196; rights-restrictive trends in, 1-3, 8, 11, 13-17, 29-30, 190-204. *See also* control/rights nexus; Liberal Internationalism; Liberal Nationalism
border/immigration control, and rights of non-citizens. *See* control/rights nexus; due process/equality rights of non-citizens; judicial oversight, of immigrant/non-citizen rights; rights-based politics; rights-restrictive policies
Boucherville, Charles E.B. de, 215*n*53
Boulay, Herménégilde, 74
Bowell, Mackenzie, 215*n*54
Bradbury, George, 99, 100
Brent, Shirley Kathleen, 165-67, 228*n*16
Brewin, Andrew, 127, 161; and *Brent* case, 166-67; and *Narine-Singh* case, 160, 227*n*2; as Pearson government critic, 174-75, 176, 177-78, 179; and Pearson government reforms, 181, 182, 185-86, 187, 188
Britain: as ally of Japan, 77, 80, 82, 83-84; East Indians' ties to, 79-80, 81, 85, 215*n*57, 217*n*85; as refuge for asylum seekers, 35-36, 49; and rights of British subjects, 81, 85, 118, 215*n*57, 219*n*18, 223*n*69; as "standard" of civilization, 102-3. *See also* liberalism, British
British Columbia, 34; and Asian immigrants, 38, 80, 82-85, 113, 118, 209*n*39, 216*n*58; and Chinese immigrants, 33, 42, 45-49, 50-55, 75, 76, 83, 119, 209*nn*39-40, 209*n*42, 209*n*45, 210*n*54; and East Indian immigrants, 79-80, 84-92, 167; and Japanese immigrants, 76-77, 84, 85, 118-20, 123-27; recent asylum seekers in, 1-2, 196-98, 200
British Columbia Supreme Court, 86, 87
British North America Act (*BNA Act,* 1867), 32, 37-38, 46, 90, 209*n*34; (s. 53), 211*n*60; (s. 95), 37, 38, 209*n*39
Brotherhood of Sleeping Car Porters, 160
Brown, John L., 107
Bryce, Peter H., 68, 207*n*19
Buchanan, William A., 222*n*68
Bunster, Arthur, 47, 209*n*40, 210*n*54
Bureau, J.O., 38
Burgess, A.M., 208*n*22
Burney, Derek, 196, 197

Calder, James A., 96-97, 99, 105, 108
Campbell, Alexander, 210*n*55
Campbell, Milton, 102
Canadian Bar Association, 201; immigration report by, 163, 164, 171, 183, 228*n*22
Canadian Bill of Rights (1960), 133, 167, 170, 173, 176. *See also* bill of rights, concept of; human rights
Canadian Citizenship Act (1946), 133
Canadian Civil Liberties Association, 1, 201
Canadian Congress of Labour, 142
Canadian Jewish Congress, 126, 140-41
Canadian League of Nations Society (later CNCR), 111
Canadian Lutheran World Relief, 145
Canadian National Committee on Refugees and Victims of Political Persecution (CNCR), 111, 121, 141-42, 143, 221*n*39
Canadian National Railway (CNR), 101
Canadian Pacific Railway (CPR), 47-48, 49, 75, 101, 193, 210*n*46
Cannon, Lucien, 105, 118
Cantelon, Reg, 175, 230*n*46
Caplan, Elinor, 194
Carling, John, 208*n*24
Cartwright, John R., 228*n*18
Cartwright, Richard J., 208*n*24, 214*n*38
Casey, George, 78-79, 215*n*48
Cassidy, Robert, 90
Castleden, George H., 222*n*60
Catherine the Great, 43
Centre for Immigration Policy Reform (CIPR), 196-97
Chance, Leslie, 147, 148-49
Chapleau, Joseph A., 75; commission co-chaired by, 49-50, 51, 210*nn*49-50
Charlton, John, 76, 78, 214*n*44
Chinese Benevolent Association of Vancouver, 160, 227*n*3
Chinese Consolidated Benevolent Associations, 118
Chinese immigrants: assimilation of, 137, 224*n*19; as asylum seekers/refugees, 1-2, 168-69, 229*n*24; British Columbia and, 33, 42, 45-49, 50-55, 75, 76, 83, 119, 209*nn*39-40, 209*n*42, 209*n*45, 210*n*54; British liberalism and, 47-49, 50-51, 53, 54, 92, 115-16, 134; control circumvention by, 83, 118, 120, 170, 229*n*29; CPR and, 47-48, 49, 75, 193, 210*n*46; disenfranchisement of, 48, 50, 51, 52, 85, 115, 210*n*50, 221*n*45; early hostility to, 47-49; and family reunification, 167, 168-69, 170; first legislation to control

(1885), 8-9, 31-32, 37, 45-47, 49-57, 115; further controls on (1887-1914), 9, 58, 62, 75-79, 82, 83, 92; Head Tax on, 50, 51-52, 55, 60, 75-78, 79, 83, 112, 114, 116; interwar controls on (1914-39), 113-18; later ban on (1923), 112, 115-18, 133, 136-40, 146; Mackenzie's defence of, 47-49, 53; naturalization difficulties of, 48, 221*n*52, 224*n*22; as perceived threats, 45, 46, 47, 50-51, 75-76, 114, 137, 214*nn*43-44; postwar (1945-52), 133, 136-40, 146, 160-61, 168-69; and rights-based politics, 84-85, 115, 117-18, 137-40. *See also entries below;* Head Tax, on Chinese immigrants
Chinese Immigration Act (1885), 8-9, 31-32, 37, 45-47, 49-57, 115; amendments to, 75-79, 82, 83, 114, 210*n*53, 216*n*64; House of Commons and, 49-52; Senate attempts to reject/repeal, 9, 32, 45-47, 52-56, 67, 134, 211*n*58, 215*n*54; and state sovereignty/racial discrimination, 46, 49, 54
Chinese Immigration Act (1900), 77-79
Chinese Immigration Act (1903), 79
Chinese Immigration Act (1923), 112, 115-18, 136; and judicial oversight, 116-17; repeal of, 133, 136-40, 146; and UN Charter, 137-38, 140, 224*n*23
Chinese Revolution, 168-69, 170
Chinese Tax Act (BC, 1878), 84-85
Choy, Wayson S., 174
Christie, Thomas, 75, 78
churches/church groups, 52, 79, 111, 120, 160; Anglican/United, 126, 161; Lutheran, 145-46
Churchill, Winston, 80
circumvention of controls: by Asians, 9-10, 46, 82, 93, 112, 113, 128, 156-57, 196-97; by Chinese, 83, 118, 120, 170, 229*n*29; by East Indians, 86, 91, 120; by Japanese, 119, 120; rights-restrictive policies and, 4, 7, 21, 22-23, 178, 180, 188, 201, 203
citizenship: expansive/realistic views of, 17, 62; Liberal Internationalist view of, 26; and literacy, 98; and rights of British subjects, 81, 85, 118, 215*n*57, 219*n*18, 223*n*69; rights-restrictive policies and, 2, 3, 14, 48, 195-96, 221*n*52. *See also entry below*
citizenship, Canadian: and appeals of rejection, 177-78; duties/responsibilities of, 96-97, 150, 153; establishment of, 127, 133; exclusion from, 96-97; revocation of, 2, 193, 195, 219*n*3; rights-restrictive

policies and, 2, 3, 14, 48, 195-96, 221*n*52. *See also* Japanese Canadians; naturalized Canadians

civil liberties movement, 120; and Japanese Canadians, 123-24, 126; and non-citizens' rights, 161, 163-64; and recent Conservative immigration bills, 1, 201

Clarke, Alfred H., 73

Clarke, Charles K., 66, 213*n*22

Clarke, Edward F., 66-67

Clemow, Francis, 215*n*53

Cloran, Henry J., 217*n*72

Cold War, 149, 151, 153, 195; end of, 2, 17, 193

Coldwell, M.J., 122, 138, 151, 222*n*61, 224*n*21

Collacott, Martin, 196, 197

Committee for the Defence of French Refugees, 144

Committee for the Repeal of the Chinese Immigration Act, 137, 140

Commonwealth, British, 132; non-white immigrants from, 112, 151, 159-60, 166, 167, 172, 175, 191, 227*n*2, 229*n*34. *See also* East Indian immigrants; West Indies, immigrants from

communism, fear of: in Cold War era, 148, 149, 164, 226*n*41; after Winnipeg General Strike, 99-100, 105, 219*n*17

Confederation era (1867-87), 8-9, 31-57; British liberalism in, 32, 34-37, 41-42, 43, 47-49, 56-57, 93; Chinese immigrant control in, 8-9, 31-32, 37, 45-47, 49-57; and development of agricultural society, 33, 34, 37-38, 56; immigration control in, 37-45; immigration trends in, 32-34; Jewish refugees in, 42, 44-45, 56; legality of control in, 37-39; limitations of control in, 39-42, 43, 46, 56; Mennonite refugees in, 34, 43, 44; and Senate defence of Chinese immigrants, 9, 32, 45-47, 52-56, 67, 134, 211*n*58, 215*n*54; US-related issues/concerns of, 33-34, 40, 41, 42, 43, 46, 53

continuous journey regulation (1908), 80-81, 82, 108, 112, 141; Armenian immigrants/refugees and, 110; East Indians and, 80-81, 85, 86-87, 89-90, 217*n*78; Jewish immigrants/refugees and, 87, 110; Oliver's reaffirmation of, 86-87

control/rights nexus, 1-11, 12-13, 17-30; Canadian literature on, 5-6, 12, 20-22, 195-97; comparative literature on, 4, 12, 16, 17-20; formulation of (alternative), 22-23; formulation of (traditional), 17-20;

and liberalism, 6-11; political discourse and, 7, 8, 13, 24-29; rights-based politics and, 1-5, 7-8, 9-11, 17-20, 22; rights-restrictive policies and, 1-5, 7, 8, 9-11, 12-13, 21, 22-23, 188-89, 201-4. *See also* rights-based politics; rights-restrictive policies

Controller of Chinese Immigration, 114, 116, 214*n*42

Co-operative Committee for Japanese Canadians, 126, 127

Co-operative Commonwealth Federation (CCF), 119, 230*n*41; and Asian immigrants, 113-20, 138; and *Chinese Immigration Act* (1923), 137-38; and Japanese Canadians, 119, 120, 123, 124, 126-27; and Jewish refugees, 122; and non-white Commonwealth immigrants, 159-60

Cornelius, Wayne A., Philip L. Martin, and James F. Hollifield: *Controlling Immigration*, 17-18, 20

Crerar, Thomas, 107, 111, 121, 136-37, 139

Crestohl, Leon D., 150-51, 154-55, 171, 172, 173, 229*n*26, 229*n*36

criminals, as immigrants, 2, 40, 45, 62, 65, 74, 78, 178, 180, 198, 213*n*23; Nazi war criminals/collaborators, 144, 223*n*1, 225*nn*35-36

Croll, David A., 135, 138, 142, 146, 151, 154, 161, 224*n*22, 225*n*25, 226*n*47

Cronyn, Hume, 97, 98

Cullen, J.S.G. (Bud), 193

Dandurand, Raoul, 105

Davies, Louis H., 50, 51

De Cosmos, Amor, 48-49, 209*n*45

Defence of Canada Regulations (DOCR), 123-24

departments, federal: Agriculture, 37-38, 41, 58, 66; Canadian Heritage, 190; Citizenship and Immigration, 147, 150-52, 174, 179; External Affairs, 131; Immigration and Colonization, 96; Interior, 58, 59-60, 83, 92, 208*n*22; Manpower and Immigration, 174, 179; Mines and Resources, 112, 136, 150; Trade and Commerce, 83

deportation: of East Indians, 81, 85, 86-87, 89-90; of "enemy aliens," 96; human face of, 70-71, 213*nn*33-34; under *Immigration Act* (1869), 45, 65-66, 67; under *Immigration Act* (1906), 68-71; under *Immigration Act* (1910), 99-100, 103-7, 108; under *Immigration Act* (1952), 152, 153-55, 161-62, 165-66, 168, 171, 173, 177-78, 180-81, 183-87; of labour

activists, 99-100, 106, 107, 219*n*14; on medical grounds, 65-67, 71, 74, 153, 154, 166-67, 228*n*18, 231*n*59; *Narine-Singh* case and, 160, 166, 227*n*2; on political grounds, 153, 226*n*45; UK legislation on, 94; under *War Measures Act*, 94-95; wartime attempt to legislate, 126, 223*n*69
Dever, James, 53
Diefenbaker, John: and *Canadian Bill of Rights*, 133, 170; Liberal Internationalism of, 133, 137-38, 165, 223*n*69, 227*n*8, 227*n*10, 229*n*25; and non-interest in immigration, 169, 229*n*26
Dinsdale, Walter G., 138, 161, 229*n*24
disenfranchisement: of Chinese, 48, 50, 51, 52, 85, 210*n*50, 221*n*45; of East Indians, 80; and "enemy alien" origin, 95, 126; of Japanese, 77, 85, 113, 118, 119-20, 126, 127, 222*n*68
Dominion By-Election Act (1919), 221*n*45
Dominion Elections Act (1920), 118
Donnelly, James J., 100
Dorion, Frédéric, 122-23, 144-45
Douglas, Tommy, 123, 222*n*61
Doukhobors, 62-63, 99, 101, 102, 108, 212*n*14, 219*n*11
due process/equality rights of non-citizens, 26; in Confederation era (1867-87), 33-34, 35-36; in immediate postwar era (1945-52), 129, 146-50, 152-57; and *Immigration Act* (1976), 191, 193-94, 195; and *Immigration and Refugee Protection Act*, 2, 191, 194, 195; and *Immigration Appeal Board Act*, 168, 183-87, 193; interwar abrogation of (1914-45), 9-10, 93-128; later institutionalization of (1952-67), 10-11, 158-69, 171, 174, 180-89, 193; in post-9/11 era, 193, 195; for refugees/asylum seekers, 194-95; rights-restrictive policies and, 1, 22-23, 27, 69, 90, 93-94, 129, 153, 156, 193; vs. state sovereignty, 9, 58-92, 106, 120, 129, 156
Dunning, Charles A., 105

East Indian immigrants, 9, 58, 74, 75, 79-82, 84-92; anti-Asian riots against, 80, 85; British ties of, 79-80, 81, 85, 215*n*57, 217*n*85; and continuous journey regulation, 80-81, 85, 86-87, 89-90, 217*n*78; control circumvention by, 86, 91, 120; disenfranchisement of, 80; hostility to, 85, 216*n*71; interwar controls on, 112-13; and *Komagata Maru* case, 82, 88-92, 217*n*77; and rights-based politics, 9, 58-59, 82, 84-92, 113, 167;

Senate support of, 217*n*72. *See also* Sikh immigrants
Edwards, John W., 97, 99
Edwards, William C., 78
Egan, William J., 111, 219*n*21
Electoral Franchise Act (1885), 50, 52
Ellis, John V., 62, 71
Empire Settlement Agreements, 102
"enemy aliens": European immigrants as, 93, 94, 95-96, 98-99, 101, 123, 218*n*8, 222*n*59; Japanese/Japanese Canadians as, 93-94, 123-28
Espillat-Rodriguez v. R., 228*n*18
ethnoracial discrimination, 13-14; in immediate postwar era (1945-52), 134, 135-36, 137, 139-40, 153, 156; in later postwar era (1952-67), 159-60, 171, 174-76, 188; Liberal Internationalists and, 47-49, 62-64, 134, 159, 225*n*26; and non-discrimination policy, 6, 10, 159, 181-83, 188, 191-93; and non-white Commonwealth immigrants, 112, 151, 159-60, 166, 167, 172, 175, 227*n*2, 229*n*34. *See also specific ethnoracial groups; entry below*
ethnoracial discrimination, Liberal Nationalism and, 28, 33, 45, 62-64, 127-28, 139-40, 188; and state sovereignty, 46, 49, 54, 78-79, 90, 93, 109, 120, 134, 140, 156. See also *Chinese Immigration Act* (1885)
Euler, William D., 98, 108-9, 220*n*35, 221*n*36, 222*n*68
European immigrants: as agriculturalists, 34, 59-61, 62, 64, 74, 98, 101, 102; and continuous journey regulation, 87; controls on (1887-1914), 9, 59-75; controls on (1914-39), 9-10, 93, 94-112; controls on (1939-45), 10, 120, 121-23; as early refugees, 32-33, 42-43; as "enemy aliens," 93, 94, 95-96, 98-99, 101, 123, 218*n*8, 222*n*59; as interwar refugees, 10, 92, 93-94, 108-12, 121-23; monetary requirement for, 65, 69, 74, 108-9, 110; as postwar refugees/asylum seekers, 10, 129, 140-46; preferred vs. non-preferred, 101-3, 110-11, 139, 219*n*21, 220*n*23; privileging of, 60-61. *See also specific immigrant groups; entries below*
European immigrants (1887-1914), 9, 58, 59-75, 92; Conservatives and, 74-75; Oliver and, 59, 63, 68-75, 77, 84, 86, 87-88, 90, 91; Sifton and, 59-68, 74
European immigrants (1914-45), 9-10, 93, 94-112, 120, 121-23; as "dangerous foreigners," 94-101; and rejection of Jewish

refugees, 10, 92, 93-94, 108, 120, 121-23, 140-41; and restrictions on refugees, 108-12; and rights-based politics, 9, 93, 95, 99-100, 101-7
European refugees/asylum seekers: from Baltic region, 145-46; early migration by, 32-33, 42-45; interwar controls on/ rejection of, 10, 92, 93-94, 108-12, 121-23, 140-41; from Iron Curtain countries, 142-43, 155, 176-77; postwar (1945-49), 10, 129, 140-46, 191, 193, 229*n*24. *See also* Jewish immigrants/refugees

Factor, Samuel, 121
Fairclough, Ellen, 140, 169-70, 171, 229*n*26; Liberal Internationalism of, 170, 172-73, 218*n*7
Fairweather, Gordon, 178, 179
family reunification/sponsorship of relatives, 14, 86, 117; difficulties of, 151-52, 162-63, 167, 170, 173, 181, 182, 184, 185; discriminatory regulations on, 230*n*39; by refugees, 168-69, 233*n*21
Favreau, Guy, 174, 179, 230*n*43
Ferguson, Donald, 213*n*33
Fleming, Donald M., 153, 155
Fleming, Gavin, 56, 208*n*32
Forke, Robert, 102
Fortier, L.M., 214*n*41
Foster, George, 61, 70, 73, 214*n*40
Fowler, George W., 219*n*17
Fraser, Duncan C., 62, 64, 76, 212*n*13
Fulton, E. Davie, 170, 224*n*18, 227*nn*5-6, 228*n*15; as immigration minister, 169; on non-citizens' rights, 151-52, 153, 161, 162-63, 165, 167-68

Galicians, 61-62, 63, 212*n*8, 212*n*10
Galt, Alexander, 44, 208*n*31
Garland, E.J., 107
Gauthier, Pierre, 122, 139
Gentlemen's Agreements with Japan: (1908), 83-84, 114; (1923), 112, 118-19
German immigrants: Cold War refugees as, 155; in Confederation era, 32, 33, 34; desirability of, 61, 212*n*8; as "enemy aliens," 95, 98, 101, 123, 218*n*8; Jewish refugees as, 109
Gibson, Colin, 144
Gibson, John L., 224*n*17
Gillmor, Arthur H., 50, 210*n*49, 215*n*53
Girroir, Edward L., 97, 100
Glen, James, 135, 136, 137, 139, 147
Gordon, David W., 75
Gordon, Wesley A., 107, 111
Gouzenko, Igor, 149

Gray, Herb, 232*n*74
Greene, John J., 178
Griesbach, William A., 222*n*68
Grizzle, Stanley G., 160

habeas corpus, right of, 88, 89, 95, 106, 171, 216*n*67, 218*n*2, 220*n*31
Haggart, John G., 217*n*75
Haidasz, Stanley, 185
Hamilton, William M., 161-62
Hanson, Richard B., 116
Harris, Walter, 150, 226*n*43, 226*n*47; and denial of discrimination, 139; and *Immigration Act* (1952), 153-54, 155; and non-citizens' rights, 148, 162, 165; and UN Convention on Refugees, 148; on weather as deterrent to immigration, 159-60
Hayes, Saul, 141, 225*nn*29-30
Haythorne, Robert P., 55
Hayward, Constance, 143
Head Tax, on Chinese immigrants, 50, 51-52, 75-78, 79, 114, 210*nn*51-53, 217*n*72; circumventions of, 83; Laurier's increases in, 60, 77-78, 79; as ostensible revenue source, 55, 211*n*60; removal of, 116; student exemption from, 112, 216*n*64
Heaps, Abraham A., 107, 121
Henderson, David, 70
Hlynka, Anthony, 142, 143
Hollifield, James F.: *Immigrants, Markets, and States*, 17, 26
Holocaust, 121, 123, 130, 223*n*2, 225*n*29
Homma, Tomey, 85
Hopkinson, William C., 84
Howlan, George, 76
Hudson's Bay Company, 37
human rights: attributes of, 130-31; and bill of rights concept/legislation, 10, 93, 119, 131, 132-33, 167, 170, 173, 176; British liberalism and, 10, 17-18, 27-28, 93, 128, 129, 131, 132, 133, 188; historical studies of, 21-22; Holocaust and, 130, 223*n*2; in immediate postwar era (1945-52), 10, 17-18, 128, 129-57; legislative protection of, 160; and national identity, 133; rights-restrictive threats to, 30, 120-27, 201; vs. state sovereignty, 130-32, 134; and UN Charter, 130, 131, 132, 138; Universal Declaration of, 2, 25, 130-32, 156, 165. *See also* postwar era, immediate (1945-52)
human smuggling, 1-2, 3, 176, 196; by Chinese, 170, 229*n*29; by Japanese, 119; legislation against, 1, 198, 199-201; of Nazi war criminals, 225*nn*35-36

Humphrey, John P., 131
Hungarian refugees, 168, 169, 191
Hunter, Gordon, 87, 217*n*78
Hutterites, 99, 101, 219*n*10

Idington, John, 216*n*70
illegal/irregular immigration, 3-4, 13, 14-15; amnesty proposal for, 229*n*30; postwar issues of, 144, 170, 174, 176-79, 180-81; recent cases of, 1-2, 196-98, 200; by ship deserters, 174, 176-77, 185. *See also* asylum seekers; circumvention of controls; human smuggling
"illiberal liberalism," 26-27, 203; of Canadian policies/proposals, 118, 152, 206*n*8, 210*n*56
immigration, international: in Confederation era, 32-34; at end of 20th century, 2-3, 13-16; in immediate postwar era (1945-52), 130-33; in late 19th- early 20th centuries, 36-37
Immigration Act (1869), 8, 38-39, 45, 60, 65-66, 67
Immigration Act (1906), 68-71, 159, 213*n*28; continuous journey amendment to, 86; deportation amendments to, 70-71, 213*nn*32-33; governmental powers under, 69-70, 213*nn*30-31
Immigration Act (1910), 9, 71-73, 87, 90, 135, 145, 152, 187, 221*n*37; deportation under, 99-100, 103-7, 108, 214*n*38, 219*n*18; exclusion amendments to (1919), 95-100; and judicial oversight, 58, 71-72, 82, 161, 226*n*45; literacy test in, 96, 98, 218*n*7
Immigration Act (1952), 10, 129, 147, 150, 152-56, 158-59, 205*n*3, 232*n*6; cases emanating from, 165-67, 227*n*2, 227*n*4; deportation under, 152, 153-55, 161-62, 165-66, 168, 171, 173, 177-78, 180-81, 183-87; and Immigration Appeal Boards, 155, 168, 173, 176, 181, 183-87, 193; limited appeal rights under, 153-55, 162-63, 164, 165-66, 171, 181; ministerial power under, 152-55, 156, 161-62, 164-65, 168, 171-72, 173, 178-79, 181, 184, 186, 187, 228*n*14; need to overhaul/replace, 170-71, 173, 174, 229*n*25; regulations under, 152-53, 155, 162-63, 165-68, 170-71, 172, 173, 177, 182-83, 230*n*39; rights-based politics engendered by, 155-56; Special Inquiry Officers under, 152, 154
Immigration Act (1976), 158, 174, 191, 193-94, 195, 205*n*3, 232*n*6, 233*n*8

Immigration Agents: reports/observations of, 39, 41, 42, 89, 208*n*31; Sifton's system of, 60, 61, 64-65
Immigration and Refugee Board (IRB), 194, 195, 196, 199-200, 233*nn*16-17; Pre-Removal Risk Assessments under, 199, 200; Refugee Appeal and Protection Divisions of, 199, 200
Immigration and Refugee Protection Act (2001), 2, 191, 194, 195
Immigration Appeal Board Act (1967), 168, 183-87, 193
Immigration Appeal Boards (IABs), 155, 168, 176, 181; Fairclough's changes to, 173; later legislation on, 168, 183-87, 193
Imperial War Conferences (1917 and 1918), 112
India, 58; British ties of, 79-80, 85; and continuous journey regulation, 81, 86, 217*n*78; independence struggle in, 85, 91, 218*n*86; and interwar controls, 112-13, 221*n*41; postwar issues involving, 147, 151; Sikh nationalism in, 89. *See also* East Indian immigrants; Sikh immigrants
International Refugee Organization, 142, 145, 147, 225*n*33
internment: of "enemy aliens," 95; of Japanese Canadians, 10, 93-94, 120, 123-28; of labour activists, 95, 219*n*14
interwar period (1914-45), immigration controls in, 9-10, 93-128; as apex of Liberal Nationalism, 93-94, 120-28; on Asians, 93-94, 112-20, 123-28; on British-born, 9, 94, 99-100; and Canadian-born/naturalized citizens, 10, 119-20, 123-28; on Chinese, 112, 113-18, 120; on "dangerous foreigners," 94-101; on East Indians, 112-13; on "enemy aliens," 93, 94, 95-96, 98-99, 101, 123, 218*n*8; on European immigrants, 9-10, 93, 94-107; on European refugees, 108-12, 120, 121-23; on Japanese Canadians, 10, 93-94, 120, 123-28; on Japanese immigrants, 112, 114, 118-20, on Jewish refugees, 10, 92, 93-94, 108, 120, 121-23; and rights-based politics, 9-10, 93-94, 101-7, 112, 113, 119-24, 126-28
Irish immigrants/refugees, 38, 41, 150
Iron Curtain countries, refugees from, 142-43, 155, 176-77
Irvine, William, 118, 138, 225*n*26
Israel, founding of, 111, 147, 169
Italian immigrants, 59, 64, 123, 212*nn*15-16

Jacobs, Samuel, 97-98, 99, 102-3, 108, 110, 121, 218*nn*6-7
Japan, 58; as ally of Britain/Canada, 77, 80, 82, 83-84, 112; Gentlemen's Agreements with, 83-84, 112, 114, 118-19
Japanese Canadian Citizens' League (JCCL), 119, 124, 126
Japanese Canadian Committee for Democracy, 126, 127
Japanese Canadians: as Canadian-born, 10, 119-20, 125, 127-28; CCF support for, 119, 120, 123, 124, 126-27; disenfranchisement of, 77, 85, 113, 118, 119-20, 126, 127, 222*n*68; as national security threat, 124-25; as naturalized, 85, 119-20, 125; and rights-based politics, 85, 119, 123-24, 126-27, 128; and "voluntary departure" policy, 125-27; wartime internment/deportation of, 10, 93-94, 120, 123-28, 132
Japanese immigrants: assimilation of, 125, 215*nn*47-48; control circumvention by, 119, 120; early controls on (1887-1914), 9, 58, 75, 76-77, 79, 92; hostility to, 76-77, 114, 118, 120; interwar controls on (1914-39), 112, 114, 118-20; Laurier's support of, 77, 80, 82, 83-84, 215*n*47; naturalization difficulties of, 221*n*52; as perceived threats, 124
Japanese Treaty Act (1913), 84
Jenson, Jane, 24-25
Jewish immigrants/refugees, 31, 43, 109, 144-45; as "Asian," 9, 75, 92; CCF support for, 122; and continuous journey regulation, 87, 110; early reception of, 42, 44-45, 56; and flight from Holocaust, 121, 123, 130, 223*n*2, 225*n*29; later controls on, 87, 110-11, 112; monetary requirements for, 65, 74, 110; rejection of, 10, 92, 93-94, 108, 120, 121-23, 140-41, 222*nn*56-57, 225*n*29; and rights-based politics, 110-11, 121-23, 160, 169
Joppke, Christian, 18, 26
judicial oversight, of immigrant/non-citizen rights: as blocked by restrictive policies, 9, 14-15, 16, 58, 71-72, 159; and border control failure, 17-18; and *Chinese Immigration Act* (1923), 116-17; East Indian activism and, 9, 58-59, 82, 84-92; and *Immigration Act* (1910), 58, 71-72, 82, 161, 226*n*45; and *Immigration Act* (1952), 153-55, 162-63, 164, 165-66, 171, 181; and increased control, 4, 19, 23; Oliver's opposition to, 71-72, 82, 87-88, 90; postwar return of, 6, 9, 10, 72, 179-80, 181-87, 188, 193-94; recent

attempts/calls to limit, 193, 197; and *War Measures Act*, 94-95
Jung, Douglas, 170

Kearney, John D., 151
Kendall, Arthur S., 67
Kenney, Jason, 1, 197-200
Kent, Tom, 179, 180
Khalsa Diwan Society (Vancouver), 79-80, 140, 160
Kidd, Thomas A., 224*n*17
King, William Lyon Mackenzie, 101, 122, 178; and Asian immigration, 80-82, 83; and *Chinese Immigration Act* (1923), 115-16; as descendant of refugee, 226*n*38; and Japanese Canadians, 123, 127; and Japanese immigration, 118, 119; and opium trade, 83, 216*n*65; on postwar immigration policy, 133-34, 150; and UN Convention on Refugees, 147, 148
Knowles, Stanley H., 122, 133
Komagata Maru (ship), case of, 82, 88-92, 217*n*77; test case for, 89-91; as triumph of Liberal Nationalism, 82, 90-92, 217*n*85

labour activists, internment/deportation of, 95, 99-100, 106, 107, 219*n*14, 221*n*37
labour market, 14, 17, 41, 58, 174, 192
Lacombe, Liguori, 122
Lambert, Norman P., 222*n*57, 222*n*68
Lapointe, Ernest, 121, 123
Lapointe, Louis A., 218*n*88
Laurier, Wilfrid, 79, 81, 86, 215*n*52, 216*n*60; and Japanese, 77, 80, 82, 83-84, 215*n*47
League of Nations, 109, 118; Covenant of, 130
League of Nations Convention Relating to the International Status of Refugees (1933), 109
Lee, Art, 193
Lemieux, Rodolphe, 80, 88, 114
Lennox, Haughton, 70
Leong Ba Chai, 161, 166
Leong Hung Hing, 161
Lewis, David, 185, 186-87, 231*n*71
liberal-democratic state. *See* border/immigration control, and liberal-democratic state; *see also entries below*
Liberal Internationalism, 7-11, 13, 24-29; attributes of, 25-26; and British liberalism, 8-9, 10, 27, 37, 46, 56-57, 92, 100, 128, 129, 131, 132, 133; in Confederation era (1867-87), 8-9, 31-32, 33-34, 43, 45-57; and defence of Chinese immigrants, 9,

32, 45-47, 52-56, 67, 134, 211*n*58, 215*n*54; in immediate postwar era (1945-52), 10, 17-18, 129-30, 131, 133, 134, 137-38, 142, 146-47, 155, 156; in interwar period (1914-45), 9-10, 95, 97-100, 102-7, 108-9, 114-15, 120, 122, 124, 126-27, 128; in post-Confederation era (1887-1914), 58-59, 62-64, 67-79, 88, 92; postwar return of (1952-67), 10-11, 17-18, 158-89, 191; in recent years, 195, 197-98, 199, 201-3; and state sovereignty, 106, 134, 165, 178. *See also* due process/equality rights of non-citizens; judicial oversight, of immigrant/non-citizen rights; rights-based politics
Liberal Nationalism, 7-11, 13, 24-29; attributes of, 26; in Confederation era (1867-87), 32, 33, 37, 45, 47-52, 57; domination of (1914-45), 9-10, 93-128; expansion/consolidation of (1887-1914), 9, 58-92; and "illiberal liberalism," 26-27, 203; in immediate postwar era (1945-52), 10, 129-57; in later postwar era (1952-67), 10-11, 159-69, 172-73, 181-82, 187, 188-89; and "privilege" of admission to Canada, 134, 164, 172, 176, 178, 181; recent turn towards, 1-3, 8, 11, 13-17, 29-30, 190-204; vs. "special interests," 54, 196; and state sovereignty, 7, 26, 27, 75, 134, 156, 162, 197. *See also* ethnoracial discrimination, Liberal Nationalism and; rights-restrictive policies; sovereignty, state, Liberal Nationalism and
liberalism: British tradition of, 34-37; as "illiberal," 26-27, 118, 152, 203, 206*n*8, 210*n*56; parliamentary debates as record of, 6-7, 10-11, 28-29. *See also entry below*
liberalism, British: attributes of, 35; and Chinese immigrants, 47-49, 50-51, 53, 54, 92, 115-16, 134; at Confederation, 31-32, 34-37, 41-42, 43, 47-49, 56-57, 93; and escaped slaves, 33-34, 43, 49, 53; and Liberal Internationalism, 8-9, 10, 27, 37, 46, 56-57, 92, 100, 128, 129, 131, 132, 133; and non-citizens' rights, 21-22, 33-34, 35-36, 94, 99-100, 103, 120, 127-28; and postwar human rights discourse, 10, 17-18, 27-28, 93, 128, 129, 131, 132, 133, 188; and rights-based politics, 9, 17, 85-92; wartime abrogation of, 120, 123, 126-28. *See also* due process/equality rights of non-citizens; Liberal Internationalism
literacy test: in *Immigration Act* regulations (1919), 96, 98, 218*n*7; in US, 94

literature, of border/immigration control: Canadian, 5-6, 12, 20-22, 195-97; comparative, 4, 12, 16, 17-20
Lougheed, James A., 67, 73, 97, 103, 104, 213*n*34, 214*n*38
Lowe, John, 38, 41, 42
Luchkovich, Michael, 102

Macdonald, Andrew A., 215*n*53
Macdonald, David, 192
Macdonald, James A., 90
Macdonald, John A., 44, 49-50, 209*n*45, 211*n*61
Macdonald, William J., 53, 55, 70, 215*n*53
MacDonnell, Samuel, 48
Machado, Gerardo, 145, 226*n*38
Mackenzie, Alexander, 47-49, 53, 209*n*41, 209*n*43
MacInnis, Angus, 124, 128, 138, 222*n*60
MacKay, Ian, 142
MacNicol, John R., 122, 135
Macpherson, Robert, 86
Magna Carta, 103, 106, 163, 219*n*15, 220*n*24, 227*n*10
Maltais, Auguste, 228*n*15
Manion, John R., 227*n*48
Marchand, Jean, 175, 179, 180, 181-87. *See also Immigration Appeal Board Act; White Paper on Immigration*
Martin, Don, 198
Martin, Paul, 133
Masella v. Langlais, 227*n*4
Masters of Vessels, 38, 39, 51, 116, 207*n*13, 208*n*32
Maude, Aylmer, 63
Maxwell, George R., 75-76, 214*n*43
McBride, Thomas G., 118, 222*n*54
McHugh, George, 98
McInnes, William W.B., 76
McKay, E.B., 140
McKenzie, Daniel D., 218*n*88
McMaster, Andrew R., 104
McMeans, Lendrum, 105
McMillan, Donald, 215*n*53
McMurray, E.J., 114
McNeill, Alexander, 62
McPhillips, Albert E., 91
McQuarrie, William G., 114
medical examinations: of Chinese immigrants, 51, 65-66, 116; and deportation, 65-67, 71, 74, 153, 154, 166-67, 228*n*18, 231*n*59; early handling of, 38-39, 40, 207*n*13, 207*n*19, 213*n*24; as later requirement of entry, 101, 166-67, 228*n*18; and quarantine process, 38, 40, 65, 66, 89, 213*n*21

Medical Superintendents, 38, 39, 40, 68, 207*n*19
Meighen, Arthur, 104, 106, 114
Mennonite immigrants/refugees, 33, 62, 98, 108, 109-10, 219*n*10; as early refugees (1873-80), 34, 43, 44, 208*nn*27-29; later ban on (1919), 99, 101, 208*n*27, 219*n*11
Michener, Roland, 161
Middle East, refugees from, 172, 192, 228*n*23, 229*n*24
Mills, David, 49, 52, 64, 77
ministers (responsible for immigration). *See* Bell, Richard; Calder, James A.; Caplan, Elinor; Crerar, Thomas; Fairclough, Ellen; Favreau, Guy; Forke, Robert; Fulton, E. Davie; Gibson, Colin; Glen, James; Gordon, Wesley A.; Harris, Walter; Kenney, Jason; Marchand, Jean; Oliver, Frank; Pickersgill, Jack; Robb, James A.; Roche, William J.; Rogers, Robert; Sifton, Clifford; Stewart, Charles A.; Tremblay, René
Mitchell, Humphrey, 222*n*66
Mitchell, Peter, 50, 51
monetary requirements, 101; Asian/East Indian immigrants and, 82, 86, 90, 112; European/Jewish immigrants and, 65, 69, 74, 108-9, 110
Mongrain, Joseph-Alfred, 187
Monteagle (ship), 86
Montizambert, Frederick, 40
More, Kenneth H., 184
Mosher, A.R., 142
Mulroney, Brian, 196
multiculturalism, 190
Munro, John C., 184, 231*n*63
Munshi Singh case, 89-90, 92, 217*n*85
Musgrave, Anthony, 47
Mutch, Leslie A., 143

Nansen passport, 109
Napoleonic Wars, 35, 37
Narain Singh case, 87, 217*n*78; aftermath of, 88-92
Narine-Singh, Harry and Mearl, case of, 160, 166, 227*n*2
National Council of Women of Canada, 137
National Emergency Transition Powers Act (1945), 126, 223*n*69
National Inter-Church Advisory Committee, 126
National Policy, 34
national security: Asian Canadians and, 118, 137; as Cold War concern, 131-32,

149; Japanese Canadians and, 118, 124-25; non-citizens' rights and, 105, 161, 164, 177, 181, 194, 186-87; in post-9/11 era, 12, 193; postwar refugees and, 141, 147, 149; recent invocations of, 2, 12, 15-16, 28, 193, 194-98
naturalized Canadians: deportation of, 219*n*18; disenfranchisement of, 48, 85, 95; internment of, 95, 125; Japanese, 85, 119-20, 125; and obstacles to citizenship, 48, 221*n*52, 224*n*22; and revocation of citizenship, 2, 193, 219*n*13; rights of, 85, 119-20, 195, 222*n*59
Nazi war criminals/collaborators, as immigrants, 144, 223*n*1, 225*nn*35-36
Negro Citizenship Association, 160
Neill, Alan, 102, 104, 115, 118, 120, 124, 125, 220*n*26, 220*n*32
The New Canadian (Japanese English-language weekly), 119, 124
New Zealand, 32, 132, 136, 150, 209*n*36
Nicholls, Frederic, 98
Nicholson, Alexander M., 225*n*24
Nicholson, George B., 98
Nielsen, Dorise W., 222*n*62
9/11. *See* September 11 (2001), terrorist attacks of
non-citizens' rights: British liberalism and, 21-22, 33-34, 35-36, 94, 99-100, 103, 120, 127-28; postwar activism on (1952-56), 159-69. *See also* due process/equality rights of non-citizens; judicial oversight, of immigrant/non-citizen rights; rights-based politics
non-discrimination, 18, 201; early discussion of, 135, 138, 140; as official policy, 6, 10, 159, 181-83, 188, 191-93
North Atlantic Trading Company (NATC), 61, 211*n*7
Noseworthy, Joseph W., 138, 159-60, 164, 170-71
Nosse, Tatsugoro, 77
Nugent, Terry, 177, 178

Ocean Lady (ship), 1, 198, 200
Oliver, Frank, 59, 63, 68-75; on Asian immigration, 91-92; and Black American immigrants, 72-73; and East Indian immigrants, 86-88, 90; on Galicians, 61-62, 212*n*8; and *Immigration Act* (1906), 68-71, 86-87, 213*n*28, 213*nn*30-31; and *Immigration Act* (1910), 71-73, 82, 87, 214*nn*39-40, 217*n*73; and Japanese immigration, 77, 84; and opposition to judicial oversight, 71-72, 82, 87-88, 90; vs. Sifton, 62, 212*n*12

Opium and Narcotic Drug Act (1929), 154
opium/opium trade, 83, 214*n*43; legislation against, 154, 216*n*65
Organisation for Economic Co-operation and Development (OECD), 14
Orlikow, David, 175, 177, 230*n*50, 231*n*56, 232*n*70

pacifist religious groups, 33, 43, 99, 219*n*11. *See also specific groups*
Pakistan, 147, 151
Palmerston, Lord, 35-36, 226*n*37
Panama Maru (ship), 87. See also *Narain Singh* case
Paquet, Eugène, 74
parliamentary debates on border control/ immigration, 6-7, 10-11, 28-29; analyses of, 158; and Conservative strategies to marginalize critics, 197-98, 233*n*15; and refugee policy, 108
Parmelee, W.S., 214*n*42
paupers, 39, 40, 42, 65, 69, 78, 207*n*15, 207*n*20, 208*n*24, 208*n*32, 213*n*23. *See also* poor immigrants
PC 27 (Order-in-Council), 80
PC 695 (Order-in-Council), 111, 136
PC 785 (Order-in-Council), 166
PC 1378 (Order-in-Council), 221*n*52, 224*n*22
PC 1962-86 (Order-in-Council), 230*n*39
PC 2115 (Order-in-Council), 113, 136, 137, 139, 140, 146, 150-51
PC 2856 (Order-in-Council), 150
Pearkes, George R., 224*n*18
Pearson, Lester B., 132, 148-49, 174, 179, 231*n*58
Pedley, Frank, 65, 213*n*21
Peters, William A., 178
Pickersgill, Jack, 155, 170, 171, 228*n*13, 230*n*47; and denial of discrimination, 139-40, 167; and family reunification, 167-68, 169; and non-citizens' rights, 164-65, 167-68, 227*n*10
points system, for immigrants, 182, 191
Poirier, Pascal, 79
political discourse, universe of, 7, 8, 13, 24-29; Canadian developments in, 56, 58, 68, 112, 129, 158-59, 182, 187, 195-98, 202. *See also* Liberal Internationalism; Liberal Nationalism
poor immigrants, 41, 56, 110, 208*nn*23-24; Galicians as, 62; vs. paupers, 65. *See also* paupers
Pope, John H., 39, 40
post-Confederation era (1887-1914), immigration controls in, 9, 58-92; on

Asians, 75-92; on Chinese, 9, 58, 62, 75-79, 82, 83, 92; under Conservatives, 74-75; on East Indians, 9, 58-59, 74, 75, 79-82, 84-92; on Europeans, 59-75; on Japanese, 9, 58, 75, 76-77, 79, 92; under Oliver, 59, 63, 68-75, 77, 84, 86, 87-88, 90, 91; under Sifton, 59-68, 74
postwar era, immediate (1945-52), 10, 17-18, 128, 129-57; and Citizenship and Immigration Department, 147, 150-52; early policy indications in, 133-40; and European asylum seekers, 10, 129, 143-46; and European refugee situation, 10, 129, 140-43; and *Immigration Act* (1952), 10, 129, 147, 152-55; and repeal of *Chinese Immigration Act* (1923), 133, 136-40, 146; repeat restrictionism in, 146-56; and UN Convention on Refugees, 10, 129, 147-50; and Universal Declaration of Human Rights, 130-32, 156, 165. *See also* human rights
postwar era, later (1952-67), 10-11, 158-89; Conservative tenure in, 169-74; continuing issues/criticisms in, 174-79; and Immigration Appeal Boards, 155, 168, 183-87; and non-citizens' rights (1952-56), 159-69; and return of judicial oversight, 6, 9, 10, 72, 179-80, 181-87, 188, 193-94; and rights-based politics, 10-11, 158-89; and Sedgwick reports, 176, 178-79, 180-81, 186, 231*n*60; and UN Convention on Refugees, 183, 188; and *White Paper on Immigration*, 150, 174, 180, 181-84, 231*n*58
Pouliot, Jean-François, 122, 143, 228*n*15
Power, Lawrence G., 52, 70, 100
Preventing Human Smugglers from Abusing Canada's Immigration System Act (Bill C-49/Bill C-4, 2010-11), 1, 198, 199
Prior, Edward G., 62
Protecting Canada's Immigration System Act (Bill C-31, 2012), 11, 199-201, 233*nn*19-22
Pugsley, William, 95
Puttee, Arthur W., 63-64

Quakers, 33, 63
quarantine, 38, 40, 65, 66, 89, 213*n*21
Quarantine Act (1872), 40
Quong-Wing v. R., 85

Rahim, Hasan, 87, 217*n*77
refugees: from Canada, 206*n*3, 226*n*38; Canadian National Committee on, 111, 121, 141-42, 143, 221*n*39; due process/ equality rights of, 194-95; early migration by, 32-33, 42-45; from Iron Curtain

countries, 142-43, 155, 176-77; later trends in acceptance of, 191-202; League of Nations Convention on, 109; parliamentary debates on, 108; postwar, 10, 129, 140-43, 172-73; recent Conservative legislation on, 1, 11, 198-201, 233*n*15; UN Convention on, 10, 25, 129, 147-50, 183, 185, 188; UN High Commissioner for, 2, 3, 15, 145, 147, 197, 201. *See also* asylum seekers; Immigration and Refugee Board; *Immigration and Refugee Protection Act; specific refugee groups*
Regier, Erhart, 229*n*24
Reid, Escott, 131, 222*n*64, 223*n*3, 223*n*6
Reid, Malcolm R.J., 89
religious discrimination. *See* Jewish immigrants/refugees; Sikh immigrants; *specific religious groups*
rights-based politics, 1-5; and border control failure, 2-3, 8, 11, 12, 17-20, 21, 23; by CCF, 113, 119, 120, 123, 126, 137, 160, 201-4; of Chinese immigrants, 84-85, 115, 117-18, 137-40; of churches/church groups, 52, 79, 111, 120, 126, 145-46, 160, 161; in Confederation era (1867-87), 8-9, 41-42, 45-57; of East Indian immigrants, 9, 58-59, 82, 84-92, 113, 167; as encouraged by rights-restrictive policies, 4, 7-8, 9-10, 22-23; of European immigrants (1921-39), 9, 93, 95, 99-100, 101-7; and increases in border control, 4, 19; in immediate postwar era (1945-52), 10, 17-18, 129-57; in interwar period (1914-45), 9-10, 93-94, 101-7, 112, 113, 119-24, 126-28; of Japanese Canadians, 85, 119, 123-24, 126-27, 128; of Jewish immigrants/refugees, 110-11, 121-23, 160, 169; judiciary and, 17-18; in later postwar era (1952-67), 10-11, 158-89; as liberal-democratic tradition, 3, 4, 5-6. *See also* due process/equality rights of non-citizens; human rights; judicial oversight, of immigrant/non-citizen rights; Liberal Internationalism
rights-restrictive policies, 1-5, 12-15; and border control failure, 3-5, 7, 8, 9-10, 11, 12, 21, 22-23, 178, 180, 188-89, 201-4; and Chinese immigrants, 8-9, 31-32, 45-47, 49-57; and citizenship, 2, 3, 14, 48, 195-96, 221*n*52; domination of (1914-45), 9-10, 93-128; vs. due process/equality rights, 1, 22-23, 27, 69, 90, 93-94, 129, 153, 156, 193; ethnoracial dimension of, 14, 28, 33, 45, 46, 109, 135-36, 156, 192, 193; expansion/

consolidation of (1887-1914), 9, 58-92; extreme nature of, 7-8, 9, 93, 106, 123, 156; historical studies of, 21, 23; vs. human rights, 30, 120-27, 201; in immediate postwar era (1945-52), 10, 129-57; in late 19th--early 20th centuries, 36-37; in later postwar era (1952-67), 10-11, 158-59, 159-69, 170, 174-79, 187; negative feedback loop of, 4, 22, 23; and opportunities for rights-based politics, 4, 7-8, 9-10, 22-23; recent turn towards, 1-3, 8, 11, 13-17, 29-30, 190-204; strategies for enforcing, 18-19. *See also* Liberal Nationalism
Robb, James A., 104, 111
Robertson, Gideon D., 100, 219*n*18
Robertson, Norman, 121
Roche, William, 99
Roche, William J., 74
Roebuck, Arthur W., 126, 134-35, 140-41, 222*n*56
Rogers, Robert, 74
Rose, Fred, 222*n*56
Rosenberg, Louis, 141, 225*n*30
Ross, James H., 105
Roxburgh, John M., 231*n*60
Royal Canadian Mounted Police (RCMP), 119, 124-25, 170, 226*n*42, 231*n*60
Royal Commissions: on Chinese immigration, 83; on Italian labour, 64
Russian immigrants, 59, 109; Doukhobors as, 62-63; as "enemy aliens," 95-96, 99, 218*n*8; Jewish refugees as, 43, 44; Mennonites as, 34, 43, 208*n*28
Russian Revolution, 95-96, 109

Safe Third Country Agreement (Canada-US), 15, 195, 196, 200
Sandwell, Bernard, 126, 141, 161, 225*n*31
Scott, Richard W., 52, 54-55, 70, 211*n*58, 215*n*49, 215*n*54, 217*n*74
Scott, William D., 68, 89, 207*n*18, 212*n*18, 214*n*41, 217*n*73
Sedgwick, Joseph, 176, 178-79, 180-81, 186, 231*n*60
Senate: and *Chinese Immigration Act* (1885), 9, 32, 45-47, 52-56, 67, 134, 211*n*58, 215*n*54; and *Chinese Immigration Act* (1923), 117; early support for Japan in, 77, 215*n*49; and East Indian immigrants, 217*n*72; and Head Tax increase, 79; and *Immigration Act* (1906) 69-71, 213*nn*32-33; and *Immigration Act* (1910), 97-100, 103, 104-6, 135, 214*n*38, 219*n*18; and Japanese disenfranchisement, 126, 222*n*68; and Jewish refugees, 122, 140-41,

222*nn*56-57; and postwar immigration committee, 134-35, 140-43, 152
September 11 (2001), terrorist attacks of, 3, 12, 14, 16, 193, 195, 196
Shakespeare, Noah, 51
Shaughnessy, Peter, 212*n*17
Shaw, Frederick D., 139, 143, 164
ship deserters, 174, 176-77, 185
Sifton, Clifford, 59-68, 74; departmental shakeup by, 59-60, 68, 213*n*27; and Doukhobors, 62-64; expanded immigration under, 59-61, 67-68; and Galicians, 61-62, 63, 212*nn*10-11; Immigration Agent system of, 60, 61, 64-65; infectious disease legislation of, 65-67; and NATC, 61; and non-white immigration, 60, 211*n*1; vs. Oliver, 62, 212*n*12; and support of increased Head Tax, 60, 77-78
Sikh immigrants, 79, 84, 85; as boat arrivals, 192-93; British ties of, 79, 85, 215*n*57; and *Komagata Maru* case, 82, 88-92, 217*n*77. *See also* East Indian immigrants
Sinclair, James, 224*n*19
Singh, Gurdit, 89, 91, 217*n*82, 218*n*86
Singh, Munshi, 89-90, 92, 217*n*85
Singh, Narain. See *Narain Singh* case
Singh, Sunder, 79, 215*n*57
Smart, James A., 56, 65, 66, 67, 211*n*2
Smith, J. Obed, 219*n*19
South Africa, 132, 150; Boers in, 78, 212*n*9; potential refugees from, 172
sovereignty, state: in control literature, 16, 17-18, 209*n*35; and imperial relations, 80-82; Liberal Internationalists and, 106, 134, 165, 178. *See also entry below*
sovereignty, state, Liberal Nationalism and, 7, 26, 27, 75, 134, 156, 162, 197; vs. due process/equality rights, 9, 58-92, 106, 120, 129, 156; and ethnoracial discrimination, 46, 49, 54, 78-79, 90, 93, 109, 120, 134, 140, 156; vs. human rights, 130-32, 134; vs. "special interests," 54. See also *Chinese Immigration Act* (1885)
Soviet Union, 131, 145, 149
Special Joint Committee on Immigration (SJCI), 178-79, 180, 183
Sproule, Thomas S., 62, 64, 71, 78, 212*n*9
St. Laurent, Louis, 150, 224*n*23
St. Louis (ship), 121
Star Chamber, 100, 161-62, 227*n*8
Stevens, Henry H., 88, 91, 98, 114, 217*nn*80-81, 220*n*28
Stewart, Alistair M., 126-27, 133, 139, 144, 152, 222*n*66, 225*n*36, 226*n*43
Stewart, Charles A., 102, 103, 105, 116, 117, 220*n*26

Stork, Alfred, 114
Sun Sea (ship), 1, 198
Supreme Court of Canada, 167, 195, 221*n*37, 227*n*4; *Brent* case, 166; *Espillat-Rodriguez* case, 228*n*18; and IAB appeals, 184, 185; *Leong* case, 161, 166; *Narine-Singh* case, 160, 166, 227*n*2; *Quong-Wing* case, 85; and "voluntary departures" policy, 127
Sutherland, Donald, 99
Syrian refugees, 9, 75, 92, 110

Taché, J.C., 39
Tai Sing v. Maguire, 84-85
Tamil asylum seekers, 1, 196-98
Taschereau, Robert, 227*n*4
Taylor, John (immigration agent), 208*n*31
Taylor, John R., 164, 171-72, 173
Thatcher, W. Ross, 136, 137, 140, 142, 143
Thompson, Joshua S., 48
Toews, Vic, 198
Tolmie, Simon F., 117, 219*n*20
Tolstoy, Alexandra, 108
Tolstoy, Leo, 108
Toronto Labour Committee for Human Rights (TLC), 160
Tremblay, René, 175, 176-77, 179
Trudeau, Pierre Elliott, 190
Tsur, Chilien, 115
Tucker, Walter A., 225*n*34
Tupper, Charles, 40, 207*n*16
Turiff, John G., 100
Tweedie, Thomas M.M., 97

Ukrainian immigrants, 95, 97, 102, 139
United Nations, 129, 131, 137, 139, 147, 160
United Nations Charter, 131, 132, 139, 225*n*25; and *Chinese Immigration Act* (1923), 137-38, 140, 224*n*23; Preamble to, 130, 138
United Nations Convention Relating to the Status of Refugees (1951), 25; early decision not to sign, 10, 129, 147-50; eventual signing of, 183, 185, 188
United Nations Declaration on the Elimination of All Forms of Racial Discrimination, 175
United Nations Economic and Social Council (ECOSOC), 147-48
United Nations High Commissioner for Refugees (UNHCR), 2, 3, 15, 145, 147, 197, 201
United States, 13, 36, 37, 110, 113, 131; control/rights nexus in, 17; early refugees to, 43, 226*n*38; and early limitations

on border control, 41, 46, 64-65, 72; as
entered through Canada, 66-67, 75, 77;
ethnoracial restrictions in, 94, 173, 174;
family immigration in, 14; history of
immigration to, 32, 43; immigrants/
refugees from, 33-34, 36-37, 42, 43, 46,
60, 66-67, 72-73, 80, 96, 101-2, 150,
219*n*10; literacy test in, 94; non-citizens'
rights in, 226*n*45; and North American
security, 15, 195, 196, 200; and postwar
border control issues, 146, 148, 149,
226*n*41; postwar immigration to, 130,
136; and postwar refugees, 145, 146; as
rival for immigration, 40, 42; Sifton's
campaign in, 60; and *St. Louis*, 121;
terrorist attacks in, 3, 12, 14, 16, 193,
195, 196
Universal Declaration of Human Rights
(UDHR, 1948), 2, 25, 165; Canada and,
130-32, 156

Vidal, Alexander, 52-55, 211*n*60, 211*n*62,
215*n*53
Vien, Thomas, 135

Wahn, Ian G., 185, 229*n*30
Wallace, Nathaniel C., 63
War Measures Act (1914), 94-95, 123, 126,
132; and Defence of Canada Regulations,
123-24

War-Time Elections Act (1917), 95
Watson, Robert, 214*n*35
West Indies, immigrants from, 159-60,
167, 172, 175, 191, 214*n*41, 227*n*1,
230*n*47; and Narine-*Singh* case, 160, 166,
227*n*2
Whidden, Howard, 99, 108
White, Peter, 196
White Paper on Immigration (1966), 150,
174, 180, 181-84, 231*n*58
Williams, Eric, 175
Wilson, Cairine, 122, 126, 135, 141,
222*n*57, 22*n*68
Wilson, John L., 165-66
Wilson, Uriah, 63, 66
Winch, Harold E., 164, 167, 172, 229*n*27,
230*n*41
Winnipeg General Strike, 9, 99-100,
219*n*14
Wong, Alice, 233*n*15
Wong Foon Sien, 170
Woodsworth, J.S., 101, 103-4, 105, 107,
114-15, 116-17, 118, 127, 220*n*34
Woolliams, Eldon M., 177-78

Zaplinty, Frederick S., 142, 225*n*33

Printed and bound in Canada by Friesens

Set in Stone by Artegraphica Design Co. Ltd.

Copy editor: Francis Chow

Proofreader: Dianne Tiefensee

Indexer: Cheryl Lemmens